Cognition and Behavior Modification

Cognition and Behavior Modification

Michael J. Mahoney
Pennsylvania State University

Ballinger Publishing Company • Cambridge, Mass.
A Subsidiary of J. B. Lippincott Company

Library of Congress Catalog Card Number: 74-13019

International Standard Book Number: 0-88410-500-8

Printed in the United States of America

Library of Congress Cataloging in Publication Data

Mahoney, Michael J
Cognitive behavior modification.

1. Behavior modification. 2. Cognition.
I. Title. [DNLM: 1. Behavior therapy—Cognition.
WM420 M215c]
BF637.B4M32 153.8'5 74-13019
ISBN 0-88410-500-8

Contents

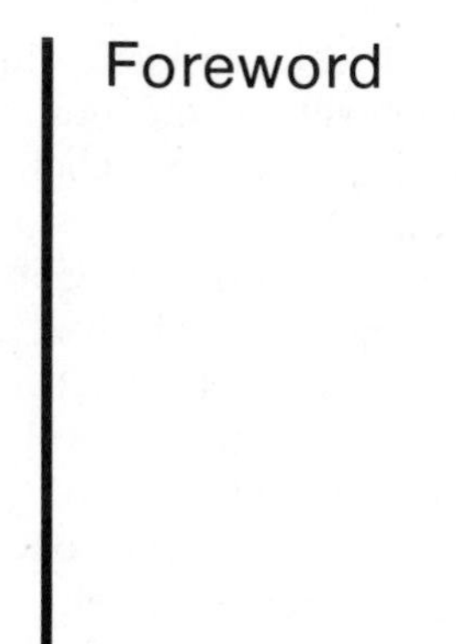

Foreword

In the summer of 1973 I was invited to give a series of lectures to a small group of experimental psychologists in Sao Paulo, Brazil. Among my topics was "cognitive behavior modification," the conceptual and empirical analysis of "private events." Since I was entering a culture dominated by animal operant research, I took great pains to prepare and document my defense of cognitive-symbolic processes as legitimate and critical foci in the experimental analysis of human behavior. Those efforts were generously rewarded. My hosts were not only receptive but warmly enthusiastic. It was their request for a tangible summary of my remarks that constituted the initial stimulus for this manuscript.

A balmy Montreal evening in August of 1973 found me enjoying a privilege which added further impetus. I had the honor of sharing a quiet evening with a man for whom my respect need hardly be acknowledged—B. F. Skinner. Although it was not our first conversation about "cognitive" topics, its content lent momentum to my conviction that the time had come for a more concerted behavioral reexamination of private events. Belief, choice, and "counter-control" were topics which Dr. Skinner lent both commentary and research encouragement.

In October, I organized a small seminar to direct and consequate my writing of a "brief" text on cognitive behavior modification. Eight bright and critical colleagues gave me generous feedback in the months that followed—Kitty Craighead, Bob DeMonbreun, Barney Feingold, Sally Goodwin, Russ Jones, Bob Kennedy, Bill Moyer, and Eliana Siebel. Their backgrounds ranged from animal operant and philosophy of science to information processing and clinical research. My indebtedness to their feedback and encouragement is substantial.

It would, of course, be impossible to do justice to the many colleagues and friends who have had impact on the present writing. Dave Rimm, Jerry Davison, Carl Thoresen, Walter Mischel, and David Rosenhan were instrumental in stimulating my early interest in cognitive behavioral research. The influence of Dick Atkinson and Gordon Bower is also readily apparent. However, my largest debt is owed to a model whose personal and professional impact defies adequate acknowledgment. Readers acquainted with social learning theory will find many familiar themes in what follows. I am deeply indebted to Al Bandura, not only for the extent to which I have drawn on his conceptual and integrative skills, but also for his modeling, encouragement, and invaluable direction. His contribution to this volume far exceeds that acknowledged in formal references.

Before embarking on this journey, the reader should perhaps be apprised of its transportation mode. My goal was effective communication, not encyclopedic boredom. What follows is therefore quite "deviant" from conventional academic style. I often employ first person pronouns and draw heavily on both anecdotal and "formal" evidence sources. My frequent delusions of humor will likewise be apparent (perhaps painfully). Although a staunch supporter of sexual equality, my conditioned rhetoric reflects a bias for male referents. Finally, I offer some value-laden suggestions late in the text which contrast sharply with "accepted" form in technical publications. I hope that these attempts to render the topic more readable, communicative, and clinically relevant have not been misdirected.

Books, I have learned, are not born in anesthetized stupor. Their maternity and birth are long and painful enterprises which often sacrifice past freedoms and social pleasures. The difficult labor of the present offspring was endured only with the assistance of several valued companions. Jim Pumphrey, Lynn Carpenter, and Duffy provided generous diversion and frequent immoral support in the wee hours of planning, writing, and revision. Several colleagues took time away from busy schedules to read chapter drafts—Walt Weimer (1-5), Al Kazdin (8), Willard F. Day (1-5), and Greg Brock (1-16). Their interest and comments are deeply appreciated.

Publishers are often portrayed as impersonal corporate giants who seldom contribute to anything but an author's headaches. Such a portrayal is fortunately diametrically inaccurate in the present endeavor. I am indebted to many Ballinger personnel for their technical assistance and warm cooperation.

In addition to her charm and humor, Sandy Ranio shared awesome professional skills in transforming illegible scribblings into near-legible prose. Likewise, Bob and Barb Kennedy were an invaluable source of encouragement, technical help, and granola cookies. All three were deeply appreciated. Finally, as reflected in the dedication of this book, I am personally and professionally indebted to a young colleague who kept my self-statements adaptive, my technical points defensible, and my evenings unproductively happy.

M. J. M.
May, 1974

Acknowledgments

The following figures were reprinted with the kind permission of the American Psychological Association:

Figure 4-3, from Spielberger, C. D., & DeNike, L. D. Descriptive behaviorism versus cognitive theory in verbal operant conditioning. *Psychological Review,* 1966, *73,* 306–326.

Figure 4-5, from Bandura, A., & Menlove, F. E. Factors determining vicarious extinction of avoidance behavior through symbolic modeling. *Journal of Personality and Social Psychology,* 1968, *8,* 99–108.

Figure 8-1, from Barlow, D. H., Leitenberg, H., & Agras, W. S. Experimental control of sexual deviation through manipulation of the noxious scene in covert sensitization. *Journal of Abnormal Psychology,* 1969, *74,* 597–601.

Figure 8-2, from Maletzky, B. M. "Assisted" covert sensitization in the treatment of exhibitionism. *Journal of Consulting and Clinical Psychology,* 1974, *42,* 34–40.

Figure 8-3, from Kazdin, A. E. Covert modeling and the reduction of avoidance behavior. *Journal of Abnormal Psychology,* 1973, *81,* 87–95.

Figure 10-1, from Mischel, W., Ebbesen, E., & Zeiss, A. Cognitive and attentional mechanisms in delay of gratification. *Journal of Personality and Social Psychology,* 1972, *21,* 204–218.

Figure 10-2, from Gerst, M. R. Symbolic coding processes in observational learning. *Journal of Personality and Social Psychology,* 1971, *19,* 7–17.

Figure 12-1, from Ross, L., Rodin, J., & Zimbardo, P. G. Toward an attribution therapy: The reduction of fear through induced cognitive-emotional misattribution. *Journal of Personality and Social Psychology,* 1969, *12,* 279–288.

Figure 13-1, which was drawn from the data of Resnick, J. H., & Schwartz, T. Ethical standards as an independent variable in psychological research. *American Psychologist,* 1973, *28,* 134–139.

Microforms International Marketing Corporation, the exclusive licensee of the copyright for Pergamon Press Journal back files, granted permission to reprint:

Figures 6-2 and 6-3, from Mahoney, M. J., Thoresen, C. E., & Danaher, B. G. Covert behavior modification: An experimental analogue. *Journal of Behavior Therapy and Experimental Psychiatry,* 1972, *3,* 7–14.

The permission of Academic Press is acknowledged for:

Figure 6-5, from Ascher, L. M. An experimental analog study of covert positive reinforcement. In R. D. Rubin, J. P. Brady, & J. D. Henderson (Eds.), *Advances in behavior therapy.* Vol. 4. 1973, pp. 127–138.

Figures 7-1 and 7-2, from Mahoney, M. J. The self-management of covert behavior: A case study. *Behavior Therapy,* 1971, *2,* 575–578.

Figure 11-1, from Meichenbaum, D., & Cameron, R. Training schizophrenics to talk to themselves: A means of developing attentional controls. *Behavior Therapy,* 1973, *4,* 515–534.

Prentice-Hall, Inc., granted permission to reprint:

Figure 4-2, from Maltzman, I. Theoretical conceptions of semantic conditioning and generalization. In T. R. Dixon & D. L. Horton (Eds.), *Verbal behavior and general behavior theory.* 1968, pp. 291–339.

The publishers of *Psychological Reports* granted permission to reprint:

Figure 6-4, from Weiner, H. Real and imagined cost effects upon human fixed-interval responding. *Psychological Reports,* 1965, *17,* 659–662.

Psychonomic Journals, Inc., granted permission to reprint:

Figure 10-3, from Kaufman, A., Baron, A., & Kopp, R. E. Some effects of instructions on human operant behavior. *Psychonomic Monograph Supplements,* 1966, *1,* 243–250.

The publishers of the *Journal of Applied Behavior Analysis* granted permission to reprint:

Figure 4-4, from O'Connor, R. D. Modification of social withdrawal through symbolic modeling. *Journal of Applied Behavior Analysis,* 1969, *2,* 15–22.

The authors' permissions to reprint the foregoing figures is likewise gratefully acknowledged. Finally, I extend my thanks to Neal E. Miller for permission to reprint Figure 4-1 from his doctoral dissertation ("The Influence of Past Experience Upon the Transfer of Subsequent Training," Yale University, 1935) and to Albert Ellis and the Institute for Rational Living to reprint material from *The Essence of Rational Psychotherapy: A Comprehensive Approach to Treatment.*

To my cognitive models
and a very special colleague-companion . . .
Kit

Cognition and Behavior Modification

Chapter One

Wherefore Cognitive Behavior Modification?

From birth to death, only a very small percentage of a person's behaviors are publicly observable. Our lives are predominantly composed of private responses to private environments—ranging from monologues in the shower to senile reveries. With the growing acceptance of cognitive behavioral research, we may expect to see progressively more promising developments toward understanding the processes and parameters of our private environs. It will be one of the main contentions of this book that the pursuit of controlled scientific inquiry in this area is not only empirically justified but ethically prescribed.

Few areas of psychological research have stimulated as much enthusiasm or controversy as that of behavior modification. In the last decade alone five different international journals have been established in order to provide an outlet for the mushrooming research in this area. Over a hundred books dealing with the principles or practice of behavior therapy have flooded the market.

The public and professional reaction to this frenzied growth has been two-sided: "Depending on one's conceptual and methodological viewpoint, behavior modification may represent an absurd and menacing delusional system or the most exciting frontier in contemporary behavioral science (Mahoney, Kazdin, & Lesswing, 1974)." The extreme and often dichotomous evaluations probably stem from a variety of sources. First, there can be little doubt that "behavioral" approaches represent a dramatically different perspective in the areas of personality and complex human functioning. Such a deviation from the traditional "trait-state" approach has stimulated extreme reactions. A second factor has been the often overzealous enthusiasm of behavior modifiers in expanding, refining, and proselytizing their efforts. Although there has been considerable empirical support for the scientific productivity and clinical promise of behavioral approaches, enthusiastic claims have often outstripped existing knowledge. Finally, a variety of philosophical and ethical controversies have been highlighted by behavior modification theory and research.

THE END OF AN ERA: THE COGNITIVE INQUISITION

The present text will not attempt to review, analyze, or evaluate the major arguments for and against "behavior modification." Such an analysis has been published elsewhere (Mahoney, Kazdin, & Lesswing, 1974). It is worth noting, however, that one of the major focal points of several arguments has been the area of "private events"—thoughts, feelings, and memories. Behavioral researchers have been repeatedly faulted for their avoidance, denial, and/or criticism of significant covert phenomena. They have often been stereotyped as a "mindless" lot of (empirically) right-wing myopics, innocently entertained by their lever-pressing rodents and stubbornly ignorant of the richness and complexity of human behavior. This image is vividly portrayed by Floyd W. Matson:

> Plainly, the differences between us must be very deep—not just technical or strategic or methodological but philosophical, and perhaps moral. For my part, I believe that Skinner and his gentle friends state the case against their own philosophy so openly and candidly that one need only cry "Hark! See there? They are exposing themselves (the Grand Conditioner has no clothes)!" On the other hand, the Skinnerians perceive themselves not only as warmly clothed but gorgeously arrayed: Wrapped in the mantle of Science, armed with the tools of the "technology of behavior," they walk the green pastures of Walden Two and marvel at their adversaries, who speak a gibberish compounded of nonsense syllables such as "freedom," "person," "choice," "responsibility," "mind," and so on (1971, p. 2).

The argument that behavior modification has ignored or deemphasized cognitive-symbolic processes has had more than intermittent justification. The outspoken relegation of private events to a "positivistic purgatory" by Watson (1913, 1924) and Skinner (1953) was instrumental in discouraging controlled behavioral analyses of such phenomena. Skinner's views on private events, however, have been frequently misinterpreted:

> No entity or process which has any useful explanatory force is to be rejected on the ground that it is subjective or mental. The data which

> have made it important must, however, be studied and formulated in effective ways. The assignment is well within the scope of an experimental analysis of behavior (Skinner, 1963, p. 958).

The avoidance of "mentalistic" phenomena within behavior modification has sometimes assumed humorous proportions. In a personality course at what was then considered "Walden Two in the desert" (Arizona State University), my instructor half-facetiously required that the word "mind" be eliminated from our classroom discussions. Such adequately communicative phrases as "re*mind* me" and "slipped my *mind*" were translated into "re-cue me" and "has left my current behavioral repertoire." The extreme semantic contortions sometimes employed to avoid covert or mental terms, however, suggested a "psyche-phobia" of less than humorous severity.

With occasional renegade exceptions (e.g., Wolpe, 1958; Bandura & Walters, 1959; Mowrer, 1960), early behavior modifiers were content to restrict their analyses and operations to discrete and blatantly observable phenomena. The terms "mental" and "unobservable" acquired classically conditioned negative connotations through association with the terms "soft," "unscientific," and "unparsimonious." The avoidance of inferred variables assumed near-religious proportions, hence the "Cognitive Inquisition." While explicitly modeling their paradigm after that of classical physics, behavioral researchers energetically criticized all forms of psychological inference. One wonders if they were aware that none of their respected colleagues in physics had ever actually *observed* an electron. The pervasiveness of this ban on mediational inferences sometimes approached that of religious dogma. After a recent colloquium on cognitive behavior modification, my host took me aside and said, "I've been waiting seven years for someone to say what you just said—that it's okay to examine covert events as factors in human behavior. We have been waiting for someone to lift the ban." Careless and wholesale reliance on unjustified inference can, of course, cripple an empirical enterprise, particularly one as young and unstable as behavior modification in the early 1960's. The fact remained, however, that critics could legitimately contend that "significant private phenomena" were functionally absent from the early behavioral framework. While their absence was often cited as an asset by enthusiastic behaviorists, their exclusion constituted a serious limitation in both the comprehensiveness and clinical relevance of the then-current behavior theory. It is interesting to note that Skinner (1953) spent a very sizeable portion of his book in speculations on covert phenomena. Unfortunately, his own cautionary proscriptions in this area forced these speculations to remain devoid of empirical research for many years.

Although he had not really changed any of his basic views about private events (see Skinner, 1945), several of his comments in "Behaviorism at Fifty" made more explicit his tolerance for their inclusion in behavioral research:

> It is particularly important that a science of behavior face the problem of privacy . . . . An adequate science of behavior must consider events taking place within the skin of the organism . . . as part of behavior itself (1963, p. 953).

By the time this stance was clarified, however, the anti-covert convention was already well entrenched.

AN EMERGING ERA: THE THINKING BEHAVIORIST

Models have a way of changing, however, and behavior modification has not been an exception. Much to its credit as an expanding paradigm, the "learning approach" has undergone significant revisions and refinements—particularly during the last decade. It is noteworthy that many of these revisions were stimulated by early critiques of the model. Of most relevance to our current discussion has been the growing interest in covert phenomena as scientifically legitimate and clinically indispensable variables.

A classic paper by Lloyd Homme in 1965 entreated behavior modifiers to apply their functional-analytic skills to "coverants"—the (covert) "operants of the mind." Homme conceptualized thoughts as important early elements in ultimately overt response chains. Since these covert events are observable to a "public of one" (i.e., their owner), they can be subjected to empirical scrutiny and experimental control. To avoid or ignore private events, according to Homme, is to set them mysteriously apart from other (publicly observable) behaviors—thereby reinforcing the very dualism (physical/mental) which behaviorists have so strongly denied.

The development of cognitive behavior modification did not proceed quickly, and many an operant eyebrow was raised at the prospect of re-entering the mentalism-introspection arena. The hard-fought struggle to be freed from the bonds of psychic tradition had left a legacy of mindless biases. Despite a relatively cool reception among their colleagues, however, the pioneers in this area set about collecting data on the relevance and scientific utility of cognitive-symbolic variables. As perceptual processing factors began receiving attention from behavioral quarters, it soon became apparent that naive realism (or the doctrine of "immaculate perception") was functionally untenable in human behavior. An individual responds—not to some *real* environment—but to a *perceived* environment. The frightened airline passenger reacts not to a purely external stimulus (loud noises after take-off) but to his perception (i.e., labeling) of those stimuli ("My God, we've lost an engine!"). The compulsive hand-washer reacts not to any real environmental contingencies, but to a perceived (but equally powerful) set (e.g., "If I don't wash my hands, God will punish me."). Data from several different lines of research offered converging evidence on the critical role of cognitive factors in human behavior.

In 1969 Bandura's classic *Principles of Behavior Modification* summarized the rapidly growing literature pointing toward cognitive-symbolic mediation. Since then, research in this area has mushroomed. The last two years have witnessed a tremendous acceleration of articles describing progressively more ambitious efforts at identifying and controlling significant mediating behaviors.

Thus, the "non-cognitive" argument against behavior modification has lost its credibility. As will be shown in the following chapters, a wide range of "significant private events" has now been empirically examined by behavioral researchers. Moreover, a technology for the modification of cognitive behaviors is being rapidly refined. The advent of this "cognitive" trend, however, has also questioned whether the term "behaviorist" can be appropriately applied to the current paradigm. In a strict "radical" sense of the term, a "behaviorist" is a scientist who restricts his inquiries to publicly observable events and conscientiously avoids inference (cf. Chapter 2). Using that definition, I would contend that there have been more unicorns than behaviorists.

PLAN OF THE BOOK

The present text presumes a familiarity with basic learning principles. It is divided into three major sections. First, we shall examine some of the *conceptual* and philosophical issues regarding inference and cognitive-symbolic processes. A brief historical sketch will outline the precedents for the currently popular "non-mediational" perspective in behavioral quarters. That model will then be examined in detail with particular focus on its logical substrata. Following an analysis of the function and justifiability of inference in behavioral science, the non-mediational model will be further scrutinized on the basis of data. Empirical evidence from a variety of areas will be presented by way of challenging this perspective.

Our second focus will entail an *empirical* evaluation of two mediational models—"covert conditioning" and "cognitive learning." Both of these models will first be outlined as conceptual paradigms, and their respective data bases will be reviewed. Greater emphasis, however, will be placed on the empirical evidence bearing on their associated therapeutic procedures.

The final section of the book is explicitly persuasive. It tentatively suggests some clinical implications and offers a general paradigm for therapeutic science. After some speculations on future directions and expanded horizons, the literature reviewed is interpreted in terms of its relevance for our own patterns of scientific inquiry. The enterprise is brought to a close with an invitation for re-appraisal of our contemporary epistemological paradigm.

One technical note bears constant acknowledgement in reading the present manuscript. Such terms as "data," "evidence," "reality," and "objectivity" should always be understood to be relativistic. It will become increasingly apparent in the chapters which follow that our efforts to align theory with "data" are substantially limited by inherent biases in our data processing. "Facts" are relativistic constructs; we do not have privileged access to reality. Thus, in all subsequent discussions of empirical assessment and theory-data congruence, the reader should remain apprised of the fallibility of our data and the relativity of our empiricism.

As indicated earlier, behavior modification is a relatively recent arrival on the applied clinical scene. *Cognitive* behavior modification is as yet a fetus. There have already been cries of "prematurity" and even "illegitimacy" from within the ranks of behavioral theory. More than a few respected workers would favor a therapeutic abortion of the accelerating trend toward a cognitive learning model. Until such a model is empirically examined and clinically evaluated, however, its critics have little to stand upon other than their own biases. It may, of course, turn out that a cognitive learning integration is neither feasible nor useful in our conceptualization and treatment of complex human functioning. If such is the case, "the data will out"—that is, the empirical evidence will so indicate. However, until data are collected and evaluated, pre-conceived notions for or against the cognitive learning perspective are unjustified and premature. To limit our knowledge by such conceptual prejudices is itself an illustration of the significance of cognitive-symbolic factors in human behavior—the radical behaviorist responds not to the exigencies of the "real" world (i.e., the data supporting mediational processes) but to his own selective processing of that world.

If the reader closes this book with more questions than

answers, it will have served its purpose. Scientific progress is marked more by questions than by any accumulation of answers. The former are the lifeblood of empiricism. Hopefully, the reader—as clinician, student, researcher, or theorist—will ask his own questions and, at some level of empirical confidence, will contribute to our expanding knowledge in cognitive behavior modification.

Chapter Two

The Behaviorisms: Metaphysical to Methodological

One of the most persistent misconceptions about behaviorism and behavior modification has dealt with the existence of a monolithic behavioral model. Thus, to the uninitiated:

1. all behavior modifiers are Skinnerians;
2. all Skinnerians presume an empty (mindless) organism;
3. the notion of an empty organism is absurd;
4. therefore, all behavior modifiers are imbeciles.

Premises (1) and (2) are patently false, which (hopefully) raises some doubts about the validity of the conclusion.

Unfortunately, critics of the "behavioral model" have long directed their arguments at a non-existent amalgam of behavioristic philosophy and clinical procedures (cf. Mahoney, Kazdin, & Lesswing, 1974). Moreover, it is ironic that many anti-behaviorism critiques have been addressed to a form of behavioristic philosophy that has long since been supplanted. Sigmund Koch (1964), for example, while legitimately faulting behaviorists for clinging to an outmoded philosophy of science (logical positivism), was himself attacking a behaviorism that was no longer contemporary. Koch's prediction about the impending demise of behaviorism ranks with Richard Nixon's 1962 prediction about his own political future:

> When the ludicrousness of the position is made sufficiently plain, perhaps it will be laughed out of existence. Behaviorists have themselves done a pretty good job in rendering this quality apparent (pp. 20–21).

> I would be happy to say what we have been hearing could be characterized as the death rattle of behaviorism, but this would be a

> rather more dignified statement than I should like to sponsor, because death is, at least, a dignified process (p. 162).

. . . And we won't have Fred Skinner to kick around anymore.

Notwithstanding Koch's dire predictions, behaviorism not only survived but flourished. Behavioristic research has mushroomed, and current speculations about its being a transient fad have lost any claim to credibility. It is ironic that some of the heated intellectual persecution directed toward early behaviorists may have actually facilitated the survival and growth of that philosophy (London, 1972). As a persecuted minority, early workers developed a camaraderie and cohesiveness that probably aided their sufferance of the ungrateful times. Their implicit slogan seemed reminiscent of other revolutionary perspectives: "If we don't hang together, we'll hang separately." Enthusiasm ran high, and party-line dedication approached that of religious reverence. As behavioristic attitudes matured, however, their adolescent enthusiasm evolved into a more conservative optimism. Critical self-examinations and theoretical revisions developed (Mahoney, Kazdin, & Lesswing, 1974).

Thus, although behaviorism has survived, it has not survived unchanged. As we shall see in the present chapter, a broad continuum of contemporary behavioristic perspectives can be described. Before examining that continuum, however, we shall turn our attention to its historical and conceptual predecessors—radical and methodological behaviorism.

METAPHYSICAL (RADICAL) BEHAVIORISM

John Broadus Watson (1878–1958) is considered the father of American behaviorism. As is usually the case with historical ascriptions of responsibility, this paternity is not entirely unchallenged. Watson's classic 1913 paper ("Psychology as the Behaviorist Views It") was undoubtedly the culmination of preceding and contemporary trends from the areas of functionalism, structuralism, and associationism (cf. Marx & Hillix, 1963). Nonetheless, Watson was the principal figure in the clarification and formalization of early behavioristic philosophy.

Two distinct subtypes of behaviorism were proposed and defended by John Watson: (a) metaphysical behaviorism and (b) methodological behaviorism. The first—metaphysical behaviorism—is concerned mainly with the concept of "mind" and the legitimate subject matter of psychological inquiry. Metaphysical behaviorism is sometimes referred to as "radical" (and often as "rabid") behaviorism due to the extreme nature of its basic postulates:

1. the existence of "mind" and "mental states" is denied;
2. all experience can be reduced to glandular secretions and muscle movements;
3. human behavior is almost exclusively determined by environmental (learning) influences (primarily along the principles of classical conditioning) rather than by hereditary or biological factors, and
4. conscious processes (covert phenomena), if they exist, are beyond the realm of scientific inquiry.

As if these postulates were not offensive enough to the conventional psychological views, Watson embellished them with some rather ambitious claims about the implications and comprehensiveness of his theory. For example, in reference to the primary significance of environmental (learning) influences rather than hereditary factors in human development, he posed his infamous challenge:

> Give me a dozen healthy infants, well-formed, and my own specified world to bring them up in and I'll guarantee to take any one at random and train him to become any type of specialist I might select—doctor, lawyer, artist, merchant-chief and, yes, even beggarman and thief, regardless of his talents, penchants, tendencies, abilities, vocations, and race of his ancestors (1924, p. 104).

The cardinal feature of metaphysical behaviorism, however, was its denial of the existence of "mind." In his energetic attack on "mentalism," Watson inadvertently resurrected the very issue which he hoped to bury—the mind-body issue. Centuries of sober and not-so-sober argumentation had been devoted to answering the question of how a non-physical entity (the "mind") interacts with a physical body. A variety of ingenious alternatives had been proposed.

1. *Cartesian Dualism* (also known as "interactionism"), formalized by Rene Descartes, stated that a non-physical mind and the physical body interacted causally with one another via the pineal gland in the brain.
2. *Psychophysical Parallelism* (also known as "Pre-Arranged Harmony"), espoused by both Baruch Spinoza and Gustav Fechner, contended that mind and body were two separate but synchronized entities, never interacting but always mirroring one another.
3. *Occasionalism,* proposed by Geulincx and Malebranche, stated that mind and body were two independent processes which were "occasionally" synchronized by supernatural intervention.
4. *Idealism,* made popular by Bishop George Berkeley, suggested a

monistic (i.e., one entity) solution—namely, that all of reality is mental ("spiritual"); there is nothing which is physical.

5. *Materialistic Monism,* formalized by Democritus and later refined by Thomas Hobbes, contended that all of reality is physical, there is no mind (this, of course, was the predecessor of Watson's position).

The centuries-old controversy, of course, focused on the logical possibility of mind-body interactions. How can a massless entity influence a physical one, and vice versa? How can a non-physical mind be confined to the area of the skull or even attached to an individual body since it is not subject to the same forces as physical objects? Behavioristic criticism of dualistic theories (those which posited the existence of both mind and body) became increasingly energetic as knowledge about physics and physiology accumulated. For example, a popular early argument (and one still defended by some contemporary behaviorists) relates to the conservation of energy principle and relativity theory in contemporary physics. It is assumed that energy can neither be created nor destroyed and that mass and energy are theoretically interchangeable ($E = mc^2$). If the mind does exert an influence on bodily processes, then the concepts of energy and force must be employed. (A glance at Freud's writings as well as most contemporary psychiatric and psychological journals attests to the frequent use of "psychic energy" and "mental forces" as presumed influences.) However, since energy can neither be created nor destroyed, the precise means by which "mental" and biological energies are interchanged and applied must be specified. (Freud, of course, contended that psychic energy was supplied and replenished through the usual biological channels of food consumption and metabolism; he shrewdly avoided the issue of how and where this interchange took place.) When "force" is used in terms of a formal physics definition (e.g., Force = Accelerated Mass), the mentalist has obvious problems to solve. Finally, Einstein's relativity theory contends that mass and energy are theoretically interchangeable. According to the behavioristic argument, this means that any reference to "psychic energy" is a reference to potential mass, thereby challenging the dualism at issue.

The foregoing arguments against "mind" and "mental" phenomena rely very heavily on theory and research in physics. It is my personal opinion that these specific arguments are logically inadequate in their efforts to invalidate mental phenomena. To begin with, many of them are relatively naive in their representation of contemporary physics. Relativity theory and the "potential mass" implication of psychic energy hold little philosophical promise for the anti-mind argument. All forces and energies, whether espoused by physicist or psychic, are inferred entities. Second, the physics-based arguments do not threaten the epiphenomenal theories of mind which explain "consciousness" in terms of wave or quanta by-products of brain activity. Finally, even if it were the case that contemporary atomic models were incompatible with mental phenomena, this would not settle the issue. If empirical evidence for such phenomena could be produced, so much the worse for contemporary physics. Our fickle "facts" and ever-changing theories should alert us to the naivete of rejecting a phenomenon because it is incompatible with our current picture of reality.

My own tentative skepticism regarding mental phenomena is based on (1) the glaring absence of testable or supported hypotheses indicating their existence, (2) the increasing percentage of behavioral processes which have been empirically reduced to physical phenomena, and (3) the arguments which suggest that the mind-body "problem" involves a linguistic rather than existential dilemma (e.g., Ryle, 1949).

John Watson's solution to the mind-body problem, of course, was a very simple one—he flatly denied the existence of mind and adopted a strict stance of materialistic monism. When challenged to explain thought processes from a physical standpoint, Watson answered by stating that all human behavior—including "thinking"—is the result of glandular secretions and muscular movements. Thinking, he said, is a type of "implicit speech" involving small but measureable contractions of the vocal chords. In an early study of this hypothesis, Jacobson (1932) reported that muscular responses could be detected in the speech apparatus of subjects who had been instructed to *think* or *imagine* various performance tasks. An ingenious extension of this line of research was described by Max (1935, 1937), who found that deaf mutes engage in subtle finger and arm movements during "abstract thinking." Since deaf mutes "speak" via hand signals, these findings again supported Watson's implicit speech hypothesis.

Not surprisingly, the public and professional reaction to Watson's "mindlessness" was extreme. Critics were quick to point out the ludicrousness of contending that the surgical removal of one's larynx would render one incapable of thought. It might be added that the converse is an equally telling criticism—politicians provide ample evidence that the possession of a well developed larynx does not insure the capacity for thought. However, Watson claimed that his critics had misinterpreted the ambitiousness of his implicit speech hypothesis: "I have never believed that the *laryngeal movement* as such played the predominating role in thought." (1924, p. 238.) As we shall see in a later chapter, the fact that laryngeal activity does correlate roughly with at least some forms of symbolic mediation may have important implications for controlled research in this area.

The contributions of John B. Watson to academic psychology were brought to a premature end in 1920. He had been criticized for the conduct of some of his private affairs and, following his divorce, was asked to resign from the Johns Hopkins faculty. He joined an advertising firm and apparently introduced Madison Avenue to classical conditioning. To some extent we may thank John Watson for the preponderance of classical conditioning paradigms in contemporary advertising (e.g., toothpaste that gives you sex appeal). However, there can be little doubt that his departure was an unfortunate event in the history of psychology: "Whatever our systematic position, we must regret the untimely loss of a figure whose vitality and clarity of expression commanded so much attention and (depending on one's bias) admiration or amazement." (Marx & Hillix, 1963, p. 139.)

Metaphysical or radical behaviorism has not survived in its original form. Although Skinner's (1974) *About Behaviorism* reiterates materialistic monism, it is a far cry from an orthodox Watsonian perspective. Few, if any, contemporary behaviorists would reduce all experience to glandular secretions and muscle movements. Although hereditary influences are still accorded a relatively minor role, their existence and relevance have been grudgingly conceded. And, although private events are far from being the bailiwick of the contemporary behaviorist, the research reviewed in this text will hopefully dispell any absolute notions about the non-cognitive myopia of all behavioral approaches.

The cardinal feature of radical behaviorism, of course, was metaphysical—it denied the existence of mind. Borrowing from Bishop Fulton J. Sheen's description of atheists, one might say that a radical behaviorist is a person with no invisible means of support. The parallels between atheism and metaphysical behaviorism are intriguing. I recently posed the following question to Dr. Skinner: "If one were to equate the 'mind' with 'God,' would you call yourself an atheist or an agnostic?" His reply was unambiguous. I paraphrase: "If by mind you mean anything other than physical-biological processes, then I deny their existence." That is, of course, consistent with the position he has maintained in the past: "Behaviorism begins with the assumption that the world is made of only one kind of stuff—a stuff dealt with most successfully by physics. . . . Organisms are part of that world, and their processes are therefore physical processes." (Blanshard & Skinner, 1967.)

The straightforward denial of mind and mental processes, however, is infrequently encountered among present-day behaviorists. This is perhaps partly due to the fact that Gilbert Ryle (1949) and other philosophers have convinced many behavioral scientists that the mind-body problem is a linguistic illusion. Their contention, sometimes referred to as the "double-language" theory of mind, asserts that mental/physical dualisms are a result of our linguistic habits. As we shall see in a later section, humans do not passively observe some "true reality." On the contrary, each individual actively constructs his own private reality by selectively attending to a very small percentage of available stimulation and by organizing this select input according to a complex system of rules. Our culture and language system have encouraged us to talk about private (covert) and public (overt) phenomena as if they were qualitatively different. Ryle (1949) offers a lengthy presentation of "linguistic analysis" as it applies to mind-body dualisms. (It is interesting to note that linguistic analysis has likewise been popular in contemporary philosophy of religion—cf. W. I. Matson, 1965.)

Adopting Ryle's position, present day behaviorists have abandoned the mind-body controversy (which has little practical bearing on their everyday endeavors anyway). A strong aversion to mentalistic terms remains, however, as a legacy of metaphysical behaviorism. For many, the aversion has generalized to virtually all mediational processes:

1. mentalistic terms and concepts are unscientific and hence bad;
2. cognitive-symbolic (mediational) concepts are mentalistic;
3. therefore, mediational concepts are bad.

Both the major (1) and minor (2) premises of the above syllogism are unjustified, as we shall soon see. Although a continuing literature is addressed to these issues (e.g., Royce, 1973; Keat, 1972; Alston, 1972; Day, 1969a,b, 1971), arguments about mind-body, mental-physical, and private-public dichotomies compromise a progressively less significant feature of contemporary behaviorisms.

METHODOLOGICAL BEHAVIORISM

It was mentioned earlier that John B. Watson proposed and defended two different subtypes of behaviorism—metaphysical and methodological. Although he was not the progenitor of the methodological variety, his outspoken defense and clarification of its crucial importance warrant his being given primary responsibility for its development and growth in the United States. *Methodological behaviorism* is concerned mainly with the procedures and methods of psychological inquiry rather than with its subject matter. Watson wanted to objectify psychology along the lines of the physical sciences and was particularly opposed to the subjectivity of the previously popular introspective methods. Observability became his cardinal criterion for scientific accessibility. If a phenomenon could be publicly observed and objectively described, then it was an allowable scientific variable. Watson explicitly recommended that psychologists restrict their theories and research to observable events—environmental stimuli and overt behavior.

Describing methodological behaviorism is about as ambitious as describing "scientific method." Just as there are few explicit boundaries to the procedures entailed in scientific research, there are few hard and fast directives for methodological behaviorism. Moreover, although the singular form of the term is often employed, a continuum of distinguishable behaviorisms should be kept in mind. Methodological behaviorisms are a culmination of both early and contemporary contributions. Although they share several basic philosophical assumptions, they also demonstrate some procedural heterogeneity. Depending on the version in question, research may be done with individual subjects or with groups. Data may be analyzed via statistics or by visual inspection. Experimental hypotheses may be deduced from comprehensive theories or induced from previous experimental findings.

From a philosophical viewpoint most methodological behaviorisms incorporate varying degrees of operationism, logical positivism, falsificationism, linguistic analysis, and pragmatism. The following general characteristics are frequently represented:

1. an assumption of macroscopic *determinism*—i.e., that systematic relationships characterize certain classes of events (cf. Mahoney, Kazdin, & Lesswing, 1974);
2. an emphasis on *observability:* when two event classes are hypothetically mediated by one or more intervening elements (e.g., physiological or enteroceptive stimuli), the first and final events must be observable;
3. a pragmatic adoption of *operationism* in which independent and dependent variables are each clearly and objectively specified according to the procedures (operations) entailed in their *measurement* (cf. Bachrach's (1965) discussion of "data language"); the objectivity of operational definitions is often assessed via measurements of *reliability;*
4. a strong emphasis on *falsifiability* (or testability) as the cardinal feature of meaningful scientific hypotheses and legitimate empirical research (cf. Turner, 1967); the methodological behaviorist must be able to specify what data would have bearing on the truth value of his hypotheses;
5. an emphasis on *controlled experimentation* as the ultimate means for accumulating and refining knowledge about behavior; the experimentation must itself incorporate the first four characteristics

and must demonstrate experimental control by reporting objective measurements of a dependent variable in both the presence and absence of an isolated independent variable (either within a single subject or between groups of subjects; cf. Campbell and Stanley's (1963) discussion of "internal validity"); the effects of an isolated independent variable may also be demonstrated via careful statistical control (although this is disputed among contemporary behaviorists);

6. a positive valuation of *independent replication* and *generalizability*: when a specified relationship has been observed by one or more independent researchers, confidence in its legitimacy is increased; when a relationship has been shown to be applicable (generalizable) to other subject populations or similar phenomena, the breadth of its relevance is enhanced.

The epistemological defensibility of the foregoing methodological conventions, however, is far from unequivocal (Weimer, in press). The contemporary behavioral researcher relies almost exclusively on a scientific metatheory which has long since been rejected by its progenitors (cf. Chapter 16). Falsification has been shown to be an indefensible criterion in the growth of knowledge (e.g., Lakatos, 1970), and "data" can hardly be considered objective arbiters in our search for "truth." In short, contemporary philosophies of science suggest that the methodological behaviorist may be sorely deluded and glaringly anachronistic in holding to his revered experimental practices. This possibility will be explored further in Chapter 16.

For the time being, I should perhaps confess my own biases. Although readily acknowledging that our "data" are always selective and distorted, my prejudices in epistemology favor "experience" over "expectancy." We like to presume that philosophy and "reality" are at least occasionally compatible. However, there will always be conflicts between data and doctrine. When they arise, I shall—perhaps naively—put my money on the data—recognizing full well that those data are distorted by my myriad information processing fallibilities. Philosophical systems are, after all, artificial, language-based strategies for describing and organizing our sensations. As such, they are fallible tools to be revised or discarded according to their utility in performing that task.

Unlike its metaphysical sibling, methodological behaviorism has not only endured but proliferated. As mentioned earlier, a variety of emphases are represented along the broad continuum which describes contemporary behavioristic methodology. Borrowing from the area of political science, one might label that continuum in terms of conservative (right-wing) and liberal (left-wing) perspectives. The right-wing behaviorist is generally less tolerant of inferred variables, statistical analysis, group research, and free love (they usually want to make the latter contingent). Left-wing behaviorists, on the other hand, are generally more flexible in terms of methodological procedures and inferred variables *so long as an empirical utility is demonstrated.* (Their love is thus not as non-contingent as they might have you believe.) I shall not extend the analogy to "John Birchers" and "bleeding-heart liberals" because of the emotional connotations of those labels. Suffice it to say that the "conservative" end of the continuum is more heavily populated by individuals who adopt a relatively strict Skinnerian (operant) viewpoint, while the "liberal" end is comprised of the "good guys." (I am at least explicit in my biases.)

Lest I misrepresent the mutual respect and reciprocal reinforcement interchanged along all points on this continuum, I shall here offer some serious comments about the relatively minor distinctions involved. Viewed against the backdrop of the fundamental assumptions shared by virtually all methodological behaviorists, their different procedural preferences appear negligible. Few would deny that the conservative paradigms of operant researchers represent some of the most exquisite and powerful applications of an empirical approach. The extensive contributions of controlled "non-operant" inquiries are equally salient. Thus, notwithstanding the above political analogy, it should be recognized that most contemporary behavior modifiers share a wide range of commonalities.

A growing number of researchers have likewise begun to defend the utility of varying procedures in diverse situations. An individual scientist may opt for a single-subject design in one instance, a controlled group design in another, and a combined design in still a third. Statistical analyses may be deemed appropriate for some types of data but less useful in other areas. My bias again lies with empirical utility. Both "conservative" and "liberal" behavioristic methods, then, have demonstrated unquestionable assets and made invaluable contributions to our knowledge about human behavior.

The fundamental principles describing infrahuman, child, and certain forms of adult behavior were established by conservative researchers. Without the conceptual and technological foundations they laid, functional analyses of more complex behavior patterns could not have evolved. However, it is the theme of this book that a mediational model—grounded firmly in empirical methodology—has demonstrated more pragmatic utility in the understanding and control of at least some human behaviors. Before discussing that perspective we shall briefly examine its historical and methodological predecessor, the "nonmediational model."

Chapter Three

Inference: The Illegitimate Leap?

The non-mediational model is sometimes referred to (especially by its critics) as "black box psychology," "stimulus-response (S-R) theory," and the "empty organism hypothesis." Its major characteristic is a very strong emphasis on *input* and *output*. Input consists of stimulation entering the organism; output consists of an observable response. No behaviorists have ever maintained that the organism is literally empty; however, their energetic avoidance of internal factors has often stimulated heated criticism. It is interesting to note that although Skinner's defenses of the non-mediational model are perhaps more widely read than others (Skinner, 1945, 1950, 1953, 1959, 1963), several other contemporary behaviorists have adopted what appear to be even more conservative stances on this issue (e.g., Gerwirtz, 1971; Stuart, 1972).

HYPOTHETICAL CONSTRUCTS AND INTERVENING VARIABLES

The term "non-mediational" should perhaps be qualified before we continue. A mediating variable is an inferred (unobserved) factor which relates stimulus input to response output. Even a radical behaviorist will concede that an animal's response to the sight of food is mediated by his nervous system and auxiliary physiological components (muscles, glands, etc.). The mediation in this example is "structural" in that it is comprised of potentially observable, physical elements. When an inferred variable is presumed to be potentially observable, it is referred to as a "hypothetical construct." (Note that "inferred" means unobserved, not unobservable.) Thus, a researcher who postulates that schizophrenia is caused by a biochemical deficiency is inferring the existence of a hypothetical construct. The "potential observability" of such a construct is determined by whether or not it *could* be discriminated by accurate measurement and/or sophisticated instrumentation, not whether it already has been observed. For most behaviorists, virtually all mediational variables are hypothetical constructs—i.e., they involve a series of neuro-chemical processes which could in principle be observed.

Another type of mediating element is called an "intervening variable." Unlike the hypothetical construct, which serves a structural function in relating input to output, an intervening variable is not potentially observable. It performs a conceptual or descriptive role in mediation. For example, Skinner's (1945) reference to his "enthusiasm" suggests an intervening variable. Unless he were to specify the structural components of enthusiasm, we must assume that he was referring to a descriptive factor relating previous stimulus input to future response production. Notice that intervening variables can often be transformed into hypothetical constructs simply by designating their (potentially observable) physical substrata.

An illustration of the distinction between these two classes of mediators might take the form of hypotheses regarding the causes of smoking behavior. Researcher A contends that after some specified interval of cigarette deprivation a nicotine deficiency develops and is followed by a smoking response. The hypothesized nicotine deficiency here is a structural mediating element and therefore a hypothetical construct. Researcher B, on the other hand, contends that cigarette deprivation simply increases one's tendency to smoke. The term "tendency" here is an intervening variable. One would not expect to surgically discover a smoking tendency lurking somewhere in the depths of the spleen. However, the term relates input (cigarette deprivation) to output (smoking) through the statistical concept of probability or likelihood. *A hypothetical construct is unobserved, while an intervening variable is unobservable.* Both, of course, are inferred and presumably perform some mediating function. A more detailed discussion of their distinction is presented by MacCorquodale and Meehl (1948).

THE NON-MEDIATIONAL MODEL

Although Skinner and other proponents of the non-mediational model would readily concede the existence of at least some hypothetical constructs (e.g., proprioceptive and enteroceptive cues, nerve pathways, etc.), their admitted assumption is that such mediators are simply structural prerequisites for behavior and hold little promise as the focus of experimental inquiry. Skinner's (1950) critique of learning theories expresses this assumption very clearly. Contrary to the popular misinterpretation of his views, Skinner's objection was not to theorizing per se, but to theorizing which posits explanations at a level which is different from that of the observed phenomenon. He criticizes "any explanation of an observed fact which appeals to events taking place somewhere else, at some other level of observation, described in different terms, and measured, if at all, in different dimensions." (Skinner, 1950, p. 193.) Explanations of behavior should be stated in terms of behavioral variables and not neural, mental, or conceptual elements. His objections to a mediational model apply equally to both physiological and psychodynamic theories.

The non-mediational model is best conceptualized as a straightforward input-output analysis. This view is illustrated in Figure 3-1. As long as a systematic relationship exists between incoming stimuli and outgoing responses, the extent of mediating factors (physiological transformations, psychodynamic contortions) is irrelevant. After entering the organism, stimulus A can perform any range of private gymnastics, but—so long as response A is produced—speculations about mediators are not functional. When invariant stimulus-response patterns are displayed, the behavioral scientist does best to restrict his conceptualization and research to them. No inferred mediators could add to the precision of his prediction or control since all of the variability in responding is adequately accounted for by observable stimulus input.

This non-mediational perspective is a direct outgrowth of early behavioristic convention. It has demonstrated unquestionable utility in the analysis of a wide range of animal behaviors and in the

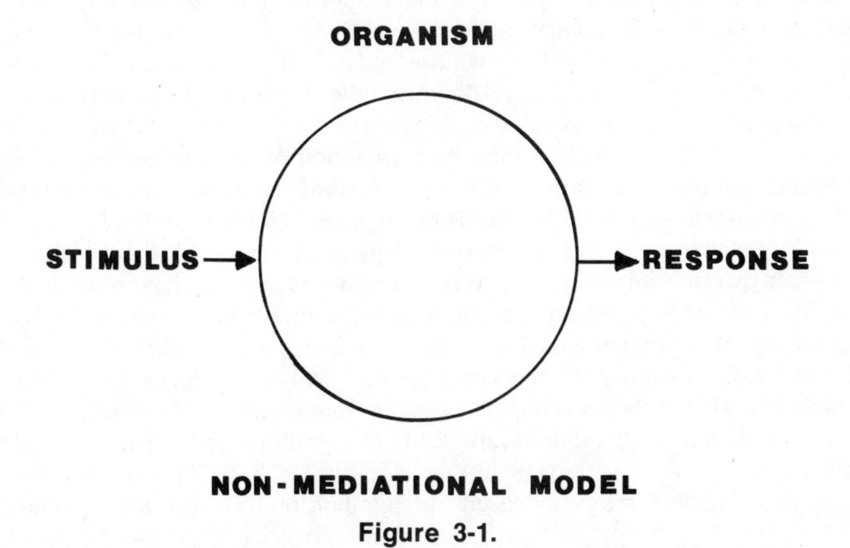

Figure 3-1.

objective examination of some human performances. The assets of the non-mediational model are readily apparent: it is simple, direct, and "parsimonious." This last asset deserves further examination.

The *principle of parsimony* states that one should avoid unnecessary inferences and nonessential complexities in explaining behavior. When two different hypotheses adequately account for some phenomenon, parsimony dictates that preference be given to the simpler, more conservative hypothesis. Thus, an unparsimonious hypothesis or theory is one which invokes superfluous influences. Because these influences are often unobserved, many behavioral scientists have viewed the terms "inferential" and "unparsimonious" as synonyms. The implication, of course, is that inferences go beyond the evidence—they are conceptual steps away from the data. This is undeniably a misrepresentation of the principle as it was first formalized:

> In no case may we interpret an action as the outcome of the exercise of a higher psychical faculty, if it can be interpreted as the outcome of the exercise of one which stands lower in the psychological scale (Morgan, 1899, p. 59).

This directive is often called "Lloyd Morgan's cannon" or "Occam's razor" (the latter giving credit to the historical originator of the principle, the fourteenth century theologian William of Occam). Morgan's formalization of the principle of parsimony was a reaction to contemporary anthropomorphism in his own field of study (zoology). It was not, as many behaviorists seem to feel, a blanket prohibition against inference or mediation. As Bannister (1966) says, "Occam's razor should be used to sharpen our wits, not to whittle away our imaginations." Some contemporary interpretations of the principle of parsimony in behavioral science are reviewed by Newbury (1954).

Notwithstanding their bastardization of its purpose, behavior modifiers continue to frantically wave the banner of parsimony as though it emblazoned a cardinal prerequisite for truth. Unfortunately, the principle of parsimony has no formal logical defense—Mother Nature doesn't owe us simplicity. If two theories are exactly equivalent in their abilities to predict and explain phenomena, we have no *logical* basis for choosing the simpler one. We do, however, have some *practical* justification in opting for the less complex. All other things equal, we might prefer that theory which is easier to understand and communicate. Moreover, since all theories are artificial symbolic representations of the world as we see (construct) it, our choice between two equally adequate models may be based on symbol preferences and similar atheoretical issues. The point, however, is that parsimony per se is not a logical virtue.

There are reasons, of course, for the continuing valuation of parsimony in behavior modification, using "parsimony" in its current terminological sense (and not in that intended by Morgan). For the contemporary behavioral researcher, parsimony implies scientific conservatism, explanatory rigor, and a close proximity to data. In contrast to more speculative models of behavior, a parsimonious model invokes a minimum of inference and "touches bases" with the data very frequently. The bulk of the model is data-based and it is careful to avoid the temptation of excessive speculation and superfluous embellishment.

From an historical perspective, there is ample support for some adherence to this variety of parsimony in behavioral science. We have repeatedly witnessed the impotence of theories which were prematurely dominated by speculative hypotheses. More important, we have learned the critical importance of a data base. In general, the further removed one gets from data, the greater the likelihood of error. Data allegedly have a way of "correcting" erroneous notions; they are an invaluable feature in the self-appraising endeavor of science.[a] Unfortunately, many psychologists spend more time looking at their theories than at the phenomena they purport to explain. They isolate themselves from data-based feedback—either through inadequate (and sometimes nonexistent) reality checks or by focusing on higher-order inferences which are comfortably removed from corrective data input.

We must be careful here, however, not to canonize "proximity to the data" (i.e., virtually complete reliance on directly observable evidence). As with most dichotomies, this one invites its own set of problems. In my opinion, the cardinal rule in choosing between two differing accounts of behavior is *not* their proximity to the data. Rather, it is their adequacy—the account which possesses more predictive accuracy and explanatory force is preferable regardless of the extent or dearth of its inferred variables. Skinner has repeatedly stated that mediational models of behavior are preferable to non-mediational ones if (and only if) they demonstrate superior utility in the prediction and control of behavior (Skinner, 1953, 1963, 1969, 1971). His contention, of course, has been that such superiority has not been demonstrated. It is the contention of this book that—in at least some areas of complex human functioning—mediational hypotheses offer a more adequate ac-

[a] The *relativity* of our data base should here be reiterated. Our data presumably "correct" our notions, but our notions often dictate and distort the data. We must remain apprised of this reciprocity and the inherent limitations in our pursuit of scientific knowledge.

count. Unfortunately, mediation and inference continue to bear negative connotations for many contemporary behaviorists. Before examining some of the shortcomings of the non-mediational model, a brief discussion of inference is in order.

INFERENCE: THE ILLEGITIMATE LEAP?

The foregoing discussion of the non-mediational model suggests what might be called the First Commandment of right-wing behaviorism: *Thou shalt not infer.* Inference involves a leap from observed to unobserved phenomena. According to early (and particularly Watsonian) behaviorisms, experimental analyses and conceptual explanations were to be restricted to directly observable events. This directive, which was even then philosophically naive, soon became an implicit badge of behaviorism. The terms "inference" and "unobserved" acquired the connotations of technical obscenities. Traditional, psychodynamic, and trait-state accounts of behavior were quickly "disposed of" by simple reference to their use of inferred variables.

The anti-inference convention continues to play a significant role in the description of contemporary behaviorists. It is both surprising and unfortunate, however, that this non-mediational bias is so often carried beyond both logical justification and practical utility. For many present-day behavior modifiers all inferences are considered "bad." Private, unobserved events are automatically classified as "mentalistic" and therefore illegitimate and unscientific. Inferred mediators, even when they are operationally specified, are often disdainfully rejected as "soft," unparsimonious, and superfluous.

It is interesting to note that Skinner (1945) rejected early forms of methodological behaviorism because of their exclusion of (inferred) private phenomena. He argued against the assertion that "public-private" distinctions are equivalent to "physical-mental" ones and objected to Boring's statement that "Science does not consider private data." The candor of this early and often overlooked defense of private phenomena is best reflected in Skinner's own words: "The irony of it is that, while Boring must confine himself to an account of my external behavior, I am still interested in what might be called Boring-from-within."

Notwithstanding this rather clear acknowledgment of private data, many "Skinnerian" behavior modifiers proclaimed a vow of strict inferential celibacy. Their avoidance of the unobserved was undoubtedly influenced by a variety of factors—the apparent impotence of earlier introspection methods, the "physical sciences" model, and so on. There is a certain irony in early and present-day efforts to emulate the physical sciences in both paradigm and theory. The irony, of course, derives from the fact that physical scientists rely very heavily on inferences. No one has ever *seen* an electron, a pi-meson, or even a quark. Moreover, many contemporary researchers who strive to emulate the methodological and conceptual purity of what has been facetiously labeled the "Holy Trinity" (Skinner, Keller, and Schoenfeld) overlook the extent to which these respected contributors have relied on inferred variables. Even the most operational of descriptions invokes a range of perceptual and conceptual leaps. Thus, Skinner's extensive discussion of "rule-governed behavior," private events, and problem-solving is highly inferential (1953, 1969). Although he goes to great terminological pains to impose operant conditioning labels on covert phenomena, calling them "stimuli" and "responses" does not obviate their inferential nature:

> Some of the objects of introspection are private (covert) responses. . . . The stimuli they generate are weak but nevertheless of the same kind as those generated by overt responses. It would be a mistake to refuse to consider them as data just because a second observer cannot feel or see them, at least without the help of instruments (Skinner, 1969, p. 242).

Instruments, of course, do not allow us to directly observe a phenomenon—they simply help us to quantify our inferences. Skinner has never directly tapped the private experiences of others (their dreams, memories, etc.) or even the "weak stimuli" which, he contends, they produce. Nonetheless, he spends hundreds of pages in meaningful scientific discourse attempting to account for them. Similarly, it is doubtful that either Keller or Schoenfeld (1950) would contend that they have actually *seen* "interoceptive" or "proprioceptive" stimuli. These phenomena, however, perform critical explanatory functions in their account of complex behavior. Finally, the doctrine of naive realism—although implicit in many behavioristic writings (Mahoney, Kazdin, & Lesswing, 1974)—cannot be logically defended by contemporary behaviorists. Converging evidence from the fields of perception, epistemology, and physics emphasizes the overwhelmingly inferential nature of everyday experience, not to mention controlled experimental observations.

Thus, inferences are not only justified but essential in behavioral science. No amount of non-mediational campaigning can totally eliminate perceptual leaps and conceptual shorthand in our analysis of behavior. The very process of empirical induction presumes a wealth of unobserved but anticipated regularities in nature. Blanket criticisms of all inferences as "unscientific" sorely misrepresent contemporary philosophies of science (e.g., Nagel, 1961; Kuhn, 1962; Kaplan, 1964; Polanyi, 1958, 1966; Lakatos & Musgrave, 1970).

The primary issue in mediational versus non-mediational accounts of behavior is not *whether* inferences are justifiable, but rather *which* inferences are legitimate and useful. As pointed out earlier, the acceptability of a hypothesis or theory is determined by its adequacy and predictive force, not by its parsimony or lack of inferences. Many behaviorists, of course, presume a strong positive correlation between these characteristics—that is, that non-inferential and parsimonious accounts of behavior are usually more capable of predictive accuracy and explanatory breadth. This is in fact the basis of Skinner's often misinterpreted stance on mediation and inference. While strongly defending the existence and importance of private experience, he contends that its difficult accessibility makes it an unpromising realm for our experimental inquiries.

It might be useful at this point to summarize some of the main behavioristic objections to conventional inferences. Skinner's (1963) article again offers a succinct and relatively straightforward presentation of this point of view. It should be borne in mind that the prohibitions against inference were specifically aimed at various *types* of inference rather than at inferences per se.

(1) Behaviorists have objected to inferences which invoke non-physical (mental) phenomena (e.g., psychic energy). Their basis for this objection is usually metaphysical, although corollary defenses from some of the subsequent arguments are also proposed.

(2) Skinner (1950) has objected to accounts of behavior that invoke variables at levels other than that of the phenomenon observed. That is, stimulus-response relationships should be explained in terms of stimuli and responses. The introduction of other elements—physical or non-physical, observed or inferred—is both unnecessary and confounding. This objection is basically terminological, requiring the theorist to maintain a specified system and level. The fundamental objection is to mediation, not inference. Its defense is based more on presumed and alleged practical advantages in theoretical explanation rather than on any formal logical defense.

(3) Objections have frequently been voiced against "explanatory fictions" (Ullmann & Krasner, 1969). An explanatory fiction is an inferred causal variable whose only justification is the effect it has allegedly produced: aggressive behavior is observed; an aggression "need" or "drive" is inferred to explain this behavior. The only justification for this inference, however, is the behavior it was invoked to explain. "She killed him out of hate. How do you know she hated him? Well, she killed him, didn't she?" The formal objection here is that

many conventional psychological inferences are logically circular. They involve analytic "truths" (i.e., are true by definition) and are therefore tautologous.

(4) An auxiliary argument criticizes the reification process which is frequent in traditional psychological inference. What the organism *does* is transformed into what it *has*. Heightened activity becomes "curiosity." Rapid learning becomes "innate intelligence." The individual does not *behave* schizophrenically—he *has* schizophrenia. As Mischel (1968, 1971) points out, the transition is from verbs to nouns, from behavior samples to psychic states. Descriptive statements evolve into "explanatory" ones (affectionate behaviors become affection-induced, schizophrenic behaviors become schizophrenia-induced, etc.). Skinner extends this non-reifying bias of behaviorism to the explanation of conscious experience: "seeing does not imply something seen." (1969, p. 234.) Thinking does not imply a thought, remembering does not require a memory.

(5) Skinner's major objection to inferred variables, however, is not based on their physical-mental, circular, or reifying corollaries. Rather, it is based on what he calls "incomplete causal analysis" (Skinner, 1959, 1963; Blanshard & Skinner, 1967). Attributing an observed behavior (Event N) to an inferred influence (Event n-1) is useful if and only if we can specify the antecedent conditions which produced the inferred influence (i.e., Events n-2, n-3, etc.). Eventually, one or more of these antecedents will be observable. Since we are presumably more accurate when our analyses rely only on observed phenomena, we might just as well avoid the intervening "mental way stations" and deal with the observed elements in the chain (Skinner, 1963). This argument might be illustrated as follows:

Observed Event	*Unobserved Events*	*Observed Event*
N-X	(n-4) (n-3) (n-2) (n-1)	N
Parental Punishment During Toilet Training (Age 2)	. . . (libidinal focus in anal area) (anal fixation) . . .	Stamp Collecting Behaviors (Age 12)

Skinner's non-mediational argument is that "explaining" event N by reference to event (n-1) is not adequate unless we can account for the latter. Also, as long as there is a lawful relationship between the two observed elements in the chain (events N and N-X), discussions of inferred mediators are superfluous—they add nothing to our analysis. Skinner's argument is basically pragmatic and has some support in practical applications. All too many significant phenomena are pursued to the point of a mental way station and then left there (Skinner, 1971, 1974). The buck gets passed to the "inner man" or to an infinite array of psychic abstractions and the scientist—deluded into thinking he has found their cause—terminates his inquiry and turns to his other delusions of relevance.

Unfortunately, the formal defensibility of Skinner's "observable cause" argument is meager. It invokes several questionable premises. Without belaboring their intricacies, they may be paraphrased as follows. To begin with, consider the assumption that an explanatory (cause-effect) statement is adequate if and only if the invoked cause can itself be explained. This suggests an infinite regress of causation and a *reductio ad absurdum* since one can never reach a first cause. To handle this dilemma, Skinner says he will accept certain *observable* causes in the chain, thereby avoiding an infinite regress and magically making the explanatory account "adequate." The supremacy of environmental causation has been recently elaborated in Skinner's (1974) reiteration of radical behaviorism: "the initiating action is taken by the environment rather than by the perceiver." (p. 73.)

This arbitrary appointment of an external "prime mover" has obvious logical flaws. We have no reason to believe that observed events are more primary or "better" causes than unobserved ones. Our preference for them comes from expediency, not logic: "A cause in the hand is worth two in the head." Unfortunately, behaviorists have a history of seeking "first causes" in the external environment and presume a one way determinism (environment to behavior). We observe a sequence of events in an endless chain of behavior-environment alterations. Our conceptual biases suggest that one is "a function of" the other. Thus, Goldiamond's (1965) representation of "behavior as a function of environment" ($B = f(x)$) implies a one way causal process. Bandura (1971c), however, has pointed out that environment is often a function of behavior ($X = f(b)$), as illustrated in many self-regulatory phenomena (Thoresen & Mahoney, 1974). If we were to adopt a strict empiricism, our only data-based contention would be that changes in the one are frequently preceded and/or followed by changes in the other. Focusing on one kind of event in a particular analysis is arbitrary. Although our research articles traditionally present figures in which behavior (a "dependent" variable) is plotted against environment (the "independent" variable), we could just as easily reverse the axes in our graphs. The relationship remains just as orderly; the "direction" of its interpretation, however, is changed. If we adopt a causality framework, there is ample evidence to suggest a *reciprocal determinism* in which the interaction between environment and behavior is bidirectional.

The second major problem with Skinner's anti-mediation argument is that we are often unable to identify an *observable* causal element. The suicidal client may not provide us with sufficient data to point to one or more previous observables which account for his wrist-slashing responses. Even if he does, these events would be historical and therefore beyond our current observability. For example, in clinical applications we often delve into causal sequences only to the extent that they are useful in our therapy. As will be substantiated later in this book, that sequence may often extend only as far as the individual's current self-stimulation—that is, his pattern of private monologues. How the suicidal client became self-critical and depressed is not as therapeutically important as the manner in which these self-stimulatory influences can be modified.

The third deficiency in Skinner's argument derives from empirical rather than logical considerations. There is now an overwhelming body of evidence indicating that a "passive organism" input-output model is sorely inadequate. Not only are there complex causal interactions among environmental and internally-based stimulations, but we now know that much of what is "external" is actually mediated. Humans do not passively register the world as it really is; they filter, transform, and construct the experiences which constitute their "reality." Some of the basic phenomena which demand this mediational perspective will be discussed at length in the next chapter. Before turning our attention to them, however, some conclusions need to be drawn about the role of inference in behavioral research.

In conclusion, the non-mediational argument against inference has little formal logical support. Its practical and empirical advantages are also limited by the complexity of the phenomenon in question (see Chapter 4). Fortunately, Skinner has not adhered to a strictly non-inferential perspective. His extensive discussion of private events (1953) and his frequent defense of their status as scientific variables leave little room for doubt. He often imposes a "language of observables" on the unobserved, which may or may not facilitate their analysis. Two things, however, are very clear regarding Skinner's stance on covert phenomena:

1. he rejects references to private experience which invoke metaphysical dualism (i.e., mentalism), discrepant levels of analysis (e.g., physiological reductionism), explanatory fictions, reification, or incomplete causal analyses; and
2. he defends covert events as mediating behaviors which are not only legitimate but necessary in a comprehensive experimental analysis of complex human behavior.

These two statements are not contradictory; they are discriminatory. Skinner defends those inferences which (he believes) are useful in our understanding of behavior, and he rejects those which are not. Deciding which is which, of course, is no simple matter.

JUSTIFIED INFERENCE: LEGITIMIZING THE LEAP

I am reminded here of the story of a wealthy businessman who walked up to an associate's wife at a cocktail party and asked her if she would sleep with him for a million dollars. After determining the seriousness of his inquiry, she paused briefly and then assented. "How about twenty dollars?" he replied. "What do you think I am, a whore?" she retorted angrily. To which the businessman calmly said, "Madam, we have already determined *what* you are. Our current dispute is your price."

Our current concern is not *whether* inferences are justified, but rather *when* and *which* inferences add to our understanding of behavior. The extensive literature in epistemology and philosophy of science leaves no doubt that inferences are not only acceptable but essential in our knowledge gathering endeavors. Even when we restrict our purview to those philosophers who have had most direct influence on behavioristic philosophy, the pervasive reliance on controlled inference is unquestionable (cf. Kaplan, 1964; Turner, 1967).

Let us first consider the purpose of inferred variables in the understanding of behavior. It was pointed out earlier in this chapter that the basic function of mediational elements is a *connective* one;[b] that is, they serve to relate two or more observable units in temporal sequence. This tying together can be either structural—as in the case of hypothetical constructs—or conceptual—as in intervening variables. Their fundamental purpose, however, is technical. We usually infer mediational factors when so doing increases the amount of evidence which can be accounted for or when such inferences improve the logical consistency (reasonableness) of our hypotheses. The latter purpose is less defensible, in my opinion, because it presumes that reality must "make sense." Inferences defended only by their conceptual elegance are expensive adornments in behavioral science; our inferences must be evaluated by the relationships they predict, not the models they polish.

At the risk of oversimplification, I shall propose that most data-induced (as contrasted with theory-induced) inferences are stimulated by four basic empirical phenomena, each of which may be thought

[b] Note here that "connection" implies reference points which, in behavior modification, are typically stimuli and responses. However, human action is an unbroken chain; it is arbitrary and misleading to give unobservables the hackwork of connection while viewing observables as the "meat" of behavior. My concession to this bias, here and elsewhere, is derived from expedience and tradition, not logic.

of in terms of variability. In the first instance, two identical stimuli produce different responses.

Case 1	Stimulus A	Response A
	Stimulus A	Response B

We "account for" this seeming violation of determinism by positing unobserved elements (e.g., stimulus differentiation via selective attention or stimulus transformation, biological differences in the organism(s), differential response availability, etc.). The second instance occurs when two different stimuli are followed by identical responses.

Case 2	Stimulus A	Response A
	Stimulus B	Response A

We "explain" this performance identity by positing a stimulus equating factor. A third data-induced inference occurs when no observable stimulus is identified.

Case 3	(no observed stimulus)	Response A

To satisfy our cause-effect (deterministic) prejudices, we posit an "implicit" stimulus. Similarly, in the fourth instance, we explain lack of observable responsiveness in terms of presumed mediational elements (e.g., lack of stimulus perception, implicit (covert) responses, etc.).

Case 4	Stimulus A	(no observed response)

The four different instances may occur within a single subject, thereby inducing *intrasubject inference*. This is undoubtedly the most popular variety in psychology, as evidenced by the voluminous writings in personality theory (Mischel, 1968, 1971). Variability between or among different individuals induces *intersubject inferences,* as in the case of intelligence disparities, dispositional differences, and so on.

The above schema does not, of course, deny the fundamental structural (physiological) mediation which is presumed to occur in all organism-environment interactions irrespective of variability. However, it points out that inferences are expediencies. They are invoked only when the exigencies of the situation so demand. The scientific enterprise, characterized by Kaplan (1964) as the "drunkard's search," is not a smoothly executed mating of experience with theory. Far from an elegant wedding ceremony, it is a shotgun affair in which we grudgingly accept new perspectives only when forced to do so by the conspicuousness of our misdeeds.

The motivation for inference, then, is basically philosophical regardless of whether our leaps have been data-induced or theory-induced. We hold a presumptuous notion—occasionally reinforced by experience—that there are regularities in nature and that reality makes sense. We make inferences when the apparent "natural order" is violated. Generally, our inferences either modify the observed data or the presumed natural order.

1. Deterministic sequences occur regularly in nature (Natural Laws 1, 2, 3, . . . n).
2. Sequence X → Y violates Natural Law n.
3. Therefore,
   a Natural Law n is invalid (and should be rejected or modified), OR
   b Sequence X → Y was illusory (due to one of the four previously discussed inferential qualifiers).

An alternative conclusion, for the more pious, is that a miracle has occurred.

The foregoing comments have examined the issue of *when* we infer. The question of *which* inferences are justified demands further exploration. It is my contention that most of the heated argument regarding inference and mediation centers around this issue. Behaviorists have not generally liked the types of inferred variables chosen by traditional psychologists. "Ego strength," "achievement motivation" and the like have not sounded as scientifically pure as "reflex reserve" and "anticipatory goal response." However, the legitimate criterion for justifying an inference is not its theoretical source or metaphorical associations. It is neither its parsimony nor its proximity to the data. The sole criterion for justified empirical inference is pragmatic. *An inference is justified if, and only if, it increases predictive accuracy or conceptual breadth.* To the extent that a presumed element can be shown to be useful in predicting, controlling or understanding systematic relationships, then it is logically warranted.

Note that "post-diction" and ad hoc explanation are not given a major role in this justification. Although after the fact accounts of an observed irregularity may illustrate some of the assets of an inference, they also invite conceptual cop-outs. For example, a theorist can isolate himself from the corrective feedback of empirical evidence by equipping himself with an ever-ready supply of ad hoc explanations. Thus, the Freudian defense mechanism of "reaction formation" and the theological notion of "divine paradox" (God works in strange ways) effectively produce closed philosophical systems. The major criterion for inference involves accurate prediction of a phenomenon rather than sense-making renditions after its occurrence.

Chapter Four

Inadequacies of the Non-Mediational Model

As we saw in the last chapter, the adequacy of a theoretical model is determined by its ability to account for or describe systematic relationships. There are actually several means of evaluating such adequacy. Prediction is undoubtedly the strongest criterion. Post-diction, or after the fact explanation, is a second criterion. When a hypothesis can account for a considerable proportion of performance variability, it is deemed adequate (cf. Sidman, 1960). If a conceptual model can neither predict nor explain some phenomenon, it is inadequate. If it can explain but not predict, it demonstrates some adequacy. When it can both predict and explain an outcome, it offers the most complete account.

In the non-mediational model, a publicly observable stimulus is presumed to be systematically followed by a publicly observable response. However, as we shall see in this chapter, such simple and straightforward relationships are rare. The same stimulus is often followed by differing responses—both within the same organism over time and across different organisms. Moreover, there are many instances in which two dissimilar stimuli produce either identical or widely discrepant responses depending on certain moderating conditions. Finally, behavior patterns involving dramatic physiological arousal frequently occur in the absence of any previous observable stimulus. These deviations from simple input-output regularities not only invite but implore some empirically testable inferences. According to the mediational model, at least a portion of this performance variability is attributable to response processes within the organism. The following broad areas of research illustrate this contention.

MEDIATED STIMULUS TRANSFORMATION

A long-recognized phenomenon in perception and psychophysics is that the organism responds not to some "pure" external stimulus, but to a "stimulus as perceived." Thus, there may be instances in which an organism responds differentially to two identical stimuli. If the behavioral scientist has some means of knowing how a stimulus will be perceived, he can increase the accuracy of his performance predictions. This fact was dramatically illustrated in an early experiment performed by Neal Miller (1935). Miller presented the symbols "T" and "4" in random sequence and asked student subjects to pronounce them aloud. Their pronunciation of "T" was consistently followed by painful electric shock; verbalizations of "4" were never shocked. In a subsequent experimental phase, subjects were presented with a series of identical dots and instructed to "think T" to the first dot, "think 4" to the second one, and so on in continuing alternation. Physiological records of their autonomic responding indicated that the students were responding to the dot stimulus as perceived (or mediated). Thoughts of "T" elicited dramatic autonomic arousal while thoughts of "4" did not (Figure 4-1).

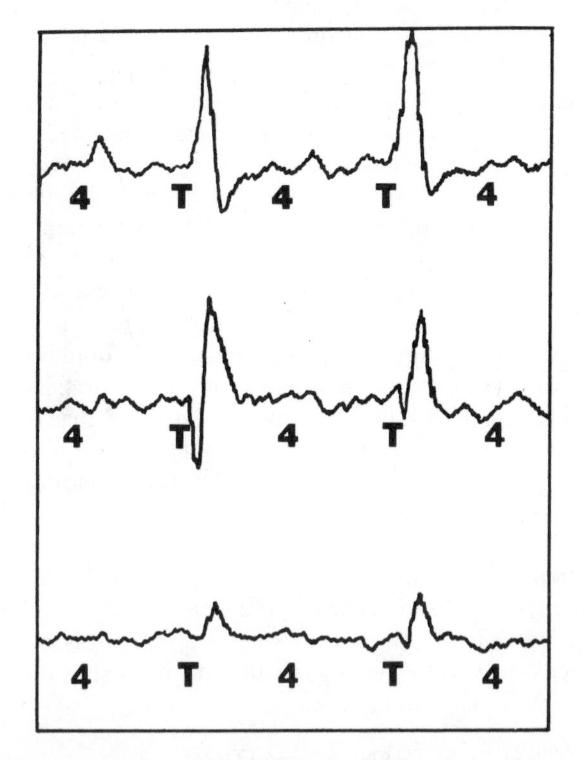

Figure 4-1. Conditioned galvanic skin responses mediated by thoughts. (Reprinted with permission from Miller, 1935.)

This experiment illustrated the extent to which knowledge of mediational processes can add to the researcher's predictive power.

The impact of mediated stimulus transformations is further demonstrated in several experiments by Dulany (1968). He placed subjects in an uncomfortably hot (110 degree) experimental chamber and presented them with a verbal learning task. On each of 100 trials subjects were to choose between two sample sentences. After a 20 trial baseline, subjects' choices were followed contingently by a blast of air which was either at chamber temperature, 40 degrees cooler, or 40 degrees hotter. This air blast was presented following choice of the one sentence in a pair which contained the article "a" prior to a key word. Some of the subjects were told that the air blast signified a correct choice while others were told that it indicated an incorrect choice or that it had no bearing on whether their choice had been correct or not. A 3 x 3 experimental design was thus employed: cool, neutral, and hot air blasts were labeled as either reinforcing, punishing, or neutral stimuli. A strictly non-mediational model might predict that the overt stimulus (air blast) would be systematically related to performance according to its physical characteristics. However, Dulany's data indicated that the effects of the air blasts were substantially influenced by the label placed on them. When subjects perceived a blast of hot air as punishing they reacted to it as an aversive stimulus by reducing their choice of the punished response. However, when subjects perceived this same stimulus as a reinforcer (signifying "correct"), they *increased* their choice of that sentence! The same was true for cool air blasts. Although this external stimulus should have been physically very reinforcing, it could be transformed into a punisher by simply programming the subject to interpret it as a sign of an incorrect choice.

The above represent only two of a multitude of studies suggesting that external stimuli are often modified through cognitive-symbolic processes. Humans respond to their perception or interpretation of a cue. Further evidence on the significant role of covert stimuli will be presented in later chapters.

SEMANTIC CONDITIONING AND GENERALIZATION

It has long been recognized (particularly by Russian investigators) that classical conditioning in humans involves much more than simple establishment of isolated stimulus-response bonds (Pavlov, 1955; Platonov, 1959; Razran, 1939, 1961, 1965). When words are used as the to-be-conditioned stimuli in respondent paradigms, some complex mediational processes come into play. For example, if the word "hare" is always followed by painful electric shock during training trials it will become a conditioned stimulus for autonomic arousal (increased pulse, respiration, etc.). During test trials, however, when no shock is presented, human subjects will display greater arousal to the stimulus "rabbit" than to the word "hair." That is, they generalize their conditioned response according to the semantic meaning of other words rather than their phonetic similarity. Maltzman (1968) presents an excellent review of the research and conceptualization in the area of "semantic generalization." Although attempts have been made to explain it in terms of complex stimulus-response associations, these accounts have necessarily become very mediational (cf. Osgood, 1953; Staats, 1968a).

As we shall see in a later chapter, extensive research has been performed in the area of human verbal learning and information processing. Some investigations have dealt with the topic of word associations. In this field of inquiry subjects are given a stimulus word such as "salt" and asked to write down the *first* word that comes to mind (e.g., "pepper," "peter," "ice," etc.). Lengthy compilations of word association norms have been published indicating the frequency with which subjects give various responses to word stimuli. In the above example, "pepper" might be a very frequent (i.e., strong) response to the stimulus "salt." Its associative strength, expressed in percentage of subjects who reported it, might be close to .90; "peter" and "ice" would probably be weaker associations. Maltzman (1968) performed an experiment in which he tested the relationship between associative strength and semantic generalization. Using a classical conditioning paradigm, the stimulus word "light" was followed by an aversive (110 decibel) noise. For some individuals the CS/UCS interval was 0.5 seconds; for others it was 10 seconds. Measures of autonomic arousal and classical conditioning were obtained through recordings of palmar GSR and peripheral vasoconstriction. During a subsequent test phase, subjects were presented with the following generalization stimuli: "dark," "lamp," "heavy," "soft," and "square." The associative value of these words to the stimulus word "light" ranges from high to low ("dark" having a strong association, "square" a weak association). The results from Maltzman's study are presented in Figure 4-2. Subjects who experienced the 10 second CS-UCS interval demonstrated little semantic generalization. However, when the 0.5 second interval was employed, an apparently systematic relationship was observed. The stronger the (mediated) association between a test stimulus and the original CS, the greater the autonomic arousal (CR). This suggested an impressive orderliness in the phenomenon. Subsequent investigations by Maltzman and others have questioned whether semantic generalization

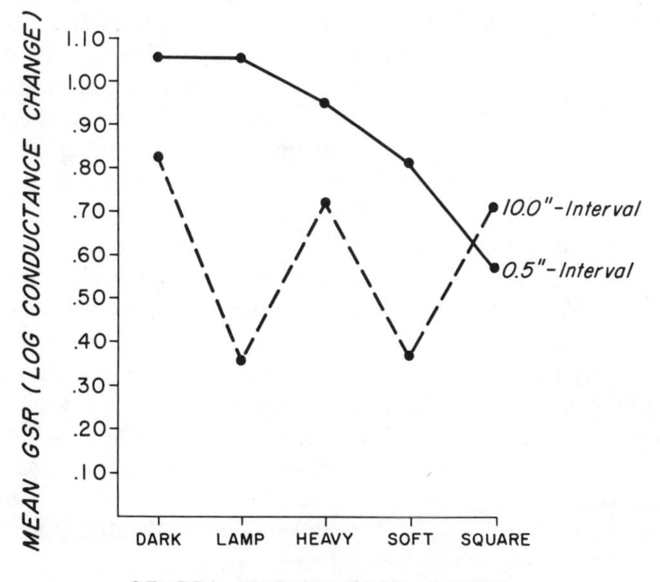

Figure 4-2. Semantic generalization of the galvanic skin response (GSR) following classical conditioning under two CS-UCS intervals. (Reprinted with permission from Maltzman, 1968.)

is as simple as all that. Factors such as order of test stimulus presentation and type of autonomic response measured have suggested more complexity than was originally encountered. However, the research in this area offers strong support for the role of mediational processes in even simple human learning paradigms.

SYMBOLIC SELF-STIMULATION

A third area of difficulty for strictly non-mediational models stems from the long-acknowledged evidence that verbal and imaginal stimuli play a very significant role in human performance. Pavlov (1955 translation) referred to language as a "second signal system" which uniquely equips the human with an almost infinite source of conditioned stimuli and the capacity for complex learning. Several of his early Russian colleagues demonstrated that words alone could elicit strong emotional reactions in subjects. For example, Platonov (1959 translation) reported that experimental subjects showed marked physiological reactions to pain-associated words (e.g., "hurt") and even to the intonation with which these words were spoken. Extensive research has subsequently shown that words can not only stimulate this arousal directly but can also become elements in chains of "higher order" conditioning (e.g., Staats, 1968 a, b; Staats & Hammond, 1972; Staats, Minke, Martin, & Higa, 1972; Staats, Gross, Guay, & Carlson, 1973; O'Donnell & Brown, 1973). In their work on attitude formation Staats and his co-workers have found that both positive and negative attitudes can be established by simply pairing to-be-conditioned stimuli with emotionally arousing words ("good," "bad," etc.). As we shall see in later chapters, words also function as significant mediators for complicated performance tasks.

The critical role of verbal and imaginal stimuli in human behavior is dramatically magnified by the fact that humans are self-stimulatory creatures. Soon after acquiring their language skills in infancy, humans begin a lifetime of overt and covert self-speech which is seldom interrupted. The audible self-instructional monologues of the toddler are gradually replaced by inaudible soliloquies which continue to direct and influence behavior. This gradual "internalization" of language behavior may be a relatively recent development in the species. Some philosophers (e.g., Jaynes, 1974) have speculated that part of Christ's charisma may have derived from his rare ability to think "to himself" (i.e., covertly). The survival value of being able to conceal performance strategies and interpersonal reactions can hardly be doubted (Terrace, 1971).

Do self-generated and covert stimuli elicit reactions comparable to those observed with external stimulation? The data are again both extensive and emphatic. When human subjects are asked to "think about" or "imagine" various stimuli or performances, measurable physiological effects are observed (cf. McGuigan & Schoonover, 1973). For example, Shaw (1940) reported that individuals instructed to *imagine* lifting weights of varying heaviness displayed arm muscle contractions proportionate to the imagined quantity of weight. When asked to imagine painful experiences (e.g., physical injury, social rejection), subjects exhibit corresponding emotional arousal (Rimm & Litvak, 1969). The documentation on symbolic self-stimulation is probably best presented by Bandura (1969), whose exhaustive and integrative literature survey repeatedly emphasizes this process in human performance. Subjects asked to imagine sexual stimuli display marked sexual arousal; those given pleasant or relaxing covert tasks exhibit calmer parasympathetic activity. Dramatic fear responses can be produced simply by cueing thoughts of an aversive stimulus.

The effects of symbolic self-stimulation can hardly be given enough credit in terms of their demonstrated importance in human functioning. Behavior modifiers have only recently begun to recognize and empirically document the pervasiveness and power of cognitive-symbolic mediation. An ever-increasing literature is providing expanded replications of covert influences as well as indicating the extent to which these influences play a role in common behavior problems (Bandura, 1968, 1969, 1971a, b, c, d, 1973; Kanfer & Phillips, 1970; Jacobs & Sachs, 1971; McGuigan & Schoonover, 1973; Thoresen & Mahoney, 1974). Indeed, the remainder of this book will be dominated by discussions of symbolic self-stimulation in behavior pathology and therapeutic procedures.

AWARENESS

A fourth area in which the non-mediational model has exhibited inadequacy is that of *awareness.* For well over a decade psychologists have debated about the role of awareness in human learning. Operationally defined, awareness is the subject's ability to verbalize or describe the contingencies imposed upon him. Non-mediational theorists have generally contended that awareness is not necessary for learning (e.g., Skinner, 1953; Verplanck, 1962). In their view, performance improvements are due to an almost automatic strengthening effect of reinforcing consequences. The antithesis of this view has been proposed by several mediational theorists, who maintain that awareness is an essential prerequisite for learning (Dulany, 1962, 1968; Spielberger & DeNike, 1966). In this latter approach, response consequences are predominantly viewed as informative cues rather than automatic "habit-stampers."

Research examining the role of awareness in human learning has been both extensive and complicated. Methodological problems in the actual assessment of this mediating response have confounded more than a few studies, and a definitive conclusion on the necessity of awareness has been elusive. However, the converging data justify a tentative statement: "The overall evidence would seem to indicate that learning can take place without awareness, albeit at a slow rate, but that symbolic representation of response-reinforcement contingencies can markedly accelerate appropriate responsiveness (Bandura, 1969, p. 577)." Awareness may not be necessary for learning, but it is undoubtedly facilitative. This conclusion is well documented by Bandura in his lengthy discussion of symbolic influences in behavior change.

In one sense, awareness represents what Skinner (1953) and others have called "rule-governed" (as contrasted with "contingency-governed") behavior (i.e., the subject responds to a symbolic representation or labeling of performance contingencies) (Terrace, 1971). The powerful role of experimenter-induced and subject-deduced awareness in both operant and respondent learning has received extensive examination (cf. Farber, 1963; Ayllon & Azrin, 1964; DeNike, 1964; Spielberger & DeNike, 1966; Spielberger, Bernstein, & Ratliff, 1966; Bridger & Mandel, 1964, 1965; Mandel & Bridger, 1967; Bandura, 1969; Grings, 1973).

A dramatic illustration of the facilitative impact of awareness was presented by Spielberger and DeNike (1966). Subjects were asked to verbalize words into a tape recorder. The dependent variable—number of human nouns produced—was measured during a baseline (operant level) phase. Subjects were then assigned to either an experimental or a control condition. In the experimental group, subsequent verbalizations of human nouns were followed by reinforcement ("Mmm-hmm") from the experimenter. Control subjects did not receive this reinforcement. Awareness of the contingencies on the part of experimental subjects was assessed by frequent probes and a post-experiment questionnaire. Figure 4-3 shows the results. The data of experimental subjects are plotted separately for aware and unaware individuals. As indicated in part A of the figure, knowledge of the reinforcement contingency dramatically influenced performance. Part B

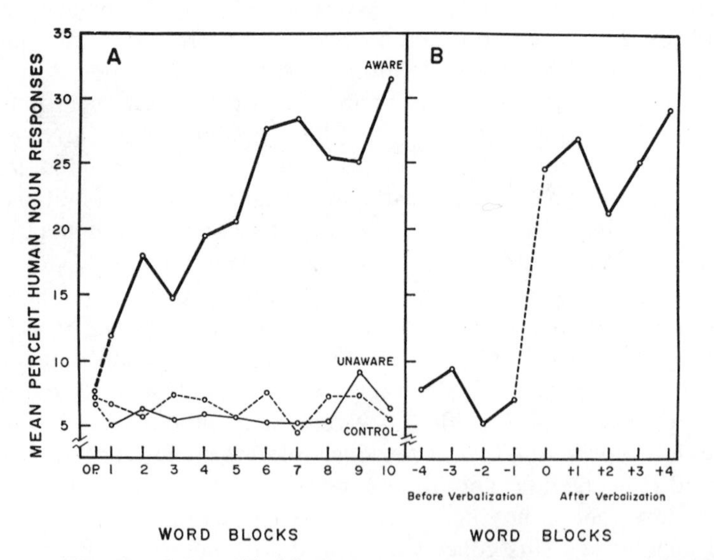

Figure 4-3. (A) Mean percent human noun responses given by aware, unaware, and control groups in the verbal conditioning task. (B) Mean percent of correct responses given by subjects in the aware group prior to and after verbalization of the reinforcement contingency. (Reprinted with permission from Spielberger & DeNike, 1966.)

illustrates the speed with which awareness had its impact. After subjects had verbalized the contingency, their mean percent of human noun production increased significantly.

Correspondingly impressive findings have been reported in the areas of classical conditioning and extinction. Notterman, Schoenfeld, and Bersh (1952), for example, paired a tone with painful electric shock. After conditioned heart rate responses were consistently elicited by the tone, extinction trials were begun. One group of subjects was informed that the shocks would be discontinued while a second group remained uninformed. In a third group subjects were told that pressing a telegraph key would subsequently result in shock avoidance. Widely discrepant extinction curves were evidenced. Informed extinction subjects and those provided with an avoidance response showed rapid extinction of heart rate conditioning in contrast to the unaware control subjects. These early findings—contributed, paradoxically, by "operant" researchers—have been replicated and extended in subsequent inquiries. Their implication of symbolic (mediational) influences in complex human behavior is both striking and heuristic.

VICARIOUS LEARNING PROCESSES

A fifth area which has seriously challenged the adequacy of the nonmediational model is that of vicarious (or observational) learning. From a survival standpoint, it is fortunate that many species do not rely exclusively on trial-and-error experience in the development and maintenance of their life-support responses. Most of the more recent members on the phylogenetic scale acquire extensive survival-relevant behaviors through indirect (i.e., vicarious) processes—namely, observations of other organisms. Animal research on the phenomenon of observational learning has shown that a wide range of behaviors can be rapidly learned through exposure to previously trained animals. Responses ranging from simple discriminations and lever presses to complex problem-solving tasks have been acquired vicariously by rats, pigeons, cats, dogs, chimpanzees, and monkeys (e.g., Morgan, 1896; Thorndike, 1898; Watson, 1908; Haggerty, 1909; Crawford & Spence, 1939; Warden, Fjeld, & Koch, 1940; Bayroff & Lard, 1944; Herbert & Harsh, 1944; Hayes & Hayes, 1952; Church, 1957; Darby & Riopelle, 1959; Corson, 1967). Valuable surveys of some of the research in this area are provided by Hall (1963), Riopelle (1967), and Bandura (1969). These reviews leave little room to doubt the power and pervasiveness of vicarious learning phenomena in infrahumans.

The amazing "savings" of both time and effort in this observational learning has been particularly impressive. When experimentally naive animals are allowed to observe the performances of previously trained subjects, they require substantially fewer trials to learn the task involved. In primates, perfect imitation is sometimes almost instantaneous. When such natural contingencies as food acquisition and predator avoidance are considered, the survival value of this "no trial learning" (Bandura, 1965) is quite apparent.

Extensive research with humans has likewise offered documentation for the significant role of vicarious processes. From birth to death a very large number of complex human skills are learned through modeling influences. The measurable effects of these influences have been categorized and described by Bandura (1969, 1971a,b,c,d).

First, an individual can acquire new responses by observing others' performances. Novel and complex skills can often rapidly be added to the individual's behavioral repertoire. Moreover, rudimentary and infrequent behaviors can frequently be refined and accelerated. A study by O'Connor (1969) illustrates some of the dramatic therapeutic potential of programmed vicarious training. Socially withdrawn preschool children were observed in a play situation. The frequency of their social interactions during pre-treatment assessment showed them to be socially deficient in contrast to a comparison group of non-isolate children. Half of the socially withdrawn subjects were subsequently shown a film depicting a child who gradually progressed from isolate to nonisolate play patterns, with corresponding peer reinforcement. The remaining group of isolate children served as controls and were shown a socially neutral film. The effects of filmed modeling are shown in Figure 4-4. Children who observed the progressively sociable model evidenced a dramatic increase in frequency of social interactions.

Observational learning involves acquisition of information about response-consequence relationships as well as performance components. An observer can learn not only how to do something but also what its probable effects will be. This motivational effect has repeatedly been documented (cf. Bandura, 1969, 1971a,d). When a model is reinforced for a specified performance, observers will subsequently increase their own rate of that behavior. Correspondingly, a response can be suppressed in one individual by allowing him to observe its punishing consequences to another person. There are notable parallels in the effects of direct and vicarious consequences. For example, individuals who observe a model being intermittently reinforced show greater resistance to extinction than observers who have witnessed continuous reinforcement (Berger & Johansson, 1968). The impact of vicarious reinforcement and punishment is not unlimited, however. Bandura (1971d) points out that factory workers would not long persist in their labors if their only reward were the occasional observation of a fellow worker receiving a paycheck.

The significance and clinical relevance of vicarious learning processes is perhaps most dramatically illustrated in the acquisition and elimination of human fears. An enormous body of laboratory and clinical evidence attests to the powerful influence of observational mechanisms in this area. For example, human subjects will readily acquire conditioned arousal to stimuli which have been paired with a model's painful experiences (e.g., Berger, 1962; Bandura & Rosenthal, 1966). Thus, the average television viewer or newspaper reader can acquire a range of debilitating fears through vicarious classical conditioning. Clinical records document the frequency with which clients display phobic avoidance patterns to stimuli with which they have never had direct or aversive contact. Many flight phobics, for example, have never flown; and, although few of you have ever directly experienced a painful snakebite, your reaction to an uncaged rattlesnake is quite predictable.

Just as autonomic and avoidance responses can be acquired

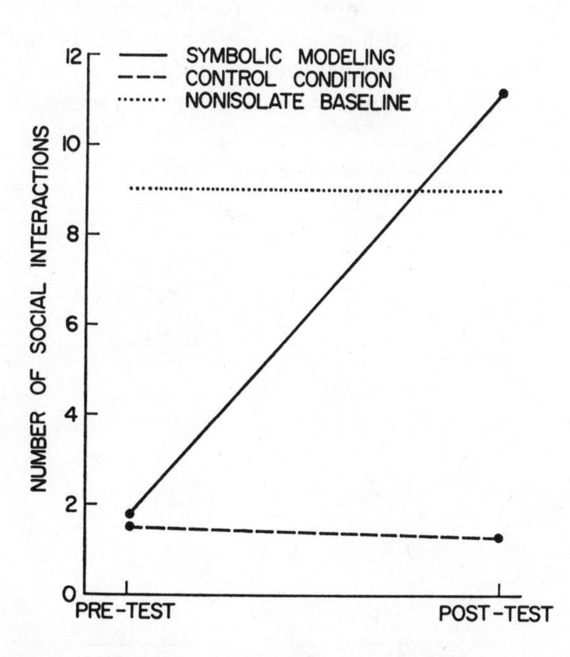

Figure 4-4. Mean number of social interactions displayed by subjects in the modeling and control conditions before and after the experimental sessions. The dotted line represents the level of interactions manifested by 26 non-isolate children who were observed at the pretest phase of the study. (Reprinted with permission from O'Connor, 1969.)

observationally, there is ample evidence that they can be vicariously extinguished (cf. Rachman, 1972; Bandura, 1969, 1971b, 1972). For example, Bandura and Menlove (1968) employed a modeling-based therapy in the treatment of dog phobic children. After a pre-treatment assessment, children were assigned to one of three conditions: (1) single model, (2) multiple model, or (3) control. Experimental subjects observed a film depicting either a single model or several different models engaging in progressively more threatening interactions with dogs. As shown in Figure 4-5, the symbolic modeling experience resulted in dramatic increases in dog-approach behaviors. In marked contrast to the post-experimental performance of control group children, subjects in both modeling conditions displayed significantly less avoidance behavior. Subsequent studies have extended and refined modeling-based therapy procedures (e.g., Bandura, Blanchard, & Ritter, 1968; Bandura, 1972).

A wide range of variables has been shown to influence vicarious learning processes. Model status, number of models, model-observer similarities, and task complexity are a few of the numerous factors which have been identified as significant.

Theoretical explanations of modeling and vicarious processes

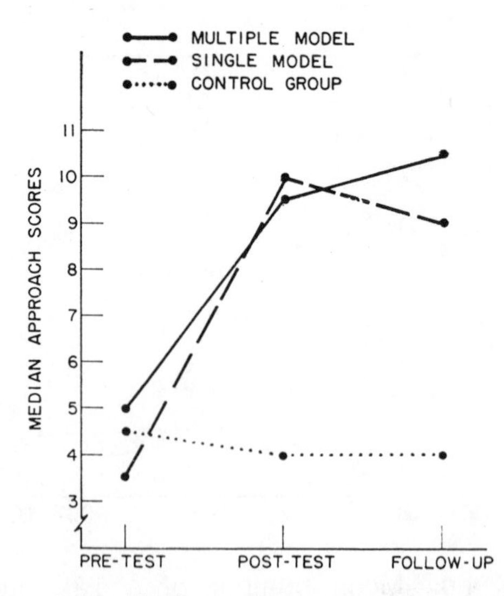

Figure 4-5. Median dog-approach scores achieved by children who received either single model or multiple model treatments or who participated in a control condition. (Reprinted with permission from Bandura & Menlove, 1968.)

have stimulated extensive research endeavors. One of the more controversial issues has dealt with its necessary conditions and underlying mechanisms. Non-mediational theorists, while readily acknowledging the evidence for observational learning, have contended that reinforcement is a necessary prerequisite for imitation (Miller & Dollard, 1941; Baer & Sherman, 1964; Gewirtz, 1971). The long-term maintenance of nonreinforced imitation has also been an issue. Non-mediational accounts have proposed that the act of imitation (i.e., the production of "matching" responses) acquires secondarily reinforcing properties due to prior learning. The organism thereby develops what is called "generalized imitation"—a high probability of future imitative performances (even with novel tasks). This hypothesis has been recently challenged by evidence on discriminative imitation, however. Bandura and Barab (1971) showed that children are not indiscriminately general in their imitation of a model. While they may initially generalize their matching responses and perform virtually every modeled behavior, they develop discriminations and imitate selectively when contingent reinforcement is given for only specified matching responses.

Actually, the "non-mediational" account of observational learning is not only inadequate but implicitly mediational. It proposes to account for actual imitative performances in terms of reinforcement contingencies but fails to give an adequate explanation of initial acquisition processes. Moreover, explanations of nonreinforced imitation and novel response matching are far from non-mediational when they invoke an inferential predisposition ("generalized imitation").

Bandura's social learning account of vicarious processes has received extensive empirical support and demonstrated considerable relevance for therapeutic applications (cf. Bandura, 1969, 1971a, b, c, d, 1972, 1973; Rachman, 1972). From this perspective, at least four subprocesses are involved. *Attentional* processes function in the discriminative observation of other organisms' performances. Information on the required response and existing contingencies must be attended to. To facilitate subsequent (and particularly delayed) imitative behavior this information must somehow be retained. *Retention* processes involving the symbolic coding and storage of performance and contingency information serve this function. *Motoric reproduction* processes deal with the organism's ability to recall and employ symbolic performance representations which can guide overt matching behaviors. Acquisition, retention, and reproduction potential are of little practical import, however, if *motivational* or incentive factors are not present. This distinction is important since it has direct bearing on the "learning versus performance" issue. An organism may be capable of a particular response but fail to perform it due to insufficient motivational influences. Theoretically, deficiencies in matching responses are attributable to deficiencies in one or more of the above sub-processes.

The social learning account of vicarious processes is noteworthy in that it is both comprehensive and extensively supported by existing evidence. As we shall see in a later chapter, Bandura draws heavily on research and theory in the field of information processing. He likewise integrates central, somatic, and autonomic nervous system components in a manner which allows complex and reciprocal interactions.

There can be little doubt that the non-mediational model has contributed generously in our preliminary understanding of learning phenomena. The fundamental principles and basic research generated by that model constitute a sturdy empirical foundation for more comprehensive analyses. As indicated by the research reviewed in this chapter, however, an increasing body of evidence poses serious challenges to the adequacy of the non-mediational model. Investigations of mediated stimulus transformation, semantic conditioning and generalization, symbolic self-stimulation, awareness, and vicarious learning processes have generated data which do not comfortably fit into a basic input-output perspective. Much as one might wish to impose such simplicity on the phenomena, the empirical "realities" voice loud objections.

The behavioral scientist has a choice. He may adhere to the conventional and long-respected model which has played such an integral role in the growth and application of contemporary behavioral therapies. In so doing, he may be placed under increasing pressure (particularly from his data) to ignore or distort phenomena which do not fit that model. Since such distortion adds to an already fallible data processing system, it may well be an exorbitant and costly option in our scientific pursuits. The second option, and one which is being pursued by a growing number of workers, is to revise the model.

Scientific knowledge progresses by competitive paradigms and practical evaluations (Kuhn, 1962; Lakatos & Musgrave, 1970). As behavioral scientists, we have grown increasingly aware of our ignorance in the face of human complexities. This reflects a maturing self-doubt in the quest for psychological knowledge. We can expect the paradox to continue—as our knowledge increases, so must our ignorance. Emerging frontiers and enduring dilemmas will feed our intellectual appetites for a long time to come. Scientific satisfaction will continue to be derived more from questions than from answers, from pursuits rather than conclusions. This enduring curiosity and pervasive self-examination are the marks of an empirical perspective:

> Men who have excessive faith in their theories or ideas are not only ill prepared for making discoveries; they also make very poor observations (Claude Bernard, 1865, p. 38).

In terms of "adaptiveness" to the data, the survival value of the non-mediational model has become questionable. We are long overdue for some evolutionary progress in our paradigm. The mediational models which we shall now examine may provide some adaptive conceptual mutations in our understanding of complex human behavior.

Chapter Five

Measurement and Theory in Mediational Research

Before examining some of the contemporary mediational models, we need to reach a consensus regarding their evaluation. How shall we decide which model or models are more adequate? This evaluation invokes two basic considerations: (1) our confidence in the data supporting a given model, and (2) our estimation of the model's adequacy as a formal theoretical system. The first consideration is one of methodology or measurement: what data constitute evidence for mediating variables? The second consideration deals with the formal scientific criteria for theory building. We shall now briefly turn our attention to these two areas.

Most of the covert mediators invoked by cognitive behaviorists differ in several significant ways from traditional psychological inferences (Mahoney, 1970). To begin with, covert mediators are often assigned an implicit "response" status which emphasizes their specific functions in a particular relationship. The unambiguous description of a mediator's role facilitates empirical evaluation of its contribution to the analysis. A second differentiating characteristic is that, in contrast to the often extensive sequence of interdependent inferences which are encountered in psychodynamic theories of personality, the inferences in cognitive behavior modification are generally more direct and proximal. The leap is often a simple, one-step inference (e.g., from verbal report to covert response). Another distinction is that the individual is often unaware of the mediating variables proposed by traditional perspectives. Libidinal cathexes and repressed impulses are beyond the purview of even their owner. With some notable exceptions in the area of information processing, however, most inferred mediators in cognitive behavioral research are observable by a "public of one" (the person who is experiencing them). They need not be inferred by their owner.

A final feature which differentiates traditional psychodynamic mediators from the inferred variables discussed in this book has to do with their active manipulation in experimental research. Personality attributes and dispositional traits are usually treated as static substrata which "explain" behavioral performances. Cognitive processes, on the other hand, are viewed as complex behavior patterns which can be measured (albeit indirectly) and whose influence on performance can be predicted and controlled through systematic experimental manipulations.

DEPENDENT VARIABLES IN MEDIATIONAL RESEARCH

On the topic of measurement, it is worth briefly previewing here some of the dependent variables employed in cognitive behavioral research. Some mediators are inferred from stimulus input; others are derived from aspects of behavioral performance. The logical processes in these two leaps are markedly dissimilar and bear further consideration. According to Reese (1971), "When the occurrence of the mediating response is inferred on the basis of the stimulus materials used, the inference is deductive (p. 25)." When the inference is based on observed performance, however, Reese contends that it is not deductive. He goes on to offer an analysis of some of the logical operations involved in inferred mediation. Deductive inferences, of course, carry sizeable risks when their major premises are equivocal. Inductive inferences also have their limitations, but most of these are at least partially ameliorated by cumulative replication and self-corrective refinement.

A common logical fallacy in inferred mediation is the act of "affirming the consequent." One cannot use a to-be-demonstrated mediational effect as a deductive defense for itself. If A has been observed to cause B, then subsequent observations of B do not necessitate the inference of A. For example, one might contend that covert rehearsal improves recall. After employing procedures designed to produce such rehearsal, the observation of improved performance is consistent with—but not demonstrative of—the inferred mediator.

The most important feature in the justification of an inference is our incremental confidence in its empirical utility. Scientific knowledge progresses according to our relative confidence in both the data and our interpretations of it. All-or-none classifications are out of place in this inductive endeavor. Inferred variables are neither good nor bad, justified nor unjustified. Rather, their employment is evaluated along a continuum of utility—we estimate our relative confidence in their usefulness.

The following are some of the more common categories of dependent variables employed in cognitive behavioral research.

1. *Mediator-induced performance differences.* The recall of items in a memory experiment may be affected by instructions on how to mediate or memorize the items. At least two inferences are invoked—one regarding actual instruction-induced differences in the mediating strategy, the other regarding observed performance differences attributable to these varying mediators. The performance differences may be measured in response magnitude, type, latency, or duration.
2. *Physiological correlates.* Research on the arousal-inducing properties of thoughts and images often employs measures of respiration, galvanic skin response (GSR), cardiovascular changes, penile volume, etc. McGuigan and Schoonover (1973) provide an illustrative representation of this research. The dual input-output inference is again invoked.
3. *Chaining elements.* When a covert event is a presumed early element in a response chain, the final (observable) component of the chain is sometimes used as indirect index of it. For example, compulsive behaviors are frequently presumed to result from obsessive ruminations, as in the case of the ritualistic hand-washer who reports a fear of contamination. If procedures designed to modify the covert elements of the chain result in changes in the later overt elements, some degree of inferential justification is claimed.
4. *Self-reports.* When the individual reports that he has experienced some covert event, this is taken as an indirect source of evidence for its occurrence. The degree of confidence assigned to this measure is affected by numerous other factors—elements which might motivate deception, supplementary evidence for the mediator, and so on.
5. *Nonverbal performance correlates.* A variety of covert phenomena are inferred on the basis of correlated performance elements such as body posture, activity level, eye contact, speech pace, facial behaviors, and so on. Recent research on depression, for example, has suggested systematic covariations between some of these measures and other indices of depression (e.g., Williams, Barlow, and Agras, 1972).

The critical problem in evaluating the accuracy of measures designed to reflect inferred variables is that no single criterion index is available. Since a covert event is by definition unobserved, all measures of it must necessarily be indirect. One can, of course, claim a "converging confidence" to the extent that an inferred mediator is implicated by various procedural operations and performance measures. The final judgment, however, rests with its usefulness rather than its epistemological elegance. Should the mediational theorist require any solace in this seemingly untidy dilemma, he may find consolation in the words of Willard F. Day:

> However, to many behaviorists the most troublesome methodological problem one faces in analyzing the role of private events in the control of behavior centers around the fact that, unlike environmental events and even behavior itself as it is often conceptualized, private events seem not to be observable in any objective way, as public events are often thought to be. For my part, on the other hand, I should want to argue that from a psychological point of view public and private events are observable, if they are observable at all, in much the same way, and that methodological difficulties appear to arise because we have a mistaken conception of precisely where it is that the scientific advantage of controlled experimentation lies (1971, p. 2).

THEORY (MODEL) EVALUATION

We are faced with a plethora of models which purport to adequately integrate and predict the principles of complex human behavior. Indeed, as scientists from other disciplines often point out, psychologists seem to have a strong penchant for fervent model building. Several possible influences encourage this theoretical fertility. One has to do with the fact that the professional pellets in our grand experimental chamber are given more generously for conceptual rather than empirical pursuits. Psychology has not fully outgrown its philosophical heritage. In addition, it deals with a topic which is very conducive to interpretation and embellishment: we hold a rare and often awkward responsibility in being both the subject and object of our own inquiry.

A second factor which encourages theorization is ignorance, a commodity we possess in great abundance. What we don't know about our world, we quickly confabulate. This blends into the third influence, which is an active tendency to organize and "make sense" out of our experiences. There is now a very sizeable literature, spanning the fields of perception, philosophy, human learning, and personality theory, which corroborates this conceptual set to integrate, hypothesize, and organize our world according to implicit and explicit conceptual models (e.g., Kelly, 1955; Kuhn, 1962; Neisser, 1967; Dulany, 1968). Psychologists do not have a monopoly on model building—it appears to be a characteristic of almost every adult human. As Jahoda (1969) puts it, "The search for order, regularity and meaning is a general characteristic of human thought processes. It is one of our salient modes of adaption to an ever-changing world (pp. 144–145)."

It should perhaps be pointed out that this "active tendency" to theorize is not necessarily *inherent* in the organism. In addition to apparent physiological limitations, many social learning influences encourage model building. When, in childhood, we acquire our culture's symbol (language) system, we likewise learn some of the rules (i.e., contingencies) that apply to its use. "Consistency" and "making sense" are often modeled and reinforced; "logical" relationships are frequently given strong positive valuation. We learn to generate hypotheses about real-world contingencies in order to predict and anticipate the consequences of our actions. When our private hypotheses closely parallel actual external contingencies, our behavior is usually more generously reinforced. We theorize, then, in order to retain knowledge derived from past experience—knowledge which plays a critical role in directing future behavior.

Making the world predictable, however, may not be the only motivation for model building. As we shall see in a subsequent chapter, there is substantial evidence pointing to our limited capacity as information processors. Theories function as condensers—they reduce the infinite complexities of experience to a streamlined set of rules. There is thus an economic advantage to theorization. Given that a model adequately summarizes the basic and most crucial relationships in a phenomenon, we can use it adaptively to guide our behavior. In essence, our private theories are crystallized contingencies—symbolic representations of an abridged reality. Provided that the rules accurately reflect "the way things are," the advantages of rule-governed behavior are apparent:

> The behavior of a person who has calculated his chances, compared alternatives, or considered the consequences of a move is different from, and usually more effective than, the behavior of one who has merely been exposed to the unanalyzed contingencies (Skinner, 1969, pp. 121–122).

The disproportionate abundance of theories in psychology may derive more from the relative complexity and ignorance in this area than from any perverse tendencies toward speculation by behavioral scientists. Regardless of its source, however, there can be little doubt that contemporary psychology boasts more models than data. The difficult and often tedious task of well controlled experimentation offers scant professional reward. Even when the behavioral scientist does turn from theory building to research, the latter is frequently restricted to innovative or model-relevant inquiries. The painstaking work of replication and refinement and the invaluable meaning of "negative results" are seldom acknowledged. Professional awards are given to the creative theorist (psychology's "armchair quarterback") rather than to the laboratory worker who pursues years of effortful replication and parametric inquiry. Our journals mysteriously consider "negative" experimental results less informative than "positive" ones, and researchers accordingly report or pursue only a select minority of issues.

The dilemma lies not in theorization per se, but in the relative valuation of model building versus exploratory research. Many of Skinner's (1950) objections to the premature proliferation of theory are relevant here. It should be reiterated that Skinner's classic paper on the utility of learning theories has frequently been misinterpreted. Far from being an "anti-theorist," he has explicitly acknowledged the need for theorization in human behavior and has offered a sizeable quantity of his own making (cf. Skinner, 1969). In a strictly philosophical sense, it is questionable whether any empirical research can be purely atheoretical. The investigator always harbors some implicit expectancies which influence his pursuits. Skinner's objection, in addition to that regarding levels of analysis (cf. Chapter 3), deals with the myopia induced by a formal theoretical set. We tend to look for the things we expect to find and to ignore those which don't fit into our model. "Give a small boy a hammer, and he will find that everything he encounters needs pounding (Kaplan, 1964, p. 28)." This theoretical bias, as Skinner rightfully points out, restricts not only what we look for but what we find and how we interpret it. Such constraints have obvious drawbacks in a science as young and rudimentary as psychology.

We are faced, then, with a dilemma. Humans seem to have a proclivity for generating hypotheses and theories about their world. To some extent, this tendency is adaptive. However, our theories significantly influence how we process our world. We are biased by our conceptual bifocals. The only solution appears to be a compromise: we must examine and evaluate our models to determine their utility and adaptiveness. More importantly, we must remain perpetually open to revisions in our theory which may be demanded by subsequent experience and we must continually acknowledge that even *that* experience has been distorted by our theoretical assumptions.

The formal criteria for evaluating a theory are beyond the scope of this text (cf. McGeogy, 1933; Estes, et al., 1954; Kuhn, 1962, 1970a, b; Marx & Hillix, 1963; Turner, 1967; Popper, 1972). However, some general practical guidelines can be briefly noted. Two broad areas of consideration may be examined: (1) the formal symbolic aspects of a theory (i.e., its terms, postulates, etc.), and (2) its empirical adequacy (i.e., summarization of existing knowledge, heuristic predictions, etc.). I am here proposing a dichotomy in which the first category deals with relationships among theoretical concepts while the second deals with the correspondence between theory and data.

Entire volumes have been devoted to the formal structure and evaluation of theories. Although a lengthy digression into systems analysis would take us far afield from the subject at hand, I think a brief summarization may facilitate our examination of the models which follow.

1. Conceptual aspects of a theory.

From the perspective of formal systems analysis, a theoretical model is often evaluated on the basis of several conceptual criteria. Among these are (a) symbolic structure, (b) terminology, (c) premises or assumptions, (d) internal consistency, (e) relationship rules, and (f) predictive derivations.

The *symbolic structure* of a model has to do with its overall conceptual architecture. Is it built vertically (i.e., hierarchically) upon several basic axioms or spread horizontally across equally weighted principles?

Terminology plays a crucial role in the formal conceptual analysis of a theory. Does it specify its terms unambiguously? Are both independent and dependent variables expressed in terms of "data language," i.e., procedures amenable to objective or quantifiable measurement? The emphasis in this requirement is communicability. Strict adherence to formal operationism (Bridgman, 1927) is seldom demanded due to the acknowledged limitations of that perspective (cf. Langfeld, 1945; Bridgman, 1954; Benjamin, 1955; Plutchik, 1963).

The *premises or assumptions* of a model are, of course, very important in its evaluation. Many theoretical controversies are reducible to disputed assumptions. This is particularly true in such areas as philosophy of religion and ethics.

The *internal consistency* of a theory refers to its conceptual housekeeping. When postulates or principles within the model contradict one another, the logical coherence of the system is threatened. This can be illustrated by an example from philosophy of religion. A model purporting to demonstrate the existence of God cannot simultaneously defend this contention with both (a) references to "order" and "design" in the universe (the teleological argument) and (b) examples of deviations from order (miracles).

Relationship rules specify the logical operations which relate the theoretical concepts or principles. These rules often take the form of technical symbolic operations ranging from deduction and induction to such things as equivalence transformations, transitivity, commutative rules, and so on.

Predictive derivations constitute the bridge between theory and reality. This is where the model "sticks its neck out." Theoretically-derived predictions provide empirical opportunities to test the model. As was pointed out earlier, all too many theories isolate themselves from data by failing to offer unambiguous predictions. This criterion is therefore one of the more significant in terms of the conceptual adequacy of a model.

2. Empirical adequacy of a theory.

The second major issue in the evaluation of a model deals with its "reality contact." How well does it correspond to and predict relationships in the real world? Several criteria are again invoked, the most fundamental of which are (a) summarization-explanation, (b) heuristic prediction, and (c) data sensitivity.

One of the primary issues in theory evaluation is that of *summarization*. Is the model consistent with our current knowledge? Does it encompass a broad range of demonstrated relationships? Does it reduce (summarize) known "facts" in a useful manner? In other words, does the model "explain" what we already know? I hesitate to use the term "explain" here because of a personal philosophical bias—namely, that science cannot explain, it can only describe. Predictions and explanations are both formal descriptions, the former preceding the event in question. Even when a proposition can be shown to be a logical consequence of postulates, principles, or laws, it does not answer the question, "Why?" I shall, however, defer to tradition and employ the term "explanation" as a reference to relationship descriptions. Suffice it to say that models are often evaluated on the basis of their ability to account for (explain or describe) known or observed relationships.

A second empirical criterion deals with the issue of *heuristic prediction*. Not only must the model generate propositions which are supported by empirical research, but it should also predict relationships not heretofore predicted. That is, the theory may be evaluated on the basis of the new knowledge it stimulates. The model should not only summarize (explain) existing phenomena as well as (or better than) competing models, but it should also advance our understanding through empirically supported new predictions.

The final assessment criterion is that of *data sensitivity*. The model must be amenable to reality testing via some form of objective experimentation or observation. Although strict adherence to falsification cannot be logically defended (cf. Chapter 16), some form of data-based theory evaluation is usually required. At some point(s), the model must make contact with the real world and these contacts must suggest some degree of congruence or compatibility between the two: "Considered in itself, the experimental method is nothing but reasoning by whose help we methodically submit our ideas to experience (Claude Bernard, 1865, p. 2)."

Evaluating a model depends not only on its sensitivity to data, but also on the types of data bearing upon it. Scientific pursuits attempt to integrate experiences that may vary tremendously in terms of our confidence in their veracity. In some ways science is a cumulative delusion—a loosely organized system of popular hunches about "the way things are." It is cumulative in that our theories often emerge out of previous paradoxes.[a] Since many of our initial conceptualizations turn out to be grossly inaccurate, their delusional character is frequently illustrated.

The empirical status of a model focuses on two aspects of data: (1) our confidence in the accuracy of existing data, and (2) the compatability of those data with the model. Different kinds of data warrant different degrees of confidence. Although there are no absolute standards for ascertaining how much confidence is warranted by various data forms, some tentative generalizations can be offered. As pointed out elsewhere (Thoresen & Mahoney, 1974), our confidence in a particular set of data is enhanced by:

1. an "objective" definition of both independent and dependent variables (e.g., treatment procedures and outcome measures);
2. objective, and preferably quantified, measurement of the independent variable;
3. objective, and preferably quantified, measurement of the dependent variable;
4. observation of the dependent variable in both the presence and the absence of the independent variable (e.g., via group comparisons or single subject designs);
5. the existence of long-term follow-up data;
6. independent replication; and
7. the evaluation and control of possible extraneous influences (e.g., subject expectancies, experimenter bias, etc.).

While the absence of these factors does not prohibit our having any confidence whatsoever in the data, it does limit that confidence. Uncon-

[a] We should be careful here not to assume that scientific knowledge involves an orderly accumulation of "facts." As we will see in Chapter 16, this perspective is seriously challenged by the historiography of science.

trolled case reports are not empirically impotent (Lazarus & Davison, 1971). Their impact, however, is more modest. We may require many such reports to produce the state of confidence effected by a single, well controlled experiment.

The procedures and merits of single subject and group experiments have been discussed by a number of workers (cf. Kazdin, 1973a; Campbell & Stanley, 1963; Paul, 1969c; Thoresen & Mahoney, 1974). Unfortunately, the dichotomization of these two methodologies has often polarized opinions about the "right" way to do research (cf. Mahoney, 1974a). Redundant polemics have argued either that single subject data are never more than suggestive or that group methodologies always ignore individuality and transition states. I shall not here belabor these arguments or their logical bases. Suffice it to say that this text will consider both controlled single subject and group experiments as uniquely invaluable contributors to scientific progress. Each is limited in the questions it may ask and the answers it provides. Moreover, there are no prohibitions against integrating the two to maximize the power of our inquiries.

The foregoing discussion has outlined some of the criteria often employed in the evaluation of a theoretical model. Whether these criteria are themselves defensible is an issue which extends far beyond our present focus. I here again propose the adoption of a pragmatic stance and invoke emphasis on relative utility and converging confidence. My own biases place heavier weight on the empirical criteria and the testable predictions derived from a model. A "firm" and frequently visited data base offers welcome security in one's theoretical ramblings.

So much for philosophy—on to the data.

Chapter Six

Mediational Model I: Covert Conditioning

The first mediational model we shall examine views private events as covert forms of overt phenomena. Moreover, as its name implies, the covert conditioning model imposes the theory and language of conditioning on private experience. Thoughts, images, memories, and sensations are described as covert stimuli, covert responses, or covert consequences. The skull becomes a rather crowded Skinner box in which such conventional principles as reinforcement, punishment, and extinction are said to describe the function and patterning of private experience. The inferred mediators in the covert conditioning model are often discussed as if they were faded representations or approximations of publicly observable events. Mental images, for example, are sometimes described as conditioned perceptions of physical objects, and thoughts are viewed as low amplitude speech.

Although its visibility has increased tremendously in the last few years, the covert conditioning perspective is *not* a recent arrival in the field. And, somewhat ironically, one of its most extensive presentations is contained in a book best known for its non-mediational views —namely, Skinner's (1953) *Science and Human Behavior.* Skinner devotes four entire chapters to private events and sprinkles covert conditioning implications through many other parts of his book. Although he does not present a formalized mediational model, he repeatedly defends the assumption that the principles and methods of operant conditioning can be applied to phenomena within the organism. This support of a covert conditioning perspective has been frequently reiterated (cf. Skinner, 1963, 1969), most recently in *About Behaviorism* (1974).

There were, of course, numerous historical predecessors who had invoked covert mediating stimuli and responses in their analyses of

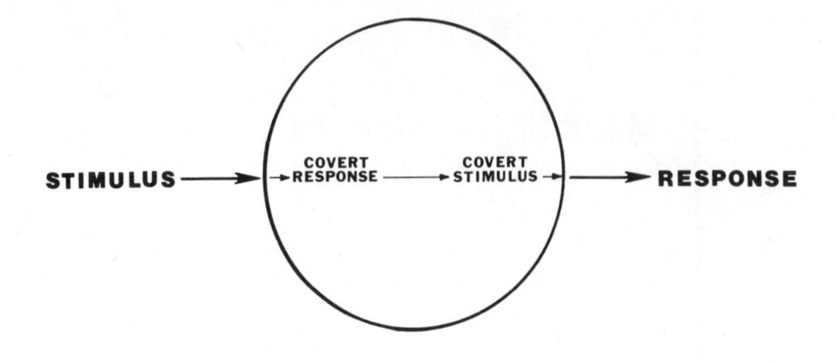

MEDIATIONAL MODEL I

Fiaure 6-1.

behavior (e.g., Pavlov, 1955; Thorndike, 1911; Guthrie, 1935; Tolman, 1932; Miller & Dollard, 1941; Hull, 1943). While the covert conditioning perspective has taken on a variety of molecular forms (cf. Osgood, 1953; Staats, 1968a,b; Cautela, 1971a), its molar premise has remained unchanged—the processes and principles which describe covert phenomena are continuous with those which describe overt behaviors.

THE CONTINUITY ASSUMPTION

The assumption of continuity or identity between overt and covert learning principles is significant, particularly with regard to the theoretical adequacy of the covert conditioning model. If we are justified in assuming such continuity, then we can make logical extrapolations from overt learning phenomena to covert processes.

The continuity assumption has been repeatedly defended by behavior modifiers (cf. Skinner, 1953, 1963; Homme, 1965; Bandura, 1969; Mahoney, 1970; Ullmann, 1970). These defenses have been predominantly based on logical inference rather than empirical demonstration. That is, we have no reason to believe that private phenomena are any different from public phenomena.

> We need not suppose that events which take place within an organism's skin have special properties for that reason. A private event may be distinguished by its limited accessibility but not, so far as we know, by any special structure or nature (Skinner, 1953, p. 257).

From the perspective of formal logic, the continuity assumption presents some rather complex issues. To begin with, it entails all of the epistemological problems inherent in the logical process of induction (cf. Turner, 1967). It implies an "order" or "rationality" in nature which may be more presumptive than real. Finally, the defense of overt-covert continuity is an argument from analogy. Briefly stated, it proposes that (1) similar events imply similar processes, and that (2) private events are similar to non-private events. Even if the first proposition were valid, we would need to substantiate the second through empirical research. The second proposition, however, invokes problems of its own. One can readily specify differences between some classes of overt and covert behavior (e.g., amplitude, frequency, etc.). On what dimensions shall similarity be evaluated? To the extent that the phenomena are dissimilar, the argument is weakened; to the extent that they are similar, we must still rest our conclusion on an epistemologically tenuous major premise.

Fortunately, we have at least some justification for circumventing these philosophical dilemmas in defending the assumption of continuity. Although its logical status is problematical, it stands in good company with an infinite array of other "formally illogical" scientific premises (e.g., falsifiability, induction, etc.). Fortunately, the contemporary scientist seldom allows logic to impede his progress. I shall again rest my defense on data rather than philosophy. The present text offers a rather extensive survey of evidence supporting the notion that covert phenomena can be described in terms of lawful relationships and systematic processes. Moreover, at least some of these processes seem to parallel those observed in overt phenomena. The following research offers illustration.

Mahoney, Thoresen, and Danaher (1972) performed two experiments designed to empirically evaluate the continuity assumption. Specifically, they differentially rewarded and punished subjects for engaging in selected covert (mediating) operations during a verbal learning experiment. The experiment presented subjects with a series of noun pairs (e.g., "pig–typewriter"). At a subsequent recall test, subjects were given the first member of a pair and asked to produce its associate. The dependent variable was the covert mediating response (associative method) employed by subjects in their memorization of the lists. Four methods of association were recorded: (1) repetition, in which the noun pairs were simply rehearsed covertly over and over again; (2) sentence generation, in which the two nouns were used together in a sentence; (3) imagery, in which the two nouns were imagined interacting in some unusual way (e.g., a pig sitting at a typewriter); and (4) other associative methods. In both experiments, the mediating response chosen for modification was imagery. This choice was based on evidence that paired associate recall is often dramatically superior when noun pairs are mediated by imagery rather than by other associative methods (cf. Bower, 1970, 1972; Paivio, 1971). Imagery, therefore, offered a covert response for which an indirect reliability check could be performed (via improved performance).

The first experiment examined the effects of external positive reinforcement on covert responding. Subjects were presented with noun pairs and asked to indicate their covert associative response by writing the letters "R" (repetition), "S" (sentence), "I" (imagery) or "O" (other) on a tablet. Their reported responses were monitored through a one-way mirror. The first 15 noun pairs constituted a baseline phase during which subjects' "operant levels" of imagery were assessed. During a subsequent reinforcement intervention, individuals who had reported low imagery were rewarded with dimes whenever they employed imagery as their covert associative method. High baseline imagers were reinforced for covert repetition during this initial reward intervention. Reinforcement continued for 15 trials, after which a reversal phase was begun. During this third experimental phase, subjects were monetarily rewarded for reporting covert responses opposite to those which had been previously reinforced. Thus, subjects who had been rewarded for imagery during the first reinforcement intervention now received reinforcement for repetition and repetition subjects were now rewarded for imagery. A final experimental phase reinstated the original (phase two) reinforcement contingencies. A recall test for all 60 paired associates was then administered. The experiment thus involved an "ABCB" design (baseline, intervention, reversal, re-intervention). After baseline, IRI subjects were sequentially reinforced for imagery, repetition, and imagery, respectively; RIR subjects experienced the converse of this sequence. As shown in the figure, self-reported imagery behavior corresponded very closely to experimental phases. When imagery was reinforced it increased; when repetition was reinforced, imagery decreased.

At this point, of course, the non-mediational theorist might object that "imagery" responses were neither reinforced nor recorded. What was observed to increase was the subject's writing of the letter "I" on a tablet. When "I-writing" was reinforced, it increased; when "R-writing" was reinforced, "I-writing" decreased. This peripheral interpretation, however, faces serious problems when subjects' recall performances are examined. The recall performance of each subject was evaluated by comparing percentage of recall on imaged versus non-imaged items. All ten subjects displayed superior recall for items which they had covertly associated via imagery ($p < .002$). The peripheralist, of course, would be hard pressed to explain why writing the letter "I"

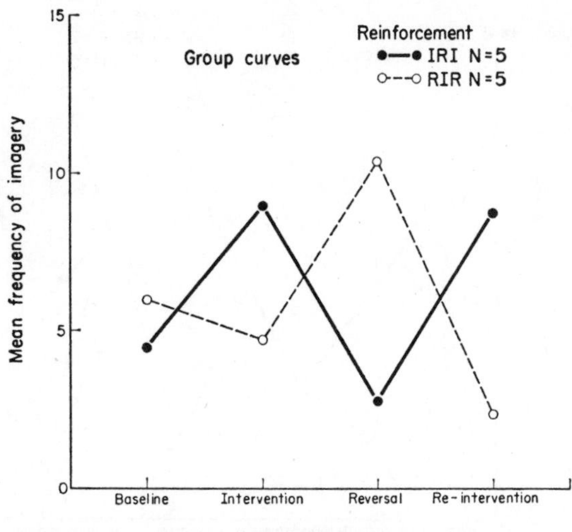

Figure 6-2. Mean frequency of imagery when subjects were alternately reinforced for self-reports of imagery (I) or repetition (R). (Reprinted with permission from Mahoney, Thoresen, and Danaher, 1972.)

should produce performances consistently superior to those observed after writing the letter "R".

In their second experiment, Mahoney, Thoresen, and Danaher (1972) utilized this same paradigm in examining the effects of punishment on covert responding. After baseline frequencies of imagery had been obtained, subjects were differentially punished for reports of imagery, repetition, and imagery (IRI condition) or the converse (RIR condition). Punishment consisted of monetary loss. The results of this experiment are shown in Figure 6-3. Again, subjects' reported covert responses were dramatically altered by external contingencies. When imagery was punished it declined; when repetition was punished, imagery increased. The recall test was again corroborative of self-reported imagery. In eleven of the twelve subjects, imagery-mediated recall was superior to repetition-mediated recall ($p < .001$).

Several other lines of research have also lent support to the continuity assumption. Experiments dealing with word associations, serial recall, and sexual fantasies have indicated that covert mediational processes are often very responsive to reinforcement and punishment contingencies (e.g., Glucksberg & King, 1967; Eriksen & Kuethe, 1956; Harsch & Zimmer, 1965; Marks, Rachman, & Gelder, 1965; Marks & Gelder, 1967; Atkinson & Wickens, 1971).

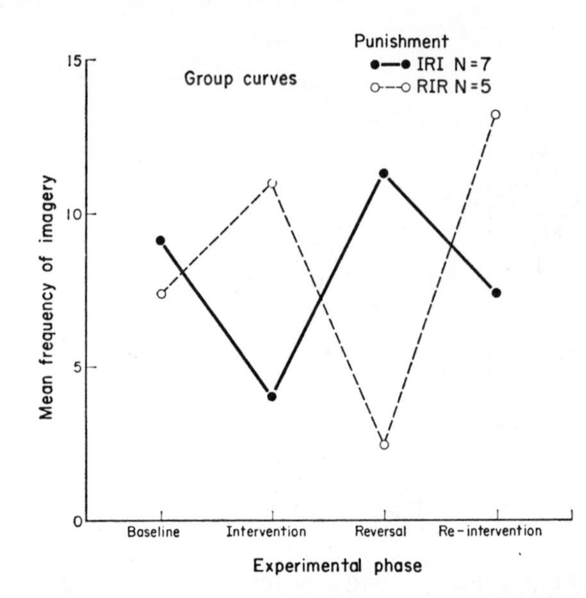

Figure 6-3. Mean frequency of imagery when subjects were alternately punished for self-reports of imagery (I) or repetition (R). (Reprinted with permission from Mahoney, Thoresen, and Danaher, 1972.)

The above preliminary evidence suggests that we are at least tentatively justified in presuming some degree of correspondence between the principles and processes of overt and covert behavior. We should, however, be cautious on this honeymoon. The fact that a handful of studies have shown specific and simplified parallels does not mean that others will be correspondingly positive. It certainly does not mean that covert responses are *nothing but* miniaturized lever presses. It is my pre-scientific hunch that the continuity assumption is only partially justified. At a molar level, and when dealing with autonomically-valenced inputs, there does appear to be rough correspondence between overt and covert processes. However, we now know that almost all behaviors are organized into complex chains or sequences and there is increasing evidence that the type of organization may depend on such factors as which nervous system predominates, hemispheric specialization, and so on (Sperry, 1973; Nebes, 1974). Systematic relationships still exist, of course, but they may not be amenable to adequate description through traditional conditioning principles.

As mentioned earlier, the covert conditioning model often categorizes private events in terms of their function: stimulus, response, or consequence. We shall now briefly address these categorizations.

COVERT EVENTS AS STIMULI

"One may generate an emotional response by recounting an emotional event (Skinner, 1953, p. 275)." Mediated self-arousal is a well documented fact. The physiological effects of symbolic activities have been long recognized and extensively replicated (e.g., Darrow, 1929; Hudgins, 1933; Miller, 1935; Menzies, 1937; Shaw, 1940; Pavlov, 1955; Platonov, 1959). Some of this documentation was presented in our previous discussion of stimulus transformation and symbolic self-stimulation (Chapter 4).

More recent studies on the phenomenon of symbolically mediated arousal suggest that it is not only well documented but relatively frequent in maladaptive behavior patterns (cf. Bandura, 1969). Physiological research with literally thousands of subjects has substantiated the arousal capacity of covert events. To cite but a few, Barber and Hahn (1964) measured pulse, galvanic skin response, and frontalis activity in subjects who either directly experienced a painful external stimulus (cold pressor) or "merely" imagined that experience. They found that subjects' self-reported discomfort and measured physiological reactions were similar regardless of whether the aversive stimulation was real or imagined. Craig (1965) likewise reported evidence supporting the autonomic effects of vicarious and imaginal stressors.

In a series of well controlled investigations, Robert M. Stern and his colleagues have likewise documented the physiological correlates of symbolic activity (cf. Stern & Kaplan, 1967; Stern & Lewis, 1968). Subjects were readily capable of voluntarily controlling their galvanic skin responses (GSRs) by imagining emotional or non-emotional events. Physiological arousal was demonstrated both *between* experimental and control groups and *within* subjects during alternating experimental phases. These researchers extended their observations to an interesting phenomenon in the field of theatre. Two broad categories of theatrical training can be delineated—(1) a somewhat traditional school in which emotional expressiveness is learned through stereotyped manners of facial and vocal expression; and (2) the "method" school of acting (founded by Stanislavsky) in which actors are taught to express emotions through the recall of emotional memories. Stern and his colleagues found that method actors were better able to control their physiological arousal than non-method actors. The imaginal re-living of stressful experiences can apparently enhance voluntary control of autonomic responses.

Several other studies have examined the relationship between covert activities and physiological responses. Grossberg and Wilson (1968), for example, reported additional evidence for the arousal capacity of imagery. Subjects who were asked to imagine fearful scenes displayed greater autonomic responsiveness than individuals who imagined neutral scenes. Similarly, Rimm and Litvak (1969) found significant differences in respiratory responses after specified covert activities. In their study experimental subjects were asked to covertly verbalize emotionally arousing triads (e.g., "I might get injured or crippled . . . this could make me ugly and incapacitated . . . what an awful thought."). Control subjects, on the other hand, subvocalized neutral syllogisms (e.g., "Inventors are imaginative . . . Edison was an inventor . . . therefore he was imaginative."). Experimental subjects showed significant increases in both rate and depth of respiration.

A recent study by Waters and McDonald (1973) compared the autonomic arousal induced by external (auditory versus visual) and imaginary stimulation in rat phobic subjects. The external stimuli consisted of taped descriptions and slides of rats, while the covert stimuli were induced via instructions to imagine graduated scenes of rat interaction. Three measures of autonomic activity revealed that imaginal stimuli often elicited even greater arousal than visual and auditory stimuli. May and Johnson (1973) have added additional evidence on symbolically induced physiological activity.

In an ingenious study on conditioned emotional arousal, Proctor and Malloy (1971) demonstrated that symbolic *concepts* can acquire autonomic arousal capacities. Subjects were trained in the use of a biconditional rule to sort complex stimuli. The biconditional rule required that a stimulus array satisfy either of two conditions. For example, if a stimulus is *both* square and red or *neither* square nor red, it is a positive instance of a square-red biconditional rule. A training criterion of 16 consecutive errorless sortings insured that each subject had mastered the concept. Biconditional sortings were later followed by painful electric shock. In a final experimental phase, subjects showed anticipatory arousal to positive instances of the biconditional concept even though unique stimuli were employed. These data strongly support a mediational interpretation.

Sexual fantasies and erotic imaginal stimuli have demonstrated control over a number of physiological responses. Although evidence is far from lacking (cf. Masters & Johnson, 1966, 1970; Annon, 1973), most of us have sufficient personal data from our own reveries to convince us of this relationship.

Further documentation of symbolically mediated arousal could be offered. For present purposes, however, the point has been made—covert events can serve as powerful controlling stimuli in human behavior.

COVERT EVENTS AS RESPONSES

The second functional role of covert events has to do with their performance as responses. In the covert conditioning model, these private responses are often viewed as mediating elements in a chain (cf. Skinner, 1953; Staats, 1968a,b). For example, a covert "urge" is sometimes posited as mediating antecedent stimulation and subsequent overt performance (Lindsley, 1969; Homme, 1965; Ackerman, 1963).

Within the confines of the covert conditioning perspective, surprisingly little research has been addressed to the response function of private events. Moreover, Skinner's (1953) operant analysis of thought has apparently influenced workers' perceptions of these events. Covert experiences are typically viewed as predominantly *operant* rather than *respondent* behaviors. An exception to this has been the work of Staats (1966, 1968a,b) who has incorporated both instrumental and classical conditioning in his theoretical account of thought and language. According to Staats' "attitude-reinforcer-discriminative" theory, a covert event can function as an emotion-eliciting stimulus, a reinforcing consequence, and/or a discriminative cue. For example, the image of a nude and receptive sex partner might elicit sexual arousal as well as reinforcing preceding thoughts and cueing the initiation of overt sexual activities.

There is considerable irony in noting the apparent double standard adopted by some operant researchers with regard to covert responses and mediation. While energetically criticizing "cognitive" accounts of problem solving, both Goldiamond (1966) and Skinner (1966) posit covert "instructional stimuli" and "precurrent responses" as if these inferences were somehow more legitimate. By systematically excluding such areas as problem solving from conventional operant research, it has been possible for the non-mediational theorist to comfortably speculate on presumed mediational processes. This strategy, of course, allows the theorist unlimited room for philosophizing without the accompanying risk of empirical disconfirmation. A much more heuristic and functional contribution would ensue if Skinner's extensive analyses of private events were subjected to controlled experimentation.

Notwithstanding the anti-cognitive convention, a number of studies have examined covert responses from a predominantly conditioning perspective. Reese's (1971) analysis of verbal and nonverbal mediation offers one example. The theory and research of Osgood (1953) and Staats (1968a,b) offer others. There has also been a recent trend toward the operant analysis of concept formation and linguistic rules (e.g., Proctor & Malloy, 1971; Catania, 1972a; Garcia, Guess, & Byrnes, 1973; Guess & Baer, 1973).

A clinically relevant avenue of research has also examined the phenomenon of experimental hallucinations (e.g., Hefferline, Bruno, & Camp, 1973; Stoyva, 1973). Hefferline and his colleagues offer a commendably straightforward definition of an experimentally induced hallucination: "an hallucination is a (verbal) report of sensory perception made in the absence of the adequate external stimulus (UCS) but in the presence of another external stimulus (CS) that in the past has occurred in close temporal contiguity to the UCS and probably to its accompanying report (p. 311)." These researchers have demonstrated that the gradual fading of an unconditioned stimulus can sometimes result in continued (hallucinatory) reports of its presence long after its deletion from the experiment. An intriguing finding reported by McGuigan (1973) suggests that the "voices" heard during schizophrenic hallucinations may actually stem from the individual's own speech apparatus. That is, the schizophrenic may be "hearing" his own subvocalizations but attributing them to external sources.

Several researchers have explored the physiological correlates of thinking (e.g., Chapman, 1973; McGuigan, 1973). Although these studies have not typically dealt with the functional properties of covert events, they have added to our methodological options for such research. For example, it has been shown that subjects display different physiological responses when asked to solve simple (2 + 7 = ?) versus complex (24 × 17 = ?) mental arithmetic tasks. As we shall see in Chapter 7, these findings may offer promise in the evaluation of some of the therapy procedures which are derived from the covert conditioning model.

COVERT EVENTS AS CONSEQUENCES

The third functional role of private events in the covert conditioning model deals with their capacity to serve as consequences of behavior. It is maintained that symbolic events can reinforce or punish overt or covert responses. Many of these covert consequences take the form of symbolic representations of external consequences.

Weiner (1965) reported one of the first laboratory studies on the effects of covert consequences. He asked two female nursing assistants to perform an instrumental task involving button pressing. For ten baseline sessions subjects were reinforced with points on a fixed interval (10 second) schedule. During the second experimental phase, ten sessions were divided in half and the abovementioned schedule (FI-10″) was randomly alternated with a punishment contingency. When the punishment contingency was in effect, each response resulted in a yellow light and the subtraction of a point from the subject's score counter. In a final experimental phase, half-sessions were again randomly alternated. However, during the punishment components of this third phase (designated by a tone), subjects were instructed to *imagine* losing a point for each button press. No yellow light was presented and their visible score counters substantiated that, in fact, they were not really being fined for responding during this phase. Results for the two subjects are depicted in Figure 6–4. Although there was marked inter-subject variability, the effects of imaginary punishment are apparent. Both subjects responded at steady rates during the initial reinforcement phase and curtailed their responding during the external punishment sessions (phase two). In the third phase (imaginary punishment), the first subject exhibited noticeable response suppression and the second displayed increased variability in performance. While these data are only suggestive in nature, they do support the notion that symbolic aversive consequences can exert some influence on human behavior.

The effects of "covert reinforcers" have received some recent experimental attention, but again the evidence is very preliminary.

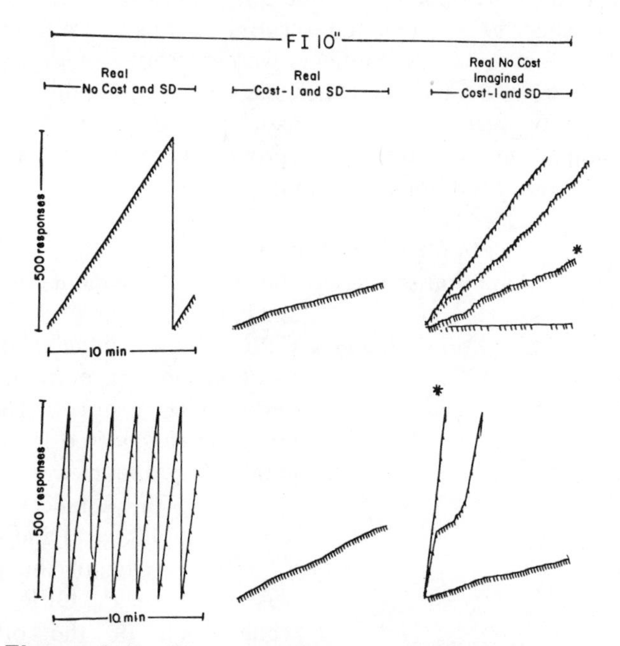

Figure 6-4. The response rates of two subjects during successive phases of fixed interval reinforcement (left), actual response cost (center), and imagined response cost (right). (Reprinted with permission from Weiner, 1965.)

Cautela and his colleagues have reported a series of studies on covert positive and negative reinforcement (cf. Cautela, 1970a,b, 1971a; Cautela, Steffan & Wish, in press; Ascher & Cautela, 1972; Steffan, 1971, 1972). In these studies, covert positive reinforcement involved training subjects to imagine pleasant experiences (e.g., "tasting one's favorite food or winning a tennis match"). Following this training, subjects were given an experimental task and were differentially cued to engage in covert reinforcement after selected responses. For example, Cautela, Steffan, and Wish (in press) utilized the cue word "reinforcement" to prompt covert positive consequences in a study involving circle-size estimations. Subjects who had received training in covert positive reinforcement (CPR) were systematically cued after either over- or underestimations. The authors found that CPR subjects displayed greater performance changes than subjects who received non-contingent CPR cueing, no feedback, or CPR cueing with less preferred imaginal reinforcers ($p < .01$, one-tailed). A comparison of CPR subjects with subjects who simply heard the word "reinforcement" after differential estimations likewise revealed predicted differences ($p < .05$, one-tailed).

Ascher (1973) employed a Taffel card task in a further exploration of the effects of CPR. Subjects were presented with cards which contained six pronouns ("I, you, he, she, we, they") and the infinitive form of a common verb. Their task was to generate a sentence using one of the pronouns and the verb. Four groups were run and each group experienced three conditions (phases):

I. *Covert Positive Reinforcement.*
 Condition (phase) 1. Baseline assessment of pronoun selection (50 trials).
 Condition (phase) 2. CPR training; imaginal reinforcement scenes were trained to the verbal cue "shift." Three pronouns were selected for reinforcement. A pronoun was reinforced by having the subject imagine it (e.g., on a billboard) and then shift to a CPR. One of the pronouns was paired with CPR 30 times while each of the other two was paired 10 times. Subjects were then given a second presentation of the 50 Taffel cards to assess any CPR effect on pronoun selection.

Condition (phase) 3. Extinction; subjects were asked to imagine the three pronouns without any cued CPR. A final presentation of the 50 Taffel cards was then given.

II. *CPR Extinction Control.* Conditions (phases) 1 and 2 were identical to those in Group I. During the third phase, subjects were not given extinction training prior to the final test series.

III. *CPR Control.* Conditions 1 and 3 were identical to those in Group II. During the second experimental phase, subjects were asked to imagine their CPRs 50 times and were then asked to imagine the three pronouns 50 times. This procedure was designed to control for the pronoun-CPR pairing experienced in Groups I and II.

IV. *Control.* All three phases involved baseline recordings.

The results of this study are presented in Figure 6-5. Statistical main effects were obtained for groups ($p < .001$), conditions (phases) ($p < .001$) and number of reinforcements ($p < .05$). As illustrated in the figure, the effect of pronoun-CPR pairing is impressive, particularly with

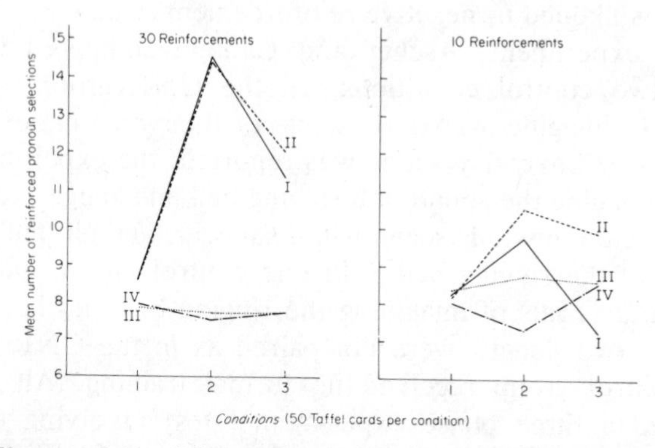

Figure 6-5. Mean frequency of pronoun selection after covert reinforcement (Groups I and II) or control procedures. (Reprinted with permission from Ascher, 1973.)

the densely rehearsed pronoun. It is worth commenting that Ascher's paradigm was more associative than instrumental. Rather than cueing CPR after the subject's selection of a specified pronoun, he paired CPR with experimenter-determined pronouns. The data suggest an enhanced attractiveness of CPR-associated pronouns, although these findings are susceptible to non-conditioning interpretations. The absence of an extinction effect and the omission of a neutral imagery (information control) group challenge the adequacy of a conditioning interpretation.

In a laboratory study investigating covert reinforcement and covert punishment, Epstein and Peterson (1973) took baseline measures of subjects' number choices (0-100). This was followed by training in positive imagery (imagining "talking with people who like you") and negative imagery (imagining "listening to country and western music"). No apologies were made to Johnny Cash. During a third experimental phase, subjects in one group were cued to generate positive imagery after selecting some numbers and to engage in negative imagery after other number choices. This contingency was reversed for subjects in the second group. Statistical analyses showed an increase in the selection of covertly reinforced numbers and a decrease in covertly punished selections. Interpretation of these findings as supportive of a covert conditioning hypothesis is once again complicated by the absence of an information control group. Two studies reported by Steffan (1971, 1972) offer mixed evidence for the effects of covert positive reinforcement.

The only existing laboratory study on "covert negative reinforcement" (CNR) was reported by Ascher and Cautela (1972). In the CNR procedure, a subject is asked to imagine an aversive scene and then to shift his attention to a to-be-reinforced image. Since the latter correlates with the termination of a (covert) aversive stimulus, the procedure is likened to negative reinforcement (Cautela, 1970a). In their laboratory experiment, Ascher and Cautela compared the effects of CNR to two control conditions. In the CNR group, subjects were instructed to imagine a noxious scene of their own choosing. When an "appropriately" aversive scene was reported, the experimenter told the subject to imagine the sound of a ringing bell and suggested that "as you imagine this, the noxious scene will disappear, and all that will remain is the sound of the ringing bell." In one control group, individuals were given separate trials of imagining the ringing bell and later the noxious scenes; the two images were not paired as in the CNR procedure. A second control group received no formal training. All subjects then experienced a three phase experimental test involving the circle-size estimation task previously employed by Cautela, Steffan, and Wish (in press). After baseline assessment of subjects' circle-size estimates, over-estimation and under-estimation judgments were followed by the experimenter's saying the word "bell." The over- and under-estimation phases were counterbalanced and the feedback cue ("bell") was presented to subjects in all three conditions.

An analysis of variance revealed predicted changes in circle-size estimation for CNR subjects but no systematic differences for either of the two control conditions. It is noteworthy that considerable variability was encountered (the ratio of variances between the two control groups in one experimental phase exceeded 25:1). The results are interpreted as providing support for the powerful effects of CNR as a covert conditioning procedure.

Unfortunately, the Ascher and Cautela (1972) study is open to several paradigmatic and methodological criticisms. To begin with, the term "negative reinforcement" usually refers to a conditioning procedure in which termination of an aversive stimulus *follows* execution of a targeted response. In the CNR procedure, however, noxious stimulus termination *precedes* response emission (Cautela, 1970a). The paradigm employed in the foregoing study adds additional complications by using a "higher order" chaining procedure—CNR was not explicitly cued after selected responses. Rather, a stimulus which had been previously associated with CNR training (the word "bell") was presented. It is not clear whether CNR subjects were instructed to imagine the ringing of the bell when they were cued during the test phase. Moreover, there was no control for the information content of this cueing word. The authors comment that some subjects (presumably controls) asked why the experimenter was occasionally saying the word "bell" during the test phase. For individuals in the CNR group, a reasonable subject-generated hypothesis would have been that this cueing indicated which direction the experimenter wanted the circle-size estimations to trend. Thus, the data might be alternatively interpreted in terms of informative feedback and demand characteristics (Rosenthal, 1966) rather than conditioning. The authors report that a brief post-experimental interview indicated that subjects had not guessed the experiment's purpose beforehand. Mention is not made, however, of whether subjects had discriminated the test-phase contingencies.

One final comment on the Ascher and Cautela (1972) experiment deals with their brief description of the imagining procedures. The lack of standardization of noxious scenes is perhaps less troublesome than the fact that imagery modality was left unspecified. Subjects presumably imaged "visual" noxious scenes but it is not clear whether they uniformly generated an "auditory," "visual," or combined image of the ringing bell. Extensive research on the phenomenon of imagery has recently suggested that its current use by behavior modifiers may be embarrassingly naive and uncontrolled (cf. Richardson, 1969; Paivio, 1971; Segal, 1971; Sheehan, 1972).

Before examining the adequacy of the covert conditioning model, we shall briefly review the therapeutic applications of this paradigm.

Chapter Seven

The Covert Conditioning Therapies: Counterconditioning, Thought Stopping, and Coverant Control

Classifying therapeutic procedures which derive from the covert conditioning model is not an easy task. The derivations from that model are often implicit, and many of the techniques we shall discuss combine strategies which could be claimed by more than one model. There are also varying degrees of mediation employed in the different techniques.

Thoresen and Mahoney (1974) point out that covert events can functionally interact with overt events in several different combinations. If we adopt the fundamental ABC conditioning sequence (Antecedent, Behavior, and Consequence), then each of these three components can be either overt or covert, and the following possibilities arise:

1. Overt Antecedent—Overt Behavior—Overt Consequence
2. Overt Antecedent—Overt Behavior—*Covert* Consequence
3. Overt Antecedent—*Covert* Behavior—Overt Consequence
4. Overt Antecedent—*Covert* Behavior—*Covert* Consequence
5. *Covert* Antecedent—Overt Behavior—Overt Consequence
6. *Covert* Antecedent—*Covert* Behavior—Overt Consequence
7. *Covert* Antecedent—Overt Behavior—*Covert* Consequence
8. *Covert* Antecedent—*Covert* Behavior—*Covert* Consequence

The complexity of the above combinations is increased when one considers sub-types of the elements (e.g., positive, neutral, and aversive consequences, discriminative stimuli, etc.). Since the covert conditioning therapies seldom use such discrete sequences as those outlined above, our review will adopt a classification schema more in line with contemporary clinical practice.

COVERT COUNTERCONDITIONING

I should, perhaps, preface this classification with a brief explanation of the term "counterconditioning." In the terminology of traditional laboratory research, counterconditioning refers to a presumed process in which the valence of a stimulus is modified through association with a stimulus of differing valence. The valences involved are usually dichotomous (positive/negative). For example, an aversive stimulus (i.e., one which the organism will work to terminate, reduce, or avoid) may be presented in attenuated form contiguous with (or immediately followed by) a strong positive stimulus (i.e., one which the organism will work to produce, increase, or maintain). In this manner, a negative stimulus can acquire neutral or mildly positive valence and a formerly positive stimulus can acquire aversive properties. For clinical purposes, of course, the counterconditioning strategy offers promise in the elimination of maladaptive avoidance behaviors (e.g., phobias) and in the production of more adaptive stimulus-response patterns (e.g., in sexual deviations, addictions, etc.).

Systematic Desensitization.

One of the earliest counterconditioning procedures to incorporate elements of a covert conditioning model was Joseph Wolpe's *systematic desensitization* (1958). In this treatment strategy, the client is asked to generate a series of imaginal fear-provoking events. These events are intended to approximate real-life stimuli or performances which are currently anxiety-inducing for the individual. A hierarchy is constructed in which the imaginal scenes are rank ordered according to their arousal potential. The client is then given training in deep muscular relaxation (Jacobson, 1938) which is intended to provide a counterconditioning element. According to Wolpe (1958),

> If a response antagonistic to anxiety can be made to occur in the presence of anxiety-evoking stimuli so that it is accompanied by a complete or partial suppression of the anxiety response, the bond between these stimuli and the anxiety responses will be weakened (p. 71).

The three ingredients in systematic desensitization, then, are (1) the construction of a graduated hierarchy of anxiety-inducing stimuli, (2) relaxation training, and (3) the gradual pairing of hierarchy items with a relaxed state. This third component, according to Wolpe, introduces the process of "reciprocal inhibition" in which prior (maladaptive) conditioning is countered physiologically.

The empirical status of systematic desensitization as a behavior therapy procedure has been extensively evaluated (cf. Bandura, 1969; Paul, 1969; Wilson & Davison, 1971; Davison & Wilson, 1973). There appears to be little dispute over *whether* the procedure is effective. Controversies persist, however, as to *why* it is effective. The current consensus seems to be that Wolpe's reciprocal inhibition (counterconditioning) formulation is inadequate. Relaxation is a facilitative but not a necessary component in the procedure.

Our current topic of discussion relates to the frequent use of imaginal stimuli in systematic desensitization. Although real life (*in vivo*) hierarchies are sometimes employed, the predominant stimulus modality in desensitization is covert. It is assumed that responses learned in the presence of these covert events will generalize to their external referents. Although there is sometimes little transfer loss, current evidence suggests considerable variability in this generalization (Bandura, 1969). The learning of adaptive behavior appears to be facilitated by the use of actual fear-provoking stimuli during treatment.

It is an unfortunate fact that behavior modifiers have devoted scant empirical attention to the role of covert events in desensitization. Despite commendable standardization and parametric refinements on other aspects of this therapeutic procedure, efforts toward examining the contribution and function of symbolic processes have begun only recently. It is noteworthy, however, that early procedural directives strongly hinted at the presumed importance of the imaginal events in desensitization. Paul (1966), for example, emphasized the importance of having the client imagine himself in the feared situation—not as if he were viewing himself in a movie, but as if he were actually there. Vivid, multi-sensory images are emphasized, presumably based on the assumption that closer approximations to real-life events will thereby be experienced.

The relationship between imagery vividness and therapy outcome has been suggested, but conclusive data are lacking (cf. McLemore, 1972). One of the problems in exploring this issue has been the absence of an accurate index of imagery. While a number of investigators have attempted to identify correlates of vivid imagery, their findings have been almost uniformly negative (cf. Rimm & Bottrell, 1969; Danaher & Thoresen, 1972; McCullough & Powell, 1972; Rehm, 1973; Paivio, 1973). Moreover, self-reported imagery vividness does not seem to correlate with therapeutic outcome (e.g., Davis, McLemore, & London, 1970; Kazdin, 1973d, in press, a,b).

A handful of intriguing studies have investigated the role of "emotive imagery" in counterconditioning paradigms. For example, although they did not adopt a conditioning perspective, Chappell and

Stevenson (1936) reported using positive imagery in the treatment of peptic ulcers. Thirty-two patients in an experimental group were trained to image pleasant scenes whenever they experienced anxiety. They reported significantly better improvements in symptomatology that did twenty control patients. A three-year follow-up revealed impressive maintenance.

Subsequent inquiries along this line were stimulated by the work of Arnold A. Lazarus and his co-workers (cf. Lazarus & Abramovitz, 1962; Lazarus, Davison, & Polefka, 1965). In treating young phobic children these researchers encountered difficulties in using relaxation as an anxiety inhibitor. As an alternative antagonistic response, the children were asked to visualize feared scenes and to incorporate positive images into them. For example, a ten-year-old had been referred for treatment of his excessive fear of the dark. Covert counterconditioning utilized imaginal scenes in which darkness was paired with comic book heroes:

> Now I want you to close your eyes and imagine that you are sitting in the dining-room with your mother and father. It is night time. Suddenly, you receive a signal on the wrist radio that Superman has given you. You quickly run into the lounge because your mission must be kept a secret. There is only a little light coming into the lounge from the passage. Now pretend that you are all alone in the lounge waiting for Superman and Captain Silver to visit you (Lazarus & Abramovitz, 1962, p. 193).

Subsequent work has extended the use of positive imagery to the treatment of pain tolerance and other avoidance patterns. Horan (1973), for example, has suggested that emotive imagery may be a useful technique for reducing the discomforts and anxieties of childbirth. In a laboratory study, Horan and Dellinger (in press) reported that subjects trained in emotive imagery were capable of tolerating painful ice water immersion far longer than control or attentional distraction subjects. Hekmat and Vanian (1971) have reported similar success in the "semantic" desensitization of snake phobia. These researchers paired the word "snake" with positive imaginal associates and found significant improvements on measures of self-reported fear, semantic differential, and behavioral approach. While these preliminary inquiries are promisingly suggestive, the therapeutic value of positive imagery procedures must await further empirical scrutiny. An interesting process issue relates to the function of emotive imagery in counterconditioning paradigms. Do images of pleasant scenes induce a general state of cognitive relaxation (Rachman, 1968) which then counteracts anxiety?

The modality of symbolic events in covert counterconditioning has received very little attention. In the clinical practice of desensitization, clients are often told to *visualize* themselves in a scene. To enhance the vividness of their cognitive rehearsal, they are often instructed to imagine *hearing* sounds associated with a particular performance, to *feel* appropriate stimulation (e.g., the contour of the dentist's chair), and to *taste* or *smell* relevant stimuli. In procedural descriptions, however, the reader is often left with the impression that "simple" visual imagery was the only method of hierarchy presentation. Symbolic representations in desensitization are far from simple, and we are delinquent in continuing to overlook their possible moderating influences.

Other uses of imaginary events have been reported in covert conditioning analogues. We shall explore some of these in subsequent discussions. Two case studies worth noting here have utilized imaginary stimuli in counterconditioning paradigms. Efron (1957) reported the successful control of epileptic seizures in a patient by employing a covertly mediated conditioned inhibition. The odor of jasmine—which appeared to inhibit seizures in this patient—was paired with a bracelet. During a later phase of treatment, the patient reported being able to inhibit seizures by merely thinking about the bracelet. Wilson (1973a) provides another example of a contiguous pairing procedure utilizing imaginary stimuli. A client who suffered urinary inhibitions (an inability to urinate publicly) was instructed to imagine the presence of other persons at the point of urinary imminence (shortly before private micturition). Significant improvement was reported.

While comparisons of real and imaginal hierarchies have not been uncommon (e.g., Agras, 1967; Litvak, 1969; O'Neill & Howell, 1969; Barlow, Leitenberg, Agras, & Wincze, 1969; Waters & McDonald, 1973), there has been virtually no exploration of the differences among covert modalities. A dissuading methodological problem here, of course, is the relative lack of control over subjects' covert activities. However, the employment of programmed covert assignments which mitigate against idiosyncratic rehearsals may offer appropriate experimental controls (cf. Bandura, Grusec, & Menlove, 1966; Gerst, 1969; Bandura & Jeffery, 1973).

As is the case with other variations of the desensitization procedure (cf. Bandura, 1969), there is scant evidence to support a physiological counterconditioning hypothesis in the covert techniques reviewed above. Whether a simple graduated extinction hypothesis is adequate, however, remains to be demonstrated. As we shall see in subsequent discussions, there appears to be more going on than just "covert stimulus exposure" in therapies employing symbolic hierarchies.

Orgasmic Reconditioning.

A second major utilization of symbolic stimuli in clinical behavior therapy has been in the area of sexual deviation. McGuire, Carlisle, and Young (1965) hypothesized that adult sexual deviance may be attributable to the use of deviant (e.g., homosexual) imagery during masturbation. According to these researchers, the pairing of such imagery with sexual orgasm may produce strong approach responses to the external referents of the images.

Pursuing this hypothesis, Davison (1968a) reported a successful case study in which sexual arousal and orgasm were oriented away from sadistic fantasies and toward more appropriate heterosexual imagery. In this study, the client was instructed to induce sexual arousal and begin masturbation with his conventional (culturally deviant) fantasies. When orgasm was imminent, the client was to shift his attention to a Playboy fold-out. Gradually, the heterosexual stimulus was introduced at earlier points in the masturbatory chain. Marquis (1970) reports success with this procedure in the treatment of a variety of sexual deviations. Several other workers have likewise found programmed masturbatory fantasies to aid sexual therapy (e.g., Lobitz & LoPiccolo, 1972). Excellent reviews of the mounting evidence for this procedure are provided by Barlow (1973), Annon (1973), and Wilson and Davison (1974).

An intriguing issue in the use of orgasmic reconditioning has to do with the role of awareness and expectancy in its success. Masters and Johnson (1970) acknowledge that premature ejaculators often resort to cognitive distraction as a means of delaying orgasm. Likely distractions might include mental rehearsals of sporting events, financial commitments, and so on. Why is it then that the Chicago Cubs and Master Charge seldom acquire erotic capacities? Many events are adventitiously associated with masturbation and orgasm, but only a select few become endowed with arousal potential. Pillows, bed covers, and thoughts about hairy palms are seldom documented as erotic stimuli.

One behavior therapist has contended that men suffer sexual deviations more frequently than women because of the fact that their sexual organ protrudes and can therefore be stimulated in accidental contiguity with a variety of stimuli. If such is the case, why do we not encounter more soap, urinal, or BVD fetishes? An automatic conditioning process does not appear to be adequate. As we shall see in Chapters 9 and 10, attentional processes appear to mediate our selective conditioning. Moreover, the fact that certain categories of stimuli (e.g., articles of clothing) tend to dominate the content of fetishes suggests the possibility that our sexual conditioning is influenced by conceptual and categorical features. These issues will be more extensively considered when we address the cognitive mediational models.

THOUGHT STOPPING

As its name implies, "thought stopping" is a procedure designed to suppress or eliminate unwanted ruminations. It was first suggested by Alexander Bain (1928) and revived by Taylor (1955, 1963) and Wolpe (1958, 1969; Wolpe & Lazarus, 1966). In this clinical strategy, the client is instructed to purposely engage in his maladaptive ruminative behaviors. When he has signaled the therapist to indicate that he is thinking undesired thoughts, the therapist loudly shouts "STOP!" This usually produces a startle response in the client, after which the therapist points out that this distraction successfully terminated the ruminative sequence. Additional trials are then presented and the client is gradually trained to subvocalize the word "STOP!" to himself.

Unfortunately, the empirical evidence on the effectiveness of thought stopping is very meager. At the time of this writing, only one controlled group study has been reported. Wisocki and Rooney (1974) compared the effectiveness of four conditions in the reduction of smoking behavior: thought stopping, covert sensitization (a technique to be described shortly), an attention-placebo strategy, and no treatment. The conclusions which can be drawn from this study are unfortunately limited by several methodological difficulties. Random assignment requirements were not met—control subjects were comprised of those volunteers who could not "schedule their time to accommodate the treatment program." No pre-treatment, post-treatment, or follow-up data are reported for controls. Moreover, although statistical analyses revealed no pre-treatment differences in smoking rates, the reported data suggest considerable variability (thought stopping and attention-placebo subjects smoked almost twice as many cigarettes per day during the pre-treatment baseline as did covert sensitization subjects). A statistical comparison of the thought stopping and covert sensitization effects was not reported. Finally, a four month follow-up indicated no significant differences among the groups. In consideration of these methodological limitations, the data provide meager support for any treatment effect.

Rimm, Saunders, and Westel (1974) reported a group study in which thought stopping was combined with "covert assertion" (the symbolic rehearsal of assertive coping responses). Subjects exposed to this procedure were much more successful in overcoming their snake avoidance than individuals in an attention-placebo control group. The active contribution of thought stopping per se, however, was not assessed.

A number of case studies have reported the successful utilization of thought stopping procedures (e.g., Wolpe, 1958, 1969, 1971; Wolpe & Lazarus, 1966; Taylor, 1963; Gershman, 1970; Stern, 1970; Gentry, 1970; Beck, 1970b; Garfield, McBrearty, & Dichter, 1969; Yamagami, 1971; Kumar & Wilkinson, 1971; Campbell, 1973; Wisocki, 1973b; Cautela & Baron, 1973; Rimm, 1973; Rosen & Schnapp, 1974). Many of these applications have combined thought stopping with a wide range of other therapeutic procedures (e.g., relaxation training, systematic desensitization, positive imagery, covert sensitization, etc.). Besides using unstandardized treatment combinations, however, most have failed to meet the methodological requirements of a controlled empirical case study. Poor operational definitions, the absence of within-subject control procedures, and lack of follow-up measurements are only a few of the methodological problems which have characterized many of the case study applications of thought stopping. Stern (1970), for example, combined drug-assisted relaxation training with thought stopping in the treatment of an obsessional patient. No quantifiable data on therapy outcome or follow-up were reported. The author, however, concluded his case report with an optimistic interpretation: although the patient "remained an obsessional personality, it was thought that his personal characteristics could now be used to a more effective end (p. 442)." This statement sounds dangerously close to many post-treatment conclusions in "psychodynamic" therapies which defend continuing behavioral maladjustment by emphasing that the client now, at least, has "insight" into its source.

The theoretical rationale for thought stopping as a "conditioning" procedure is not entirely clear. Few rats or pigeons have experienced an analogue version of this strategy. Several therapists have suggested that abrupt cognitive distraction and incompatibility constitute the presumed underlying processes. If attention can be distracted from covert ruminations, they will (theoretically) terminate. Moreover, the subvocalization of an imperative self-instruction may be incompatible with other (maladaptive) subvocalizations (cf. Bergin, 1969; Wisocki & Rooney, 1974). In an attempt to evaluate the attentional distraction feature of thought stopping, Mahoney (1971) asked an obsessive client to count backwards by 7's from a four digit number whenever he experienced undesired ruminations. This strategy was borrowed from the field of information processing research. Unfortunately, the distractional procedure appeared to increase rather that decrease obsessional thinking. Campbell (1973) combined a backward counting procedure with positive imagery training and reported more successful results.

A research-worthy speculation is that thought *substitution* procedures may prove more effective than simple termination or distraction strategies. Moreover, researchers in this area might do well to consider the use of psychophysiological measurement in the evaluation of thought-alteration procedures. As noted earlier, there is evidence suggesting that gross categories of thinking can be discriminated on the basis of vocal chord EMG and other physiological responses (cf. Jacobson, 1973; McGuigan, 1973). A straightforward evaluation of thought stopping techniques might be obtained via use of such dependent variables.

It is again interesting to note our naivete regarding human mediational processes. Almost without exception, thought stopping has been applied as if all ruminative mediations were *verbal*. Little interest has been paid to the possible differences between therapeutic termination of maladaptive subvocalizations and maladaptive *imagery*. Although we now know that both thoughts and images can induce dramatic physiological arousal, we know very little about the most effective means for abruptly terminating these private events. Recent laboratory studies by Horowitz and his colleagues corroborate that stressful experiences increase the frequency of repetitive and maladaptive thoughts (Horowitz & Becker, 1971a, b, c; Horowitz, Becker, & Moskowitz, 1971). Thought stopping represents a preliminary attempt to develop means for controlling and eliminating these covert sequences. However, as the foregoing discussion has indicated, our knowledge and procedures at this time are rudimentary and lacking strong empirical support. Extensive methodological improvements are long overdue in the standardization and systematic exploration of mediator-terminating strategies. Unless such improvements are forthcoming, we will remain in our present state of relative ignorance, plodding along with a therapy procedure which has little to support it other than tradition.

COVERANT CONTROL

A third covert conditioning therapy was suggested in Homme's (1965) classic article on "coverants, the operants of the mind." The term *coverant* is an abbreviation of *covert operant* and accurately depicts Homme's perspective. According to this viewpoint, thoughts are early elements in a response chain. Subvocalizations such as "I'm dying for a cigarette" may precede and functionally activate an undesired target behavior (i.e., smoking). Utilizing Premack's (1965) differential probability definition of reinforcement, Homme suggested a programmed sequence for the modification of maladaptive coverants. According to this "coverant control" paradigm, stimuli which have previously elicited inappropriate coverants can become cues for coverants which are incompatible with the undesired target behavior (TB). For example, the individual can be trained to generate anti-TB coverants in the presence of TB stimuli. This is represented in the first two phases below.

1. TB stimuli	2. anti-TB coverant	3. pro-non-TB coverant	4. reward
smoking stimuli	"smoking causes halitosis"	"I'll save money by not smoking"	coffee

To avoid terminating the response chain on an aversive element (phase 2), Homme recommends that a reinforceable behavior be inserted and then some reward (high probability behavior) experienced. Thus, an individual might encounter a cigarette machine. To counteract his usual "urge" for a cigarette, he engages in an anti-smoking coverant (e.g., "smoking causes cancer"). This is followed by a thought which is compatible with *not* smoking (e.g., "my food will taste better if I don't smoke"). This positive coverant is reinforced by engaging in a high probability (rewarding) activity, such as drinking a cup of coffee.

Some of the theoretical problems in Homme's coverant control sequence have previously been discussed (Mahoney, 1970, 1972). Briefly, there is a strong possibility that thoughts relevant to the target behavior might frequently be cued by the reinforcing activity rather than by target behavior stimuli. Thus, an individual who had chosen to use coffee as his reward for an anti-smoking coverant sequence might find himself inadvertently reminded of his smoking reduction efforts by coffee stimuli. There is evidence in the area of delay of gratification that this fortuitous cueing might actually interfere with cigarette avoidance (cf. Mischel, in press). A second speculative problem has to do with the close temporal pairing of negative coverants and reinforcers. This contiguity approximates a counterconditioning sequence and might jeopardize the suppressive effects of the negative coverant. Additionally, Homme's coverant control sequence implies that reinforcers have an *automatic* strengthening effect. In essence, the client is told to get maximum mileage out of daily reinforcers (e.g., meals) by inserting to-be-reinforced responses before them. This automaticity assumption will be discussed at greater length at the end of Chapter 8. For the time being, suffice it to say that it has little empirical support.

A final objection to the strategy proposed by Homme has to do with his misapplication of Premack's (1965) reinforcement theory. According to Premack (1965, 1971), high probability behaviors (HPBs) can be used contingently as reinforcers for low probability behaviors

(LPBs) and, conversely, the latter can be used as punishers for the former. An important distinction must be made here, however, between response *probability* and response *frequency*. Premack's use of the term probability refers to an operation in which the organism has free (i.e., non-contingent) access to various behaviors. Their probability is determined by the relative amount of time spent engaging in each of the available activities. Response frequency, on the other hand, refers to the rate of occurrence of a behavior regardless of whether its availability is contingent or non-contingent. Domestic chores and paying taxes may be relatively frequent responses, but few would argue that they are inherently reinforcing. Their high frequency is a result of the contingencies placed upon them. Homme (1965) and several other researchers have employed trivial high frequency behaviors (e.g., use of a particular office chair, turning on a water faucet, answering the telephone) as if they were Premackian reinforcers. The fact that a few of these inquiries have reported promising results may derive more from the *cueing* function of these activities than from any inherent reinforcing properties. There is, of course, the empirical possibility that even onerous high frequency behaviors can be reinforcing due to their instrumental role in a response chain which is ultimately reinforced. One can conceive of situations in which a person might work very hard to earn the opportunity to take out the garbage or wash a floor. Such negative reinforcement, however, presents a very different picture from what is usually denoted as Premackian reinforcement.

The conceptual and theoretical complexities of applying Premackian strategies to adult human behavior require more space than our present discussion will allow. Suffice it to say that inadequate analogues seriously challenge these extrapolations, particularly as they have been reported in the literature to date. A more detailed discussion of these problems has been been presented elsewhere (Mahoney, 1972; Danaher, in press).

Empirical evidence for the effectiveness of Homme's suggested coverant control strategy is meager. Although several researchers have reported its examination, they have either modified the sequence proposed by Homme or omitted a procedural description (e.g., Tooley & Pratt, 1967; Rutner, 1967; Keutzer, 1968; Lawson & May, 1970; Tyler & Straughan, 1970; Gordon, 1971; Chapman, Smith & Layden, 1971). A number of recent studies have provided more direct examination of coverant control effectiveness.

Horan and Johnson (1971) assigned 96 obese females to four experimental conditions: reinforced coverants, scheduled coverants, information and encouragement, or delayed treatment control. Individuals in the first two groups were given negative/positive coverant pairs to subvocalize (e.g., "obesity shortens one's life span," "if I lose weight, my clothes will fit better"). "Reinforced" coverants were followed by a high frequency event which occurred at least seven times per day (e.g., "sitting down on a particular chair"). Subjects in the scheduled coverants group were simply told to recite the coverant pairs to themselves at least seven times per day. After eight treatment weeks, individuals in the reinforced coverant group had lost 5.66 pounds as compared with mean losses of 2.72, 3.13, and 0.02 pounds in the scheduled coverants, information, and control groups, respectively. Self-reported coverant frequencies suggested that, at least initially, subjects in the reinforced coverant group engaged in the coverant pairs more frequently than did scheduled coverant subjects. This finding, however, is also compatible with a cueing interpretation. It is worth noting that neither experimental procedure resulted in sustained frequencies of these covert behaviors.

In a subsequent study, Horan, Baker, Hoffman, and Shute (1974) compared the effects of positive and negative coverants, eating and non-eating rewards (HPBs), and group versus individual counseling. A 2 × 2 × 2 design was employed and weight loss again constituted the dependent variable. Positive coverants were reported to produce significantly greater reductions than negative coverants. Eating versus non-eating HPBs did not result in significantly different effects.

Danaher (1974) examined the role of cueing versus consequation in the treatment of smoking via coverant control. A 2 × 2 design was employed in which type of cue (smoking urge versus reward stimuli) was crossed with type of consequence (frequent event versus valued response). A control group was also included. Dependent variables consisted of number of cigarettes smoked daily, frequency of smoking urges, and intensity of urges. Data analyses after three weeks of treatment revealed significant smoking reductions on the part of subjects in all groups. No intergroup differences were encountered. Follow-up measurements after eight months showed significant relapse to pre-treatment smoking levels. It is worth noting that Danaher included daily self-rewards for experimental subjects who attained a ninety percent criterion of adherence to their respective coverant control strategies. Despite this additional feature, coverant control subjects were not impressively successful in their smoking reduction.

Several other studies have examined the effectiveness of coverant control training in the treatment of smoking (e.g., Johnson, 1968; Hark, 1970; Gardiner, 1971). Their findings again lend relatively meager support to the therapeutic promise of this strategy. It should be mentioned, however, that cigarette smoking represents one of the most difficult clinical problems thus far encountered by behavior modifiers (cf. Bernstein, 1969). The relative ineffectiveness of coverant control in its treatment should be viewed against the backdrop of other therapies which have been equally unsuccessful.

Homme's contribution to cognitive behavior modification does not rest solely on the clinical efficacy of his proposed coverant control sequence. In addition to defending the empirical status of private events, he placed long overdue emphasis on the role of covert activities in the regulation and modification of overt responses. The heuristic contribution of this emphasis can hardly be overlooked.

Recent efforts to analyze and re-program covert "repertoires" have often received impetus from Homme's (1965) suggestions. For example, Ackerman (1972, 1973) has presented an intriguing operant analysis of the conditions complicating the modification of covert impulses. According to Ackerman, impulses (covert events involving imaginal representations or topical subvocalizations) mediate many consummatory stimulus-response sequences. Thoughts and images of food, for example, may perform this function. On a relatively continuous reinforcement schedule, the impulses are maintained at high frequencies by actual occurrences of the consummatory behavior. When the individual resolves to reduce or terminate a consummatory behavior, an extinction process develops. Covert impulses continue but may quickly terminate if total abstinence is effected (e.g., abrupt cessation of smoking). If such abstinence is not encountered, partial reduction in consummatory behavior may actually increase impulse frequency. Since the impulse is a covert discriminative stimulus for the overt response, this intermittent reinforcement effect exacerbates the problem. The individual gradually resumes the consummatory behavior, thereby making the impulses even more resistant to extinction during subsequent self-regulatory enterprises. These speculations suggest the clinical implication that preconsummatory impulses may often merit direct modification. In instances where a consummatory response cannot be totally suppressed (e.g., eating), it may be helpful to program a temporal separation between the impulse and the consummatory response. Eating, for example, might be artificially cued (using a timer) and not be allowed to immediately follow the occurrence of an eating impulse. The promise of such a strategy, of course, awaits empirical evaluation.

The clinical use of programmed coverants has been illustrated in a number of case studies. Categorically, it is difficult to distinguish some of these applications from those described under the "cognitive therapies" in a later section of this book. However, most of those mentioned briefly here have described their rationale as a modified form of coverant therapy. Johnson (1971), for example, reported the successful treatment of two clients with a procedure involving programmed subvocalizations. Jackson (1972), Todd (1972), and Ince (1972) have likewise adapted coverant conditioning procedures in successful clinical applications for the treatment of depression. A modified coverant strategy was employed by Mahoney (1971) in the case of a 22-year-old male who complained of uncontrollable self-critical obsessions. After a baseline assessment of obsessional frequency, the client was instructed to count backwards by sevens whenever he experienced undesired ruminations. This distractional strategy appeared to increase inappropriate thoughts, so a "tactile aversion" strategy was introduced. This consisted of the client's wearing a heavy gauge rubber band on his wrist and snapping it whenever he obsessed. Reported ruminations decreased markedly and remained absent for the remainder of therapy (Figure 7-1). A strategy designed to "prime" and reinforce positive self-thoughts was also employed. The client wrote positive self-statements on three cards attached to his cigarette package. Each time he reached for a cigarette, he was to read the top card, move it to the bottom of the stack, and then have his cigarette. A fourth card required the client to generate an original and spontaneous positive self-thought. Gradual removal of the

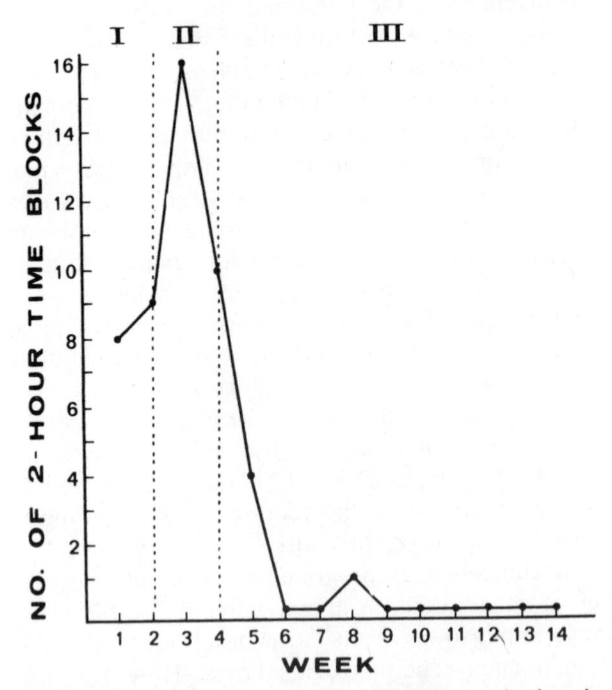

Figure 7-1. Frequency of obsessions during baseline assessment (Phase I), a backward counting intervention (Phase II), and self-punishment (Phase III). (Reprinted with permission from Mahoney, 1971.)

priming cues resulted in progressive increases in reported positive coverants (Figure 7-2). A four month follow-up contact suggested adequate maintenance and impressive improvements in other areas of functioning (employment, family dependency, heterosexual relations).

A few current thoughts on the foregoing case study are in order. A three year follow-up indicated that the client was continuing to function independently and was gainfully employed. Two years after the termination of therapy he had had a brief suicidal episode and was hospitalized for two weeks. During the subsequent year he had shown no signs of further maladjustment. These data suggest a more conservative optimism than the original case report. It is my own current opinion that the theoretical model adopted in this case was relatively naive and overly simplistic. While the modification of covert self-statements continues to demonstrate powerful clinical promise (as several forthcoming chapters will attest), simple conditioning principles may not be optimal for effecting such changes. The rubber band strategy may reduce clinical equipment costs, but it is questionable whether it effects the conditioned

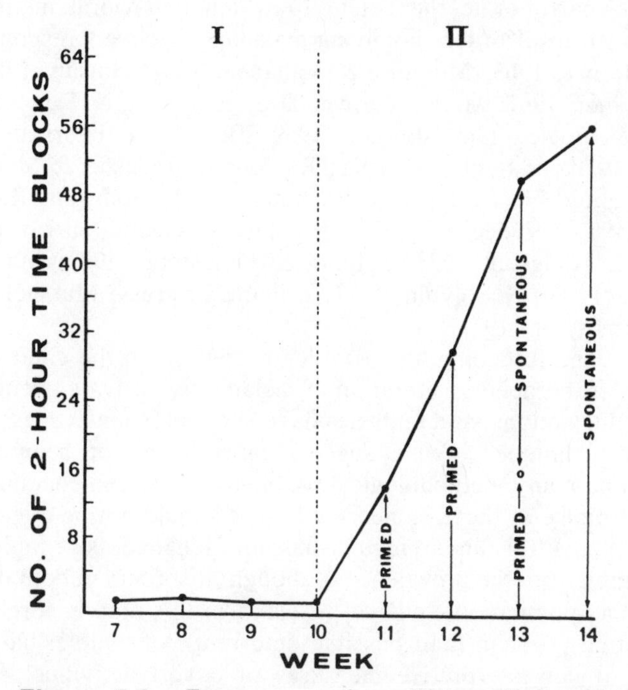

Figure 7-2. Frequency of positive self-thoughts during baseline assessment (Phase I) and coverant control (Phase II). (Reprinted with permission from Mahoney, 1971.)

"tactile aversion" which was suggested. Similarly, the cigarette procedure may have produced a frequent cueing for subvocal rehearsals rather than any automatic reinforcement effects. It is my current speculation that attentional factors and rehearsal operations may have accounted for many of the cognitive behavior changes reported in the above case, and even these appear to have been inadequate judging from the ambivalence of the follow-up data. Similar conclusions are suggested by a recent replication of the rubber band technique (Bass, 1973). These speculations deserve closer empirical scrutiny in future clinical research.

The covert conditioning perspective has, of course, been liberally applied in the behavioral treatment of a variety of thought disorders. Obsessions, hallucinations, and delusions have been viewed as modifiable covert responses which are sensitive to external contingencies. Self-recording, desensitization, aversion therapy, extinction, and selective reinforcement have been among the many therapeutic strategies employed in their treatment. Although an extensive discussion would take us far afield from our current topic, the following selected references corroborate the extent to which behavioral methods have been applied to disorders involving maladaptive covert responses: Walton & Mather, 1963; McGuire & Vallance, 1964; Haslan, 1965; Mees, 1966; Weiner, 1967; Marks, Crowe, Drewe, Young, & Dewhurst, 1969; Rutner & Bugle, 1969; Bergin, 1969; Bucher & Fabricatore, 1970; Mather, 1970a,b; Rachman, 1971; Rachman, Hodgson & Marks, 1971; Alumbaugh, 1971; Hodgson & Rachman, 1972; Hodgson, Rachman & Marks, 1972; Nydegger, 1972; Haynes & Geddy, 1973; Rachman, Marks, & Hodgson, 1973; Solyom & Kingstone, 1973; Marks, 1973; Kenny, Solyom, & Solyom, 1973; Hallam, in press; Marshall, 1974, in press, a; Taylor, 1974.

The foregoing literature lends support to the clinical feasibility of direct therapeutic alteration of maladaptive private events. Obsessions, hallucinations, and fantasies have shown responsiveness to a wide range of techniques. While success rates have not been invariably positive and many methodological problems have been encountered, the clinical promise of these pioneering efforts should not be overlooked. It is suprising that this line of inquiry has not escalated more rapidly than it has. Judging from the prevalence of thought disorders in both out-patient and chronic populations, clinical research in this area is sorely needed. A persisting problem (and possible deterrent), of course, has been the absence of non-interpretive measures of covert activities. Hopefully, recent efforts toward such measurement (e.g., Lowe, 1973) will stimulate increased experimental activity in this area.

Chapter Eight

The Covert Conditioning Therapies: Covert Sensitization, Reinforcement, Extinction, and Modeling

In terms of a technical referent, the label "covert conditioning" is probably applied most frequently to the theory and research of Joseph R. Cautela. In a series of heuristic theoretical and procedural contributions, Cautela has suggested the extrapolation of covert therapy procedures from laboratory conditioning paradigms (Cautela, 1966, 1967, 1969a, b, 1970a, b, c, d, 1971a, b, 1972, 1973). The present chapter will explore some of these extrapolations and examine the evidence for their clinical efficacy.

COVERT SENSITIZATION

The earliest and most widely adopted form of covert conditioning was that of *covert sensitization.* In this procedure imaginal rehearsals of a problem behavior are paired with aversive symbolic events (e.g., scenes of nausea, pain, social ridicule). Impetus for its clinical application was provided by several early reports of "hypnotically induced aversions" (cf. Strel'chuk, 1957; Lazarus, 1958; Miller, 1959, 1963). Hypnotized clients were instructed to imagine engaging in some problematic performance and to experience feelings of nausea and discomfort while doing so. This technique was reportedly successful in the treatment of alcoholism, sexual deviation and compulsivity.

In 1966 Cautela formalized this symbolic aversion procedure and gave it the label "covert sensitization." Two successful cases were reported involving alcoholism and obesity. In a subsequent paper Cautela (1967) offered a more formal theoretical defense of covert sensitization and provided a vivid description of the procedure. For example, after relaxation training, the covert sensitization of overeating might incorporate a scene such as the following:

> I want you to imagine you've just had your main meal and you are about to eat your dessert, which is apple pie. As you are about to reach for the fork, you get a funny feeling in the pit of your stomach. You start to feel queasy, nauseous and sick all over. As you touch the fork, you can feel some food particles inching up your throat. You're just about to vomit. As you put the fork into the pie, the food comes up into your mouth. You try to keep your mouth closed because you are afraid that you'll spit the food out all over the place. You bring the piece of pie to your mouth. As you're about to open your mouth, you puke; you vomit all over your hands, the fork, over the pie. It goes all over the table, over the other people's food. Your eyes are watering. Snot mucus is all over your mouth and nose. Your hands feel sticky. There is an awful smell. As you look at this mess you just can't help but vomit again and again until just watery stuff is coming out. Everybody is looking at you with a shocked expression. You turn away from the food and immediately start to feel better. You run out of the room, and as you run out, you feel better and better. You wash and clean yourself up and it feels wonderful (Cautela, 1967, p. 462).

The escape scene, in which terminating the target behavior is followed by immediate relief, is emphasized as a crucial component in the therapy.

The theoretical foundations for covert sensitization raise some interesting conceptual issues. We shall explore some of them in more detail at the end of the chapter. For the time being, it should be noted that Cautela has vacillated as to whether the procedure involves a covert classical aversion paradigm (1966) or a covert punishment analogue (1973). Moreover, a strict conditioning parallel is challenged by the fact that the effects of covert sensitization do not appear to be reduced when a backward rather than a forward conditioning sequence is employed (e.g., Ashem & Donner, 1968; Sachs & Ingram, 1972).

Empirical evidence for the efficacy of covert sensitization and other covert conditioning procedures has received several reviews (cf. Cautela, 1971a, 1972, 1973; Agras, 1972; Wisocki, 1972; Thoresen & Mahoney, 1974). Our present discussion will summarize that evidence and suggest some of the possible sources of its marked variability. We shall deal separately with applications to specific problem areas.

Alcoholism

The treatment of alcoholism by covert sensitization was pioneered by the early work of Strel'chuk (1957) and Miller (1959). Using a hypnotic aversion procedure, for example, Miller found that 24 treated alcoholics were impressively successful in maintaining abstinence during a nine month post-treatment follow-up. Cautela (1966) reported the successful treatment of a 29-year-old nurse who drank excessively to allay social anxieties. Further positive results were suggested by Anant (1967) who treated twenty-six institutionalized alcoholics. Follow-up contacts of varying intervals indicated impressive maintenance. Unfortunately, the absence of experimental controls and the often meager data presentations in the foregoing studies limit their contribution to the assessment of covert sensitization.

Several more recent studies have remedied at least some of these methodological problems. Ashem and Donner (1968), for example, included a no-treatment control group in evaluating the effects of forward and backward covert sensitization procedures. In the backward paradigm, nausea was induced prior to (rather than following) the imaginal rehearsal of problematic behaviors. Treatment results indicated no differential effectiveness between the two experimental groups. At a six month follow-up, forty percent of the contacted experimental subjects reported being abstinent. All control subjects were drinking at that time. These findings, which are much more conservative than those reported in previous studies, must also be interpreted cautiously due to the absence of an attention-placebo control group. It is worth noting that the authors interpreted the equivalence of forward and backward conditioning groups as indicative that subjects in the latter group were making forward associations during treatment.

In a 1970 study Rohan (cited by Wisocki, 1972) compared the effects of covert sensitization and electrical aversion in thirty hospitalized alcoholics. A three month follow-up suggested better maintenance by individuals who had received electrical aversion therapy. As Wisocki points out, however, a number of methodological inadequacies appear to have reduced the informative value of this inquiry. In a more controlled laboratory experiment, Wilson (1974a) examined the suppressive effects of covert sensitization and electrical aversion on the drinking behavior of gamma level (severe) alcoholics. Actual alcohol consumption was measured in a live-in laboratory environment. Data from six brief studies suggested that both treatment strategies were about equally effective and that neither was impressively successful in its suppressive effects.

The above studies offer meager evidence for the effectiveness of covert sensitization in the treatment of alcoholism. Tremendous variability in findings and equally salient procedural diversities warrant a suspension of judgment until more adequate empirical evidence is available. The fact that at least some alcoholics appear to benefit from the technique invites a closer examination of predictor variables and treatment components.

Smoking

The pairing of external aversive stimulation (e.g., electric shock) with imaginary smoking performances has been reported (e.g., Steffy, Meichenbaum, & Best, 1970; Berecz, 1972) but controlled comparisons with covert sensitization have yet to be explored. Studies addressed to the efficacy of the latter have again deviated procedurally from the treatment guidelines suggested by Cautela (1972). Methodological problems have additionally threatened the empirical import of these inquiries.

Tooley and Pratt (1967) combined covert sensitization with coverant control and contingency contracting in the treatment of a smoking couple. They report that covert sensitization was effective during the early stages of treatment but that its therapeutic power declined rapidly. Following a preliminary report by Wagner (1969), Wagner and Bragg (1970) compared the efficacy of desensitization, covert sensitization, a combined group, relaxation alone, and counseling. The combined group received systematic desensitization to a standardized hierarchy of cigarette deprivation. When subjects signalled discomfort, they were instructed to imagine a covert sensitization scene. There were no inter-group differences after four treatment weeks. A ninety day follow-up, however, revealed that subjects in the combined group had relapsed less than individuals in the other groups. Interestingly, covert sensitization subjects demonstrated the most relapse at that interval.

Similarly pessimistic results were reported by Lawson and May (1970) in a study comparing covert sensitization, coverant control, contingency contracting, and self-monitoring. A very small subject sample (N = 12) and the absence of follow-up data limit the conclusions which can be drawn from this inquiry. However, post-treatment analyses revealed no significant differences among the four procedures. Sachs, Bean, and Morrow (1970) utilized an attention-placebo control group (self-monitoring) and compared its efficacy to that of covert sensitization or a self-control procedure. After three weeks, no treatment effects were found. A one month follow-up revealed that that only experimental subjects had reduced their smoking from baseline levels. Unfortunately, a high attrition rate (35%) may have inflated treatment effects. A study by Gordon (1971) likewise failed to demonstrate any differential superiority of covert sensitization. Two unpublished studies (Mullen, 1967; Viernstein, 1968) suggested some short-term suppression of smoking but the absence of attention-placebo control groups and long-term follow-up assessments limit the conclusions which can be drawn. Finally, the import of Wisocki and Rooney's (1971) comparison of thought stopping and covert sensitization is obscured by several methodological inadequacies (cf. Chapter 7).

As mentioned earlier, the lack of standardized procedures and a host of methodological problems prohibit any definitive conclusions at the present time. While we cannot affirm the null hypothesis, it is apparent that the efficacy of covert sensitization in the treatment of smoking has not yet been adequately demonstrated.

Obesity

Cautela (1966) reported the successful treatment of obesity with covert sensitization in a female client. An impressive loss of 66 pounds was maintained at a seven month follow-up. This report stimulated the incorporation of covert sensitization into several behavioral programs for obesity (cf. Stunkard & Mahoney, in press). Unfortunately, only one of these programs has attempted to isolate the contribution of covert sensitization to weight loss. Manno and Marston (1972) compared a control group, covert sensitization, and covert reinforcement (a procedure to be described shortly). Both of the covert conditioning therapies achieved significantly better reductions than the control group; the former did not differ from one another. A three month follow-up revealed a maintained loss of 8.9 pounds in each of the two treatment groups. While this magnitude of loss does not approximate that reported by Cautela, differences in pre-treatment weight and therapeutic procedure might moderate some of this variability.

In a well controlled group study, Janda and Rimm (1972) compared the effects of covert sensitization to an attention (relaxation) control group and a no-treatment control. Overall analyses after six treatment weeks failed to differentiate the three groups but a subsequent six week follow-up revealed highly significant differences. Covert sensitization subjects had lost 11.7 pounds as compared with a loss of 2.3 and a gain of 0.9 pounds by attention and control subjects. Interestingly, Janda and Rimm found that individual weight losses in covert sensitization subjects correlated significantly with their subjectively reported discomfort during aversive imagery ($r = .53$).

The therapeutic promise suggested by the above studies, however, must be evaluated in light of several other studies, which have failed to demonstrate the efficacy of covert sensitization. Meynen (1970), for example, compared relaxation, covert sensitization, and a modified version of systematic desensitization. After eight treatment weeks, all three groups had lost significant amounts of weight and no inter-group differences were apparent. Lick and Bootzin (1971) reported similarly pessimistic findings. They assigned forty overweight females to one of four groups: (1) no-treatment control, (2) covert sensitization with relief (escape) scene, (3) covert sensitization without relief scene, and (4) covert sensitization with "automatic immunization" instructions. The latter group involved a presentation of the therapy procedures in terms of classical conditioning principles. Treatment was conducted for four weeks and a five week follow-up was conducted. Although treatment subjects reported reductions in the attractiveness of favorite foods, data analyses revealed very little weight loss (four pounds over 10 weeks) and no inter-group differences

It was mentioned earlier that Sachs and Ingram (1972) found no differential effects between forward and backward covert sensitization procedures. Using a counterbalanced design with ten subjects, self-reported food consumption declined significantly regardless of treatment procedure. Data on subjects' bodyweights were not reported. A series of three studies have recently been reported by Wilson (1974b) in an effort to evaluate the effects of covert sensitization on food consumption and weight loss. In one study, the addition of aversive imagery and relaxation to a behavioral treatment package (stimulus control, self-monitoring, etc.) did not produce greater weight loss. A second study utilized an ingenious and relatively unobtrusive "taste test" to evaluate the effects of covert sensitization. Subjects were given access to snacks and told to rate their palatability. The addition of covert sensitization to a self-monitoring procedure had no effect on actual food consumption. In a final study, Wilson and his colleagues found covert sensitization to be relatively ineffective as an isolated method for weight reduction.

A well controlled study by Foreyt and Hagen (1973) lends further doubt to the therapeutic sufficiency of covert sensitization in weight management. Thirty-nine obese females were assigned to one of three groups: covert sensitization, attention-placebo, or no-treatment control. Eighteen sessions were administered over nine treatment weeks. Using standardized food approach scenes, sensitization subjects were directed to engage in aversive (nauseous) imagery. These same scenes were followed by positive imagery in the attention-placebo group. After nine weeks there were no significant differences among the three groups. Attention-placebo subjects had lost 8.5 pounds as compared with 4.1 and 3.7 (covert sensitization and control groups, respectively). These findings were interpreted by the authors as suggestive of expectancy influences.

The addition of the foregoing studies suggests that the clinical efficacy of covert sensitization in the treatment of obesity is not entirely clear. Contradictory findings suggest that outcome variability may be due to procedural differences, varying populations, or unspecified factors in the treatment strategy. We are again obliged to defer conclusions until more adequate and extensive evidence is available.

Sexual Deviation

The use of covert sensitization in the treatment of sexual deviations has received rather extensive examination. A number of case reports have indicated its clinical promise with such varied disorders as homosexuality, sadistic fantasies, and pedophilia (e.g., Miller, 1963; Gold & Neufeld, 1965; Kolvin, 1967; Davison, 1968a, 1969; Cautela & Wisocki, 1971; Kendrick & McCullough, 1972; Curtis & Presly, 1972; Farr & Tucker, 1974). The ingenuity of therapists applying covert sensitization to sexual deviation is well illustrated in Davison's (1968a) treatment of a client with sadistic fantasies:

> With his eyes closed, he was instructed to imagine a typical sadistic scene, a pretty girl tied to stakes on the ground and struggling tearfully to extricate herself. While looking at the girl, he was told to imagine someone bringing a branding iron toward his eyes, ultimately searing his eyebrows. A second image was attempted when this proved abortive, namely, being kicked in the groin by a ferocious-looking karate expert. When he reported himself indifferent to this image as well, the therapist depicted to him a large bowl of "soup," composed of steaming urine with reeking fecal boli bobbing around on top. His grimaces, contortions, and groans indicated that an effective image had been found, and the following 5 minutes were spent portraying his drinking from the bowl, with accompanying nausea, at all times while peering over the floating debris at the struggling girl (p. 86).

Controlled experimental analyses in this area have been provided by a series of well designed single subject inquiries. Barlow, Leitenberg, and Agras (1969) reported the successful treatment of two clients via covert sensitization. A pedophile and a homosexual were each asked to subjectively rate the arousal potential of deviant sexual scenes. These ratings were quantified by a sorting procedure in which more arousing scenes received greater weighting than those which were less arousing. The clients were also instructed to record the frequency of deviant sexual urges between therapy sessions. Finally, galvanic skin responses (GSRs) were measured during all experimental phases. After five baseline sessions, covert sensitization procedures were instituted. The authors provide commendable specification of procedure (e.g., scene duration, intertrial intervals, and total number of pairings). Following covert sensitization, baseline conditions were reinstated. This extinction phase was described to the clients as "the best course of action at this time" and no explicit reversal expectancies were presented. In a final reacquisition phase, covert sensitization procedures were again employed. Figure 8-1 shows the subjective arousal ratings and sexual urge frequency of the pedophilic client. These measures correlated very well with experimental phases. GSRs displayed similar phasic patterns. Corresponding results were obtained with the homosexual client. While this study did not report follow-up assessments or naturalistic performances, it provided preliminary laboratory support for the efficacy of covert sensitization in sexual deviation.

A replication and refinement of the above study was reported by Barlow, Agras, Leitenberg, Callahan, and Moore (1972). Four male homosexuals were treated with a somewhat modified paradigm. Penile circumference was measured via a mechanical strain gauge which provided a more direct assessment of sexual responsiveness. To evaluate the role of expectancy and demand characteristics, the previous experimental procedure was altered. Phase one (baseline) was presented as a therapeutic strategy in which clients were led to believe that they would learn to substitute a relaxed response for their former arousal to homosexual scenes. Phase two (covert sensitization) was introduced with *negative* instructions in which expectancies of increased sexual arousal were conveyed: "To obtain the best effects we are going to heighten the tension by pairing the sexually arousing scenes with images of vomiting. You will probably notice an increase in your sexual arousal to males and in your homosexual urges but don't be alarmed, this is part of the treatment (pp. 412-413)." Extinction (Phase three) was presented

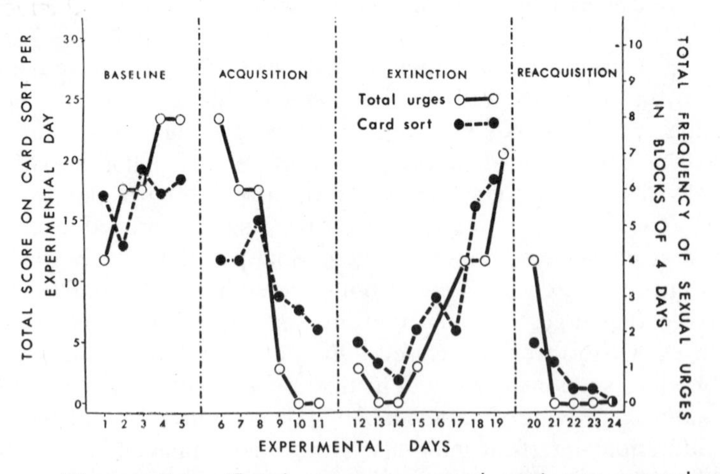

Figure 8-1. Total score on card sort per experimental day and total frequency of pedophilic sexual urges in blocks of 4 days surrounding each experimental day. (Reprinted with permission from Barlow, Leitenberg, & Agras, 1969.)

as a therapeutic reversal during which sexual arousal would decline. Finally, the re-introduction of covert sensitization (Phase four) was presented with positive expectancies. Despite the above counter-therapeutic instructions, clients' sexual responses conformed to the actual experimental phases. Penile circumference decreased during both covert sensitization phases.

The clinical promise of these findings was borne out in a subsequent inquiry reported by Callahan and Leitenberg (1973). Using counterbalanced, within-subject designs, six sexual deviants were treated with covert sensitization and electrical aversion. Measures of penile circumference revealed no differences between the two procedures. However, subjective ratings of sexual urges and deviant fantasies suggested a marked superiority of covert sensitization over electrical aversion. Follow-up contacts ranging from four to 18 months indicated very favorable data on the absence of actual deviant performances in five of the six cases.

A series of inquiries by Maletzky has offered promising evidence for an "assisted" covert sensitization procedure (Maletzky, 1973, 1974, in press; Maletzky & George, 1973). The conventional procedure was altered by adding an aversive odor (valeric acid) to the covert nauseous scene. This technique was impressively successful in the treatment of ten exhibitionists (Maletzky, 1974). Therapy outcome was evaluated on the basis of (1) self-reported covert activities (urges, fantasies, and dreams), (2) self-reported occurrences of exhibitionism, (3) arrests, and (4) performance during a "temptation test" executed by an experimental confederate (e.g., an attractive female was paid to tempt the client by walking seductively past his car). Figure 8-2 illus-

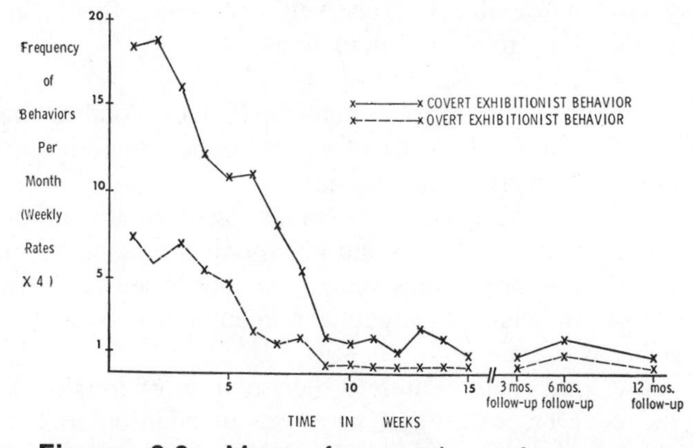

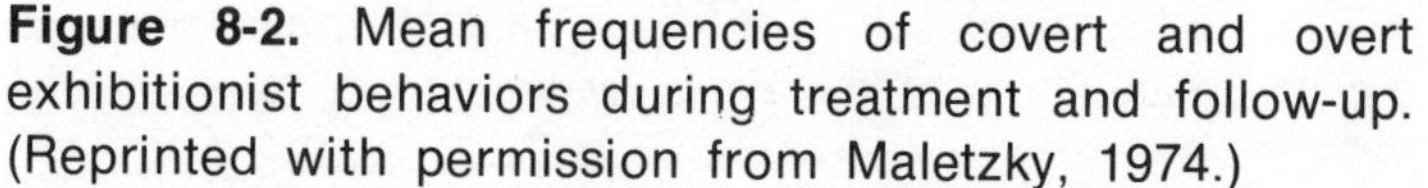
Figure 8-2. Mean frequencies of covert and overt exhibitionist behaviors during treatment and follow-up. (Reprinted with permission from Maletzky, 1974.)

trates the effects of treatment on overt and covert exhibitionistic behaviors. The correlation between these two indices is noteworthy. A twelve month follow-up indicated total elimination of exhibitionistic behaviors in all subjects. No legal apprehensions had been made and all clients passed their one year temptation test with flying colors.

The foregoing results suggest that covert sensitization may offer considerable clinical promise in the treatment of a range of sexual deviations. Although we are faced with an unfortunate paucity of controlled investigations, the few which are available offer an optimistic omen. Procedural variations such as that described by Maletzky (1974) may prove useful in reducing some of the apparent variability in responsiveness to treatment. Notwithstanding our cautious optimism, the need for empirical replication and refinement in this area is readily apparent.

A handful of studies have examined the efficacy of covert sensitization in the treatment of disorders such as drug addiction and compulsions (e.g., Kolvin, 1967; Cautela, 1966; Steinfeld, 1970; Wisocki, 1970, 1973b). Although heuristic, their evaluation must await controlled experimental scrutiny.

In summary, covert sensitization has been mainly applied to four clinical problems—alcoholism, smoking, obesity, and sexual deviation. Although sparsity of evidence and frequent methodological inadequacies limit the conclusions which may be drawn, the preliminary data are suggestive:

1. covert sensitization has not shown any consistent or impressive effectiveness in the suppression of alcohol consumption or smoking;
2. it has shown variable success with obesity; and
3. it has shown impressive and relatively consistent efficacy in preliminary applications to sexual deviation.

Before turning our attention to the remaining covert conditioning procedures, brief note should be made of several conceptual and procedural issues relating to covert sensitization.

First, the absence of a standardized treatment procedure discourages empirical replication and unequivocal outcome evaluations. Specific quantifiable operations should be developed to form a procedural basis from which therapeutic refinements and treatment outcomes can be assessed.

A second issue relates to the isolation of treatment components in the covert sensitization package. In addition to the role of relaxation training, self-monitoring, and therapist reinforcement, the covert components of the package need to be separately evaluated—

covert rehearsal of a problem behavior, symbolically-induced nausea, covert escape from an aversive scene, covert reinforcement, and so on. The contribution of therapeutic expectancy needs continued evaluation.

The differential effects of other forms of aversive imagery are likewise in need of examination. While nauseous scenes have conventionally been used, little attention has been given to the promise of utilizing imagery of other forms of aversive experiences (e.g., physical injury, social ostracism, etc.). An intriguing sub-issue relates to whether or not "naturalistic" covert consequences are more effective than artificial ones. Nausea is a conceivable consequence of certain activities (e.g., consummatory responses) but a less likely occurrence in others (e.g., compulsive checking).

An even more critical issue concerns the contribution of autonomic arousal to successful covert aversion. Must an individual experience negative physiological activity in order to develop avoidant associations? Is the nature of that arousal an important feature? One potential study might induce autonomic activity (e.g., with drugs) and then manipulate its label (positive/negative—e.g., excitement/anxiety) to determine whether the physiology or its cognitive label plays a larger part in covert aversion. This speculation derives from some research which will be reviewed in a later chapter as well as from the previously cited work on semantic generalization in attitude formation.

A final issue is suggested by the trend evidenced in our foregoing review of the covert sensitization literature. At the present time, it appears that the effectiveness of covert sensitization may correlate positively with the extent to which imaginal (visual) fantasies precede the problem behavior. Sexual deviations are very frequently mediated by fantasized performances and erotic imagery. The prevalence of food-related imagery in obesity has not been formally addressed, although clinical reports suggest wide individual differences. Smoking and alcoholism, on the other hand, have rarely been described as imaginally-mediated behavior patterns. As a matter of fact, clients in these last two categories often report that they are unaware of *any* form of mediation preceding their execution of the problem behavior. This may be due partly to the fact that these patterns involve relatively swift and often private consummations (which distinguishes them from most sexual acts). If covert sensitization is aimed at therapeutically altering symbolic representations (mediators) of undesired performances, the naturalistic occurrence and functional role of those mediational activities need to be determined. The establishment of aversions to an imaginal performance seems futile if symbolic events do not play a functional role in the execution of a particular behavior pattern.

COVERT REINFORCEMENT

A second covert conditioning procedure involves pairing an imaginal performance and an imaginal reinforcer (Cautela, 1970a,b). Two variations of this covert reinforcement procedure have been delineated: positive and negative. In covert positive reinforcement, the individual is trained to generate imagery of a pleasant activity (e.g., eating a favorite food). After this initial training, symbolic response–consequence pairings are instituted. The individual is asked to imagine performing some desired response (e.g., asserting himself) and then to shift to a reinforcing image. The imagery shift is initially cued by the therapist via pronouncement of the word "Reinforcement." Clients are later requested to practice the technique on their own.

An illustration of covert positive reinforcement is provided by Cautela (1970b) in the treatment of a test anxious graduate student. The client had flunked his doctoral qualifying examination three times and was very anxious about the success of his final opportunity. He was first trained to imagine "skiing down a mountain feeling exhilarated" in response to the therapist's pronouncement of the word "Reinforcement." Pairings of this positive image with imaginal performances were then instituted:

> Now let's work on the examination situation. It is the day of the examination and you feel confident ("Reinforcement.") You are entering the building in which the exam is going to be given. ("Reinforcement.") You remember that in all these scenes you are to try to feel confident. Now you enter the building and go into the classroom. ("Reinforcement.") You sit down and kid around with another student who is taking the exam. You feel good; you know you are ready. ("Reinforcement.") The proctor hands out the exam. ("Reinforcement.") You read the questions and you can answer all of them. ("Reinforcement.")
>
> Now let's do that again. This time you look the questions over and you are not sure about one question, but you say, "Oh well, I can still pass the exam if I flunk this one question." ("Reinforcement.") All right, this time you look over the exam, and you can see two questions about which you are in doubt, and you say, "Well, I can still pass this exam if I take my time and relax." ("Reinforcement") (1970b, p. 39).

After ten treatment sessions, the client passed his doctoral examination and reported being both confident and relaxed while doing so.

Cautela (1970b) reports that the covert positive reinforcement procedure has become his main therapeutic approach, occasionally supplemented with other behavior therapy procedures. He states that he bases his confidence in the power of this covert conditioning procedure on (1) demonstrated efficiency of other behavior modification procedures (e.g., desensitization), (2) the fact that it is not contradicted in the writings of learning theorists such as Pavlov, Hull, and Guthrie, and (3) observations of its clinical effectiveness. We now turn our attention to an evaluation of the latter.

Two laboratory studies offering suggestive evidence on the effectiveness of covert positive reinforcement were discussed in Chapter 6 (Cautela, Steffan, & Wish, in press; Ascher, 1973). A few studies have been reported in which this covert conditioning procedure was employed in an effort to produce attitude change. Cautela, Walsh and Wish (1971), for example, attempted to modify college students' attitudes about mental retardates. Experimental subjects were trained to pair positive imagery with thoughts about retardates, while control subjects were simply told to imagine the retarded person. Questionnaire responses suggested an increase in the positive attitudes of the experimental group. An attention-placebo control procedure was again omitted. Krop and his colleagues have reported two studies in which covert positive reinforcement was used to improve the self-concepts of emotionally disturbed children and psychiatric patients (Krop, Calhoon, & Verrier, 1971; Krop, Perez, & Beaudoin, 1973). In their 1971 study, 36 children were given 34 items from the Tennessee self-concept scale. They then repeated the test with either (1) overt reinforcement (a token and a gum drop) after positive self-concept statements, (2) covert positive reinforcement after these statements, or (3) no procedural change (control group). Re-administration of the test immediately after these manipulations and at a two week follow-up indicated greater improvements on the part of the covert and overt reinforcement groups. In a subsequent study (1973), sixty-nine psychiatric patients were given sixty-two items from the self-concept scale and then assigned to a control, non-contingent reinforcement, or covert reinforcement group. Individuals in the latter two groups received training in positive imagery. During a second administration of the test, non-contingent subjects were cued to reinforce themselves covertly after randomly selected items. Experimental subjects were cued only after positive self-concept statements. Data analyses followed the third administration of the test. Covert positive reinforcement was again correlated with a nominal (3.99 point) increase in self-concept. These increments were statistically significant. Data on the frequency of reinforcement in the non-contingent group were not presented. Unfortunately, neither of the above studies employed an information control group. The failure of other researchers to produce similar improvements in self-concept responses through direct verbal conditioning suggests the need for further empirical scrutiny (Babladelis, 1973). Moreover, a study reported by Kingsley (1973) raises some questions about the role of imaginal consequences in covert conditioning. Using positive self-evaluative statements as the dependent variable, subjects were trained in the contingent self-presentation of neutral, reinforcing, or aversive imagery. Despite salient differences in the nature of the covert consequence, covert reinforcement and covert punishment (sensitization) subjects did not differ from neutral image controls in subsequent self-evaluation.

Wisocki (1973a) reported a study with thirty-two college students in which test anxiety was treated via covert positive reinforcement. After filling out a self-report scale on text anxiety, experimental subjects received five sessions of covert conditioning over a four week period. Control subjects received no treatment. Analyses after a second administration of the self-report scale indicated that covert reinforcement subjects had reduced subjective anxiety more than controls. Imagery vividness was reported as correlating significantly with anxiety decrement. A six week follow-up elicited reports of improved relaxation, better grades, and more self-confidence on the part of experimental subjects. Unfortunately, this follow-up occurred two weeks after final examinations and the possibility of spontaneous improvement was not assessed—control subjects were not contacted. Wisocki notes that the post-treatment anxiety reports of five experimental subjects who attended only three treatment sessions did not differ from their matched controls. Since there were only five total sessions, the impact of two absences is noteworthy. Wisocki acknowledges that the above study does not control for placebo effects. Measures other than self-reported anxiety might also have enhanced its clinical import.

Flannery (1972a) found that three sessions of covert positive reinforcement were sufficient to produce therapeutic improvements in rat phobic nursing students. After pre-treatment measures, covert conditioning was presented either *in vivo* (during an attempted approach toward a rat) or in the standard imaginal fashion. A control group received brief training in covert positive imagery but no intervening stimulus exposure. Post-treatment measures of behavioral approach and subjective fear indicated significant improvements on the part of both experimental groups, with a superiority on the part of *in vivo* subjects. Generalization and follow-up data were not presented. Congruent with other research suggesting extinction processes in "counterconditioning" procedures (cf. Bandura, 1969), the variable of *in vivo* exposure appeared to be very important in Flannery's experiment. While less than seven percent of the standard covert reinforcement subjects were able to hold the rat after treatment, 73% of the *in vivo* subjects did so. The absence of exposure-only and attention-placebo controls is once again unfortunate.

In a four week treatment program for obesity Manno and Marston (1972) found that covert positive reinforcement and covert sensitization were both more effective than a contact control group. Significant changes in self-reported food preferences and actual eating habits were found only in the covert reinforcement group. It is worth noting that the treatment procedure for subjects in this group involved "coping" imagery and response-relevant reinforcement. For example, scenes involved food temptations followed by covert rehearsals of adaptive responses (saying "I don't want it," putting it down). The realistic consequences of this pattern were then imagined—praise from friends, improved physical appearance, etc.

The previously summarized study by Foreyt and Hagen (1973) utilized positive imagery as a "placebo" strategy in the evaluation of covert sensitization. Overweight subjects were told to imagine food approach scenes and then switch to very pleasant imagery (e.g., walking through a field of beautiful flowers on a warm summer day). Despite the fact that attention-placebo subjects engaged in covert positive reinforcement for symbolic rehearsals of food approach, they did not end the study heavier than they began. On the contrary, their weight *losses* were nonsignificantly greater than those in the covert sensitization and no-treatment control groups. Moreover, covert reinforcement subjects reported significant *decreases* in subjective palatability ratings of their favorite foods. Context and expectancy factors are again prime candidates for further empirical scrutiny.

In a project designed to improve performance on remedial reading tasks, Schmickley et al. (1974) compared the effects of covert positive reinforcement and a control procedure which utilized neutral imagery. After three weeks, data analyses on measures ranging from reading performance, task valuation, and comprehension showed no differences between the two groups.

A well controlled single subject experiment by Blanchard and Draper (1973) attempted to evaluate the relative contribution of symbolic stimulus exposure in the covert reinforcement procedure. A 20-year-old female was treated for rat phobia. Measures of behavioral approach, physiological arousal, and subjective fear were obtained by an assistant who was unaware of the treatment conditions. After a baseline of insight-oriented psychotherapy, three hours of standard covert positive reinforcement were administered. These were followed by 1.5 hours of covert exposure (imagining rat scenes without any associated reinforcement), 1.5 hours of covert reinforcement, a brief extinction phase, and 1.5 hours of participant modeling. Behavioral, physiological, and self-report measures indicated therapeutic improvements which were maintained at a 4.5 month follow-up. The addition of a covert reinforcer to covert exposure alone did not appear to enhance behavioral approach substantially although subjective measures suggested that this may have served a facilitative therapeutic function. These findings are consistent with those reported by Kazdin (1973d) in a group study discussed below.

Marshall and his colleagues have reported a series of studies examining the contribution of positive imagery in covert conditioning. One investigation found that pleasant imaginal scenes were as effective as muscular relaxation in desensitization (Marshall, Strawbridge, & Keltner, 1972). Two other inquiries specifically addressed covert positive reinforcement. The first (Marshall, in press, b) found this procedure about as effective as systematic desensitization in the treatment of snake phobia. A second study compared covert positive reinforcement with a reversed procedure in which a pleasant scene was imagined prior to the symbolic rehearsal of the target behavior (Marshall, Polgrin, & Boutilier, 1974). A direct extrapolation from the covert conditioning model suggests that this backward covert reinforcement strategy was actually an imperfect analogue to "covert response cost"—i.e., a pleasant stimulus was terminated shortly before the emission of a target behavior. (The fact that stimulus termination preceded, rather than followed, the symbolic performance makes the analogue only approximate.) Despite this procedural reversal, Marshall and his colleagues found no difference between the two covert conditioning procedures. It appears that strict adherence to sequential contiguity is not a necessary element.

A number of case study reports have described the use of covert positive reinforcement, often in combination with other treatment strategies (e.g., Wisocki, 1970, 1973b; Cautela, 1970b; Kendrick & McCullough, 1972). Evaluation of the contribution of this therapy component is therefore difficult.

Before summarizing the covert reinforcement findings, we should briefly note the few applications of covert *negative* reinforcement. As described in Chapter 6, this procedure involves the termination of a covert aversive image contiguous with the imagined rehearsal of a desired response. For example:

> A boy with a school phobia was asked to imagine that his arm was bleeding (aversive stimulus). He then shifted to the image of walking to school and saying to himself, "It doesn't matter if the teacher criticizes me. I am going to school to learn what I can."
>
> A man who was impotent was asked to imagine that his boss was yelling at him (aversive stimulus). Then immediately he switched to

a scene in which he was lying in bed naked next to his wife and feeling relaxed.

A homosexual imagined a rat approaching his throat (aversive stimulus); and then shifted to hugging a naked girl (Cautela, 1970a, pp. 275–276).

Data on the clinical effectiveness of covert negative reinforcement are virtually nonexistent. Although Cautela (1970a) estimates a ninety percent success rate, no supportive evidence is cited. The Ascher and Cautela (1972) study reviewed in Chapter 6 offers very modest support both methodologically and in terms of task relevance (circle size estimation). A study by Cautela and Wisocki (1969) attempted to modify the attitudes of college students toward elderly people. After filling out an attitude questionnaire, experimental subjects were instructed to imagine a scene in which they were bleeding and comforted by an elderly person. After ten days of home practice, experimental subjects reported more negative attitudes. The implications of this study are again obscured by methodological inadequacies.

In the previously described study by Marshall (in press, b), covert negative reinforcement was found to be approximately equivalent to a "non-contingent" procedure in which the sequence of covert performance and covert reinforcer images was randomized.

It is worth noting that two studies have apparently employed a variant of the covert negative reinforcement procedure as an experimental control. Ashem and Donner (1968) and Sachs and Ingram (1972) utilized a *backward* covert sensitization technique in which aversive scenes were imaged prior to symbolic rehearsal of undesired behaviors. Both of these studies reported no difference between the *suppressive* effects of covert sensitization and the covert negative reinforcement strategy. Cautela (1973) interprets these findings as indicating that nausea should not be employed in covert negative reinforcement. Other aversive stimuli more capable of abrupt termination are recommended. However, the evidence on "backward" covert sensitization might alternatively be interpreted as suggesting the possible influence of "expectancy" factors in observed outcome. The same clinical procedure has apparently opposite effects depending on whether it is presented as a suppressive or facilitative treatment. Moreover, data from a number of other studies lend support to the speculation that much of the variance in covert conditioning may result from cognitive processes rather than "orthodox" conditioning (e.g., Kingsley, 1973; Foreyt and Hagen, 1973; Schmickley et al., 1974; Marshall, Polgrin, & Boutilier, 1974).

In summary, the empirical evidence on the efficacy of covert reinforcement is considerably more modest than some of its proponents suggest. With notable exceptions, the studies devoted to its examination have relied solely on paper-and-pencil measures of performance. The paucity of well controlled research with clinically relevant dependent variables is unfortunate. Exploration of two main themes of inquiry is sorely overdue—one dealing with whether or not covert reinforcement procedures reliably effect therapeutic improvement, and the other addressed to an analysis of the processes involved (e.g., symbolic stimulus exposure, covert rehearsal of appropriate responses, specification and emphasis of realistic performance consequences).

COVERT EXTINCTION

A third covert conditioning procedure was suggested by Cautela (1971b) and labeled "covert extinction." In this strategy, the client is asked to imaginally rehearse an undesired behavior without any associated covert consequences. Treatment is usually preceded by a brief explanation of rationale and a suggestion that this covert rehearsal will effect a decrease in the problem behavior. Covert extinction scenes are then employed. For example, a stutterer was told:

> You are sitting in your school cafeteria. Choose a place in which you usually sit. (Pause) You can hear and see students walking around, eating and talking. (Pause) You are eating your favorite lunch. (Pause) There is an empty seat near you. (Pause) A pretty blond girl comes over and asks you if she can sit down. (Pause) You stammer, "Ya . . ya . . ya . . ya . . yes." She absolutely reacts in no way to your stuttering (Cautela, 1971b, pp. 193–194).

It is not clear whether the girl in the above scene walked away, sat down, or remained motionless. Cautela (1971b) presents seven other case illustrations of the covert extinction procedure. Of these eight cases, the outcome of one was reported as successful. Results of the other seven treatments are not indicated. In the one successful case, covert extinction was supplemented with external contingencies (threatened expulsion from school) to reduce a boy's disruptive classroom behaviors. Cautela recommends the combination of covert extinction with other procedures (e.g., covert sensitization, covert reinforcement) to enhance its effects.

Empirical evidence on the efficacy of covert extinction is nominal. Cautela (1971b) cites Ascher's (1973) laboratory study on covert reinforcement as providing supportive analogue evidence since it incorporated an extinction phase. However, as indicated in Chapter 6, Ascher (1973) did not find an extinction effect. Gotestam and Melin

(1974) reported using covert extinction in the treatment of four hospitalized amphetamine addicts. The clients were trained to imaginally rehearse amphetamine injections without experiencing pleasant physiological "flashes." Eight to fifteen trials per day were administered. All four clients absented themselves without leave (went "AWOL") after treatment periods ranging from twelve trials (one day?) to one hundred trials. In subsequent injections of actual drugs, all clients reported at least one instance of not experiencing a flash after shooting up. Follow-up assessment at nine months indicated that two of the clients were drug abstinent, one had relapsed after 2.5 months, and the third had discontinued drugs but increased alcohol consumption.

No other direct experimental tests of covert extinction have been reported. It should be noted, however, that "exposure only" control groups in standard systematic desensitization research employ a procedure which is very similar to Cautela's covert extinction. Subjects are instructed simply to imagine feared scenes or performances (without concomitant relaxation or positive imagery). The imagery instructions differ somewhat—in covert extinction the absence of consequences is highlighted—but their similarities are salient. Evidence on the effects of covert stimulus exposure suggest the possibility of an extinction process (e.g., Cooke, 1968; Crowder & Thornton, 1970; Nawas, Welsch, & Fishman, 1970; Foxman, 1972; Wolpin & Raines, 1966; Craighead, 1973). A few studies, however, have questioned the equivalence of covert exposure alone and covert exposure paired with relaxation (Davison, 1968b; Lomont & Edwards, 1967; Paul, 1969b). "The various findings, taken as a whole, indicate that relaxation is a facilitative rather than a necessary condition for elimination of avoidance behavior (Bandura, 1969, p. 439)."

Data on the efficacy of "implosion therapy" and symbolic flooding procedures might also be construed as relevant to covert extinction processes (Stampfl & Levis, 1967). In this strategy, anxiety-arousing scenes are imaginally embellished and extensively rehearsed. Rather than terminating an aversive image (as in desensitization), the client maintains the image and exaggerates its intensity.

> A person afraid of a snake would be requested to view himself picking up and handling a snake. Attempts would be made to have him become aware of his reactions to the animal. He would be instructed to feel how slimy the snake was. Next, he would be asked to experience the snake crawling over his body and biting and ripping his flesh. Scenes of snakes crushing or swallowing him, or perhaps his falling into a pit of snakes would be appropriate implosions (Hogan, 1966, p. 26).

The embellishments often assume psychoanalytic themes suggested by the therapist (cf. Stampfl & Levis, 1967). For example, a person who is afraid of contamination might be told to imagine falling through the seat of an outdoor toilet, swimming in the malodorous cesspool of stale urine and maggot-infested feces, swallowing lumpy fecal matter, and so on. A driving phobic is told to transform an image of an approaching vehicle into one of a gigantic breast or a penis on wheels. No efforts are made to restrict these embellishments to realistically probable or even possible real-life experiences. (Our declining petroleum resources discourage the use of gasoline-powered sexual organs.)

The differences between implosive therapy and covert extinction are marked. Moreover, the equivocal evidence for the effectiveness of the former suggests that it has little to offer in the defense of covert conditioning procedures (cf. Morganstern, 1973).

In summary, the evidence on covert extinction is equivocal. Only one study has formally addressed the clinical procedure suggested by Cautela (1971b) and its findings are not impressively supportive (Gotestam & Melin, 1974). Relevant research from the area of desensitization has suggested that covert stimulus exposure may effect reductions in subjective arousal and behavioral avoidance. The facilitative role of positive associates (e.g., relaxation) and the relative superiority of *in vivo* and participant modeling procedures should, however, be noted. Conclusions about the clinical promise of the covert extinction strategy must again be deferred until sufficient empirical data are available.

COVERT MODELING

One other covert conditioning procedure suggested by Cautela (1971c) is that of "covert modeling" in which the client is directed in the symbolic rehearsal of appropriate behavior. Since contemporary modeling formulations often do not incorporate a strict conditioning perspective (cf. Bandura, 1969, 1971a), the theoretical subtrates of this procedure as a covert conditioning paradigm are not unequivocal.

Empirical evidence on the effects of covert modeling is as yet preliminary. Cautela (1971c) and Flannery (1972b) report successful case histories but the active therapeutic components in these applications are unclear. Cautela, Flannery, and Hanley (in press) performed a group study in which the effects of live (overt) modeling were compared to covert modeling. Reductions in avoidance behaviors were obtained by both of these methods. Maultsby (1971a) suggests the use of "rational emotive imagery" based on Ellis' (1962) model but no effectiveness data are offered.

By far the most impressive evidence on the power of covert modeling has been provided in a series of well controlled studies by Alan Kazdin (Kazdin, 1973b,d, in press, a,b). In the first study (1973b), sixty-four snake phobic college students were matched on pre-treatment snake avoidance and randomly assigned to one of four experimental conditions: (1) covert "coping" model, (2) covert "mastery" model, (3) scene control, and (4) delayed-treatment control. A coping model is one who shows "initial reticence" similar to the avoidant observer, but actively copes with this anxiety, relaxes himself, and eventually completes the task. In contrast, a mastery model is fearless and competent throughout his performance. The "coping" versus "mastery" model differentiation was suggested by evidence that perceived similarity between model and observer increases the probability of imitation (Bandura, 1969, 1971a). A previous study by Meichenbaum (1971a) had demonstrated that a coping model film was more effective in reducing snake avoidance than a mastery model film. A typical coping model scene in the Kazdin (1973b) study was:

> Imagine that the person (model) puts on the gloves and tries to pick up the snake out of the cage. As the person is doing this he sort of hesitates and avoids grasping the snake at first. He stops and relaxes himself, feels calm, and picks up the snake (p. 89).

The last two snake interaction tasks in both modeling conditions were identical. An exposure-only control group visualized 14 scenes of snake approach without any model interaction. Delayed-treatment control subjects simply received pre- and post-assessments. The study was conducted by four experimenters who were blind to the experimental hypotheses; each experimenter saw an equal number of subjects in each condition.

Post-treatment data analyses revealed that the two covert modeling groups achieved significant improvements in snake approach performances and subjective indices of fear. Both modeling groups were superior to the exposure-only and delayed-treatment control conditions. Moreover, the coping model condition was significantly more effective than the mastery model group in improving behavioral performance. Subsequent to post-assessment, the delayed-treatment control group received covert modeling therapy without any description of model affect (coping versus mastery). Significant increases in approach responses were obtained. A three week follow-up revealed maintained improvement on the part of covert modeling subjects (cf. Figure 8-3) and no change on the part of exposure-only controls.

Besides providing a commendable model of experimental

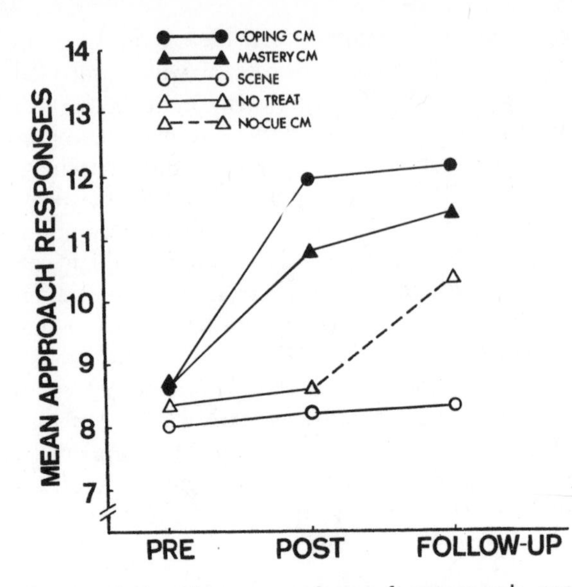

Figure 8-3. Mean number of approach responses performed before, immediately after, and 3 weeks subsequent to treatment. (Reprinted with permission from Kazdin, 1973b.)

rigor, the Kazdin (1973b) study offers suggestive evidence on some of the processes which may mediate success in other covert conditioning procedures. For example, the failure of the exposure only control group to demonstrate significant improvements suggests that simple "symbolic extinction" may not account for much of the outcome variance in other covert strategies. One possibility, of course, is that the coping model provides relevant information on adaptive stress-reducing responses.

This hypothesis was explored in a second study involving seventy snake phobic subjects (Kazdin, in press, a). Using a similar assessment format, a 2×2 experimental design was employed: fear-irrelevant model similarity (age and sex) was crossed with fear-relevant similarity (coping versus mastery). An exposure-only control group was again utilized. Post-treatment and follow-up findings indicated that age-sex similarities between model and observer were more important than the coping-mastery distinction. Greatest improvement tended to occur in the group which maximized similarity (both age-sex and coping). The exposure only control group again failed to evidence improvement. These findings lend support to the efficacy of covert modeling procedures and suggest that model characteristics may influence clinical outcome. Whether these influences are moderated by differential attention to similar models remains to be explored.

A subsequent replication study (Kazdin, in press, b) found that imagining oneself as the covert model did not effect greater avoidance reduction than imagining another person. Covert modeling again produced significant improvements in snake phobic subjects, and a coping model was more effective than a mastery model.

In a fourth study Kazdin (1973d) examined the effectiveness of covert modeling in the development of assertiveness. Forty-five unassertive volunteers were assigned to one of four experimental conditions: (1) covert modeling, (2) covert modeling plus covert reinforcement, (3) no-model control, and (4) delayed treatment control. Self-rating of assertiveness, actual performance during a behavioral role-playing test, and compliance with a demanding post-treatment phone solicitation constituted the dependent variables. Therapy scenes were divided into context (e.g., receiving an overcooked steak at a restaurant), assertive response (e.g., sending the steak back), and reinforcing consequences (e.g., apologies from the waiter and receipt of an appropriate steak). No-model control subjects visualized only the context; covert modeling subjects imagined both the context and the assertive model's response. Individuals in the covert modeling plus covert reinforcement group visualized all three scene components. Post-treatment and follow-up analyses revealed significant improvement on the part of both covert modeling groups, with occasional slight superiority on the part of individuals who had received covert reinforcement. The realistic nature of anticipated positive consequences in this procedure is noteworthy.

The foregoing research presents some impressively consistent preliminary evidence on the clinical promise of covert modeling procedures. Independent replications and parametric refinements will facilitate more definitive conclusions. Several research issues are in particular need of empirical scrutiny. For example, the contribution of component processes in the therapy procedure deserves examination. Kazdin's studies have already suggested that disinhibitory (extinction) processes may not play a major role in successful outcome. An alternative process involves the expansion of clients' behavioral repertories through systematic response clarification and description. Covert rehearsals of these "cognitive blueprints" may facilitate both maintenance and generalization of response improvements. The imaginal rehearsal of motoric activity needs to be evaluated. What would happen if covert modeling subjects imagined passive rather than active exposure (e.g., the feared object being brought closer to them rather than their approaching it)?

Comparisons of covert modeling with overt and participant modeling procedures might also provide more information on the processes and relative efficacy of these strategies.

The procedural differences between covert extinction and covert modeling are in need of more accurate specification. In some studies using "exposure only" control groups (e.g., in desensitization research), the exact nature of covertly rehearsed events is far from clear. Based on Kazdin's findings, there may be differential effects when stimulus elements are imagined in the absence of symbolic performance rehearsals.

The role of covert consequences deserves further exploration. As mentioned earlier, the real-life relevance of symbolic reinforcers may play a role in their effectiveness. Cautela and his colleagues often use target-irrelevant covert reinforcers. Other workers (e.g., Manno & Marston, 1972; Kazdin, 1973d) have employed realistic anticipated consequences. Further inquiries are needed to assess any differential effects of these two strategies.

A supplementary research issue deals with the personage of the covert model. To date, the symbolic performer has been predominantly a similar but separate person rather than the client himself. Kazdin's (in press, b) article is the only existing report of a personage analysis. Further inquiries will hopefully examine other contributing factors in covert model characteristics (e.g., the effects of covert models who are successively more similar to the client).

Still another issue relates to the intriguing lack of correlation between imagery vividness and the effectiveness of covert modeling (Kazdin, 1973d, in press, a,b). Whether this non-correspondence reflects a true relationship absence or the crudeness of our imagery assessment methods remains to be seen. If the non-correspondence is veridical, we are faced with a complex question regarding the manner in which symbolic rehearsals effect therapeutic behavior change.

Judging from the initial evidence on covert modeling, a substantial percentage of the variance in other imagery-based procedures (e.g., desensitization, covert sensitization) may be accounted for by symbolic rehearsal processes rather than "counterconditioning." The effects of subtle imagery manipulations may be considerable, as indicated in the Meichenbaum and Kazdin studies. These findings implore more objective procedural specifications in the imagery therapies, as well as an analysis of behavior change processes. Three nervous systems are operative in the avoidant client—central, somatic, and autonomic. Are inputs to one more important than inputs to others? Are there sequential or interactive combinations which might facilitate therapeutic success?

Two final comments conclude our discussion of covert modeling. First, the conditioning basis of this procedure is very tenuous. As we shall see in subsequent chapters, a cognitive information-based model appears to more adequately describe the processes in modeling therapies. Therefore, the preliminary promise of covert modeling techniques may reflect the adequacy of cognitive mediational models rather than that of the covert conditioning model. Secondly, covert modeling procedures are neither new nor indigenous to behavior modification. For example, an early self-improvement regimen recommended the mental rehearsal of successful performances prior to their attempt (Pelman, 1919). Beck (1970b) and Singer (1972) have documented the extensive use of "mental practice" and "eidetic imagery" in activities ranging from athletic practice to psychotherapy. Athletes frequently employ covert modeling strategies to refine and improve their performance (e.g., Suinn, 1972a). Anecdotal evidence of the extensiveness of these symbolic rehearsals can be easily obtained. In a series of informal interviews, I asked competitive wrestlers, gymnasts, and Olympic weightlifters to describe their thought processes prior to and during competition. All eight interviewees spontaneously reported the use of covert rehearsals, with a salient emphasis on imagery (e.g., "I picture myself at the next stage of my (parallel bars) routine while I'm still at the previous stage," "I go over the different movements in my head before I approach the barbell," etc.). Considering their easily quantifiable performance measures, it is somewhat surprising that behavior modifiers have not devoted more research attention to athletics.

A COVERT COMMENT

My own sense of humor and the suggestions of several colleagues prompt me at this point to proffer some innovative covert techniques (e.g., covert lobotomy, covert nude marathon). One associate has even predicted that we will soon be publishing covert articles in covert journals. These comments, of course, speak to the recent increase in the transformation of overt therapeutic techniques into covert conditioning strategies. While it is probably an adaptive skill to be able to occasionally view our scientific pursuits as a comedy of errors, we must be careful not to overlook the heuristics and determinants of our innovative binges. Efforts to expand and refine our therapeutic techniques reflect a humane and empirical dedication. Our enthusiasm, however, sometimes favors innovation at the expense of experimental validation.

As we have seen in the last two chapters, the covert conditioning therapies have presented a mixed and generally modest empirical picture. The limited experimental evidence on thought stopping, coverant control, covert negative reinforcement, and covert extinction has not lent support to the contention that these procedures consistently effect reliable or clinically significant therapeutic improvement. The remaining techniques, with the exceptions of covert modeling and some forms of covert sensitization, have generally demonstrated mixed or marginal efficacy. In covert sensitization, efficacy has been most impressive in the treatment of sexual deviations. The covert counterconditioning therapies (desensitization and orgasmic reconditioning) have reported favorable applications, but simple conditioning processes do not appear adequate to account for their effectiveness. Covert modeling, which is perhaps more appropriately classified as a cognitive information-based strategy, stands alone as the most consistently effective procedure. In this instance, as with all the others, however, our tentative evaluations are based on very sparse research. Notwithstanding the extensive use of covert conditioning therapies in behavior modification, controlled empirical evaluations and refinements have lagged embarrassingly behind clinical applications. Since current journal publication policies seem to selectively expose us to "successes" and obscure our knowledge of negative results, the modesty of the foregoing findings is even more noteworthy.

The above comments do not contend that covert conditioning techniques are ineffective. Rather, they address the fact that the efficacy of many of these procedures is as yet undemonstrated. Further inquiries will hopefully provide more definitive and extensive bases for making clinical treatment recommendations. As behavioral scientists, we again find ourselves in the familiar position of deferring judgment until more data are available.

Before concluding our discussion, some brief comments on the adequacy of the covert conditioning model are in order. In Chapter 5 we discussed some general guidelines for evaluating such adequacy. Examination of the covert conditioning model in terms of those guidelines suggests the following evaluative remarks.

Conceptual Aspects of the Theory

The covert conditioning model presents a basically horizontal set of principles, most of which are directly borrowed from traditional theory and research on conditioning.

The terminology of the model is often operationally vague and extensively metaphorical. Covert events are called "stimuli" and "responses" without acknowledging the salient referent differences in these applications. Glaring ambiguities regarding the nature of covert events threaten objective communication and empirical replication of covert conditioning phenomena. Almost all symbolic activity is dichotomized into covert auditory (subvocal) or visual (imaginal) categories. Programmed covert activities are often only vaguely specified, and the correspondence between requested and performed mediation is seldom evaluated. Treatment procedures and explanatory accounts are often couched in conditioning terminology when significant operational discrepancies exist (e.g., in covert negative reinforcement and covert extinction). This ambiguity is illustrated in the vacillation between classical and operant conditioning rationales in the description of some covert conditioning procedures.

It should be noted that the metaphorical nature of covert conditioning terminology is not inherently problematical. Metaphorical thinking is a valuable and perhaps necessary element in model building. However, the theorist must constantly acknowledge and evaluate the utility of borrowed metaphors. In covert conditioning, many borrowed terms have come to denote veridical rather than metaphorical meaning. Such illegitimate equivalence translation has been exacerbated by ambiguous and contradictory usage.

The covert conditioning model makes several implicit assumptions about human behaviors. Two of the most significant are the continuity assumption and the automaticity assumption. The continuity assumption contends that covert behaviors obey the same principles as overt behaviors. While preliminary evidence has provided tentative support for this assumption, the extensive extrapolation of conditioning parameters to symbolic phenomena goes well beyond existing data. Clinical recommendations for the use of intermittent covert consequences, for example, have no basis in current experimentation.

While usually left implicit, the pervasiveness of the "automaticity assumption" is readily apparent. Simply stated, this assumption contends that "A reinforcer has an effect even though the behavior it follows does not produce it (Skinner, 1974, p. 134)." Covert conditioning techniques presume that imaginal events (and their external counterparts) are automatically endowed with positive or negative qualities through simple association with strongly valenced experiences. For example, Homme's coverant control strategy and the orgasmic reconditioning procedure both invoke an automatic conditioning premise. As our brief review of the awareness literature indicated (Chapter 4), this automaticity appears to be the exception rather than the rule. Most adult human learning is mediated by symbolic processes rather than being patently produced by stimulus-response contiguities. The specificity of behavior change in covert conditioning likewise challenges an automaticity assumption.

It should, perhaps, by noted that Skinner has both supported and challenged an automaticity assumption in human learning (cf.

Mahoney, 1970). We would not, for example, expect to find that the paranoid schizophrenic developed his persecutory delusions by the repeated accidental pairing of suspicious thoughts and meals. Recent findings in animal research have even begun to question whether operant reinforcement works as "simply" as theory suggests. Staddon and Simmelhag (1971), for example, attempted to replicate the early work of Skinner (1948) on "superstition" in the pigeon. Skinner observed that the presentation of reinforcement after regular intervals (and irrespective of behavior) resulted in the development of bizarre response patterns in pigeons (e.g., turning in circles, exaggerated neck stretching). He suggested that these responses had been accidentally strengthened by being followed by reinforcement. The attempted replication by Staddon and Simmelhag (1971), however, failed to support Skinner's contention. In this later study it was found that many of the behaviors Skinner had attributed to superstitious reinforcement actually *followed* rather than preceded grain delivery. It appears that our behavior as experimenters may sometimes be more superstitious than that of our subjects.

As for internal consistency, the covert conditioning model proffers at least one apparent self-contradiction. The sequence of imagining an aversive scene and then switching to a symbolic performance is defined as both an accelerative (covert negative reinforcement) and decelerative (backward covert sensitization) strategy. This ostensive contradiction suggests the operation of other moderating influences in these two therapy procedures.

Empirical Adequacy of the Theory

The covert conditioning model does not purport to summarize or integrate current knowledge. However, its correspondence with at least some aspects of that knowledge is equivocal. The evidence on selective covert conditioning (e.g., in orgasmic reconditioning) again implies that a simple experimental contiguity is not sufficient. The model likewise fails to account for spontaneous symbolic rehearsals of unpleasant experiences (traumatic memories, nightmares, etc.). If symbolic events are exactly parallel to extrinsic phenomena, one might expect the virtual absence of negative ruminations and very frequent engrossment in pleasant covert reveries.

Since it draws very heavily on laboratory conditioning phenomena, the adequacy of the covert conditioning model rests in part on the adequacy of its progenitor. While "contemporary learning theory" is a difficult amalgam to evaluate (Mahoney, Kazdin, & Lesswing, 1974), some broad generalizations can be offered. Until the past few years there was consensus regarding a few "fundamental" learning principles such as reinforcement, immediacy of consequences, and so on. Although the processes and conceptual breadth of these regularities in learning were occasionally challenged, the basic principles were not. Reinforcement increases behavior; immediacy of consequences facilitates learning; intermittency of consequences strengthens resistance to extinction. These were the unquestioned foundations of the conditioning model. Their empirical validity had been borne out in extensive replications.

However, the last few years have witnessed a growing number of reports regarding exceptions and contradictions to "accepted" laws of learning. While an historical documentary would take us far afield, some of the more salient works are worth noting. Breland and Breland (1961), for example, presented an early article on "the misbehavior of organisms" which documented anecdotes of failures in the operant reinforcement of animals. It was their impression that certain categories of instinctive behaviors may place limitations on the modifiability of species-specific response patterns. Brown and Jenkins (1968) described an innovative laboratory procedure called "auto-shaping" which produced rapid response acquisition in the absence of painstaking experimenter reinforcement of successive approximations. Auto-shaping has now become a familiar and well replicated laboratory procedure despite its ostensible violation of peripheral principles. In a subsequent series of well executed laboratory experiments, Williams and Williams (1970) demonstrated that operant learning phenomena may be far more complex than we had anticipated. Their research on "negative automaintenance" showed that pigeons will peck a key for thousands of trials despite the fact that key-pecking produces *removal* of otherwise available food. Their data again suggest the possibility of ethological factors in pigeon behavior.

The work of Neal Miller and his colleagues on the operant control of autonomic responses raised serious doubts about the revered dichotomy between instrumental and classical conditioning (Miller, 1969). A pair of studies by Neuringer (1969, 1970a) indicated that animals will work in the presence of free food and in the absence of deprivation. Evidence began to accumulate suggesting that immediacy of reinforcement can sometimes impair rather than facilitate learning (cf. McKeachie, 1974) and the findings of Staddon and Simmelhag (1971) suggested that molecular reinforcement processes are neither automatic nor simple. Rumblings of a conceptual revolution regarding the "basic laws of learning" grew progressively louder as we entered a new decade (cf. Estes, 1971; Bolles, 1972; Dember, 1974).

The foregoing studies do not, of course, overthrow the conditioning model. They simply emphasize that our scientific "laws" are expedient, descriptive summaries of contemporary evidence. As new evidence accrues, old laws must be re-evaluated and refined. Universal generalizations are an alluring but deceptive goal. Even infrahuman behavior is more complex than our current empirical models acknowledge. Operant reinforcement and classical conditioning do not provide sufficient accounts. While we may still pursue a "liberated" learning model in our unavoidably biased approach to reality, we should at least adopt a justified humility in that endeavor.

The covert conditioning model has wed itself "for better or for worse" to laboratory conditioning phenomena. Although recent findings have not refuted "basic learning theory," they have certainly suggested that the processes of behavior change are far more complicated than most learning theories have thus far acknowledged. Thus, the indirect support derived from laboratory conditioning research must be viewed as "under current review." We do not have a comprehensive and unequivocal model to account for overt human behavior, let alone one which can be directly extrapolated to covert events.

Finally, the empirical adequacy of the covert conditioning model rests most directly on its own accountability. Since it is addressed primarily to clinical therapeutics, outcome evaluations offer some indication of its promise. As indicated in the last two chapters, the empirical evidence on the effectiveness of procedures derived from the covert conditioning model tentatively suggests that its clinical utility may be problem-specific and summarily modest.

With this evaluation in mind, we turn to a second mediational model—that based on cognitive (information processing) research.

Chapter Nine

Mediational Model II: Information Processing

As its name implies, the *information processing* model places emphasis on the acquisition, storage, and utilization of information. Although stimulus *input* and performance *output* are still employed as anchors, the information processing viewpoint invokes very different mediators in relating these two events. Rather than positing covert stimulus-response mechanisms, it borrows structural and functional features from several other disciplines. Cybernetic theory, linguistics, perception and computer analogues are generous contributors to the information processing model.

I should, perhaps, point out that the term "information processing" is only one of several frequently applied to this model. "Cognitive psychology," "verbal learning" and "human memory" are terms which occasionally overlap in their referents. The term information processing, however, captures what I believe to be two cardinal features of this model—namely, (1) its use of information as the basic element in learning and (2) its recognition of active processes in such learning.

The present description of information processing will necessarily be both brief and selective. Volumes have been written about phenomena to which we can afford only limited attention. The interested reader is urged to consult original sources for a more detailed presentation. Of particular utility are Ulric Neisser's (1967) classic *Cognitive Psychology* and the texts by Adams (1967) and Norman (1969). Several recent books provide valuable summaries of contemporary trends and recent evidence in this area (e.g., Kintsch, 1970; Hall, 1971; Melton & Martin, 1972; Anderson & Bower, 1973). My rendition of information processing utilizes a model similar to that proposed by Atkinson and Shiffrin (1971). As indicated in the Foreword, I am indebted to Dick Atkinson and Gordon Bower for my conceptual approach to this field.

Let us begin by dealing with a difficult definition. What is information? The basic currency of the present model, of course, relies exclusively on the concept of states and manipulations of this entity. Information is said to be *acquired*, to be *transformed* into complex codes. This coded information is *stored* until it is *retrieved* and *utilized* in performance. Drawing from the field of computer science, information is often described as being stored in the form of "bits." Unfortunately, the technical definition of "information" is not a simple matter. A proposal made by George A. Miller (1956) suggests that information is the reduction of variance or uncertainty. Utilizing a binary (dichotomous) categorization in which an event can assume one of two forms (e.g., on/off, positive/negative), Miller suggests that information is anything which reduces the uncertainty associated with the state of the event in question. There are, of course, problems with this definition. First, the uncertainty-reducing feature of information is not inherent in the input; it is an interaction of the input and its utilization by the perceiver. For example, two individuals might be given a clue toward the solution of a riddle. The physical input is identical but its information value is influenced by whether or not it is appropriately processed and utilized by the two players. Second, the definition of information must be broad enough to span the range of potential inputs in human behavior. Although most of us are unaware of the myriad of homeostatic physiological processes that characterize our biology, few would argue against the existence of an information feedback loop in the maintenance of our life support systems. We unconsciously respond to changes in our own blood glucose, osmolarity, and so on. Thus, it is apparent that information need not involve "higher mental processes" or awareness.

At this point, I would like to be able to offer an objective and unequivocal definition of information that circumvents these problems. Unfortunately, I am not aware of any such definition and readily concede my present incapacity to offer one. We need not, however, abort our journey because of these ostensible difficulties in fundamental terminology. From a pragmatic rather than semantic perspective, there appear to be few real problems in the effective communication of information processing research. Even a cursory glance at the technical journals in this field will attest to the facility with which information-based inquiries are objectively pursued (cf. *Cognition*, *Cognitive Psychology*, *Journal of Verbal Learning and Verbal Behavior*). Perhaps one reason for this is the use of operationally defined inputs in such investigations. While the rather global term "information" is employed in broad theoretical conceptions, the actual research is carried out with objectively specified variables.

The information processing model is heavily mediational: i.e., it posits that an awful lot is going on between input and output. According to Miller, Galanter, and Pribram (1960), this perspective offers a favorable alternative

> to nickel-in-the-slot, stimulus-response conceptions of man....(It is so reasonable to insert between the stimulus and the response a little wisdom. And there is no particular need to apologize for putting it there, because it was already there before psychology arrived)(p. 2).

In criticizing the covert conditioning analysis of complex human performance, these authors state that invoking covert responses and covert stimuli, "does nothing but parallel objective concepts with subjective equivalents and leaves the reflex arc still master—albeit a rather ghostly master—of the machinery of the mind (p.19)." An appealingly straightforward defense of mediational research is presented by Neisser (1967) who states that the reason for examining cognitive processes is "because they are there (p. 5)."

The information processing theorist takes a basic view of man as an active processor of experience rather than a passive or functionally vacuous composite of stimulus-response linkages. The organism is seen responding not to a "real world" but to his own mediated rendition of it. This mediation often takes the form of stimulus selection, distortion and transformation. There are obvious parallels between the mediated reality of information processing and the epistemological writings of several philosophers (e.g., Immanuel Kant).

According to this model, the organism's responses are influenced by his information processing—that is, the way he mediates stimulation. Four broad categories of processing are posited:

1. *attention*, which deals with selective orientation toward and assimilation of specific stimuli,
2. *encoding*, which involves symbolic codification of the stimulus according to various factors (physical features, semantics, etc.),
3. *storage*, which is simply the retention of encoded information, and
4. *retrieval*, which involves the subsequent utilization of stored information to guide performance.

A distinction must be made between the functional *processes* of information transfer and the *structural* elements which are involved. These structural features often take the form of hypothetical constructs—they are inferred substrata which make information transfer possible. There are three popular structural features in the information processing model:

1. a *sensory register*, which receives stimulation (internal and external),
2. a *short-term memory*, which offers brief storage of selected input, and
3. a *long-term memory*, which serves in the more enduring retention of information.

For those familiar with the fundamentals of computer science, some metaphors and analogues should be apparent. The nervous systems (autonomic, central, and somatic) constitute the "hardware" of the human computer—i.e., its physical machinery. Three major parts are delineated—a sensory register, a short-term memory, and a long-term memory. The "software" of the system is that extensive set of "programs" which control information transfer and storage. Four basic programs are posited (attention, encoding, retention, and retrieval), each with a vast number of "sub-routines." I have presented this computer analogy in a very simplified and abbreviated form. More detailed accounts may be found in Feigenbaum and Feldman (1963) and Apter (1970).

To emphasize the complex system integration in the information processing model, we shall discuss each of the functional processes in conjunction with associated structural elements. It should be kept in mind that Figure 9-1 offers a dramatically simplified representation of the model.

ATTENTION ENCODING RETENTION RETRIEVAL

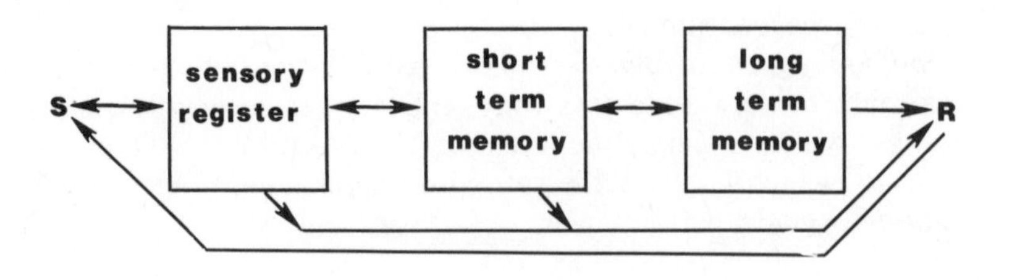

MEDIATIONAL MODEL II

Figure 9-1.

ATTENTION AND THE SENSORY REGISTER

Simply stated, the process of attention appears to be a frequent prerequisite for learning. Given that learning involves performances associated with various situations, the acquisition of performance-relevant information demands some form of selective experimental focusing. We attend not only to the antecedents of a performance, but also to its consequences. The organism is in intimate contact with the continuous reciprocal interactions between himself and his external environment. As stimuli impinge on his sensory receptors, he attends to their variations and sequencing.

An issue which has long dominated the interests of researchers in this area is that of "selective attention." From among a virtual bombardment of impinging stimuli, the organism selects and assimilates only a small fraction. In reading this page, for example, you are attending to an array of visual symbols and probably ignoring many other impinging stimuli (e.g., the tactile stimulation of your clothing or chair, the faint hum of a light or appliance, the sight of your hand on the sides of the book, etc.). We are perceptual bigots, attending to only a select minority of available information. Moreover, we seem to have some control over our own selectivity. The reader may now find, for example, that he or she is attending to some of the stimulation cited above. Another illustration of this controlled selectivity is the "cocktail party" phenomenon (Cherry, 1953; Treisman, 1964). When standing in a room full of conversing people, we can often "switch channels" and sample several of the conversations which are going on. Despite the drone of noises and the relative distance of some of the speakers, we can single out one or more voices. This is particularly true if our name has been mentioned by someone across the room! We smile and obligingly nod our head to the monologue of someone in our physically proximal group, while covertly listening in on a conversation going on several feet away.

The evidence for selective attention is much more sophisticated and extensive than that provided by cocktail parties. A sizeable body of research has been devoted to this phenomenon and several theoretical models have been proposed to account for it (cf. Norman, 1969; Neisser, 1967). Its relevance for clinical phenomena and therapeutic procedures will be explored more fully in Chapter 10.

There appear to be some attentional processes, however, which precede formal recognition of a stimulus. These inferred processes—called "pre-attentive mechanisms" (Neisser, 1967)—allow the organism to carry on a range of activities without consciously attending to them. For example, most of us have probably had the experience of "unconscious driving." We are startled by the sudden realization that we have been driving without "paying attention." Many minutes and miles may have passed while we drove on in distracted reveries. Despite this inattentiveness, however, we apparently stayed on our intended course, obeyed traffic regulations, and managed to avoid collisions. Many other examples could be cited from everyday experience: we often perform relatively complex tasks while attending to other stimuli (daydreams, conversations, television, etc.). Workers with relatively monotonous tasks are probably experts in this duality (e.g., assembly line workers). Some of us would like to believe that it occurs less frequently among selected professionals (e.g., surgeons and airline pilots).

Although the phenomena of pre-attentive mechanisms have been empirically explored in laboratory perceptual tasks, little has been done in naturalistic everyday settings. Subjective accounts suggest that they are encountered only when a task is relatively simple or routine. The individual who is just learning to drive is seldom distracted from his perceptual-motor assignments. Interestingly, pre-attentive features seem to filter and assimilate some inputs without our directed attention. While performing a routine task, we may be abruptly brought out of our reveries by a relatively minor discrepancy in the task situation. For example, walking pensively down a familiar hall or sidewalk, we may suddenly terminate our reveries and focus on the external situation only to find that something has been changed. Alterations in the routine seem to stimulate focused attention. This detection of discrepancies suggests that we have, in fact, been "unconsciously" assimilating stimuli. Pre-attentive processes are not, of course, invariably operative. Many changes in routine (e.g., a spouse's hairdo) may go temporarily unnoticed until more prominent input is provided (e.g., a hairdresser's bill). The occasional operation of these mechanisms however should not be overlooked. Naturalistic explorations of their controlling influences are sorely needed.

The physical substrata of attention and perception have been examined extensively. Although the sensory register is a metaphorical construct, its component parts have presumed physiological referents (receptor systems, afferent and reticular pathways, etc.). Two intriguing topics in this realm are the concepts of "iconic" and "echoic" storage. There is evidence that almost all impinging stimulation is retained very briefly prior to being further processed or discarded. When the presented stimulus is visual, this storage is said to be "iconic"; when it is auditory, the term "echoic" is employed. Some of the strongest evidence for the existence of iconic storage has been reported by Sperling (1960) who used an ingenious experimental strategy. Subjects were exposed to a 3×3 matrix of stimulus letters for a very brief interval (50 milliseconds). For example:

KRZ
NFB
DJH

Their task was to recall as many of these letters as possible. When a standard recall test was administered, individuals could usually produce fewer than half the letters. An alternative recall test used a sampling procedure in which a post-exposure tone cued the subject to recall only one of the three rows of letters. In this situation, the stimulus matrix was presented, a tone was sounded, and the subject's recall performance was recorded. By randomly sampling (cueing each of the different matrix rows within subjects), Sperling was able to demonstrate the brief (iconic) store of all stimuli. Presumably, subjects given a standard recall test are able to report only a portion of the stimuli due to the very rapid decay of the iconic store. A real-life analogue to echoic storage might be the "what did you say?" phenomenon. We frequently ask someone to repeat himself only to find that the repetition is unnecessary. Sometimes, before even completing our request, we have performed a private "instant replay," possibly via scanning echoic storage.

There are many topics in the area of attention for which we have neither time nor space. For example, an extensive literature has been addressed to the competing theories of "template matching," "feature detection," and "constructive synthesis" (cf. Neisser, 1967). In template matching, perceptual recognition is thought to occur when an incoming stimulus corresponds to a stored "template" or image. This suggests a passive "match-to-sample" process. An alternative theory is that of feature detection, in which critical attributes or features of a stimulus are extracted and processed (e.g., linearity, size, etc.). A third model—and one which may have relevance for clinical disorders—suggests that human perception invokes constructive synthetic processes—that is, that the organism actively creates (and distorts) much of its own "input." In this last perspective, perception is not a passive matching operation but an active and biased processing pattern.

One final topic which does have immense relevance for behavior pathology and therapeutic improvement is that of "expectancy." Briefly stated, the information processing research on expectancy strongly suggests that our perceptions are dramatically influenced by such factors as prior learning and stimulus context. For example, a vertical line will be perceived differently depending on its perceptual context. When preceded or followed by letters of the alphabet, it will be "seen" as the letter "l." In a mathematical series, however, this same stimulus will register as the digit "one." In a geometric display, on the other hand, it might be perceived simply as a vertical line segment.

Our private experiences are neither naive nor independent. We perceive and label stimulation differentially. Some of the factors which appear to influence our perceptual set or expectancy include immediate physical context (e.g., surrounding stimuli), temporal context (the extent and nature of preceding experiences), familiarity with the stimulus, and conceptual categories. If we are informed ahead of time that a series of ambiguous stimuli are distorted letters rather than geometric symbols, our perception of them will be biased in the direction of letters. Professional proofreaders provide an excellent example of the effects of perceptual expectancy. I can recall with belated amusement a proofreader's impact on a short story published during my high school days. With my perversity for puns, I had laboriously constructed a plot centering around a suspected romance between heroine Spring Heatherton and the local undertaker. Spring was a wisp of a girl and the undertaker was a rather corpulent fellow. I painstakingly developed a theme of small town gossip about their clandestine romantic involvement and led up to the critical pun-accentuated scene in which short-armed Spring was seen hugging the undertaker. My punch line was, "And there it was for all to see—Spring was just around the coroner." As you might *expect* from our preceding discussion, the well-meaning proofreader at the newspaper changed the spelling of "coroner" to "corner" (a much more familiar word in that context) and totally removed any semblance of wit or social redemption from my short story (assuming it had any).

As we shall see in Chapter 10, the term "expectancy" is used in a parallel but significantly different manner in discussions of clinical phenomena. The perceptual foundations and information theory substrata of that concept, however, are worth bearing in mind.

ENCODING AND SHORT-TERM MEMORY

The fact that a stimulus has received our attention does not insure that it will be stored in memory. The processes and parameters of information transfer from the sensory register to our "memory banks" have occupied the research interests of numerous investigators for many years. It was mentioned earlier that a distinction is often drawn between relatively brief "short-term" information storage and more enduring "long-term" memory. The viability of this distinction has not gone unchallenged (Melton, 1963; Wickelgren, 1973). The differentiation of iconic/echoic storage, short-term memory, and long-term memory is apparently more procedural than conceptual. Test intervals vary with each of the three. For iconic/echoic storage, performance is evaluated after very brief intervals (milliseconds). In studies of short-term memory, tests are administered after an interval of elapsed seconds. The duration of long-term storage, however, is often evaluated hours, days, or even months after initial learning. Different types and methods of learning appear to influence the duration of information storage. For example, it is likely that you can now recall what you ate for breakfast, your current phone number, and the scene of your first sexual intercourse. However, can you remember what you had for lunch a week ago Tuesday, the poems that you recited in fourth grade, or your drivers license number? Why is it that we remember some things and forget others?

An extensive body of evidence in information processing has identified several factors which influence short-term storage (cf. Melton & Martin, 1972). To begin with, the duration of stimulus exposure appears to correlate positively with subsequent recall. This variable is often referred to in terms of *rehearsal processes* (Atkinson & Shiffrin, 1971). The longer an item occupies out "attentional limelight," the more likely it is to be remembered. Note that the term "rehearsal" as it is used here does not mean simple repetitive practice. *Repetition*, or the frequency with which an item is either presented to or retrieved from memory, also enhances recall. Thus, we often repeat a new phone number or street directions while we are performing our phoning or finding task. A third factor in short-term memory has to do with the temporal *primacy or recency* of an item. If we are introduced to a number of people when we first enter a party, our ability to recall their names may be affected by the order of introductions. People whom we met first (primacy) and last (recency) will probably be remembered better than people in the middle of the introductions chain. Atkinson and Shiffrin (1971) account for the primacy-recency effect by suggesting that initial items in a list receive more rehearsal while final items are still in short-term storage.

A fourth variable which significantly influences recall is the processes of encoding. We often transform stimulation into a private "code" to facilitate and economize its memorization. The nature of these various coding processes has been extensively explored (cf. Melton & Martin, 1972). For example, many of our codes seem to rely on symbol systems (e.g., language) and conceptual categories. According to psychologist George A. Miller (1956), we are limited capacity processors who can handle only so much information at one time. Miller has hypothesized that the average human can process about seven "bits" of information at a time. In a classic paper on the "magical number seven, plus or minus two." Miller contended that our limited information processing capacities force us to abbreviate and condense information through a process called "chunking." In chunking, we use a sort of mental short-hand to code and store memory items. Mnemonic aids, for example, serve such a purpose. Rather than memorize the number of days in each month, we memorize an informative jingle ("Thirty days hath September . . ."). Language rules are also often stored in the form of economical chunks (e.g., " 'i' before 'e' except after 'c' or when pronounced as an 'a' as in 'neighbor' and 'weigh' ").

Not all mnemonics are exclusively verbal. Miller, Galanter, and Pribram (1960), for example, illustrate a mnemonic aid which utilizes imagery. The individual is first trained to learn a series of number-image associations:

> one is a bun, two is a shoe, three is a tree, four is a door, five is a hive, six are sticks, seven is heaven, eight is a gate, nine is a line, and ten is a hen.

To memorize a list of up to ten nouns all you have to do is generate a novel image which combines each of the respective components. For example, suppose you have to remember to pick up some cigarettes, mail a letter, and stop at the cleaners. After learning the above mnemonic "peg" system, you might conjure up vivid images such as the following: a smoking cigarette sticking out of a *bun*, a letter sticking out of a *shoe*, and a cellophane-wrapped suit hanging from a *tree*. This system is a very efficient mnemonic aid. The individual can remember a number of items by simply checking his mnemonic "pegs" periodically (bun, shoe, etc.) to see if he has stored any recent information on them. As we shall see in our later discussion of the cognitive therapies, coding strategies and performance-cueing mnemonics can provide helpful therapeutic assistance.

RETENTION, RETRIEVAL, AND LONG-TERM MEMORY

We remember some things for a brief period of time (e.g., until final exams are over). Other information seems to be retained almost indefinitely. What makes the difference?

At least four different processes have been suggested to account for the phenomenon of forgetting. First, the *decay hypothesis* suggests that memory "traces" gradually fade away (or erode) unless they are occasionally re-stimulated. Like an old photograph, the memory of our second grade teacher may fade into oblivion unless it is revived by occasional cueing (e.g., via a scrapbook). The *interference hypothesis*, on the other hand, suggests that we forget because of other experiences which interfere with the stored memory. Our "mental filing system" gets cluttered with a myriad of inputs and many memory traces get lost in the shuffle. From this perspective, the name of our second grade teacher does not fade away so much as it becomes less accessible. We have trouble "finding it" due to the number of other intervening experiences and memories which have followed it (e.g., other names, other teachers, etc.). Another information loss process is that of *directed forgetting*. If we are instructed to disregard selected stimuli or experiences, the likelihood of their subsequent recall is dramatically reduced.

The fourth hypothesis speculates that we occasionally exhibit *motivated* forgetting. Memories which are associated with very painful experiences may become less accessible. This, of course, is parallel to the psychodynamic process of "repression." Pursuing our second grade teacher, we may forget her name because it is associated with very aversive experiences. The clinical relevance of motivated forgetting should be readily apparent. It has received some preliminary support in a handful of laboratory investigations (cf. Zeller, 1950; Eriksen & Kuethe, 1956; D'Zurilla, 1965; Glucksberg & King, 1967). In the study described by Glucksberg and King (1967), for example, subjects initially learned a list of paired associates (e.g., "MYV-fruit"). They then read a list of words which were implicit associates of the response words (e.g., "tree") as indicated by word association norms. Some of these associates were followed by shock. During a subsequent recall test, subjects' performances were significantly worse on items which had been implicitly associated with shock. The clinical relevance of motivated forgetting is well illustrated in several case studies reported by Marks and his colleagues (Marks, Rachman, & Gelder, 1965; Marks & Gelder, 1967). These investigators used electrical aversion in the reduction of disturbing thoughts and deviant sexual fantasies. Clients were instructed to actively generate these maladaptive ruminations in the laboratory and when they signaled a clear image a painful electric shock was administered. Interestingly, clients displayed progressively longer latencies in producing deviant images until they eventually reported total inability to activate these symbolic events. Corresponding improvements in daily behavior patterns suggested that they were being honest in their reported "repression" of the deviant images. A case study by Thomson (1971) also lends some very indirect support for the phenomenon of motivated forgetting. During desensitization a client spontaneously recalled a long-forgotten traumatic experience related to one of the requested hierarchy scenes. While the foregoing studies are only suggestive, they encourage further inquiries into this type of forgetting. One question which needs to be addressed deals with whether traumatic experiences affect encoding or retrieval operations (Holmes & Schallow, 1969). Recent findings on the tendency of individuals to symbolically rehearse recent trauma must be integrated with motivated forgetting hypotheses (Horowitz & Becker, 1971a,b,c). We obviously do not "repress" all of our aversive memories. As a matter of fact, many individuals seem to dwell on such events. What are the variables which moderate trauma recall and motivated forgetting? We are again faced with an intriguing question and a paucity of data.

The status of unretained information poses another relevant question. Do forgotten items somehow "vanish" from our heads or do we simply lose accessibility to them? That is, is it possible that forgotten information is actually "still there" in storage but that we are unable to retrieve it? Relying again on the filing system analogy, is it possible that files are never destroyed, only misplaced? The question of the permanence of memory has intrigued psychologists for several decades. Some of the most impressive support for memory permanence comes from the anecdotal case records of a brain surgeon, Wilder Penfield (1959). His early work involved the surgical treatment of focal epilepsy via craniotomies. In this procedure, a section of the skull is removed to allow the ablation of portions of the temporal lobe. The patient is given a local anesthetic and remains both awake and conscious throughout the operation. In applying electrical stimulation to portions of the exposed brains, Penfield found that patients reported vivid subjective experiences often involving long forgotten memories. In over a thousand such operations, Penfield collected extensive reports of this nature and eventually formulated a theory of memory permanence. The current status of that theory, however, is far from unequivocal (cf. Adams, 1967; Neisser, 1967). It is worth noting, however, that the hypothesis (if not its memory) appears to be permanent. John B. Watson (1924), for example, hinted at such an hypothesis when he described the Freudian unconscious as the aggregate of an infant's experiences prior to his acquisition of language (pp. 263-265). The implication of Watson's speculation, of course, is that we may respond to stimuli but fail to recall the original learning circumstances due to the relative disarray of our infantile filing systems.

The transfer of information from short-term to long-term storage has raised several other intriguing research questions. For example, what are the physiological processes in memory formation? Investigators often talk about a memory *engram*, the basic unit of storage. The nature of the engram is far from clear, however. Does it involve structural changes in the connections between nerve cells (e.g., at synapses)? Is it chemically stored as an intracellular protein? The process of stabilizing or establishing the relative permanence of an item is often termed the *consolidation* of a memory. Is this consolidation process dichotomous or incremental? That is, do we store information in all-or-none fashion (either we retain it or we don't)? Or is the engram initially "weak" but gradually strengthened by specific consolidation processes (rehearsal, repetition, etc.)? Some evidence for incremental storage is provided by the phenomenon of retrograde amnesia after severe head injuries. A sharp blow on the head will sometimes result in memory losses, most of which are related to very recent experiences. This suggests, of course, that recent experiences have not yet been consolidated into a larger and more enduring memory store and that the head injury may have interfered with that consolidation.

Much of the research in memory and information processing has distinguished between the performances of *recall* and *recognition*. In recall procedures, the subject is given an open-ended question and asked to generate the correct answer (e.g., Richard Nixon's middle name is_______). A recognition performance, on the other hand, inserts the correct answer among several presented alternatives (e.g., Richard Nixon's middle name is: (a) Mitchell (b) Milhouse (c) Mischievous (d) Melvin). Recognition performance is usually far superior to recall, which suggests that different processes may be involved. In a recall test situation, the individual is seldom given cues telling him where to "look" in his memory stores, so he presumably must engage in *search* procedures. Recognition, on the other hand, only requires that the individual compare the presented alternatives to those in his memory stores—he need only "match" the stimulus.

The modalities of information storage are an intriguing topic, and one which has tremendous relevance for clinical applications. Conventional experimentation has generally addressed two major forms of information storage: visual imagery and auditory/verbal encoding. The parallels and differences between these two have received quite a bit of recent empirical attention. For some types of information (e.g., concrete noun pairs), imaginal storage appears to be superior (cf. Bower, 1970, 1972; Paivio, 1971). Subjects demonstrate better recall when they mediate a noun pair such as "turtle–phonograph" with a vivid image (e.g., a dizzy tortoise on a rotating turntable) rather than with other associative methods (e.g., simple repetition). This was illustrated in the study reported by Mahoney, Thoresen, and Danaher (1972) (cf. Chapter 6) and in the mnemonic peg system suggested by Miller, Galanter, and Pribram (1960). Few reports of the functionality of imaginal memory have equalled that of Francis Galton (1883) who described a skillful associate. Galton's friend was reportedly capable of conjuring up a vivid image of a slide rule and then adjusting it symbolically to perform accurate imaginal calculations!

Imagery does not always produce superior retention, however. Verbal—and particularly "organizational"—encoding procedures are often more effective in the memorization of abstract and more complex information. Items may be stored according to relationships (e.g., cause-effect, spatial), categories (e.g., supraordinates), and so on. I shall preview here a speculation which will receive more attention in Chapter 14—namely, that some of the differences between imaginal memory and verbal memory derive from their respective evolutionary histories. Visual imagery was presumably an earlier form of mediation—the cave man could store memory items (particularly spatial and temporal) via "mental pictures." As a language system developed, the nature of environmental input and information storage changed dramatically. It is now not uncommon to encounter individuals who report difficulty or total inability to generate visual imagery. This is well documented in the literature on desensitization and covert conditioning. Whether this phenomenon suggests the gradual evolutionary extinction of imagery-based memory is an intriguing but speculative hypothesis. We shall take it up again in Chapter 14 when speculation is our explicit task.

Information which has been adequately coded and stored is more likely to be retrieved and utilized in subsequent performance. The basic issues in memory retrieval seem to center around search, selection, and response generation processes. If an individual can recognize correct items, we assume that his search "sub-routines"—to borrow from computer science—are adequate. If he can recall the item, we infer proficiency in both search and retrieval operations.

Some of the most intriguing data on memory retrieval is illustrated by the "tip of the tongue" phenomenon (Brown & McNeill, 1966). Each of us has had the painfully frustrating experience of trying to recall a name or word which we know we have stored but cannot retrieve. Brown and McNeill operationalized this phenomenon by presenting subjects with definitions of uncommon words and asking them (1) if they thought they knew the word, (2) whether they could supply it and (3) given that they knew it but could not recall it immediately (i.e., that they were in the "tip of the tongue" (TOT) state), whether they could provide *any* information on the word (e.g., letters it contained, number of syllables). Those subjects who reported being in the TOT state were impressively successful in providing partial information. In forty-seven percent of the reported TOT instances, subjects were able to give the number of syllables a word contained accurately, and fifty-one per cent correctly reported its initial letter. Further evidence on this type of phenomenon is provided by Hart's (1965) research on "the feeling of knowing." After failure to recall test items, subjects were asked whether they had the "feeling" that they knew the missed item. In a subsequent recognition test, subjects were much more successful on items they felt they had known.

The tip of the tongue phenomenon suggests that there may be instances in human information processing wherein we "know that we know" but are unable to meet strenuous performance demands (e.g., recall). Polanyi's (1964) speculations on "tacit knowledge" are suggestive parallels. However, the major impact of the Brown and McNeill (1966) findings relates to specific aspects of human information storage. These researchers suggest a cognitive filing system in which memory items are tagged with various features (e.g., phonological, semantic, associative, etc.). They suggest the metaphor of punched keysort cards in the head. During retrieval operations, the individual searches according to these various features (e.g., "begins with the letter 'f', three syllables, a type of bird, rhymes with 'bingo' "). The more features (search clues) available, the more successful the retrieval operation.

It is interesting that most of us utilize imaginal as well as verbal search routines. For example, if you are asked what you were doing last New Year's Eve, it is likely that you will generate an imaginal rehearsal of your holiday experiences. More intriguing perhaps is the fact that we often employ extraneous cues to aid our memory. For example, while you are cleaning up in the kitchen you may think of something you need to do. Upon walking into the living room, you find that you have forgotten what your task was. To facilitate its recall, you return to the kitchen and retrace your activities. Accidentally-associated cues may be the key to this operation.

The phenomenon of "accidental retrieval" is probably familiar to most of us. Although we have not purposely initiated a search routine, we find ourselves retrieving items or fantasies from the past. For example, during infrequent visits to relatives or old neighborhoods, the frequency of childhood memories and dreams is probably much greater. This is presumably due to the cueing function of environmental stimuli. An impressively large percentage of our everyday reveries is probably induced by accidental retrieval. Analyzing the associations and antecedents of such retrievals can be an intriguing challenge. You are driving to work and suddenly recall the houses on a childhood paper route or the name of a long-forgotten playmate. Immediate analyses of these retrievals often reveal current cues or associates that led to the recalled memory—the sight of an old mailbox, a song on the radio, etc. A strict reinforcement analysis of retrieval might predict that we spend most of our time in pleasant reveries. However, experimental data (e.g., Klinger, 1971) and our own introspection challenge this prediction. Most of our retrievals appear to be associative or instrumental (e.g., in problem-solving).

Perhaps the aspect of memory retrieval with which we are most familiar is that of frustration. We try to recall someone's name or an unfamiliar address and are upset at our inability to retrieve it. We "strain" cognitively and find that this only makes matters worse. After giving up in frustration, we often find that the forgotten item is retrieved almost automatically. The extensiveness of this experience is attested to by the frequent recommendation to "stop thinking about" something we are having trouble remembering. One possible explanation for this phenomenon suggests that we perseverate in our first search routine. If we have asked the wrong "question" of our memory stores, it is very hard to modify that question during an active search operation. However, when we drop this inappropriate search routine, we increase the likelihood that our next attempt to locate that memory item will use alternative search cues.

A final issue in long-term memory has to do with the retrieval versus *reconstruction* of stored information. Sir Frederic Bartlett (1932) has suggested that we often impose an idiosyncratic organization on recalled material. In a series of investigations, Bartlett asked subjects to reproduce a prose passage or story after varying intervals of time. His data suggested that individuals "reconstructed" information rather than recollecting it. They often gave quite distorted versions of the original material and failed to discriminate accurate from confabulated elements. Many subjects even generated elaborately creative reports to buttress their idiosyncratic versions of the passage or story. According to Bartlett, these findings reflect an active reconstruction process in memory (cf. Zangwill, 1972). The extent of distortion and reconstruction appears to increase with progressively longer time intervals. Norman (1969) suggests that this phenomenon is consistent with much of our knowledge on short- and long-term memory—namely, that individuals often impose an organization on the material (e.g., via mnemonics, categorical encoding, etc.). The impressive relevance of reconstruction for clinical self-reports need hardly be elaborated. However, we should take particular notice of the apparent role of organization in memory. If we expect clients to learn and enduringly retain information from therapy, its presentation in a systematic and organized fashion may be very important.

The foregoing presentation of the information processing model has been necessarily brief. For the reader familiar with this area of research, my generalizations and glaring omissions will be obvious. For the neophyte, the foregoing may appear unnecessarily complex. Having therefore alienated all but my closest relatives, I shall add insult to injury by offering a brief general summary.

The information processing model views man as an active mediator of stimulation. Processes of information acquisition, transfer, storage, retrieval, and utilization are emphasized. Three basic structural elements are conventionally proposed: a sensory register, a short-term memory, and a long-term memory. Between environmental input and response output are posited four broad categories of processes which influence information transfer: (1) attention, (2) encoding, (3) retention, and (4) retrieval. A well established finding in attention research relates to our selectivity in stimulus processing. The storage of memory items appears to be influenced by a number of features: (a) imaginal versus verbal encoding, (b) the nature, context, and meaningfulness of the stimulus, (c) rehearsal duration, (d) exposure frequency (repetition), (e) temporal factors (e.g., primacy/recency), and (f) associated affective experience (e.g., reinforcement or punishment). There is some evidence that our capacity for information processing is limited. To accommodate this limitation, we often chunk or group memory items and impose economical organizational schema on them (e.g., via mnemonics). Information retrieval appears to be influenced by the adequacy of various search operations and the saliency of feature clues (e.g., phonological, semantic, etc.). Active reconstruction processes may characterize at least some types of memory retrieval. Our current knowledge about the permanence of memory, its physiological bases, and the nature of forgetting is still inadequate. While analogies from computer science and cybernetic theory have been heuristic in this area, the limitations of these analogues bear our continued examination.

An extensive evaluation of the information processing model would be an ambitious and equivocal endeavor, not only because of the complexities and extent of the literature, but also because of the plethora of different models within the field. Man's propensity for theorization is seldom as visible as in this area. We are faced with not only an abundance of general models, but an almost infinite array of sub-theories on various issues (e.g., attention, short-term storage, etc.).

Some perspective on the adequacy of an information model may be derived from its brief comparison with the covert conditioning model. It will be recalled that the latter was described as a basically horizontal set of principles. The information processing model, on the other hand, combines both horizontal and vertical aspects. Memory is conceptualized in terms of horizontal (same-level) transfer as well as vertical (hierarchical) organization. While the covert conditioning researcher is likely to invoke fewer and more conservative inferences, the information processor often posits extensive mediational variables. Although he frequently gets "further away from the data," however, the information theorist ostensibly addresses a more comprehensive and complex subject matter. He supplements associative principles with functional rules describing other relationship variables (e.g., attentional selectivity, categorical encoding, etc.). Both models use metaphors extensively in their procedural and explanatory language. The covert conditioning model borrows its metaphors from theory and research on laboratory conditioning; covert events are viewed as relatively discrete stimulus and response units. In the information model, metaphors are drawn more heavily from cybernetics, systems theory, and computer science. In place of discrete stimuli and responses, we encounter sequences of events ("processes") which are patterned and interwoven in substantial complexities. Despite these differences in the nature and form of inferred mediators, however, both the covert conditioning and information processing models adhere to a methodological behaviorism in the exploration and evaluation of their hypotheses.

One of the assumptions of the information processing model which has recently been challenged relates to its implication of a closed feedback loop (von Bertalanffy, 1967). According to the computer analogue of human behavior (cf. Miller, Galanter, & Pribram, 1960; Hilgard & Bower, 1966; Newell & Simon, 1972), the organism pursues instrumental behavior to reduce the discrepancy between actual and adaptive states of the system. That is, man seeks homeostasis, not only physiologically but in terms of information feedback and learning. It is von Bertalanffy's contention that man is an open, growing system, a creative synthesizer of experience. He does not seek a steady-state, but is rather in constant pursuit of system expansion. This critique is at least partly justified if we restrict our attention to the model discussed in the present chapter. However, passive information storage and equilibrium-seeking do not accurately characterize all informational models of the human being. An extensive literature is devoted to the phenomena of curiosity, creativity, and instrumental problem solving (cf. Spivack & Shure, 1974; Davis, 1973; Newell & Simon, 1972; Bourne & Dominowski, 1972). Cognitive homeostasis is an assumption rarely encountered in human learning research.

Another conceptual criticism of the information processing model relates to its "implicit dualism." Many of the behaviorist's mentalistic fears are elicited by discussions of our "covert computer." Skinner (1969), for example, takes repeated exception to the assumption that "seeing implies something seen":

> The Inner Man is often said to store and recall memories. . . . A man need not copy the stimulating environment in order to perceive it, and he need not make a copy in order to perceive it in the future. When an organism exposed to a set of contingencies of reinforcement is modified by them and as a result behaves in a different way in the future, we do not need to say that it stores the contingencies. What is "stored" is a modified organism, not a record of the modifying variables (p. 274).

Skinner, however, appears to be inconsistent in his use of denial of stored environments. When the cognitive theorist is speaking of information storage, Skinner readily attacks this metaphorical inference. However, in his own account of rule-governed behavior, Skinner relies explicitly on symbolic contingency storage:

> A person . . . constructs comparable stimuli for himself when he makes resolutions, announces intentions, states expectations, and formulates plans. The stimuli thus generated control his behavior most effectively when they are external, conspicuous, and durable—when the resolution is posted or the plan actually drafted in visible form—but they are also useful when recreated upon occasion, as by recalling the resolution or reviewing the plan (pp. 123-124).

It is noteworthy that Skinner (1969, 1974) defends the recall of a "response" as less problematical than the recall of a symbolic label or stimulus for that response. An extensive body of literature suggests, however, that representational storage is the rule rather than the exception. Moreover, as our discussion of retrieval processes attests, response generation is significantly influenced by search cues and feature questions.

The crux of Skinner's objections to cognitive and information-based perspectives lies in interpretation, not data. While readily acknowledging the phenomena of selective attention, classification and so forth, Skinner (1974) cautions against their reification as cybernetic entities rather than covert behaviors:

> Human beings attend to or disregard the world in which they live. They search for things in that world. They generalize from one thing to another. They discriminate. They respond to single features or special sets of features as "abstractions" or "concepts." They solve problems by assembling, classifying, arranging, and rearranging things. . . . They . . . extract plans and rules which enable them to respond appropriately without direct exposure to the contingencies. They discover and use rules for deriving new rules from old. In all

> this, and much more, they are simply behaving, and that is true even when they are behaving covertly (p. 223).

His evaluation of the theoretical trappings of the information processing model, however, leaves little room for doubt:

> The metaphor of storage in memory . . . has caused a great deal of trouble. The computer is a bad model. . . . The assumption of a parallel inner record-keeping process adds nothing to our understanding of this kind of thinking. (It is not the behaviorist incidentally, but the cognitive psychologist, with his computer-model of the mind, who represents man as a machine.) (1974, p. 110)

It is interesting that Skinner (1974) seems to equate all mediational models as deriving from a "mentalistic" framework. He repeatedly employs "cognitive psychology" and "information theory" as if they were synonymous with mentalistic perspectives and energetically contends that they have "cost us much useful evidence (p. 118)" and wreaked inestimable havoc (p. xiii) on our scientific endeavors.

Selective data processing and reluctance to step outside of a paradigm to evaluate its adequacy are readily discernible features in the operant critique of information processing. After presenting lively arguments against the feasibility of the cognitive psychologist's telling us what *is* going on inside the organism, the operant critic extensively elaborates what is *not* going on. He denies the operation of encoding, search, and retrieval mechanisms, but then argues for the existence of contingency-induced covert behavior. It is ironic and perplexing to examine the relative abundance of operant speculation on thought processes and the corresponding dearth of operant research in this area. The ratio of theory to original data in their writings would probably embarrass many a cognitive theorist. If there are *data* to support the operant analysis of thinking, they are long overdue for communication. Continued theoretical dialogues merit substantiation by research and the operant critic might do well to concede that his "privileged knowledge" about what is and is not going on inside the organism is probably less data-based than that of the cognitive theorist. Extrapolations from skeletal operant research lose their heuristic value when they are uncritically adopted as "explanatory" rather than empirically evaluated for adequacy. As reviewed in the present and following chapters, the existing data are less than timid in challenging the operant analysis of mediation.

The argument that cognitive theories are "mentalistic" is sometimes defended by reference to homunculus metaphors in information models. We are sometimes given the impression that our processing operations are coordinated and controlled by an overworked cognitive controller, a faded descendant of the "little man in the head" who was posited by philosophers several centuries ago. In Neisser's (1967) intriguing theory of human information processing, he posits an "executive routine" which regulates our processing operations. Cognizant of the homunculus problem and its infinite regress (i.e., who controls the controller?), Neisser defends the executive routine as a viable and non-dualistic solution. Cognitive bootstrapping is not illogical. Complex computer systems are frequently regulated by an executive routine which monitors various operations *including its own.*

I tend to agree with Neisser's defense of the "executive" and am particularly impressed with its heuristic promise. A further comment on the dualism argument in information theory is, however, in order. Specifically, I would suggest that the homunculus issue in the cognitive (memory) model is again indicative of the linguistic muddles which frustrate our perception of the way things are. Effect implies cause; control implies a controller. The cognitive computer implies a cognitive computer programmer. We are forever looking for the "agent" of purposive action rather than viewing such action as a part of the system itself. Just as self-knowledge need not imply an existential entity (the "self"), information processing does not necessitate an information *processor.* We must continue to examine and differentiate those instances in which our metaphors and linguistic biases are useful and those in which they are not.

The empirical status of the information processing model has received little substantiation in the present chapter. However, as reflected in the prolific literature in this area, supporting data are not hard to find (cf. Neisser, 1967; Adams, 1967; Norman, 1969; Kintsch, 1970; Hall, 1971; Melton & Martin, 1972; Anderson & Bower, 1973). Since this model is not specifically addressed to clinical phenomena, its relevance for the practicing therapist and clinical researcher may not be readily apparent. In the next chapter we shall consider some revisions and extensions of an information-based model of human behavior. Particular emphasis will be placed on the possible role of various cognitive principles in the development, maintenance, and alteration of maladaptive response patterns.

Chapter Ten

Mediational Model III: The Cognitive Learning Model

The model which will be presented in the present chapter is far from revolutionary. It represents an attempted integration of several varied perspectives ranging from the formalized theories of Bandura (1971c) and Bem (1972) to the clinical models of Ellis (1962), Kanfer (1971), and Thoresen and Mahoney (1974). Metaphors and analogies will be drawn from both "learning theory" and information processing perspectives.

While the analysis of clinical phenomena from a cognitive, information-based perspective is not new (cf. Kelly, 1955; Rotter, Chance & Phares, 1972), recent years have witnessed a salient increase in efforts toward refining and operationalizing a "cognitive learning" approach (e.g., Bandura, 1969; Breger, 1969; Estes, 1971; Kanfer & Karoly, 1972; Staats, 1972; Mischel, 1973, in press). A rapidly accumulating body of evidence suggests that this convergence toward a cognitive-behavioral perspective holds substantial clinical promise. It should be kept in mind, however, that the model is both embryonic and tentative at the present time. Continued empirical explorations must decide its refinement, maturation, or abortion.

The basic features and conceptual flavor of the cognitive learning model have permeated many of the foregoing chapters and can be informally summarized as follows. Man is viewed as a complex organism capable of impressive adaptation. He is in a continuous reciprocity relationship with his environment, a relationship which might be analogized as a cybernetic feedback loop. Behavior changes are influenced by the current physiological state of the organism, his past learning history, the existing environmental situation, and a variety of interdependent cognitive processes (e.g., selective attention, anticipated consequences, etc.). Part of man's awesome complexity derives from his extensive evolutionary differentiation. Three interdependent nervous systems (central, somatic, and autonomic) affect the organism's adaptive performance. Under many circumstances the autonomic nervous system—which is most closely associated with basic life support functions—appears to override and dominate man's actions. However, we now know that the three systems interact in complex and reciprocal fashion.

One of the cardinal characteristics of the cognitive learning perspective is its view of man as an active element in his own growth and development. He is both a controlled and controlling organism; a product and a producer of environmental forces. The unending sequence of his experiences is not passively etched on a *tabula rasa*. The "raw data" of experience are selectively filtered, transformed, categorized, and stored. At a theoretical level, learning is induced by the experience of systematic relationships in time and space. These regularities may be experienced directly, vicariously, or via symbolic processes. While initial learning may derive primarily from perceived contiguity, subsequent performance is often moderated by a variety of influences (e.g., motivational factors, recency of learning, etc.).

The most significant feature of the cognitive learning model, however, is its emphasis on mediation in human learning. A brief analysis of the evolution of cognitive-symbolic processes lends support to the contention that they possess survival value (cf. Chapter 14). Although I shall not defend the human brain as the most efficient or supreme biochemical computer in existence, its evolutionary complexity can hardly be ignored. The functions of an elaborately developed central nervous system are probably varied. However, it is apparent that we utilize memory and thought processes to (a) mediate temporal intervals, (b) impose regularities on experience, (c) anticipate the consequences of our actions, and (d) economize our problem solving efforts. The nonmediating organism has difficulty profiting from the experience of temporally separated events. Through symbolic representational processes and information storage skills, the mediating organism can adaptively "connect" disjoined experiences. Likewise, as Chapter 9 indicated, we often impose an organization on experience which may facilitate both its learning and retention.

Suffice it to say that the adult human being thinks a lot. This symbolic activity involves complex sequences of neuronal behavior, much of which remains unexplored by contemporary science. As with many other evolutionary developments, mediation carries both adaptive and unadaptive features. In some ways, the thinking organism may be its own worst enemy. Our symbolic representations of reality are frequently naive and inaccurate.

Although the cognitive learning model encompasses both adaptive and maladaptive performances, the remainder of this chapter will address clinical and experimental illustrations of dysfunctional mediation. Four foci of behavioral variance will be suggested: (1) attentional (perceptual) factors, (2) relational processes, (3) response repertoire features, and (4) experiential feedback. Since the distinctions among these areas are complicated by their frequent interactions and inevitable overlap, their separate treatment here should be viewed as an attempt to facilitate their processing by the reader.

ATTENTIONAL FACTORS

As previewed by our discussion in Chapter 9, the human organism responds to a selectively filtered world. There is some evidence to suggest that this selectivity is forced upon us by our physiological limitations as information processors. We are continually bombarded by far more stimuli than receive our focused attention. Through an intricate interaction of receptor system influences and our own learning history, we acquire the ability to impose a perceptual funnel on our experiences—we selectively attend to events and sensations which have innate or acquired importance in our adaptation.

Empirically controlled research on the important role of attentional factors in human performance is far from lacking. One illustrative area deals with the research on "endurance" and pain tolerance (Thoresen & Mahoney, 1974). In experiments on subjects' abilities to tolerate prolonged or incremental aversive stimulation, the importance of attentional factors has been apparent. Kanfer and his colleagues, for example, have found that individuals can tolerate significantly longer durations of painful ice water immersion when they are provided with attentional distractions (cf. Kanfer & Goldfoot, 1966; Kanfer, Cox, Greiner, & Karoly, in press). When subjects are given control of self-presented distractive cues (travel slides), for example, their endurance capacities are greatly enhanced (Kanfer & Seidner, 1973). Subsequent research by Horan and Dellinger (in press) has replicated and extended this finding, suggesting that the nature of the distractive stimulus may be important. Subjects who were told to count backwards from 1000 were no more successful in their pain tolerance than control subjects. Individuals who distracted with positive imagery, however, endured painful stimulation for dramatically longer intervals.

Resistance to temptation is an analogous phenomenon in which attentional factors play a significant role. The extensive work of Mischel and his colleagues on "delay of gratification" is noteworthy and illustrative (cf. Mischel, in press; Mischel & Ebbesen, 1970). In this paradigm, children are given their choice between an immediate small reward and a delayed larger reward. For example, a child is asked his preference between a marshmallow and a pretzel. He is then told that he can have his less preferred choice immediately, or he can wait and have the more preferred one later. If the child chooses to await the delayed reward, the experimenter provides him with a signal bell and leaves the room. The subject can terminate his delay interval at any point and receive his less preferred choice simply by ringing the bell. If he waits (fifteen minutes) until the experimenter returns on his own, however, he is awarded the preferred incentive. Mischel's research has identified a series of factors which influence children's abilities to successfully defer gratification. Among the most significant of these have been attentional processes (Mischel, Ebbesen, & Zeiss, 1972). For example, one variable is the perceptual presence or absence of the tempting object. If the deferred reward is physically present and readily visible, children's delay capacities are reduced. This lack of restraint, however, can be dramatically altered through cognitive training. Children who are trained to distract themselves during the delay interval by thinking about "fun things" demonstrate considerable improvement. If they think about the awaited object, however, their delay ability is impaired. Figure 10-1 illustrates the impact of cognitive-attentional factors in this paradigm. It

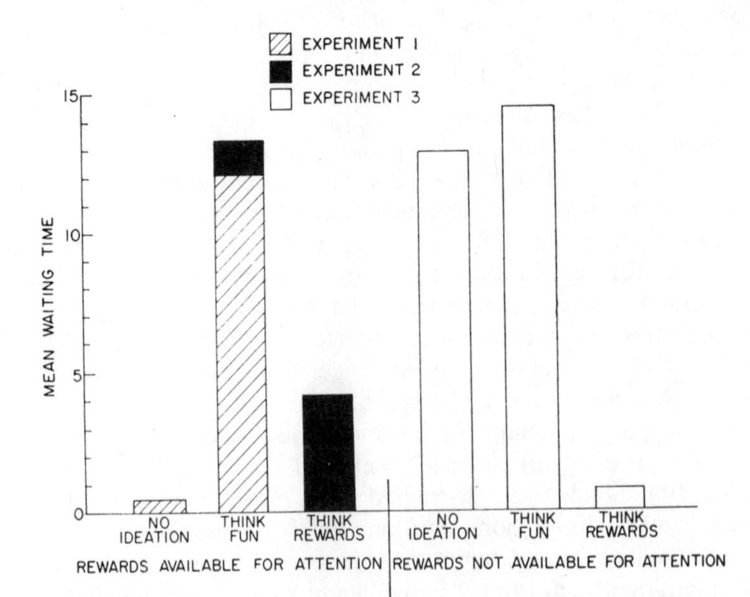

Figure 10-1. Mean number of minutes of voluntary waiting time in three experiments comparing different ideational instructions. (Reprinted with permission from Mischel, Ebbesen, & Zeiss, 1972.)

is noteworthy that positive symbolic distractions seem to be more powerful than the actual physical presence of a stimulus. In both the presence and absence of awaited rewards, "thinking fun" results in virtually perfect restraint.

Restraint, of course, is only one of many behavior patterns which are apparently influenced by attentional mechanisms. As we shall see in Chapter 11, training in covert self-instruction can effect impressive improvement in a range of clinically relevant dysfunctions.

A third area of research bearing on the role of attentional processes spans the literature on "stimulus control" and self-monitoring (Thoresen & Mahoney, 1974). The role of antecedent events in maladaptive behavior patterns is well recognized in behavior modification. The smoker's indulgence in his "filthy habit" is often cued by the sight of an ashtray, completion of a meal, or the smell of someone else's cigarette. We eat in response to temporal cues (e.g., the noon whistle) and a wide range of not-so-hidden persuaders (e.g., a bountiful bowl of taco chips, the sight of one last cookie in the package, and a spouse's remonstration that we paid $8.00 for the steak we have not yet finished). Researchers in the area of self-regulation have drawn extensively on the literature of stimulus control in their treatment recommendations. Smokers, for example, have been instructed to limit their cigarette consumption to specified times or places in an effort to reduce the number of events which can cue the behavior. Weight watchers have been similarly instructed to limit the availability and prominence of food stimuli and to restrict their eating to circumscribed locations. Thoughts about a target behavior and accurate attention to the act itself have been singled out as possible factors in successful self-regulation (Ackerman, 1973; Mahoney, Moura, & Wade, 1973; Gaul, Craighead, & Mahoney, in press). Individuals can be given training in attentional distraction to facilitate their restraint capacities. Although the bulk of existing evidence on stimulus control strategies has emphasized cues external to the organism, the relevance of selective attention and self-stimulation should be readily apparent. Research on the effects of simple self-observation lend additional support to the contention that perceptual factors introduce considerable variability in human behavior (Kazdin, 1974b; Thoresen & Mahoney, 1974). Performance can be appreciably influenced not only by the existence of self-monitoring operations, but also by their differential focus.

A fourth area of attentional relevance is that of "expectancy." The impact of context and set on perception is well documented. However, in the realm of research methodology and behavioral dysfunction, the term "expectancy" claims a much broader range of referents. Wilkins (1973) has appropriately critiqued the enduring ambiguity and *ad hoc* expedience of many contemporary uses of the term. The concepts of "demand characteristics," "placebo effects," "implicit communication," "set," "expectancy," and "nonspecific influences" have all been invoked as potential moderators of performance variance. According to Orne (1969), "demand characteristics" are those cues which influence a subject's perception of his role in an experiment. A large body of evidence has shown that both the experimenter's and the subject's performance can be dramatically affected by their respective hypotheses about the experiment (Rosenthal, 1966; Rosenthal & Rosnow, 1969). Individuals exhibit greater avoidance behavior when the same task is presented as fear assessment, for example, rather than communications research (Bernstein, 1973). Similarly, individuals will often demonstrate substantial clinical progress after receiving only "suggestions" of therapeutic improvement (i.e., in the absence of formal treatment) (Kazdin, 1973c).

Placebo effects are neither new nor rare in psychotherapy (Frank, 1961; Goldstein, 1962; Shapiro, 1971). A placebo is an inert chemical or procedure which, despite its actual impotence, effects therapeutic improvement in its recipient. The history of medicine has been characterized as a history of the placebo. A substantial percentage of "curing" is done through inactive drugs, medical ritual, and professional pizzazz. Not only do patients show greater progress when they *think* their physician or therapist is skilled, but the helping professional is himself affected by his perceived potency. If he *believes* he is administering a strong drug or powerful therapeutic strategy, his perception of clients' responsiveness and improvement will be biased. The amount of outcome variance accounted for by these expectancies and beliefs presents a controversial and difficult issue.

It is worth noting that researchers in behavior modification have often taken a very defensive stance regarding the role of placebo and expectancy factors in their clinical procedures (Mahoney, 1974a). The terms themselves have come to connote "illegitimacy" and poorly controlled methodology. Despite a growing body of literature indicating that such factors are involved in both the outcome and assessment of many behavior therapy techniques (cf. Jacobs & Wolpin, 1971; Wilkins, 1971; Davison & Wilson, 1973; Hamerlynck, Handy, & Mash, 1973), their importance is often either minimized or totally denied. The placebo effect is treated as if it were a medieval demon lurking in the darkness of our laboratories, ever ready to devour the well-intentioned efforts of the dedicated behavioral scientist.

It should be obvious from the above paragraph that I do not concur with the view that the effects of expectancy are somehow illegitimate or indicative of sloppy research. There are no "nonspecific" influences in a deterministic science (only unspecified ones), and there is nothing mysterious about placebo effects. A closer examination reveals these factors to be inferred mediators—i.e., cognitive-symbolic processes. Although we have already spent considerable time on this topic, I shall briefly suggest that the entire lot of "artifacts" in behavioral research—expectancy, placebo, role-playing, and demand characteristics—are moderated by parallel cognitive processes. Specifically, it is very likely that these factors describe instances in which the individual's patterns of information processing are systematically altered. He selectively attends to specific stimuli and retrieves an organized (and biased) subset of possible response options. His anticipated consequences are dramatically affected by the perceptual schema imposed (intentionally or unintentionally) by the therapist/experimenter. In short, the procedures which induce expectancy appear to operate via their influence on perceptual and mediational processes. To say that these processes are operative in behavior modification is very different from asserting that the discipline is "nothing but" placebo, etc. Even if perceptual/mediational factors are extensively involved in the therapeutic impact of many behavioral treatment strategies, this does not call into question their validity or their clinical promise. It questions only our knowledge of their contributing elements. Judging from the comparative outcome data among the various therapeutic perspectives, behavior modifiers appear to be thoroughly skilled at inducing these processes in their clients. Our future functional analyses of the active ingredients in successful behavioral treatments will, hopefully, address some of these skills. Is the presentation of a cogent rationale important? How critical is the fact that behaviorally-oriented therapies often involve discrete, graduated, and goal-specific "expectancies"?

The foregoing research has documented the pervasive role of attentional factors in many forms of human behavior. On the "adaptive" side, selective information processing appears to facilitate an individual's ability to endure painful stimulation, "resist" temptation, and optimize therapeutic improvements.

Unfortunately, attentional processes may also contribute to maladaptive patterns which exacerbate performance dysfunctions. Among these maladaptive patterns are the following.

(1) Selective inattention involves the ignoring of performance-relevant stimuli. This phenomenon occurs when environmental cues are adequate but unattended. Striking examples of inattention can often be found in mental patients. I can recall one experience, as an undergraduate psychiatric aide, during which I naively attempted to persuade a patient out of his delusion that he was Jesus Christ. After

I had laid out some logical premises and set up a crucial test of his supernatural powers, the patient agreed that he would abandon his delusion if he were unable to make me disappear. The experiment was prepared, and I made the critical request, "Make me disappear." With supernatural suave, he slowly closed his eyes and said, "Okay, you're gone."

(2) Misperception occurs when impinging stimuli are attended to but inaccurately labeled. Bruch (1973), for example, documents the frequency with which emaciated anorexic patients perceive themselves as obese. In anorexia nervosa, the individual often refuses to eat; and instances of fatal self-starvation are not infrequent. Even though they can report accurate knowledge of their physical dimensions, patients label these dimensions as corpulent.

> When Lynn was fourteen years old she noticed suddenly that she was developing a pot belly. . . . Her weight was 110 lbs. at the time, appropriate for her height, but she decided to lose weight . . . six months later her weight was down to sixty-eight lbs (Bruch, 1973, pp. 247–248).

Another illustration of the effects of misperception is offered in a recent study by Wooley (1972). In comparing the effects of physiological and cognitive factors in food regulation, Wooley gave normal and obese subjects liquid "preloads" prior to an experimental meal. Half the time these drinks were presented as rich milkshakes, and half the time they appeared to be low-calorie diet liquids. Their actual calorie content was experimentally varied (200 versus 600 calories). Food consumption during the subsequent experimental meals was determined by subjects' perceptions, not by veridical preload intakes. When individuals believed that they had consumed a milkshake, they reduced their subsequent eating and reported feeling fuller. It was their perception rather than actual calories which determined performance.

A third example of misperception occurred on the psychiatric ward of a Catholic general hospital. We had a second Jesus Christ who continually ordered the nuns around and kept most of the patients awake at night by lying in a cruciform position and screaming at the top of his lungs. The permissible limits of medical sedation and rational entreaty were unsuccessful in reducing his noise. In an act of desperation, I returned to the nurse's station, channeled the intercom to the patient's room and transmitted, "This is God the Father—GO TO SLEEP!" The patient was immediately silent, and his night-long tirades were not again encountered. His apparent misperception produced a welcome improvement in behavior.

(3) Maladaptive focusing occurs when the individual attends to external stimuli irrelevant or deleterious to performance. This often occurs in conjunction with selective inattention. The literature on "impulsivity" suggests that impulsive and hyperactive children may attend to distractive stimuli. As we shall see in Chapter 11, preliminary research has demonstrated substantial promise in the alteration and improvement of this maladaptive pattern (Meichenbaum & Goodman, 1969a, b, 1971). A recent speculation by Kathryn Craighead (personal communication) has addressed the moderating influence of maladaptive focusing in the behavioral treatment of avoidance patterns. Many phobic clients seem to remain totally engrossed in their autonomic arousal during treatment rather than attending to external stimulus factors. Whether training in more appropriate focusing might enhance therapeutic improvement remains to be examined.

(4) Maladaptive self-arousal involves the generation of private "stimuli" which are either irrelevant or detrimental to performance. This, of course, is analogous to maladaptive focusing except that the attended cues are "internal" rather than "external." Self-arousal processes have been extensively documented using both laboratory and clinical phenomena (cf. Chapter 4). Many instances of personal distress and maladjustment are effected and maintained via symbolic self-arousal. Fear of the dark, for example, offers a clear illustration of this phenomenon. In the virtual absence of external stimulation, many individuals experience dramatic and painful autonomic stress due to self-generated cues.

The foregoing discussions have dealt with only a few of the many topics which have direct bearing on the role of attentional factors in behavior dysfunction. I have omitted, for example, the extensive literatures suggesting that such disorders as schizophrenia are characterized by perceptual deficits (Marshall, 1973). The deleterious effects of psychiatric labeling have likewise been omitted (Ullmann & Krasner, 1969; Stuart, 1970; Rosenhan, 1973). An entire volume could easily be consumed documenting the extent to which we squeeze reality into organized perceptions. Selective attention characterizes not only many forms of behavior disorder, but also our performance as scientists. We focus on a biased subsample of reality and often maintain our funneled perception long after its empirical utility has been disconfirmed. Recent refinements in methodological assessment procedures have forced a glaring awareness of the extent to which "objective data collection" operations are perceptually biased.

Suffice it to say, then, that attentional factors—broadly defined—appear to exert extensive impact on human behavior. Although our emphasis has been on the role of perceptual dysfunction in "abnormal" behavior, there are ample data to suggest a pervasiveness which does not recognize our labels of social deviance. The therapist is often as perceptually bigoted as his client. The most salient effects of attentional dysfunction seem to accrue when the individual (a) assimilates inaccurate information (via mislabeling, selectivity, etc.) and/or (b) focuses on stimuli which are either irrelevant or detrimental to performance in a given situation. Many maladaptive attentional cues appear to be self-generated.

RELATIONAL PROCESSES

The possibilities for mediational dysfunction do not end when a stimulus has been attended and encoded. Registration is only the beginning. After it has "checked in" to our metaphorical computer, a cue may undergo extensive processing in the form of transformation, relational comparisons, and so on. It will be recalled that one inference-inducing situation is that in which two identical stimuli occasion varying responses. This may result from the application of different "computer programs" to the two events. In the present section we shall briefly examine a few of the complex mediational processes which may influence performance variability. The metaphorical nature of the following "program error" illustrations should be borne in mind.

A first programmatic dysfunction overlaps some of the encoding operations previously discussed. Specifically, an attended stimulus may be translated inaccurately in such a way that a *classification error* impedes adaptive performance. For example, a spouse's ostensible grunt following our quiet "Good morning" might be classified as a negative social reaction rather than a poorly timed response to the bitterness of the coffee. Many such categorical errors involve comparator and equivalence operations which are dramatically affected by the classifications we entertain. "Dichotomous thinking," for example, is a common but dysfunctional process in human mediation. Events are categorized in all-or-none fashion without recognition of the graduated continuum which might more appropriately reflect the situation. Individuals often seem to impose a binary reality on their experience. A marriage is either "good" or "bad"; we are "on" or "off" a diet. The data are either "strong" or "weak" and a model is either "adequate" or "inadequate." Dichotomization, of course, presumes a point of demarcation—a comparator fulcrum which decides classification.

Comparator processes are a pervasive element in human thought. The literatures of personality theory, achievement research, and human learning readily reflect the consensus that the *homo sapiens* is an evaluating organism. Impinging stimuli—particularly when they constitute experiential feedback on previous performance—are subjected to extensive comparison operations. There is some evidence to suggest that performance feedback alone has little impact in the absence of standard setting (cf. Locke, Cartledge, & Koeppel, 1968; Mahoney, Moore, Wade, & Moura, 1973). According to Bandura (1969, 1971c, d), we apparently set comparison standards relative to at least three referents: (1) our own previous experience, (2) the observed performance of other individuals, and (3) socially acquired performance criteria. In a sense, then, our private evaluations are made relative to past, vicarious, and ideal standards. The preliminary research on comparator processes has suggested that vicarious (social) referents often dominate. Given a culture which values supra-normal deviance, the ramifications of this fact for personal evaluation are distressing. If an individual's happiness is determined by percentile rank relative to his peers, then the majority of our population should be perpetually dissatisfied. Clinical experience suggests that this generalization may not be grossly inaccurate.

The significance of evaluation in human behavior is well documented in the literatures on depression, suicide, and performance anxiety. Beck and his colleagues, for example, have reported data suggesting that depressed individuals set higher performance standards than non-depressed controls (cf. Beck, 1967, 1972b; Loeb, Beck, Diggory, & Tuthill, 1967). Even though their proficiency on an experimental task was equal to that of normal subjects, depressed individuals exhibited lower self-evaluations and more pessimistic expectancies about future performance. Neuringer (1974) has similarly reported that suicidal patients are dramatically more negative in their self-appraisals than are other hospitalized individuals.

The debilitating impact of fear of evaluation is extensively documented in the research on test anxiety (cf. Allen, 1972). Clinical records are often replete with illustrations of the extreme measures taken by clients to avoid evaluation. Perpetual procrastination, somatic complaints, and self-protecting excuses are not uncommon features. Bruch's (1973) descriptions of perfectionistic striving in anorexic clients offers further evidence on this phenomenon. These self-emaciated patients often report long histories of academic excellence and disciplinary perfection. Progressively inflated performance standards, however, often turn their childhood reinforcers into a "sweet sabotage" in later life—they can never do enough to earn positive evaluations. Replication of past excellence becomes routinely expected and future endeavors must always set new highs. Like Jonathan Livingston Seagull, their lives are often dominated by evaluative comparison, which "satisfy" only when they are superlative. Striving for a balanced competence is replaced by anxious avoidance of any hint at imperfection. This accelerating cycle of inflationary self-evaluation is not restricted to clinical disorders, however. As most of us can readily attest, comparator processes and evaluative striving are a pervasive, and often pernicious, component of everyday life.

Retentional deficiencies constitute a third form of mediational dysfunction which may contribute to maladaptive behavior patterns. It was previously suggested that thought and memory derive some of their presumed survival value from their "linkage" and storage functions. Disjoint temporal events can be symbolically connected and organized to economize and refine future performance. If the organism can recall prior mistakes and intervening successes, his chances of adaptation are enhanced. It should be noted that deficiencies in retention may involve inadequate storage of (a) stimulus and context information, (b) response elements, (c) consequence features, and/or (d) the various relationships among the above. Recent research has applied knowledge from the field of information processing to behavior disorders. For example, formalized training in rehearsal operations has been shown to dramatically improve memory deficiencies in retardates (cf. Belmont & Butterfield, 1971; Butterfield, Wambold, & Belmont, 1973).

Bandura and his colleagues have likewise demonstrated that encoding operations may significantly influence the retention of response-relevant therapeutic information (cf. Bandura, Grusec, & Menlove, 1966; Bandura & Jeffery, 1973; Bandura, Jeffery, & Bachicha, 1974). In a study by Gerst (1971), individuals were exposed to the manual language (hand signals) employed by the deaf. Three different coding strategies were compared to a control group: (1) summary labeling, in which selected "key" features were encoded, (2) imaginal coding, in which visual retention was attempted, and (3) verbal description, which involved detailed itemization of component features. Subjects' abilities to reproduce the modeled response were assessed immediately after exposure and once again following a 15 minute delay. The results are illustrated in Figure 10-2. Different coding operations effected wide variability in retention. Summary labeling produced significantly more enduring storage of response information than the other two procedures.

In a recent review article, Zimmerman and Rosenthal (1974) provide an excellent summary of the extensive research implicating encoding and retentional processes in complex human learning. The relevance of these processes for clinical behavior change can easily be extrapolated. Provision of mnemonic aids, rehearsal assignments and a meaningful conceptual context may substantially enhance clients' acquisition and retention of performance-facilitating information.

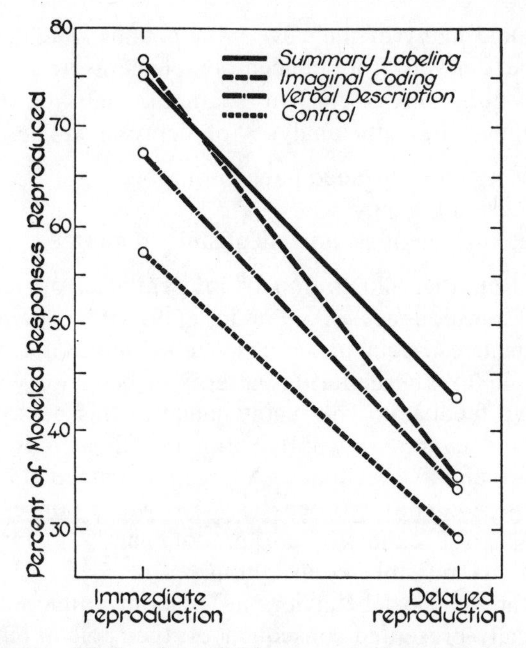

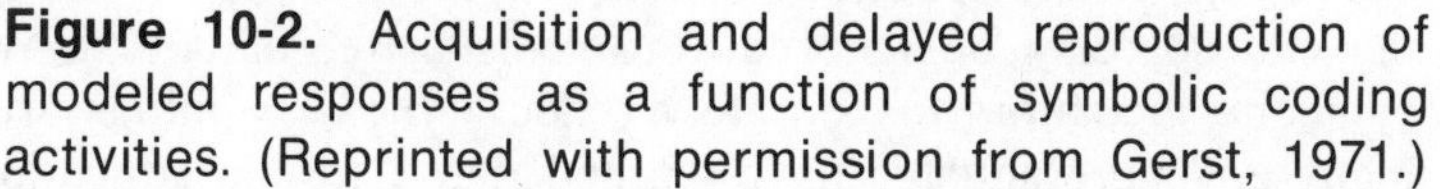
Figure 10-2. Acquisition and delayed reproduction of modeled responses as a function of symbolic coding activities. (Reprinted with permission from Gerst, 1971.)

Inferential errors comprise still another possible form of mediational dysfunction. We are often forced to go beyond available information or to distill performance directives from rudimentary input. This general process of going from experiential "raw data" to implications and response programs might be roughly classified as a form of inference. Many of our private inferences seem to parallel some of the classical forms of logic. We use inductive reasoning, for example, in drawing generalizations from isolated events. Inductive dysfunctions are probably pervasive elements in a wide range of human thought, both deviant and "normal." We often infer conclusions poorly supported by our personal data. A spouse's occasional tardiness is generalized to an indictment of rejection or infidelity. Occasional failures readily become transformed into a summary label of incompetence.

Analogical errors may also be involved in dysfunctional inference. "An eye for an eye" thinking, for example, may accelerate negative interaction patterns through encouragement of restitution rather than resolution. Deficiencies in deductive logic are also apparent. As we shall see in our later discussion of Albert Ellis's (1962) therapeutic rationale, it appears that some individuals rely on implicit and explicit premises to guide many of their everyday actions. Deductive inference errors may be derived from inaccurate elements (e.g., premises) or deficient reasoning processes. An example might be the deduction implicit in some behavioral analyses of depression:

1. All happy people are adequately reinforced.
2. My client is not happy.
3. Therefore, my client is not adequately reinforced.

Still another illustration of inferential errors deals with the anticipation of consequences. As Bandura (1971d) has pointed out, most human performances occur in the absence of immediate consequences. We exhibit complex and enduring patterns of behavior with only occasional incentive feedback. The maintenance of this behavior is often a result of symbolic events—the anticipation of ultimate consequences and of interim self-evaluative feedback. A large percentage of our actions are mediated by these cognitive processes. My own responses in generating this manuscript, for example, are predominantly maintained by the anticipation of its possible contribution.

Although most behaviors are seldom a function of "nothing but" symbolically-presented consequences, their role in human functioning can scarcely be ignored. Problems arise, of course, when these symbolic mediators inaccurately reflect "the way things are." All too many college graduates have learned that a formal education does not necessarily improve one's financial or occupational status. The blissful newlywed may soon discover that a marital relationship incurs many unanticipated responsibilities. Accurate knowledge about the ultimate consequences of our actions is an important element in adaptive functioning. The temporal gradient as well as nature of those consequences is also important. Individuals under treatment for obesity, for example, often entertain unrealistic anticipations regarding the immediacy of dramatic weight loss (Stunkard & Mahoney, in press).

The significance of anticipated consequences for human function and dysfunction can hardly be overemphasized. Being mediating organisms, one of our primary symbolic processes appears to focus on "personal prediction." Based on prior experience, vicarious learning, current (e.g., instructional) inputs, and a range of private inferences, we anticipate the consequences of our actions. This anticipation appears to dramatically influence our behavior and enables us to endure long temporal separations between performance and pay-off. Persevering and often "masochistic" response patterns can be thereby produced. Examples from religious history—ranging from martyrdom to lifetime vows of celibacy and silence—attest to the power of an anticipated incentive. Laboratory research has further documented this phenomenon (cf. Bandura, 1969, 1971d; Bolles, 1972). Interestingly, some of that research has suggested that the nature of one's anticipation may dramatically influence the effect of an actual consequence. Buchwald's (1959a, b, 1960) explorations of "reinforcement and punishment contrast," for example, indicate that identical consequences may either increase or suppress performance depending on the individual's prior experience (and presumed anticipation). After generous reinforcement for a response, a modest reward actually suppresses performance; after severe punishment, a milder aversive stimulus may increase responding.

The ability to accurately predict the consequences of our actions, of course, is an adaptive mediational skill. Unfortunately, many of our personal predictions are inaccurate, and a large number are never tested. Clinical records and personal experience offer ample documentation of the pervasiveness of dysfunctional expectancies. We often anguish over aversive events whose actual probability of occurrence would stymy a statistician. Worrying, "catastrophizing," and similar anticipatory responses are often culturally transmitted patterns. Conversely, the sweepstake entrant, Las Vegas gambler, and stock broker bear frequent witness to the effects of improbable positive consequences on human performance.

Mediational processes, whether functional or dysfunctional, result in symbolic "products" which might be abbreviated as *cognitive contingencies*. These representations of alleged regularities and relationships constitute our assumptive worlds. They are the "rules" or "plans" which organize stimulus-response-consequence combinations (Skinner, 1969). From a speculative survival analysis, the acquisition, storage, and utilization of cognitive contingencies might serve a variety of adaptive functions. As limited processors of information, we are forced to impose regularities on experience. Given that "consistency" facilitates learning, this abridged reality may be adaptive in the sense that our perceived world is much tidier than its referent. Moreover, since we are finite organisms whose experiences are spread over time and space, the ability to "connect" disjoint events may be important. In any case, there is a broad consensus among psychologists and philosophers alike that most human action is occasioned by a mediated rather than direct reality.

In their imposition of order and regularity on experience, cognitive contingencies perform an ostensibly adaptive function. However, their "survival value" is moderated by the accuracy with which they reflect real-world relationships.[a] Perceived regularities are often

[a] It may be time to reiterate here that the therapist should not be deluded into thinking that he has "privileged access" to the "real world." Although it is probably adaptive to adopt some form of "pragmatic" (rather than naive) realism, we must remain apprised of our own limitations in differentiating between perceived and "veridical" contingencies.

quite discrepant from actual ones. As our subsequent discussion will illustrate, the detection of these discrepancies often occurs slowly, if at all. We continue to respond to our cognitive contingencies until their dysfunctional misalignment becomes painfully expensive. In many classical forms of behavior pathology, the discrepancy is never experienced because the symbolic representation of reality is never tested.

The literature on superstition provides ample illustration of the dramatic role of cognitive contingencies in maladaptive behavior. Congruent with the foregoing analysis, Jahoda (1969) comments that

> superstition is part of the price we pay, an inevitable by-product of the constant scanning for patterns in which we are engaged. . . . The major difference between scientific thought and other kinds which shade imperceptibly into superstition is not in the initial weaving of the patterns, but in the obligation imposed by the scientific ethos to verify the products of thinking by well-established methods linking it to empirical phenomena (pp. 143-145).

An intriguing early analysis of superstition focused on the role of perceptual errors and retentional deficits in the phenomenon (Lehman, 1898). Lehman offered some preliminary evidence implicating cognitive distortions in the generation and maintenance of nonveridical belief. Although they are largely anecdotal, anthropological accounts of "faith healing" and "voodoo deaths" have likewise lent further illustration (cf. Cannon, 1942, 1957; Frank, 1961; Sargant, 1957; Huxley, 1969; Metraux, 1972; Leacock & Leacock, 1972; Gonzalez-Wippler, 1973). Laboratory experiments on both animals and humans have shown that tenacious and maladaptive response patterns can be generated through adventitious contiguity of responses and rewards (cf. Skinner, 1948; Morse & Skinner, 1957; Catania & Cutts, 1963; Neuringer, 1970b; Boren, 1970). It is interesting to note that we, as experimenters, selectively apply the label "superstition" to laboratory paradigms in which we have purposively programmed "adventitious reinforcement." When an accidental contiguity occurs without our informed consent, we may exhibit some extensive filtering and superstition in our own inferences (cf. Crosby & Caboon, 1973). While the learning processes and professional manifestations of superstitious responding are not unequivocal (cf. Staddon & Simmelhag, 1971), the phenomenon itself is well documented.

An illustrative study of cognitive contingencies in humans was performed by Kaufman, Baron, & Kopp (1966). Subjects participating in a "concept formation" experiment were given varying instructions about the task contingencies. Minimal instructions (control) subjects were simply told that the experiment dealt with concept formation.

Response instructions subjects received information regarding the critical response. In addition to the above, individuals in three experimental groups were told that their responding would be reinforced on either a fixed interval (FI = 1′), variable interval (VI = 1′), or variable ratio (VR = 150) schedule. In actuality, all subjects were rewarded after variable intervals of one minute. The impact of experimenter-induced cognitive contingencies is well illustrated in Figure 10-3. Letters refer to experimental conditions and digits to subject numbers. Individuals who believed they were being reinforced on fixed interval (FI) and variable

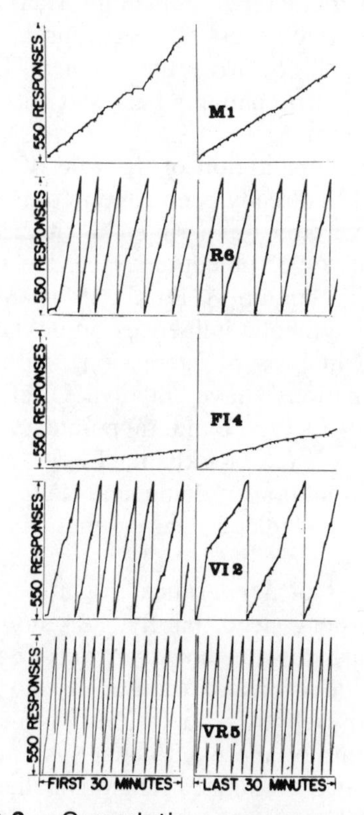

Figure 10-3. Cumulative response records from a representative subject in each of the five experimental conditions. From the top, the conditions illustrated are Minimal Instructions (M), Response Instructions (R), Fixed Interval (FI), Variable Interval (VI), and Variable Ratio (VR) Instructions. Digits refer to subject number. The records are taken from the first and last 30 minutes of performance during a three hour experimental session. (Reprinted with permission from Kaufman, Baron, & Kopp, 1966.)

ratio (VR) schedules responded at rates which were widely discrepant from one another. Despite the fact that they were experiencing identical real contingencies, the median number of responses per minute for the three experimental groups ranged widely (fixed interval = 7, variable interval = 43, variable ratio = 269). Bandura (1971d) points out that a gradual process of "reality testing" would probably bring most discrepant cognitive contingencies into better alignment with "veridical" regularities. However, the frequent absence of such reality testing in behavioral disorders should be kept in mind. Moreover, the selectivity and distortion which characterize human information processing suggest that "reality testing" may necessitate a comprehensive alteration in the individual's patterns of cognitive functioning. Tens of thousands of institutionalized psychiatric patients bear sad witness to the tenacity of dysfunctional mediation.

Further documentation of the role of symbolic mediation in human performance has already been cited in our discussion of Dulany's (1968) work. Moreover, post-experimental interviews have shown that the nonconformity of some subjects may be due to their misperception of contingencies (e.g., Bandura & Barab, 1971). More dramatic illustration of the impact of symbolic influences on deviant behavior is offered in Bandura's (1973) analysis of aggression. With only one exception, presidential assassinations have involved delusional contingencies (Weisz & Taylor, 1970). As Bandura points out, the fact that most assassins are "loners" (cf. Kirkham, Levy, & Crotty, 1969) may exacerbate their dysfunction: "Being unusually seclusive in their behavior, they effectively shielded their erroneous beliefs from corrective influences (p. 179)."

Occurrences of nonveridical cognitive contingencies in classical behavior disorders need hardly be enumerated. The schizophrenic's delusions are deviant, however, only in the sense that they do not agree with the delusions of the society at large. Moreover, the untestability of "psychotic" delusions is hardly an adequate criterion—many culturally approved belief systems are no less immune to experiential feedback. Organized religious beliefs offer but one example. As Chesen (1972) points out, the criterion of accountability is seldom applied to contemporary religions despite the fact that they are marketed in much the same manner as other products of public consumption. From the standpoint of their own survival, this immunity to empirical evaluation may be quite adaptive. In a classic study titled "Statistical Inquiries Into the Efficacy of Prayer," Francis Galton (1872) compared the longevity of the clergy and other occupations. Generalizing from a modest sample of 6473 subjects, Galton found the average life expectancy of poor farmers to exceed that of the clergy.

However, the adequacy of this "test" (or any other) would probably be energetically attacked by the undeluded theist.

Our lavish cultural reinforcement of religious beliefs may partially account for their extensive appearance in behavior pathology (cf. Walters, 1964; Chapman, 1967). The following case study from Kushner (1967) illustrates the extreme actions which can be induced by such beliefs. A 37-year-old patient had engaged in a brief homosexual encounter. Disgusted with his sinful behavior, he resolved to "excommunicate" himself.

> He said that he had read the Bible and was deeply impressed with Matt. xix. 12: "and there be eunuchs which have made themselves eunuchs for the Kingdom of Heaven's sake" . . . he performed a bilateral orchidectomy on himself. He applied a ligature to his scrotal skin, and arrived at the hospital carrying his testes in a box; and claimed that he had castrated himself as "a freewill offering to God" (pp. 294–295).

The pervasiveness of dysfunctional cognitive contingencies could consume several volumes of documentation. It should be noted that these perceptions often involve complex interactions of attentional deficits and mediational errors. The individual may not only selectively filter impinging stimuli, but he may also engage in a combination of maladaptive "sub-routines" (e.g., erroneous inference, dichotomous thinking, inaccurate anticipation of consequences, maladaptive self-evaluation).

The clinical implications of the foregoing discussion bear brief consideration. As a skilled observer of behavior, it is the therapist's role to discriminate dysfunctional mediational processes in his client and to assist in their alteration. When these processes involve maladaptive cognitive contingencies, he must be able to detect and communicate the "real" contingencies in a manner which will enhance therapeutic cognitivve realignment.[b]

An amusing clinical example of misperceived contingencies is provided in an anecdote from G. C. Davison. After a frustrating and expensive failure with psychoanalysis, a mother consulted a behavior therapist for assistance in the reduction of indiscriminate swearing on

[b] The "real" contingencies, of course, are unknowable. Since many clinical disorders involve socially-defined "deviance," however, the therapist can offer his own acculturated perception of the contingencies involved. More accurately stated, then, the therapist's task may involve the perceived congruence between his own and the client's cognitive contingencies. We make the (perhaps naive) assumption that the clinician is in "better contact with reality" than his client, which is to say that his assumptive world is probably more congruent with current social consensus.

the part of her two young sons. The behavior therapist began his therapeutic program with a brief synopsis of two learning principles. "First," he said, "it is important that you use immediate and severe punishment each and every time the swearing behavior occurs. Second, you can maximize the impact of your punishment by making sure that both children are present whenever one of them is punished. This is called 'vicarious learning'; the second child will learn from example." Enthusiastic over this refreshingly straightforward recommendation, the mother returned home to implement her newly acquired knowledge. At breakfast the next morning, she sat down ready and raring to modify behavior. The older son opened the day with the request that she "pass the fucking Cheerios." With lightning fury, the mother lunged across the table, hit her son, and sent both him and two chairs sprawling to the floor. The younger son helped her replace the furniture and the two of them sat back down. Pleased with her skillful execution of modern learning theory, she turned to her second breakfast partner and said, "Well, what will *you* have?" With ample indication that he had learned something from the preceding slaughter, he sagely remarked, "You can bet your sweet ass it isn't Cheerios!"

It is the therapist's responsibility not only to correct dysfunctional cognitive contingencies, but also to provide skills training for the client's subsequent self-improvement of mediation. As we shall see in Chapters 11 and 12, this often involves an initial treatise on the role of cognitive factors in personal distress and maladjustment. The client will hardly be motivated to examine or modify his private monologues and mediational processes unless he perceives them as critical elements in his therapeutic improvement. After presenting the rationale and evidence for "cognitive behavior modification," the therapist may provide training in accurate self-observation. Subsequent procedures often involve vicarious learning, guided performance, and systematic refinement of "thinking styles" (e.g., standard setting, logical inference, etc.).

It should be kept in mind that relational processes may influence attentional factors, response selection processes, and the nature of experiential feedback. Like the "self-fulfilling prophecy," mediational dysfunctions may tenaciously prevent or distort accurate processing of information. By selectively attending to those stimuli which conform to his cognitive contingencies, an individual may not only maintain but adventitiously "support" his fallacious assumptions. The paranoid patient, whose belief system automatically precludes corrective external feedback, provides a familiar illustration. By insulating himself in a closed personal theory of reality, he effectively sacrifices an invaluable learning source. Maladaptive mediational processes—in such forms as classification errors, comparator dysfunctions, retention deficiencies, and unwarranted inference—may perpetuate an enduringly painful pattern of maladjustment. Their modification presents a therapeutic challenge of considerable dimension.

RESPONSE REPERTOIRE FEATURES

The adequacy of attentional and relational processes does not insure adaptive performance. The individual must also be capable of exhibiting the requisite responses in a given situation. If this response repertoire is deficient, his performance will necessarily be inadequate. Response deficiencies may be a result of physiological limitations, insufficient learning, poor retention, or inappropriate response utilization. Using the analogy of retrieval processes in human memory, one might speculate that the immediate response options in a given situation are influenced by search, storage, and retrieval operations. We select, execute, and evaluate various action "plans" (Miller, Galanter, & Pribram, 1960). There is a growing consensus that we draw upon generalized performance *strategies* in performance rather than upon discrete and isolated units (Estes, 1971). If a response strategy is in our repertoire but is not utilized, inadequate performance is still exhibited.

Our previous discussion of retentional deficits and encoding operations has already offered some evidence on the importance of repertoire features in adjustment. Inadequacies may also result from the failure to integrate component skills in adaptive fashions. A colleague recently related an unsuccessful case history which emphasizes the importance of repertoire considerations in behavior modification (Sirota, 1974). Despite commendable operationalization and procedural specification, the report has yet to be accepted for publication. It involved the operant reinforcement of flying in a 9-year-old, 87 pound boy. Flying was defined as elevation off of a horizontal plane by at least 12 centimeters for a minimum of ten seconds. Having employed sampling procedures to identify a reinforcer, raisins were ultimately selected. Following 14 one hour sessions in which successive approximations to arm-flapping behavior were reinforced, no observable learning had occurred. These negative results were interpreted as reflecting a poor choice of reinforcers, although repertoire limitations offer an alternative explanatory candidate.

Recent research in the area of problem solving has lent ample support to the notion that repertoire deficiencies often characterize maladjustment (Spivack & Shure, 1974). Extensive investigations with emotionally disturbed children, delinquents, and psychiatric patients have shown that these individuals often lack the skills necessary for the generation of appropriate problem solving options. For example, Shure and Spivack (1972) found that children classified as "maladjusted" were inferior in both the number and diversity of their suggested solutions to a social conflict. Their resolutions were marked by impulsive and aggressive features. As we shall see in Chapter 11, systematic training in problem solving skills can produce dramatic improvement in response repertoires. The modeling therapies have likewise shown impressive clinical promise in expanding clients' performance options (Bandura, 1969, 1971a,b,c,d).

Since the next two chapters will be predominantly concerned with repertoire-enhancing therapeutic strategies, a detailed treatment of this topic will be deferred. For the present, suffice it to say that our "behavioral blueprints" tremendously affect adaptation capacities.

EXPERIENTIAL FEEDBACK

Until now we have talked about three possible foci of performance variance—attentional factors, relational processes, and response repertoire features. A final candidate is experiential feedback. Motivational factors cannot be excluded from a comprehensive analysis of human action. While their role in learning has been repeatedly disputed, their contribution to performance is seldom questioned.

In many ways, the history of behavior modification research is a history of experiential feedback. Disproportionate emphasis has been placed on the role of consequences in human behavior, sometimes to the virtual exclusion of other factors. I shall not long belabor a point which is already documented *ad absurdum*—that behavior is influenced by its consequences. However, the different kinds of consequences bear brief mention.

Most behavioral research has dealt with tangible incentives which are externally administered. Tokens and food have been the most common examples. Motivational influences can also be exerted by vicarious learning—i.e., the observed receipt of consequences by others (Bandura, 1971a,b). A third significant source of experiential feedback is self-generated. That is, we often supply our own evaluative consequences. Self-presented incentives may be either tangible or symbolic and their effects appear to be similar to those of externally applied incentives (Thoresen & Mahoney, 1974).

A consequence, of course, cannot work "backward" on behavior. Its impact—if it has one—can only accrue to future actions. The processes of this "futuristic causation" are usually overlooked by the radical behaviorist, and with good reason. A past event cannot exert influence on a future event *unless* the two are deterministically connected (this premise admittedly invokes some causal assumptions which have occupied philosophers for several centuries—cf. Hook, 1958). That is, we cannot contend that the rat's receipt of reinforcement 72 hours ago has influenced his current behavior unless we posit some form of experiential retention. Either the rat or his environment has changed. The rat, you say? We are then left with the potential processes of change in the rat. Presumably, at least some of those changes have occurred in his nervous system. Now then, moving back to his not-so-hairy relative, the man, let us concur in the defensible inference that many of those changes involve the central nervous system (Bandura, 1969). Based on the foregoing comments and a virtual plethora of both laboratory and phenomenological evidence, it is a short step to the contention that past consequences influence future behavior through a neurochemically based mechanism called "anticipation" (Bolles, 1972). While the neurology of that pattern has yet to reveal itself, its phenomenology and pervasiveness are readily ascertained.

This topic raises the intriguing issue of mediational contiguity in learning. We respond to experiential regularities which are more symbolic than real. Thus, the actual contiguity of events may be far less important in learning than their perceived relationship. In administering delayed consequences to a child, for example, symbolic reinstatement of the targeted behavior and/or the contingency may be sufficient to effect learning. Blackwood (1970) has shown that children in a token economy who are trained to mediate (covertly verbalize) performance contingencies demonstrate greater responsiveness than untrained children. Many formalized religions invoke a type of "retrospective conditioning" in much the same manner. Following the occurrence of affectively pleasant or unpleasant events, we are told that they constituted supernaturally mediated consequences for our past deeds (or misdeeds).

Experiential feedback, then, constitutes a transitional feature in complex human performance. It plugs into our metaphorical computer as a source of information on the probable consequences of various actions in specific situations. As we shall see in our discussion of the cognitive therapies, the pervasiveness of symbolic self-evaluation in human behavior emphasizes the role of mediational events in both dysfunctional and adaptive performance. Meichenbaum (1974a) reminds us of Shaffer's (1947) definition of therapy as a "learning process through which a person acquires an ability to speak to himself in appropriate ways so as to control his own conduct (p. 463)."

The present chapter has presented an admittedly tentative attempt to integrate several converging perspectives into a cognitive learning model. That model is characterized by a heavy emphasis on mediational processes in complex human behaviors. Four foci of performance variance were suggested: (1) attentional factors, (2) relational processes, (3) response repertoire features, and (4) experiential feedback. A pervasive assumption in the model is the premise that input-output variabilities are moderated by intervening mediational processes which can be operationally specified and empirically examined.

The adequacy of the cognitive learning model is still under evaluation. Because of its recency and the heterogeneity of contributing perspectives, a definitive and monolithic evaluation is both premature and extremely difficult. As the present chapter will readily attest, the "model" is yet evolving. Formal "systems" criteria (cf. Chapter 5) are a long way off. We can at the present time, however, offer some preliminary generalizations.

At the conceptual level, the cognitive learning model offers both horizontal and vertical structure. It invokes both sequential and hierarchialized patterns in human behavior, and suggests incremental organizational complexities in performance. Like its conceptual sibling and partial progenitor, the information processing model, it relies extensively on metaphorical terminology borrowed from the disciplines of cybernetics and computer science. It is likewise highly inferential and addresses an ambitiously broad range of behavioral phenomena. In place of the molecular and discrete stimulus-response units of the covert conditioning perspective, the cognitive learning model posits complex molar sequences and organized response "processes." Its most striking theoretical assumption proposes that behavior-environment relationships are pervasively influenced by inferred mediational events. While it does not explicitly adopt an assumption of continuity between the principles describing overt and covert behavior, it does invoke the premise of orderly relationships (i.e., determinism) in cognitive-symbolic processes. One noteworthy aspect of the cognitive learning perspective is its attempt to integrate interdisciplinary knowledge. Evidence is drawn from the fields of physiology, anthropology, sociology, philosophy, and epistemology.

The conceptual adequacy of the cognitive learning model can be more definitively evaluated only after its maturation. While its conceptual embryonics are currently optimistic, a reasoned systems evaluation must await its elaboration and refinement. The empirical adequacy of the model, however, has already begun to receive scrutiny. Some of this research has been reviewed by way of illustrating the model. The next two chapters will be devoted to detailed evaluations of the clinical and experimental evidence bearing on the cognitive learning model.

Chapter Eleven

The Cognitive Therapies: Cognitive Restructuring and Self-Instruction

The therapy procedures which will be discussed in the present and subsequent chapter share a common emphasis on the role of cognitive behavior change in therapeutic improvement. It should be kept in mind, however, that their development has been largely independent. Likewise, although they are compatible with and partially responsible for the cognitive learning model, none of them derive historically from that perspective. The model is itself an attempted integration of recent trends represented by such developments as the cognitive therapies. Finally, we should bear in mind the distinction between the conceptual adequacy of a model and the empirical adequacy of a therapeutic procedure. The latter may have direct bearing on the former, particularly when a straightforward derivation has been made. That is, if the model has suggested a procedure as one of its empirical reference points, then the effectiveness of that procedure has direct implications for the empirical adequacy of the model. However, the conceptual inadequacy of a model has no necessary bearing on the utility of its associated procedures. While we can make judgments about a theory based on the effectiveness of its clinical derivatives, we cannot evaluate the latter solely on the basis of theoretical criteria. A model stands, staggers, or falls depending on the ebb and flow of relevant data. The "data," of course, are not independent of the model, but the model must remain subservient to experience. In short, while the efficacy of the various cognitive therapies has relevance for the adequacy of the cognitive learning model, their individual clinical utility rests solely on their own respective merits (i.e., data)—not the final status of the model

COGNITIVE RESTRUCTURING

In terms of both historical precedents and popular adoption, the rationale and procedures of Albert Ellis merit our extended consideration. Their presentation is likewise warranted by the recent expansion of efforts to integrate that perspective into behavior therapy (cf. Ellis, 1969, 1973a; Beck, 1970a; Lazarus, 1971; Meichenbaum, 1972a; Rimm & Masters, 1974; Goldfried, Decenteceo, & Weinberg, 1974). While these efforts have not gone unchallenged (cf. Bergin, 1970; Ullmann, 1970; Nawas, 1970), their continued acceleration is noteworthy.

Ellis's "rational-emotive psychotherapy" takes as its major premise a contention which can be traced as far back as the stoic philosopher Epictetus (60 A.D.): "Men are disturbed not by things, but by the views they take of them." Maladaptive feelings result from maladaptive thoughts. The conceptual framework and philosophical flavor of Ellis's perspective is well illustrated in his 1970 summary, which is here reprinted:

> Rational-emotive psychotherapy is a comprehensive approach to psychological treatment that deals not only with the emotional and behavioral aspects of human disturbance, but places a great deal of stress on its thinking component. Human beings are exceptionally complex, and there neither seems to be any simple way in which they become "emotionally disturbed," nor is there a single way in which they can be helped to be less self-defeating. Their psychological problems arise from their misperceptions and mistaken cognitions about what they perceive; from their emotional underreactions or overreactions to normal and unusual stimuli; and from their habitually dysfunctional behavior patterns, which enable them to keep repeating nonadjustive responses even when they know that they are behaving poorly.
>
> PHILOSOPHICAL CONDITIONING
>
> Rational-emotive therapy is based on the assumption that what we label our "emotional" reactions are caused by our conscious and unconscious evaluations, interpretations, and philosophies. Thus, we feel anxious or depressed because we strongly convince ourselves that it is terrible when we fail at something or that we can't stand the pain of being rejected. We feel hostile because we vigorously believe that people who behave unfairly to us absolutely *should not* be the way they indubitably are, and that it is utterly insufferable when they frustrate us.
>
> Like stoicism, a school of philosophy which existed some two thousand years ago, rational-emotive therapy holds that there are virtually *no* legitimate reasons why human beings need make themselves terribly upset, hysterical, or emotionally disturbed, no matter what kind of negative stimuli are impinging on them. It gives them full leeway to feel strong emotions, such as sorrow, regret, displeasure, annoyance, rebellion, and determination to change social conditions. It believes, however, that when they experience certain

self-defeating and inappropriate emotions (such as guilt, depression, anxiety, worthlessness, or rage), they are almost invariably adding an unverifiable hypothesis to their empirically-based view that their own acts or those of others are reprehensible or inefficient and that something would better be done about changing them

The rational-emotive therapist—often within the first session or two of seeing a client—can almost always put his finger on a few central irrational philosophies of life which this client is vehemently propounding to himself. He can show the client how these ideas inevitably lead to his emotional problems and hence to his presenting clinical symptoms, can demonstrate exactly how the client can forthrightly question and challenge these ideas, and can often induce him to work to uproot them and to replace them with scientifically testable hypotheses about himself and the world which are not likely to get him into future emotional difficulties.

12 IRRATIONAL IDEAS THAT CAUSE AND SUSTAIN EMOTIONAL DISTURBANCE

Rational therapy holds that certain core irrational ideas, which have been clinically observed, are at the root of most emotional disturbance. They are:

(1) **The idea that it is a dire necessity for an adult to be loved by everyone for everything he does**—instead of his concentrating on his own self-respect, on winning approval for practical purposes, and on loving rather than being loved.

(2) **The idea that certain acts are awful or wicked, and that people who perform such acts should be severely punished**—instead of the idea that certain acts are inappropriate or antisocial, and that people who perform such acts are *behaving* stupidly, ignorantly or neurotically and would be better helped to change.

(3) **The idea that it is horrible when things are not the way one would like them to be**—instead of the idea that it is too bad, that one would better try to change or control conditions so that they become more satisfactory, and, if that is not possible, one had better temporarily accept their existence.

(4) **The idea that human misery is externally caused and is forced on one by outside people and events**—instead of the idea that emotional disturbance is caused by the *view* one takes of conditions.

(5) **The idea that if something is or may be dangerous or fearsome one should be terribly upset about it**—instead of the idea that one would better frankly face it and render it non-dangerous and, when that is not possible, accept the inevitable.

(6) **The idea that it is easier to avoid than to face life difficulties and self-responsibilities**—instead of the idea that the so-called easy way is invariably the much harder in the long run.

(7) **The idea that one needs something other or stronger or greater**

than oneself on which to rely—instead of the idea that it is better to take the risks of thinking and acting independently.

(8) **The idea that one should be thoroughly competent, intelligent, and achieving in all possible respects**—instead of the idea that one would better *do* rather than always need to do *well* and accept oneself as a quite imperfect creature, who has general human limitations and specific fallibilities.

(9) **The idea that because something once strongly affected one's life, it should indefinitely affect it**—instead of the idea that one can learn from one's past experiences but not be overly-attached to or prejudiced by them.

(10) **The idea that one must have certain and perfect control over things**—instead of the idea that the world is full of probability and chance and that one can still enjoy life despite this.

(11) **The idea that human happiness can be achieved by inertia and inaction**—instead of the idea that humans tend to be happiest when they are vitally absorbed in creative pursuits, or when they are devoting themselves to people or projects outside themselves.

(12) **The idea that one has virtually no control over one's emotions and that one cannot help feeling certain things**—instead of the idea that one has enormous control over one's destructive emotions if one chooses to work at changing the bigoted and unscientific hypotheses which one employs to create them.

MAIN DIFFERENCES FROM OTHER SCHOOLS

1. **De-emphasis of early childhood.** While RET accepts the fact that neurotic states are often *originally* learned or aggravated by early inculcation of irrational beliefs by one's family and by society, it holds that these early-acquired irrationalities are *not* automatically sustained over the years by mere lack of counter-propagandization, but that they instead are very actively and creatively re-instilled by the individual himself. In many cases the therapist spends very little time on the client's parents or family upbringing; and yet helps him to bring about significant and permanent changes in his disturbed patterns of living. The therapist demonstrates that no matter what the client's basic irrational philosophy of life is, nor when and how he acquired it, he is presently disturbed because he *still* believes this self-defeating world- and self-view; and if he will observe exactly what he is telling or signalling himself in the present, and will challenge and question these self-verbalizations, he will usually improve significantly.

2. **Emphasis on deep philosophical change and scientific thinking.** Because of its belief that human emotional disturbance is essentially ideologically or philosophically based, RET strives for a thoroughgoing philosophic reorientation of a person's outlook on life, rather than for a mere removal of any of his mental or psychosomatic

symptoms. It teaches the client, for example, that human adults do not *need* to be accepted or loved, even though it is highly *desirable* that they be. RET encourages the individual to be appropriately sad or regretful when he is rejected, frustrated, or deprived; but it tries to teach him how to overcome feelings of intense hurt, self-deprecation, and depression. As in science, a client is shown how to question the dubious hypotheses that he constructs about himself and others. If he believes (as alas, millions of us do), that he is a worthless person because he performs certain acts badly, he is not merely taught to ask, "What is really bad about my acts?" and "Where is the evidence that they are wrong or unethical?" More importantly, he is shown how to ask himself, "Granted that my acts may be mistaken, why am I a totally bad person for performing them? Where is the evidence that I must always be right in order to consider myself worthy? Assuming that it is preferable for me to act well rather than badly, why do I *have* to do what is preferable?"

Similarly, when an individual perceives (let us suppose, correctly) the erroneous and unjust acts of others, and becomes enraged at these others, he is taught by the rational-emotive therapist to stop and ask himself, "Why is my hypothesis that the people who committed these errors and injustices are no damned good a true hypothesis? Granted that it would be better if they acted more competently or fairly, why *should* they have to do what would be better?" RET teaches that to be human is to be fallible, and that if we are to get on in life with minimal upset and discomfort, we would better accept this reality—and then unanxiously work hard to become a little less fallible.

3. **Use of psychological homework.** RET agrees with most Freudian, neo-Freudian, Adlerian, and Jungian schools that acquiring insight, especially so-called emotional insight, into the source of his disturbances is a most important part of corrective teaching. It distinguishes sharply, however, between so-called intellectual and emotional insight, and operationally defines emotional insight as the individual's knowing or seeing the cause of his problems and *working,* in a determined and energetic manner, to apply this knowledge to the solution of these problems. The rational-emotive therapist gets the client to acknowledge that there is no other way for him to get better but by *his* continually observing, questioning, and challenging his own belief-systems, and by *his* working and practicing, to change his own irrational beliefs by verbal and behavioral counter-propagandizing *activity.* In RET, actual homework assignments are frequently given to individual and group therapy clients: assignments such as dating a girl whom the client is afraid to ask for a date; looking for a new job; experimentally returning to live with a husband with whom one has previously continually quarrelled; etc. The therapist quite actively tries to persuade, cajole, and to undertake such assignments as an integral part of the therapeutic process. (Reprinted with permission from Ellis, 1970.)

The irrational beliefs posited by Ellis have undergone some revision and expansion since their initial development (cf. Ellis & Harper, 1961; Ellis, 1962). However, the basic contention that "I think, therefore I feel" has remained unaltered.

To supplement Ellis's rather straightforward presentation of his theoretical assumptions, several recent workers have outlined some broad categories of dysfunctional thought. Beck (1970a), for example, suggests four common distortions in the thought patterns of distraught clients. *Arbitrary inference* involves "drawing a conclusion when evidence is lacking or is actually contrary to the conclusion." An example would be the individual who interprets an unreciprocated letter as evidence of personal rejection. *Overgeneralization* occurs when a single incident generates a general rule. Thus, failing in one heterosexual relationship implies total social incompetence. The tendency to exaggerate the meaning of an event is called *magnification* and is similar to Ellis's "catastrophizing." In the health-conscious 40-year-old male, indigestion, numbness, and shortness of breath are quickly interpreted as omens of imminent cardiac arrest. As humorously illustrated by Redd Foxx in the television series *Sanford and Son,* virtually every deviation from routine sensation is dramatized as the "big one." According to Beck, *cognitive deficiency* involves "disregard for an important aspect of a life situation." Individuals with this deficiency fail to attend, integrate, or utilize relevant experiential information.

In addition to suggesting some original cognitive retraining strategies, Lazarus (1971) adds the categories of *dichotomous reasoning* and *oversocialization* to the above mediational dysfunctions. In dichotomous reasoning, the individual allows only two possible evaluations of an event—good/bad, right/wrong, etc. Rather than recognizing the continuum of confidence which is probably more appropriate for personal beliefs, the dichotomous thinker forces evaluations into discrete and separate classes. Oversocialization is often reflected in the failure to recognize and challenge the arbitrariness of many cultural mores. For example, the logical bases of prohibitions against masturbation, extra-marital sex, and suicide are seldom examined.

It should be noted that Ellis's theory and the above classification schema relate to several of the mediational dysfunctions discussed in the last chapter. Selective inattention, inaccurate anticipation of consequences, and logical errors are prevalent elements. Performance inadequacies and subjective distress are viewed as resulting from deficiencies in information processing. The world is either misperceived or misinterpreted.

The procedures involved in the therapeutic improvement of mediational processes have been variously termed "cognitive restructuring," "rational-emotive therapy (RET)," and "rational re-evaluation." Their essence is symbolized as an **A-B-C-D-E** sequence (Ellis, 1971). **A** refers to an objective experiential event (e.g., receiving a failing grade on an examination). **B** symbolizes the self-statements which follow that event (e.g., "This is horrible! I'm going to flunk this goddam course and get kicked out of school; then everybody will know how stupid I am."). The negative emotions generated by these thoughts are represented by **C**. In phase **D**, the cognitive therapist exerts his impact on the future probability of **B** responses. Specifically, he provides systematic training in their discrimination, evaluation, and therapeutic alteration. In our current illustration, this might involve discussions of logical errors (flunking one examination does not necessarily imply failure of the course; failure of a course does not invariably result in dismissal from school; and dismissal from school does not logically justify the inference of stupidity). It would probably also address some of the implicit premises in the client's self-statements (e.g., that competence in school is a necessary condition for feeling good about oneself and that other people's opinions are crucial in personal happiness). The beneficial effects of this cognitive restructuring are symbolized by phase **E**.

A relevant tangent here is the use of mnemonic aids in the client's acquisition and naturalistic utilization of cognitive restructuring skills. In my own clinical experimentation with this strategy, I have used mnemonic labels such as **Adapt** to cue and assist implementation of the sequence. Each of the letters in the word **Adapt** represents a cognitive performance element:

A *Acknowledge* the sensation of distress (anxiety, depression, anger),
D *Discriminate* the private events (both thoughts and images) which have just occurred (i.e., do a "covert instant replay"),
A *Assess* the logical bases and adaptive functions of your images and self-statements,
P *Present* alternatives (i.e., generate private monologues or imagery of more appropriate, coping content) and then
T *Think* praise (!) (i.e., reward yourself for having executed the entire sequence).

An illustrative therapist-client interchange in cognitive restructuring is presented below:

CLIENT: I got really depressed on Wednesday night—almost called you but I felt too bad to even do that.

THERAPIST: Did you remember to use any of the "cognitive" skills we have been talking about in the last few sessions?

CLIENT: You mean the ADAPT stuff? Yeah, I tried it but couldn't seem to figure out what was bothering me. You know, it just seemed like everything was shitty.

THERAPIST: Had anything happened earlier in the day that made you feel bad?

CLIENT: Nope . . . it was one of my routine crappy days. Two classes in the morning, bussing trays at the cafeteria all afternoon, and a boring evening of television and books. I called the Self-Report Service[a] at about 11:30 and turned in before midnight.

THERAPIST: Yes, I listened to your self-monitoring messages just before coming in here. It seems to me that you had said something about Sally being over Wednesday night . . .?

CLIENT: Oh, yeah, she came over. We watched *All in the Family* and listened to a couple of albums.

THERAPIST: Is that it? No arguments? discussions? sex?

CLIENT: Yeah, we balled a little.

THERAPIST: What does "a little" refer to?

CLIENT: Well, it was pretty short. I mean I had studying to do and she had to get going.

THERAPIST: When did you first notice that you were depressed?

CLIENT: Um . . . let's see . . . I'd been kind of mellow all day; not high or low . . . until the evening.

THERAPIST: Before or after Sally?

CLIENT: I see what you're getting at. Yeah, it was after she left. We had made love and then she had to go right away to catch her bus. But why would that make me depressed? Balling is a high.

THERAPIST: You had no problems or disappointments in making love? Both of you enjoyed it and felt good afterward?

CLIENT: Well, like I said, it was brief. I had to come pretty quick, even though I could have waited.

THERAPIST: Did Sally enjoy it?

CLIENT: I don't know . . . I guess so. She didn't say much before she left.

THERAPIST: And did that bother you . . . the fact that she didn't say much?

CLIENT: Well, kind of. I was a little worried about whether I had done okay . . . you know. It wasn't as if I didn't want her to feel good or couldn't have held off my climax until she came.

THERAPIST: You say you "worried" about it . . . Give me some specifics. What do you mean?

[a] An automated phone answering device which allows clients to call in self-monitoring data on a twenty-four hour basis. The therapist can review these reports at his convenience.

CLIENT: Well, I thought about it a lot. Couldn't get back to the books. I kept . . . Hey! I see what you're getting at! I *was* saying a lot of negative things to myself! Like "Jesus, she is going to think I'm a premature ejaculator or a 'slam-bam' baller—somebody who just wants to get their rocks off and doesn't care about how she feels."

THERAPIST: Good . . . you're getting pretty "insightful." Now let's see how well you've done your cognitive homework. Give me a brief summary of what happened and why you may have felt depressed.

CLIENT: Well, Sally is usually pretty expressive. You know, telling me that I made her happy and that she enjoyed it. I initiated sex and she reminded me that we only had a little time before her bus arrived. We "had at it" . . . very little foreplay . . . I came, we washed up, and she left. Then I started feeling kind of bad; worried about whether Sally had enjoyed it and what she was thinking of me. I gave myself hell for being a horny klutz who couldn't wait until we had more time for love-making.

THERAPIST: Excellent! Now that we have some of the facts on what probably made you depressed, let's look at whether or not you *should* have felt bad. Is occasionally being a "horny klutz" grounds for feeling totally wiped out? Should your sexual performance be an absolute standard for self-acceptance?

The diversity and clinical flavor of cognitive restructuring strategies are difficult to convey in brief session excerpts. Ellis's extensive descriptions are illustrative (cf. Ellis, 1962, 1971, 1973b). Rimm and Masters (1974) also offer some exemplary cases. As indicated in the previous material from Ellis (1970), heavy emphasis is placed on Socratic dialogue and logical self-examination.

Although Ellis's therapeutic procedures have been existent and professionally "visible" for well over a decade, there is a sparsity of controlled experimental data bearing on their effects. Research interest has accelerated in the last few years, however, and we are now in a position to offer some preliminary empirical evaluations. First, the data.

To begin with, there is an extensive body of evidence supporting the contention that symbolic events may play a significant role in behavioral disorders (cf. Chapters 4 and 6). Not only can thoughts and images induce painful physiological distress, but mediational deficiencies can generate and maintain maladaptive performance patterns (cf. Chapters 9 and 10). Illustrative of this evidence is a study by Rimm and

Litvak (1969) which was specifically directed toward an evaluation of Ellis's contentions. These researchers found that negative self-statements induced substantial physiological arousal. Their analysis also pursued an interesting sub-issue in rational-emotive theory. Ellis's (1962) model suggests a quasi-deductive sequence in emotional self-arousal:

(A) observed event	People often ignore me
(B) inference	I must be ugly or uninteresting
(C) self-evaluative conclusion	How terrible!

Rimm and Litvak (1969) presented their subjects with sentence triads in the above format and found no differences in emotional responsiveness to the three components. A replication and interpretation of this finding has been recently reported by Russell and Brandsma (1974) in a study which offers additional physiological data on symbolic self-arousal.

Further supportive evidence on the role of mediational deficiencies in clinical disorders is far from lacking. Our discussion of cognitive contingencies has already documented the pervasiveness of inaccurate beliefs in behavior pathology. Additional support is provided by recent findings on the role of dichotomous thinking in certain maladaptive behavior patterns (e.g., Plummer & Das, 1973). Finally, the extensive case illustrations provided by Beck (1970a, b, 1971, 1972a; Beck, Laude, & Bohnert, 1974), Lazarus (1971), and Ellis (1962, 1971) provide suggestive support. While some efforts have been made to develop quantifiable means for assessing "irrational" beliefs, few of these have related their assessment to observed clinical dysfunction (cf. Zingle, 1965; Gustav, 1968; Hartman, 1968; Argabrite & Nidorf, 1968; Jones, 1969; Fox & Davies, 1971; MacDonald & Games, 1972; Trexler & Karst, 1973; Goodman & Maultsby, 1974).

Our primary evaluative focus, of course, lies with the documented effectiveness of cognitive restructuring in the treatment of behavior disorders. First, there is a plethora of successful case studies. In addition to those offered by Ellis (1957, 1962, 1971), numerous case reports from other clinical researchers have suggested therapeutic improvement following rational-emotive therapy (cf. Davison, 1966; Beck, 1970a, b, 1974; Beck & Greenberg, in press: Rosenthal & Meyer, 1971; Maultsby, 1971b; Watts, Powell, & Austin, 1973; Goodman & Maultsby, 1974). While most of these reports have involved relatively uncontrolled methodologies (poorly specified procedures, inadequate assessment, etc.), their converging optimism should be borne in mind. Once again, although a poorly controlled case study may offer more modest "empirical returns" than its more rigorous siblings, its possible contribution to our incremental confidence should not be overlooked.

Group studies involving cognitive restructuring have also offered some data on its clinical efficacy. Several have unfortunately limited their empirical contribution because of methodological inadequacies. McClellan and Stieper (1973), for example, combined rational-emotive therapy with psychodrama and failed to employ a control group. Ellis's (1957) comparison of psychoanalysis and RET suffered not only from possible assessment biases but also temporal and sampling errors (172 clients were spread across several years with psychoanalysis being received by earlier clients and—as Ellis's theoretical model matured—later clients receiving RET).

Baker (1966) evaluated the effects of cognitive restructuring on the self-statements of 105 University of Illinois undergraduates. Five groups were employed: (1) cognitive restructuring ("verbal instructions using reason and information processing"), (2) reinforcement, (3) cognitive restructuring plus reinforcement, (4) cognitive restructuring plus an immediate post-test, and (5) control (non-contingent reinforcement). Positive self-references during an interview constituted the dependent variable. The results indicated significant increases on the part of subjects who received cognitive restructuring. Operant reinforcement did not significantly accelerate the emission of positive self-reference statements. However, data from several psychometric tests suggested that generalization of cognitive restructuring effects may have been enhanced by the addition of reinforcement.

The impact of cognitive restructuring on test anxiety was evaluated in a study summarized by Rimm and Masters (1974):

> Maes and Heimann (1970) compared the effectiveness of RET, client-centered therapy, and systematic desensitization with test-anxious high school students. Treatments were administered during 10 training sessions covering a 5-week period. Response measures included an anxiety self-report, heart rate, and galvanic skin response. Following treatment, the subject was required to imagine he was about to take an examination, at which time the anxiety inventory was administered. Following this, he was given a concept-mastery test (described as an intelligence test), and as he responded, physiological measures were taken. Although the anxiety inventory failed to distinguish among the treatment groups, for both physiological measures, desensitization and RET subjects showed significantly less emotional reactivity than either the client-centered subjects, or subjects in a fourth, nontreated control group. No follow-up was reported (p. 427).

In a laboratory analogue study, Burkhead (1970) exposed subjects to the threat of shock and compared the stress-reducing effects of live RET (a therapist was present), taped adaptive RET (in which an attempt was made to challenge and modify stress-relevant irrational beliefs), taped maladaptive RET ("designed to reinforce subjects' irrational beliefs"), and a no-treatment control group. Both physiological and subjective measures of arousal showed the two therapeutic groups (live and adaptive RET) to effect significantly greater anxiety reductions. Subjects receiving maladaptive RET reported increases in anxiety.

A preliminary study by Karst and Trexler (1970) compared the effects of RET, Kelly's (1955) "fixed role therapy," and a no-treatment condition in the alleviation of speech anxieties. The dependent variables were five self-report and two behavioral measures. Unfortunately, adequate inter-observer reliabilities were obtained with only one of the behavioral measures (a Speech Disruptions Checklist). Post-treatment data analyses indicated no group differences on this behavioral measure. Three of the five self-report measures showed both therapies to be superior to no-treatment, and a fourth approached significance. At a six month follow-up, 80% of the contacted experimental subjects reported their speech anxiety to be "much" or "somewhat" less than it had been prior to treatment. The omission of an attention-placebo group in this study was remedied in a subsequent partial replication (Trexler & Karst, 1972). In this second study, speech anxious subjects received either RET, an attention-placebo procedure (relaxation training), or no treatment. Three behavioral measures revealed no inter-group differences, two self-report measures favored RET over the other groups, and a subjective anxiety rating found relaxation training to be significantly more effective than RET. Following this assessment, the relaxation and control groups were given RET training and a third measurement battery was performed. Pairs of groups were statistically collapsed on this third assessment and compared to the remaining group's performance during the second assessment. While these analyses tended to favor RET over the other two procedures, their interpretation must take into account the resulting differences in time and intervening practice. A repeated-measures analysis of all subjects' improvements from pre-treatment to post-RET-treatment indicated significant progress on all measures. The absence of an untreated comparison group, however, again limits the conclusions which are warranted.

Comparable findings were reported in a study by Montgomery (1971) dealing with test anxiety. Individuals who received systematic desensitization, implosive therapy, or cognitive restructuring reported less anxiety following therapy than did no-treatment controls. Three paper-and-pencil measures of anxiety failed to discriminate the groups, although systematic desensitization did demonstrate significant superiority on a fourth assessment tool (an Achievement Anxiety Test). The poor correspondence between self-report and behavioral indices of anxiety again allows little clinical inference from these results.

DiLoreto (1971) assigned 100 volunteer subjects to five experimental groups: (1) systematic desensitization, (2) client-centered therapy, (3) rational-emotive therapy, (4) attention-placebo, and (5) no contact control. Self-report measures and therapists' ratings of interpersonal anxiety constituted the dependent variables. All three treatment groups were significantly more successful than the two control groups, with systematic desensitization effecting greater anxiety reduction and rational-emotive therapy producing larger increases in interpersonal activity. Some of the outcome variance was apparently related to a counselor effect. The clinical significance of this study is limited, however, by the absence of direct performance measurements.

A study by D'Zurilla, Wilson, and Nelson (1973) employed a procedure labeled "cognitive restructuring" to control for "nonspecific factors" in two formal experimental groups (systematic desensitization and graduated prolonged exposure). A no-treatment control group was also employed. In this study, cognitive restructuring involved a "perceptual relearning" and relabeling of the fearful situation (rat phobia). Subjects were given theoretical explanations for their fear (conditioning, avoidance learning, vicarious processes, cognitive labeling, and perceptual learning). They were encouraged to perceive and modify the irrational bases of their own fears. While this therapeutic strategy was similar but not equivalent to "orthodox" rational-emotive therapy, its effects bear consideration. On a behavioral approach measure, only the graduated prolonged exposure group effected significant reductions in avoidance. However, the cognitive procedure resulted in improvements which approached significance ($p < .10$), while the systematic desensitization group did not differ from no-treatment controls. Interestingly, on a self-report measure of anxiety, only the cognitive group demonstrated significant improvements over control procedures.

One final source of clinical data is an article by Goldfried, Decenteceo, & Weinberg (1974) whose main purpose was to integrate rational-emotive therapy into a learning framework. In offering justification for that integration, the authors cite evidence from four speech-anxious subjects who were given training in cognitive restructuring. Despite treatment brevity and this very small sample, questionnaire responses indicated significant reductions in self-reported speech anxiety. Data from a controlled study in progress further suggested that cognitive restructuring was significantly more effective than an imaginal exposure group. While admittedly preliminary, these findings are interpreted by the authors as offering support for the possible clinical promise of cognitive restructuring.

In terms of research on "orthodox" rational-emotive therapy, the foregoing summary has reviewed existing clinical and laboratory investigations. However, as we shall see in the next section, several researchers have employed isolated components from RET (e.g., training in the discrimination and alteration of dysfunctional self-statements). Before examining their effects, some brief evaluative comments on RET are warranted.

First, the experimental research evaluating the efficacy of cognitive restructuring has been sparse, methodologically poor, and summarily modest in its implications. Two studies have employed analogues which placed limitations on their clinical relevance (Baker, 1966; Burkhead, 1970). Three studies have limited their outcome assessments to subjective reports of improvement and paper-and-pencil responses (Montgomery, 1971; DiLoreto, 1971; Goldfried, Decenteceo, & Weinberg, 1974). Finally, in the four studies which have included both self-report and performance measures of improvement, three have suggested that the effects of cognitive restructuring may be most salient in the realm of private phenomenology (subjective distress) rather than task performance (Karst & Trexler, 1970; Trexler & Karst, 1972; D'Zurilla, Wilson, & Nelson, 1973). The fourth (Maes & Heimann, 1970) showed RET effective in the reduction of physiological arousal but less powerful in its impact on subjective distress.

In short, the extent, quality, and findings of the existing experimental work on cognitive restructuring do not warrant an evaluative conclusion. This, of course, means that the clinical efficacy of RET has yet to be adequately demonstrated. Depending on one's own conceptual biases, empirical criteria, and perhaps clinical experience with RET, the foregoing evidence may be viewed as tentatively promising or pessimistic. In either case, we are obliged to suspend a more confident judgment until further data are available.

In addition to empirical evaluation of its clinical impact, several other issues in RET warrant scrutiny. The active components in cognitive restructuring constitute one of those issues. Even a cursory reading of Ellis's therapeutic recommendations suggests the operation of at least the following components:

1. didactic persuasion toward a belief system that emphasizes the role of irrational thoughts in subjective distress and deficient performance; a value system is also communicated—its main premise being that of non-contingent self-acceptance irrespective of performance competencies;

2. training in the discrimination and systematic observation of self-statements;
3. training in the logical and empirical evaluation of self-statements;
4. graduated performance assignments;
5. immediate and often candid social feedback on (a) actual performance progress, (b) standard setting, and (c) the logical and adaptive nature of private monologues (logical inferences, self-evaluations, etc.);
6. explicit instructions and selective reinforcement for the therapeutic alteration of self-statements; and
7. extensive therapist modeling of prescribed mediation styles (via self-disclosure, role-playing, etc.).

As we shall see in the next section, many of these components have also been included in the cognitive strategy labeled "self-instruction." Controlled research on this latter procedure has already begun to isolate the contribution of several components. Before looking at that evidence, however, a few brief comments on some of the philosophical assumptions of orthodox cognitive restructuring are warranted.

An implicit but salient premise in Ellis's (1962, 1970) view of the human organism deals with the role of logic in thought patterns. RET assumes a logical organism. It is suggested that the discovery of "irrationality" in one's self-statements will automatically motivate their alteration. Presumably, this valuation of logical coherence is at least partially learned. However, in his critique of DiLoreto's (1971) study, Ellis contends that the tendency to believe irrational self-statments is probably inborn rather than acquired (p. 215). The social psychology of cognitive consistency and logical belief seriously questions whether we are inherently logical organisms (McGuire, 1960, 1968). While there does seem to be a high frequency of socially influenced organization in our mediational processes, its structure often deviates markedly from formal logical criteria. My own clinical experience has revealed instances in which a client's discovery of irrationality in his self-statements produced either negligible or negative reactions. One individual, for example, said, "Okay, so I'm being illogical. I still *believe* what I am saying to myself." Two other depressed clients interpreted their newly discovered irrationality as further evidence of their incompetence. As I will reiterate at the end of the next section, our future experimental inquiries might profitably address the tentative speculation that Ellis' appeal to logic is but one procedural *means* toward effecting what may be the most critical element in RET—namely, the modification of maladaptive cognitive behaviors.

A second implicit philosophical assumption suggests that

virtually all forms of subjective distress are unreasonable. It is always irrational to be extremely upset. While he acknowledges the individual's freedom to feel regret and dissapointment, Ellis maintains that there are virtually no events which can evoke justifiable fear, panic, or depression. Thus, in his rational analysis of the fear of flying, Ellis (1972) contends that a fear of death is irrational:

> Stop the crap! When you are dead, you're really *dead*. Yes: unliving, unfeeling, unknowing (p. 31).
>
> Take, by way of illustration, your demand that, "I *ought* to live forever and it would be horrible if I didn't." You can challenge this idea logically by asking whether it makes any sense (p. 51).
>
> The logical corollary of "death is horrible" is the conclusion that "therefore I must do every *possible* thing to avoid dying" (p. 53).

Similar arguments are used to challenge the assumption that the death or loss of a loved one ought to induce severe feelings of depression. While our professional values may motivate efforts to reduce such personal distress, an appeal to logical analysis may not be the most powerful strategy. A depressed philosopher might want to offer Ellis some suggestions in the logical analysis of his own premises. There is nothing inherently more logical about personal happiness—it just feels better.

SELF-INSTRUCTION

The role of "private monologues" in emotional experience and performance regulation has been recognized for several centuries. Eastern writings dating back thousands of years stress the role of covert speech in adaptation and growth (e.g., the Vedas, the Bhagavad Gita, etc.). This emphasis has continued into more contemporary strategies of personal self-improvement. The French psychotherapist Émile Coué (1922), for example, popularized the optimistic self-statement, "Day by day, in every way, I am getting better and better." In his formal self-improvement program Pelman (1919) stressed that "Every Thought, especially Thought charged with Feeling tends to become an action (p. 30)." Bain (1928) suggested specific strategies of thought control for the improvement of personal adjustment. Dale Carnegie (1948) offered similar suggestions, and Norman Vincent Peale (1960) described the impressive "power of positive thinking." In a treatise which predated current information-based approaches to clinical disorder, Maxwell Maltz (1960) proffered "psycho-cybernetics" as cognitive therapeutic strategies.

Fifth Avenue, of course, is forbidden territory for the respectable scientist and efforts toward the empirical evaluation of the foregoing thought control procedures have been slow in evolving. It is noteworthy that the clinical researcher shows such alacrity in attacking popularized therapeutic strategies and such stubborn reluctance to subject those strategies to controlled evaluation or to offer the public more effective and empirically supported alternatives. Until very recently, the behavioral scientist was considered almost "tainted" if he addressed himself to the lay public, let alone the trade book market.

As "self-statement" psychologies grew in popularity, laboratory research on "covert speech" continued along its separate path. Much of the early work in this area was dominated by the Russian psychologists Luria (1961, 1963) and Vygotsky (1962). Luria suggested three stages in the internalized control of behavior. The child's performance is first controlled by the verbal instructions and reactions of external agents (e.g., parents). He then begins to regulate some of his own actions through audible self-talk. Finally, these self-statements become covert and expand their extensive regulatory influences.

The role of verbal self-instructions in complex performance gradually became a topic of experimental interest (cf. McGuigan, 1970; Wine, 1971). Sandra L. Bem (1967), for example, showed that 3-year-olds' performance on a number concept task could be appreciably improved via training in covert verbal mediation. O'Leary (1968) similarly showed that self-instruction significantly reduced transgressions in a laboratory analogue to morality training. Replications and refinements with a wide range of subject populations and target behaviors were soon forthcoming (cf. Palkes, Stewart, & Kahana, 1968; Blackwood, 1970; Ridberg, Parke, & Hetherington, 1971; Monahan & O'Leary, 1971; Palkes, Stewart, & Freedman, 1972; Sarason, 1973; Denny, 1972; Hartig & Kanfer, 1973).

Some of the most extensive and clinically impressive work in the area of self-instructional training has been that of Donald Meichenbaum and his colleagues at the University of Waterloo. Several recent reviews summarize their work and survey both collaborative evidence and some of the salient conceptual and clinical issues in this area (cf. Meichenbaum, 1973a; 1974a,b; Meichenbaum & Cameron, 1974). While a detailed presentation of the numerous studies performed by Meichenbaum et al. would consume a volume in itself, their procedures and impressive effectiveness data merit more than cursory review.

Meichenbaum first became interested in the performance effects of self-statements following his (1969) dissertation research on the modification of schizophrenics' "crazy talk." In that study he observed that many of the patients who had been trained to emit "healthy talk" maintained their performance improvements by engaging in overt self-instructions similar to the experimenter's previous directives (e.g., "be coherent," "be relevant"). This observation stimulated several subsequent inquiries into the effects of systematic training in self-instruction. The mediational deficiencies of "impulsive" children became an early focus of this research (cf. Meichenbaum, 1971b; Meichenbaum & Goodman, 1969a, b, 1971). "Impulsivity" describes a response pattern characterized by extremely brief response latencies and a high frequency of errors. Previous research had suggested that a significant factor in this pattern is immature and inadequate private speech. The impulsive child does not appear to have learned how to appropriately direct his attention and guide his performance in many task situations. In a series of well controlled laboratory experiments, Meichenbaum was able to show that the response latency and performance accuracy of impulsive children could be dramatically improved via training in self-instruction. The training sequence involved an abbreviated developmental progression which paralleled some of the probable elements in the "normal" child's internalization of speech:

1. an adult model first performed the task while talking to himself outloud (cognitive modeling);
2. the child then performed the same task under the directions of the model's instructions (overt external guidance);
3. the child next performed the task while instructing himself aloud (overt self-guidance);
4. the child then whispered the instructions to himself as he went through the task (faded overt self-guidance); and finally,
5. the child performed the task while guiding his performance via private speech (covert self-instruction).

In a task which required the copying of line patterns, an example of the modeled self-instructions was:

> "Okay, what is it I have to do? You want me to copy the picture with the different lines. I have to go slow and be careful. Okay, draw the line down, down, good; then to the right, that's it; now down some more and to the left. Good, I'm doing fine so far. Remember, go slow. Now back up again. No, I was supposed to go down. That's okay. Just erase the line carefully . . . . Good. Even if I make an error I can go on slowly and carefully. Okay, I have to go down now. Finished. I did it (Meichenbaum, 1971b, p. 8)."

It should be noted that in his "thinking out loud" the model displays several performance-relevant skills: (a) problem definition ("what is it I have to do?"), (b) focused attention plus response guidance ("be careful . . . . draw the line down"), (c) self-reinforcement ("Good, I'm doing fine . . ."), and (d) self-evaluative coping skills plus error-correcting options ("That's okay . . . . even if I make an error I can go on slowly").

The contribution of several of the above training components was examined in a series of controlled laboratory studies (cf. Meichenbaum, 1971b). In one experiment, for example, it was found that cognitive modeling alone was not as effective as cognitive modeling plus self-instructional training. Children were much more successful when they not only observed a model's verbal self-guidance but also received training in the rehearsal and personal use of similar private speech. Dependent measures ranging from Porteus Maze performance, response latency, covert speech content (egocentric versus instrumental), scores on the Matching Familiar Figures Test, and performance IQ (prorated WISC) revealed consistent and impressive improvements following self-instructional training. These improvements were significantly greater than those obtained in no-treatment and attentional control groups.

The above results stimulated further expansions and refinements of self-instruction procedures. Meichenbaum, Gilmore, and Fedoravicius (1971), for example, developed an "insight-oriented" therapy procedure for the treatment of speech anxious clients. In this strategy, individuals were (a) apprised of the role of self-defeating private monologues in speech anxiety, (b) trained to discriminate and label these maladaptive self-statements, and (c) encouraged to produce more adaptive self-verbalizations. The effects of this self-instructional training were compared to desensitization, desensitization plus self-instruction, attention-placebo, and a no-treatment control group. Two behavioral measures of actual speech performance and four measures of self-reported anxiety were employed. The results indicated that both the desensitization and the self-instruction groups effected significant improvements on behavioral, cognitive, and self-report measures. Although the cognitive training in this study can be procedurally differentiated from that employed in orthodox rational-emotive therapy, their parallels should be kept in mind.

A study on snake avoidance (Meichenbaum, 1971a) evaluated the effects of "coping" versus "mastery" self-instructions. It will be recalled from the Kazdin studies on covert modeling (Chapter 8) that a coping model is one who shows initial anxiety similar to the avoidant observer but gradually copes with his fears and eventually completes the task. A mastery model, on the other hand, is one who is competent and fearless throughout his performance. Previous research on vicarious learning (Bandura, 1969, 1971a) had suggested the possibility that subjects would be more likely to imitate the behaviors of coping models due to their greater similarity to the observer. Meichenbaum's (1971a) study compared the effects of (1) mastery behavior modeling (fearless and unhesitating snake approach without modeled self-verbalizations), (2) mastery behavior modeling plus mastery self-verbalizations, (3) coping behavior modeling (snake approach with marked hesitancy and occasional physical withdrawal), and (4) coping behavior modeling plus coping self-verbalizations (e.g., describing their initial fears, self-instructions to take deep breaths and relax). Both behavioral and self-report measures indicated that exposure to coping models (verbalizing and non-verbalizing) effected significantly greater improvement than observation of mastery models. Moreover, the addition of coping self-instructions dramatically enhanced the effects of exposure to nonverbal coping performances. The coping, self-verbalizing models were most effective in reducing avoidance behavior. The implications of these findings for the "therapist as a model" will be more fully explored in subsequent chapters.

Self-instructional training has likewise been applied to the treatment of test anxiety. Meichenbaum (1972b) compared the effects of desensitization, a modified self-instruction procedure, and no treatment in the alleviation of college students' test anxiety. In this study, self-instructional training was combined with a desensitization procedure which employed coping imagery. Measures of actual test performance, self-reported anxiety, and changes in grade point average revealed that the cognitive training strategy was most effective. Three other studies have likewise reported dramatic reductions in test and speech anxiety following self-instructional training (Wine, 1971; Sarason, 1973; Norman, 1974).

One of the most clinically impressive demonstrations of the effects of this cognitive strategy is presented in an article titled "Training Schizophrenics to Talk to Themselves" (Meichenbaum & Cameron, 1973a). Two studies addressed the impact of self-instructional training on the attention, thought, and language behaviors of institutionalized schizophrenics. The first experiment found that the cognitive training strategy significantly improved schizophrenics' performance on two perceptual tasks (digit symbol substitution and auditory distraction digit recall). A second study evaluated the effects of extended training in self-instruction. The performances of five cognitively trained schizophrenics were compared to those of five yoked practice controls. Assessment was made by an experimenter who was blind to subjects' condition assignments. The results are presented in Figure 11-1. Measures of rater reliability on "sick talk," proverb abstraction, and inkblot responses ranged from 0.82 to 0.91. As illustrated in the figure, cognitive training effected significant improvements on all dependent measures except digit recall in the absence of distraction. Although the two groups

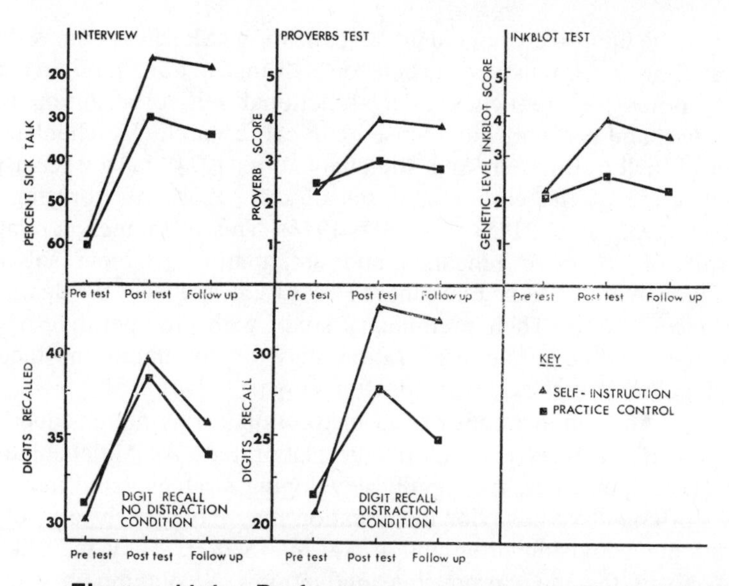

Figure 11-1. Performance measures at pre-treatment, post-treatment, and follow-up assessment. (Reprinted with permission from Meichenbaum & Cameron, 1973a.)

were equivalent prior to treatment, self-instructional training produced significant decreases in "sick talk" during a standardized interview ($p < .005$) and effected improvements in proverb abstraction, rated perceptual integration, and digit recall under distraction conditions. A three week follow-up revealed that improvements in these four areas not only maintained, but actually improved relative to yoked controls. Differences in the frequency of "sick talk" at follow-up, for example, were statistically significant at the .0005 level. Although further inquiries are sorely needed, the above results suggest considerable promise in the application of cognitive training strategies to classical behavior disorders.

Subsequent investigations of self-instructional strategies have taken Meichenbaum and his colleagues into the areas of creativity, anxiety relief, geriatrics, and worrying. In a comprehensive study which measured creativity from several different theoretical perspectives, Meichenbaum (1973b) found that cognitive training effected significant improvements in creative performance (divergent thinking, unusual uses, originality, etc.). An experiment on anxiety relief (Wolpe & Lazarus, 1966) found that snake phobics' rehearsals of both adaptive and avoidant self-statements resulted in significant therapeutic improvements regardless of whether shock offset coincided with emission of either the adaptive or avoidant verbalization (Meichenbaum & Cameron, 1973b). A provocative article on self-instructional training in the elderly notes the frequency of dysfunctional self-verbalization in this population and recommends focused clinical research (Meichenbaum, in press). Finally, Burstein and Meichenbaum (1974) have recently extended some of the earlier analyses of the "work of worrying" (cf. Marmor, 1958; Janis, 1958; Breznitz, 1971). This phenomenon relates to the role of cognitive rehearsal and anticipatory problem solving in individuals who are facing imminent stress (e.g., surgery, the death of an ailing friend, etc.). Their preliminary study with pre-operative children suggested that cognitive preparation may be an important factor in reducing the stress experienced after surgery.

The ramifications of self-instructional training for educational and clinical practices need hardly be elaborated. As Meichenbaum & Turk (1972) point out, the rapidly developing strategies and impressive results of cognitive behavior modification may have much to offer such educational television programs as *Sesame Street*. They may likewise offer one of the most promising innovations in contemporary clinical practice.

The empirical status of self-instructional training offers a much brighter picture than does its partial progenitor, rational-emotive therapy. In addition to the clinically significant results of Meichenbaum's own research, independent replications and refinements corroborate a growing confidence in the internal and external validity of these strategies (e.g., Bem, 1967; O'Leary, 1968; Palkes et al., 1968, 1972; Blackwood, 1970; Ridberg, Parke, & Hetherington, 1971; Denny, 1972; Sarason, 1973; Hartig & Kanfer, 1973). Many of these corroborative studies have restricted their focus to experimental analogues in children. Further replications in the realm of more applied clinical problems are sorely needed. The work of Wine (1970), Sarason (1973), and Norman (1974) has already lent preliminary replicative support in the treatment of test and speech anxiety. Likewise, although they have not isolated the contribution of cognitive training, several studies have apparently included self-instructional variations in successful treatment packages (cf. Tori & Worell, 1973; Mahoney, 1973; Rimm, Saunders, & Westel, 1974).

Empirical analyses of the component features, maintenance, and therapeutic transfer of self-instructional training are also needed. Examination of Meichenbaum's (1974c) "Therapist Manual for Cognitive Behavior Modification" suggests the possible operation of at least the following components:

1. didactic presentation and guided self-discovery of the role of self-statements in subjective distress and performance inadequacies;

2. training in the fundamentals of problem solving (e.g., problem definition, anticipation of consequences);
3. training in the discrimination and systematic observation of self-statements;
4. graduated performance assignments;
5. explicit suggestions and self-reinforcement for the modification of self-statements along the lines of "coping" adaptation and performance-relevant attentional focusing;
6. structured modeling of both overt and cognitive skills;
7. modeling and encouragement of positive self-evaluation (self-reinforcement), and
8. depending on the treatment package employed, relaxation training combined with the use of coping imagery in a modified desensitization procedure.

A comparison of the above itemization with our previous component analysis of Ellis's rational-emotive therapy reveals striking similarities. Both strategies emphasize the role of private monologues in subjective distress and provide training in (and reinforcement for) systematic observation and alteration of dysfunctional thought patterns. In addition to didactic instructions and guided self-discovery, both strategies rely on graduated performance tasks and modeling processes. Their procedual distinctions appear to center around the relative emphasis placed on formal logical analysis (e.g., isolation and evaluation of premises), the concomitant presentation of a value system (unconditional self-acceptance), and the authoritarian directiveness with which the therapeutic rationale and procedures are presented.

As mentioned earlier, an important performance focus in both RET and self-instructional training involves modification of dysfunctional thought patterns. Their respective *means* for effecting this goal, however, vary in emphasis. Ellis relies predominantly on Socratic dialogue and logical self-examination. Meichenbaum, on the other hand, places greater procedural emphasis on graduated tasks, cognitive modeling, and directed mediational training. He likewise encourages self-reinforcement of improvement. The existing evidence on RET is unfortunately both insufficient and inadequate to allow a comparative evaluation between these two approaches. Future inquiries will hopefully examine not only the relative effects of these training strategies, but also their potential combination. My own clinical experience has reinforced an initial preference for Meichenbaum's emphases, with occasional resort to logical examination in clients for whom didactic instructions, graduated tasks, and cognitive modeling have appeared inadequate.

The publication of actual clinical transcripts and operationally defined procedures (e.g., Meichenbaum, 1974c) will undoubtedly assist in our further analysis of the commonalities and differences between RET and self-instructional training. Until then, the rational-emotive model can claim only tentative and indirect support from the rather impressive preliminary research on self-instruction.

In addition to component analyses, the processes involved in self-instructional therapy warrant empirical scrutiny. Is there any clinical utility in distinguishing between imagery-based and verbalization-based mediational therapies? Are those disorders characterized by imagery arousal, for example, better suited to imaginal strategies? Are combinations of auditory, visual, kinesthetic, and other symbolic activities more powerful than unimodal procedures? Recent work in the field of information processing suggests that it may be very difficult to differentiate private events on the basis of sense modality. We must therefore keep in mind that our contemporary terms reflect procedures rather than processes. Moreover, it may be heuristic to remain apprised of the fact that many private phenomena may neither be "conscious" nor restricted to the popular imagery-verbalization dichotomy (cf. Chapters 13–14).

The relationship between Meichenbaum's self-instructional procedures and Kazdin's "covert modeling" strategies (Chapter 8) may offer an exciting avenue for future inquiry. Although the former places more explicit emphasis on covert verbalization and the latter has focused predominantly on visual imagery, their commonalities are apparent. (As mentioned in Chapter 8, I would argue that covert modeling fits more comfortably into a "cognitive" than a "conditioning" paradigm.) Are these two therapeutic strategies based on a common foundation? Although admittedly speculative, it seems reasonable to suggest at this point that both of these operations rely on essentially the same processes in effecting their therapeutic impact. Future comparisons and component analyses will hopefully facilitate our understanding of those processes.

Before closing the present discussion, the differences between self-instructional training and popularized entreaties to "positive thinking" bear consideration. While a detailed differentiation might prove exceedingly lengthy, some general conceptual and procedural discrepancies can be noted. In contrast to the global and often unrealistic "autosuggestions" popularized by several best-sellers, self-instructional training emphasizes specific, task-relevant self-statements. It similarly highlights the importance of concomitant attempts at graduated performance tasks. This distinguishes it from several "miracle working" thought control systems which place major therapeutic responsibility on cognitive performances alone. Finally, the cautious but optimistic prose and preliminary but promising data associated with self-instructional training offer an easy demarcation from the often unsubstantiated and unbridled claims of popular "self-statement" psychologies. Sensationalism may not win the hearts of clinical researchers, but it sure does sell books.

Having reviewed both the rationale and empirical evidence for therapeutic self-instructional training, Meichenbaum (1974b) reminds us of two timely quotations:

> The world is such-and-such or so-and-so only because we tell ourselves that that is the way it is . . . . You talk to yourself. You're not unique at that. We carry on internal talk . . . I'll tell you what we talk to ourselves about. We talk about our world. In fact we maintain our world with our internal talk (Carlos Castaneda, *A Separate Reality,* 1972, pp. 218-219).

> The one thing psychologists can count on is that their subjects or clients will talk, if only to themselves; and not infrequently, whether relevant or irrelevant, the things people say to themselves determine the rest of the things they do (Farber, 1963, p. 196).

AMEN.

Chapter Twelve

The Cognitive Therapies: Coping Skills Training, Problem Solving, and Attribution

The therapeutic strategies discussed in the present chapter are much more heterogeneous than cognitive restructuring and self-instructional training. Their relevance to the cognitive learning model, however, is no less apparent. After a brief examination of their derivations and associated evidence, a more general summary and evaluation of this clinical relevance will be presented.

COPING SKILLS TRAINING

As mentioned in Chapter 10, an individual's ability to function adaptively in both stressful and non-stressful situations is dramatically influenced by his response repertoire. If he has acquired the component skills and integrative capacities to "cope," satisfactory adjustment is a much more likely occurrence.

Bandura (1969) emphasized that the acquistion of coping skills in humans is probably a complex, centrally-mediated process involving direct, vicarious, and self-stimulatory experience. However, as its critics will readily attest, early behavior modification research was predominantly focused on discrete, situation-specific responses. In desensitization, for example, hierarchy themes were often very circumspect. The behvior therapy client was frequently diagnosed in piecemeal fashion and problem-specific procedures were selected (cafeteria-style) to treat compartmentalized behavioral dysfunctions.

In 1971, Goldfried suggested that systematic desensitization be reconceptualized as a broader and pervasively mediational therapeutic strategy. According to Goldfried, the desensitization client may be acquiring a general self-relaxation skill rather than experiencing a passive counter-conditioning process. In a subsequent case study, Goldfried (1973a) illustrated some of the possibilities for transforming desensitization into an even more comprehensive "coping skills" training. Emphasis was placed on (1) describing the therapeutic rationale in terms of general, skills training, (2) the use of relaxation as a multipurpose coping strategy, (3) the use of a multiple- (rather then single-) theme hierarchy, and (4) training in "relaxing away" scene-induced anxiety (rather than the conventional method of terminating an imaginal scene at the first sign of client distress). The use of heterogeneous arousal scenes is intended to increase therapeutic generalization: "the client is being taught to cope with his proprioceptive anxiety responses rather than with situations which elicit the tension (Goldfried, 1971)." Similarly, the act of maintaining an anxiety-arousing image and then "relaxing it away" is designed to emphasize an active, coping orientation toward stress. Self-instructional methods and stimulus labeling strategies have been incorporated in later refinements of the coping skills package (cf. Goldfried, 1973b). Supporting evidence for the effectiveness of coping skills training is unfortunately very sparse. In addition to his case study (1973a), Goldfried documents the frequent effectiveness of "relaxation-only" control groups in desensitization. The data on the sufficiency of relaxation training in fear reduction, however, are far from unequivocal (Bandura, 1969). A group study by Goldfried and Trier (in press) has offered preliminary evidence suggesting that the manner in which relaxation training is presented may affect its therapeutic impact. Speech anxious subjects were given training in deep muscular relaxation along with instructions that (a) their subsequent relaxation skills would enable them to actively cope with their anxieties, or (b) relaxation training would almost automatically reduce their overall tension level. A third, attention-placebo group met for discussions of speech-irrelevant topics. Measures of actual speech performance, subjective anxiety, and self-reported generalizations did not reveal significant intergroup differences. However, within-group analyses found the coping skills group to have improved significantly in actual speech performance. Subjective anxiety improvements (relative to their own pre-treatment levels) and therapeutic transfer were reported within each of the three groups. A six week follow-up questionnaire, however, suggested more enduring and generalized improvement on the part of coping skills subjects.

Additional evidence on the effects of coping skills training is offered in a series of reports on "anxiety management training" (Suinn & Richardson, 1971; Suinn, 1972b; Richardson & Suinn, 1973). This procedure, which was developed almost simultaneously with Goldfried's (1971) strategy, also emphasizes heterogeneous arousal stimuli and relaxation training as an active coping skill. In their preliminary study, Suinn and Richardson (1971) found anxiety management training approximately equivalent to desensitization in the reduction of subjectively reported test anxiety. Both treatments were superior to a no-treatment control group. Unfortunately, the latter was comprised of non-anxious students and subjects from a study two years previous. A successful case study (Suinn, 1972b) was supplemented with a comparison between the 1971 anxiety management subjects and two desensitization groups run in a subsequent study (Richardson & Suinn, 1973) . Since only one controlled study has examined the effects of anxiety management training, and it omitted a matched control group, it need hardly be said that the current data on this specific strategy are sorely inadequate.

Still another coping skills training package is that described by Meichenbaum and Cameron (1973c) as "stress inoculation." This package draws heavily on Meichenbaum's self-instructional research (cf. Chapter 11) and includes (a) a discussion of stress reactions (with emphasis on labeling, attribution, and arousal-inducing self-statements), (b) relaxation training (presented as an active coping skill), (c) instructed practice in the emission of coping self-statements (cognitive self-monitoring, preparation for stress, self-reinforcement, etc.), and (d) supervised practice in utilizing the above coping skills in an actual stress situation (e.g., an unpredictable shock situation). To test the efficacy of this package, Meichenbaum and Cameron assigned rat and snake phobic subjects to five groups: stress inoculation, self-instructional training, systematic desensitization, anxiety relief, and a no-treatment control group. Individuals in the self-instructional group received training identical to that in stress inoculation except for the omission of supervised practice in an actual stress situation. For half of the subjects in both the desensitization and anxiety relief groups, a snake hierarchy was employed; the other half were exposed to a rat hierarchy. All subjects underwent pre-, post-, and follow-up assessments involving actual approach behaviors (to both animals) and subjective measures of distress. Data analyses of approach behavior found the stress inoculation group most effective. Terminal approach behavior at both post-test and follow-up was exhibited by 83% of stress inoculation subjects, as compared with 50% for desensitization, 33% for anxiety relief, 16% for self-instructional training, and 0% for controls. Moreover, approach responses to the untreated (generalization) object favored stress inoculation, self-instruction, and anxiety relief over desensitization and control subjects. Self-report measures of subjective distress reflected a similar efficacy pattern with stress inoculation producing greatest fear reduction. It is worth noting the contrast in the effects of the present self-instructional group and those cited in Chapter 11. Individuals who received self-instructional training in the current study were dramatically less successful on both approach and self-report measures than subjects in the previous studies. However, as the authors note, the self-instruction training utilized in the 1973c study did not allow any opportunity for practice or exposure to potential stressors (e.g., shock, a modeling film, etc.). Interestingly, subjects in this group began their post-test approach sequences with minimal levels of anxiety but soon reported sharp increments in arousal as their performance tasks became more demanding. The authors conclude that self-instructional training—in the absence of stress-relevant opportunities for practice—may effect only mild and temporary benefits. In the presence of an actual stress experience, these benefits quickly dissipate. However, when systematic modification of cognitive behavior is accompanied by relevant performance opportunities, impressive therapeutic results are obtained.

The Meichenbaum and Cameron (1973c) study offers some preliminary supportive evidence for the clinical promise of coping skills training. Further support is suggested in a study by Tori & Worell (1973) which combined a variety of ostensibly broad-based coping procedures ("cognitive" relaxation, practice in relaxing away anxiety without terminating aversive imagery, use of fear-irrelevant imaginal stressors to practice tension control, etc.). Although these components were not procedurally isolated, the effectiveness of two cognitive therapy groups employing them offers some partial corroboration.

The fact that coping skills training has often involved multi-component "treatment packages" deserves further comment. Depending on one's methodological biases, a treatment package may be viewed as either a clinical asset or an empirical liability (Mahoney, 1973). It should obviously not be employed as a euphemism for vague and poorly evaluated "shotgunning." However, assuming that its components have been adequately specified, the treatment package often offers an invaluable clinical strategy, both during initial therapy developments and where broad-based skills training is desired. In the development or unprecedented application of therapeutic procedure, a pragmatic rule of thumb is: First show an effect, then isolate its cause. All too many researchers have spent months of painstaking work attempting to isolate a single independent variable only to find it clinically impotent.

A second defense of broader coping approaches to therapy stems from the increasingly popular assumption of multi-determinism in complex human behavior. Personal adjustment problems are seldom circumscribed and their determining factors are often varied and numerous. To the extent that a therapy procedure addresses itself to only a portion of the relevant causal factors, its success and permanence are jeopardized. Likewise, the provision of coping skills training may enhance maintenance and generalization through over-learning and the provision of skills relevant to future adjustment-relevant problem solving.

After developing a data-based confidence in the efficacy of a treatment package, one can pursue a component analysis. Once active contributors to therapeutic impact have been identified, the package may be refined and its underlying processes of change may be better understood. It should be kept in mind, however, that package components may interact complexly. Not only may there be no single active ingredient, but various components may effect therapeutic results only when combined with other package elements. This would, of course, add justification to the use of the package. A more frequent phenomenon, perhaps, is that of various treatment components contributing differentially to an effect. Component A may enhance initial motivation and continuation of therapy; component B may effect short-term or situation-specific progress while the more enduring or general effects of component C are awaited, and so on.

The evidence reviewed above on the clinical efficacy of coping skills training is extremely meager. Behavioral researchers have only recently begun to address themselves to less circumscribed clinical phenomena (cf. Mahoney, Kazdin, & Lesswing, 1974). While snake phobics and enuretic children have served admirably in the methodological assessment of isolated therapy procedures, the next few years will hopefully witness a continuing liberalization of both clinical targets and therapeutic programs. Until broader-based coping strategies receive their empirical due, our confidence in them must remain suspended and tenuous.

PROBLEM SOLVING

Few areas of psychological interest can claim the enduring tenacity of theoretical and empirical attention which has accrued to the phenomenon of "problem solving." Its history can be traced to a lineage long preceding William James (1890), and few major learning theories have escaped its pervasive allure (cf. Hilgard & Bower, 1966). As an applied research area, however, problem solving has only recently been explored.

Except for generally speculative and predominantly operant analyses, contemporary behaviorists have virtually ignored the phenomenon (cf. Skinner, 1953, 1966, 1969; Staats, 1966, 1968a; Goldiamond, 1966). In a timely article outlining the relevance of problem solving for clinical behavior modification, D'Zurilla and Goldfried (1971) have recently suggested the need for a long overdue functional analysis of the therapeutic promise offered by systematic training in problem solving skills. As indicated in the previous section, the general tenor of early behavior therapy applications was quite circumscribed. Discrete presenting complaints were often treated with problem-specific interventions and little emphasis was placed on the acquisition of more versatile coping skills.

One possible reason for the longstanding de-emphasis of problem solving in behavior modification may have been its mediational flavor. Although animal problem solving research dates back to the last century (cf. Riopelle, 1967), its frequent reliance on inferred variables and speculative cognitive processes has apparently kept it alien to the interests of the applied behavior therapist. A second possible influence may have been the difficulties inherent in the operational definition and measurement of the phenomenon (cf. Gágne, 1964; Davis, 1966, 1973). An unequivocal definition of problem solving has yet to be offered. As Gagne (1964) points out, workers in this area have relied upon specification criteria ranging from the external stimulus situation to inferred conceptual operations and various aspects of observed performance (latency, number and type of errors, cross-situation transfer, etc.). Davis (1973) defines a "problem" as "*a stimulus situation for which an organism does not have a ready response* (p. 12)." Unfortunately, the "readiness" of a response presents its own definitional difficulties (and it need hardly be mentioned that even the terms "stimulus" and "response" incur referential problems). D'Zurilla and Goldfried (1971) define "problem solving" as:

> *a behavioral process, whether overt or cognitive in nature, which (a) makes available a variety of potentially effective response alternatives for dealing with the problematic situation and (b) increases the probability of selecting the most effective response from among these various alternatives* (p. 108).

Again, however, the component terms share definitional problems and ambiguities which jeopardize unequivocal acceptance. The absence of a formal lexical agreement on the general term "problem solving" has not, however, impeded empirical inquiries into specific instances of the phenomenon. As with many other areas of sectarian science, workers in the field seem to have less difficulty describing their tree than their forest. Procedural specifications and operationalized performance measures have facilitated an apparently adequate exchange of communication.

As reflected in the valuable reviews of Sheerer (1963), Gagne (1964), and Davis (1966, 1973), the theory and research on problem solving have nourished a vast literature. While a detailed excursion would take us far afield, a brief synopsis of major directions and general findings is warranted. The relevance and clinical promise of problem solving strategies will then be evaluated.

Animal Problem Solving

The ability of animals to resolve problematic situations has long intrigued behavioral scientists. In Riopelle's (1967) edited volume on *Animal Problem Solving*, this enduring interest is documented in the writings of both 19th and 20th century researchers. Some of the earliest reports in this area stemmed from the work of Gestalt psychologists. Investigators such as Wolfgang Köhler (1925) have examined the response sequences and inferred mediational operations of problem solving apes. With impressive ingenuity and what Köhler termed "insight," these primates were able to solve a wide range of perplexing food-gathering problems. For example, in a set of tasks in which bananas were suspended out of reach from the ceiling,

> the apes learned to (1) release the free end of the string from a tree, thus dropping the basket; (2) place a bamboo pole vertically under the banana, and instantly climb up to twelve feet before the pole fell, and (3) push a box (or stack of several boxes) under the bananas to use as a footstool. In one creative version of the latter solution, chimp Sultan pulled Köhler under the banana, climbing the famed psychologist as he would a ladder. In still another variation, the chimps learned to use each other as footstools. Unfortunately, with increasing sophistication, all wanted to be climbers and none stools, resulting in noisy battle among the chimpanzees (Davis, 1973, pp. 30-31).

The occasional absence of overt trial-and-error performance and vicarious learning led Köhler to speculate about perceptual re-organization and "insight" in primate problem solving. The sudden and often serendipitous appearance of a solution was not infrequent:

> The most difficult task of all was the two-stick problem, to which Sultan, the most famous of the chimps, lent his talents. To reach the banana, the smaller bamboo stick had to be fitted into the end of a slightly larger one, creating a single stick long enough to reach the distant goal object. For the first *fruitless* hour, Sultan committed 'bad' errors, such as dragging a box from the rear of his cage and placing it directly in his own way, and 'good' errors, pushing one stick with the other toward the banana. Finally, ignoring the perturbing banana, Sultan played carelessly with the two sticks; and when he accidentally slipped the little one neatly into the bigger one, the

> light blinked on and he instantly dashed to rake in his dinner (Davis, 1973, pp. 31-32, italics added).

There are two broad generalizations which can be made from the extensive documentation of animal problem solving. First, it exists. Although it has been reported most frequently in primates, its occurrence in "lower" phylogenetic forms has also been acknowledged (Riopelle, 1967). Well controlled studies have shown animals to be capable of a wide range of response differentiation and integration. The operant researcher need hardly be convinced of this phenomenon—informal laboratory observations and *ex cathedra* anecdotes readily demonstrate the cunning ability of rats, pigeons, and monkeys to sabotage the best laid plans of an experimenter. The ingenious "guerilla warfare" tactics I have observed in my own animal research have ranged from perverse pigeons who learned to cover a photoelectric cell with one wing (rendering it functionally inoperative) to ingenious Capuchin monks who not only developed the skillful ability to catch and hold a raisin-filled food hopper (making reward removal impossible) but also learned to disassemble their experimental chamber by using their fingernails as screwdrivers. These feats, of course, motivated counter-influencing problem solving on the part of their frustrated "controller."

The second broad generalization which can be made about animal problem solving is that it appears to involve some complex mediational processes. Vicarious learning, for example, has been well documented in infrahumans (cf. Chapter 4). Speculations and research on active "hypothesis testing" in animals have likewise suggested that some cognitive relational processes are involved (Riopelle, 1967). While the nature and forms of these inferred mediators are far from unequivocal, there is little argument about the fact that "something is going on" between the stimulus and the response in many animal learning situations.

Human Laboratory Problem Solving

Much of the formal experimental work on human problem solving has focused on the conceptual skills and component processes of the phenomenon rather that its adaptive functions (cf. Gagne, 1964; Kleinmuntz, 1966; Davis, 1966). The influence of prior experience, instructions, varied forms of stimulus presentation, and erroneous logic has been extensively examined. Perceptual, mathematical, and verbal tasks are frequently employed. For example, a subject is asked to connect 9 dots in a 3 x 3 matrix using only four straight lines and without lifting his pencil from the paper:

*	*	*
(1)	(2)	(3)
*	*	*
(4)	(5)	(6)
*	*	*
(7)	(8)	(9)

Most subjects given the above problem have great difficulty until they realize and correct their erroneous assumption that the lines may not extend past the dots. (One correct solution would be four straight lines, A, B, C, and D, with A connecting dots 1, 5, and 9; B connecting 9, 8, and 7 and then extending beyond 7 until an appropriate angle will allow line C to run back through 4 and 2; C likewise extends beyond 2 and allows line D to complete the task by connecting 3, 6, and 9).

In a valuable Appendix referencing tests and measures of problem solving and creativity, Davis (1973) documents the vast number of tasks which have been employed. Riddles are sometimes used to assess subjects' skills at information gathering and hypothesis testing. An informative first-hand exploration of other people's thinking styles, for example, can be obtained by presenting a friend with something like the following:

> A physician on his way to church stops a one-armed beggar and hands him a large sum of money. Sometime later, a messenger delivers a box to four men. The men open the box, find that it contains a well scrubbed human arm, and subsequently dispose of it.

The task is to determine the "plot" of the above riddle by asking questions of the experimenter—who can only respond with one of three answers: yes, no, or irrelevant. Measure the time it takes to solve the riddle and tally the frequency of redundant or irrelevant queries. More interestingly, categorize the content of questions (information-gathering, motivational, etc.) and note the dramatic impact of several "discoveries" on the direction of interrogation. (For example, ascertaining (1) that the arm was not diseased, (2) that the physician had paid the beggar to allow its amputation, (3) that the four recipients had no current use for the appendage, and (4) that the four men were each missing an arm.) Through an often extensive series of questions, the subject will usually zero in on the solution—namely, that the four men and the physician had shared a near-fatal survival trauma in which each contributed a cannibalized limb in succession to prevent group starvation. Being the only qualified surgeon in the group, the physician had not amputated his own arm. After they returned to civilization and went their separate ways, the physician assuaged his guilt feelings over escaping at the expense of his peers' appendages by perpetrating their perception that he had voluntarily sacrificed his own arm as a symbolic gesture of gratitude.

The critical role of perceptual and relational processes in effective problem solving has been extensively examined. Subjects often fail to observe multiple uses for an object or fixate upon irrelevant aspects of the problem situation. Moreover, logical reasoning processes have occupied considerable theoretical and empirical attention (cf. Bruner, Goodnow, & Austin, 1956; Piaget, 1955; Piaget & Inhelder, 1969). The diversity of paradigms, tasks, and emphases in experimental problem solving is quite substantial (cf. Sheerer, 1963; Gagne, 1964; Davis, 1966, 1973). Foci have ranged from simple anagram solutions to the computer simulation of problem solving (Feigenbaum & Feldman, 1963; Newell & Simon, 1972). Similarly, mathematical models in "decision theory" have generated extensive research on the component process in reasoned choice (cf. Slovic & Lichtenstein, 1971).

A related and equally vast literature has been addressed to the phenomenon of "creativity," which is sometimes differentiated from problem solving on the basis of solution originality, functional flexibility, and so on. As many introductory psychology texts proffer, creativity seems to be more often attributed to hereditarily-influenced factors and temporal variables. The fact is often cited, for example, that famous individuals frequently make their major scientific discoveries and intellectual contributions before the age of 30. The implicit decay of creative abilities after that age is seldom noted as correlating very well with the removal of many professional performance requirements at about that same age (i.e., with the granting of tenure).

The generalizations to be drawn from laboratory experiments on human problem solving are difficult to crystallize. One warranted statement seems to be that the *homo sapiens* is an extremely complex problem solver with simultaneous capacities for innovative and diversified performance as well as tenacious and dysfunctional biases. The human being shows awesome abilities to adapt, as well as a frequently distressing incapacity to remove his perceptual, learned, and symbolically-mediated "bifocals." This paradoxical combination of flexibility and fixation appears to be moderated by a perplexing array of variables.

A second generalization relates to some of the component processes in human problem solving. Although an unequivocal consesus has yet to be reached, D'Zurilla and Goldfried (1971) suggest that the available data converge on five basic elements or stages: (1) the generation of a problem solving "set" or orientation, (2) definition of the problem, (3) generation of alternative solutions, (4) tentative selection of a solution, and (5) testing of that solution (verification).

A third generalization from human laboratory experiments relates to the consensus that both "vertical" and "horizontal" response processes appear to be involved (Kendler & Kendler, 1962; Gagne, 1964; Davis, 1966). That is, successful performance in problemmatical situations often seems to require relatively sequential (horizontal) response chains as well as integrated and hierarchialized (vertical) skills. The problem solver must often combine sequential operations with highly organized "second order" conceptual processes:

> Second-order rules for manipulating first-order rules are derived from empirical discoveries of the success of certain practices or from an examination of the contingency-maintaining systems which the first-order rules describe. . . . Second-order rules are discovered inductively when they are found to produce effective new first-order rules or deductively (possibly tautologically) from an analysis of first-order rules or of the contingencies they describe.
>
> Second-order, "heuristic" rules are often thought to specify more creative or less mechanical activities than the rules in first-order (possibly algorithmic) problem solving, but once a heuristic rule has been formulated, it can be followed as "mechanically" as any first order rule (pp. 144-145).

The separate convergence upon such organization in mediational processes by many theorists and investigators in the area suggests a contemporary consensus in their existence. The foregoing block quote, by way of illustration, is taken from Skinner (1969).

A final generalization relates to a distinction emphasized by Davis (1966) between overt and covert problem solving. The former involves actual trial-and-error interactions with stimulus materials and probably offers an invaluable source of information about response options, probable consequences, and so on. Covert problem solving, on the other hand, presumably entails symbolic stimulus transformations, cognitive rehearsals and tests of alternate solutions. While this latter strategy has often been documented as an effective and relatively economical problem solving approach, it requires prior acquisition of accurate situational information and skills necessary for innovative response generation or integration.

It should be noted in closing this section that laboratory experiments on human problem solving have often employed tasks and paradigms with very little practical relevance. The problems themselves are often artificially simple and substantially removed from the genre of conflicts which are faced in everyday experience. Recent efforts to employ more realistic and relevant problem tasks have already begun to remedy this limitation (e.g., Shulman, 1965; Spivack & Shure, 1974).

Industrial Problem Solving

Edwards (1968) and Davis (1973) review several lines of research and evaluation in the use of systematic problem solving training in industry. Creativity workships and personnel/management courses on instrumental thinking are popular and profitable features in the contemporary market place. Large corporations devote millions of dollars to the improvement of their creative marketing and management skills. While the empirical evaluation of these programs has often been less than optimal, their heuristic contribution and subjectively reported impact warrant brief discussion.

Three major approaches to creativity training have dominated the industrial market: *Brainstorming, Synetics,* and *Bionics*. Brainstorming is a relatively structured program developed by Alex Osborn (1963) in which major emphasis is placed on flexible idea production. Based on the assumption that both criticism and hasty decisions threaten the generation of original and effective solutions, the Brainstorming format encourages wild, "no-holds-barred" speculation and deferred judgment. Four ground rules are suggested (Osborn, 1963):

1. **Criticism is ruled out.** Group members are told to encourage creativity by accepting even bizarre suggestions. Fault-finding and adverse judgment are viewed as inhibitory to the expression of original ideas. Constructive criticisms of suggested solutions are deferred until a later problem solving stage.
2. **Freewheeling is welcomed.** The more bizarre and original the idea the better. "It is easier to tame down than to think up."
3. **Quantity is welcomed.** It is presumed that quality will distill from quantity. The greater the total number of ideas, the higher the likelihood of useful and original solutions.
4. **Contribution and improvement are sought.** Group members are encouraged to integrate and refine suggested ideas.

The Brainstorming approach has been adopted by a number of large corporations and widely disseminated in personnel and management workshops. Its documented impact has included substantial savings in man-hour usages as well as creative marketing "firsts" (e.g., the Sylvania "Flash Cube" for cameras).

Synetics was developed by William Gordon (1961) and emphasizes the use of analogical processes in creative thought. Three problem solving strategies involve direct, personal, and fantasized analogies. A direct analogy often involves a parallel problem. Davis (1973) cites, for example, a problem Gordon and his colleagues encountered in designing a roof which automatically changed colors with the seasons (white in the summer to reflect heat, black in the winter to absorb it). One possible solution was suggested by use of the direct analogy method, recognizing that pigmentation changes are often encountered in some animals (e.g., the flounder). In personal analogy problem solving, the individual is instructed to imagine himself as being the problem object. A third analogical method encourages active, and often bizarre, fantasizing. This latter strategy was credited with the generation of an innovative vaporproof closure device for use in space suits. As Davis (1973) points out, the creative processes involved in Synetics are much more extensive and complex than the above three methods would suggest.

A somewhat similar approach is that of Bionics, which has been described as "the use of biological prototypes for the design of man-made systems (Papanek, 1969)." Sensory organs and transducer systems have been popular foci for extrapolation. In way of illustration, Davis (1973) informs us that the extremely sensitive infrared sensors of the rattlesnake "led to the appropriately named *Sidewinder* missile, a device which indifferently trails the hot exhaust of a target aircraft, exploding in its tailpipe (p. 130)." It need hardly be added that problem solving training offers a systematic *means* for resolution, and that its *ends* are often far from unequivocal. (Was it the cartoon character Bullwinkle who said that "military intelligence" is a self-contradiction?)

A long list of popular books on creative thinking have also been published. Among them are Polya's (1957) classic *How To Solve It,* which is a very readable guide for both student and teacher. Although its illustrations are predominantly mathematical, its methods can be applied to a wide range of phenomena. Likewise, de Bono's (1970) *Lateral Thinking* offers a concise but comprehensive review of practical and empirically supported problem solving stategies.

The demonstrated relevance of industrial problem solving for clinical applications may be less apparent than its heuristics. An impressive array of practical strategies offers some support for its own impact—i.e., creativity programs have, in fact, been quite creative.

Problem Solving in the Classroom

A number of recent studies have addressed the significance of providing systematic instruction in problem solving skills as a part of formal education. While the recommendation for the inclusion and encouragement of "inquiry activity" in education dates back to Dewey (1933, 1938), controlled evaluations of this enterprise have only recently been reported. Among these have been the work of Suchman (1960, 1969) who has divised and evaluated a series of projects involving "inquiry training" in the physical sciences. In these programs, children are systematically taught to formulate problems, gather relevant information, and generate and test hypotheses. In a sense, they are given training in formal logic and scientific method. Similar programs have been developed and assessed by several other workers (e.g., Butts, 1965; Butts & Jones, 1966; Burmester, Garth, Koos, & Stothart, 1970). Several projects addressed to less circumscribed topics have emphasized broader academic problem solving skills (cf. Torrance & Myers, 1970; Covington, Crutchfield, & Davies, 1966; Olton & Crutchfield, 1969; Feldhusen, Treffinger, & Bahlke, 1970; Davis & Scott, 1971). Davis's (1973) text once again provides a valuable review of this literature.

The overall findings of classroom problem solving training have been encouraging. While some studies have suffered from possible methodological problems, their independent replication and relatively consistent convergence has suggested that a valid and often enduring impact has accrued. On various measures of creativity, conceptual skills, and performance flexibility, systematic training in problem solving and scientific method has resulted in substantial improvements. Moreover, subjective measures of "curiosity" and personal attitudes toward "inquiry activity" have suggested that the impact of such training may have a very broad and enduring effect on the child. In emphasizing the need for re-aligning educational objectives toward training students *how* to think rather than *what* to think, Olton and Crutchfield (1969) pose the problem very succinctly:

> Since today's education emphasizes mastery of the *known*, it does very little to prepare an individual to cope effectively with the *unknown*. Yet many of today's school children will be spending more than half their lifetime in the unknown world of the twenty-first century. To cope effectively with the unknown, an individual must have a well-developed ability to think. Thus, an education that will prepare today's student for a useful, fulfilling life in the twenty-first century must provide him with extensive, systematic instruction in the skills required for original, independent thinking and problem solving (p. 69).

Problem Solving Deficiencies in Behavior Disorders

The frequency with which clients exhibit grossly inadequate and often self-defeating methods for dealing with personal distress need hardly be documented for the experienced clinician. Case records are replete with illustrations of tragic inadequacies. As D'Zurilla and Goldfried (1971) point out,

> much of what we view clinically as "abnormal behavior" or "emotional disturbance" may be viewed as ineffective behavior and its consequences, in which the individual is unable to resolve certain situational problems in his life and his inadequate attempts to do so are having undesirable effects, such as anxiety, depression, and the creation of additional problems (p. 107).

A recent series of experiments by George Spivack and his colleagues has added some preliminary empirical documentation to the above contention (cf. Spivack & Shure, 1974). In comparisons of a variety of "normal" and "deviant" populations, these researchers have found consistent differences in problem solving abilities. Tests of *means-ends thinking,* which have featured prominently in these inquiries, were designed to measure both the quantity and form of suggested solutions (means) as well as the individual's ability to accurately anticipate the probable consequences (ends) of various response options. In the Preschool Interpersonal Problem-Solving Test (PIPS), for example, children are presented with a variety of hypothetical problem situations (using pictures and verbal descriptions). They are then asked to tell the experimenter all of the possible things a child could do in that situation. A second test (called "What Happens Next?") evaluates anticipated consequences:

> Today G wants to use the swing but H is already on it. Who is already on the swing? Right, H. Who wants a chance on the swing? That's right, G. What can G do so he can have a chance on the swing? (p. 194)
>
> A had a truck and he was playing with it. B wanted to play with that truck. So B grabbed—you know, snatched—that truck. Tell me what happens next (Spivack & Shure, 1974, p. 198).

A behavioral rating scale has also been used in some of the Spivack et al. research. This seven item scale focuses on the child's overt performance in the areas of (1) delay of gratification, (2) emotional upset (tantrums, etc.), and (3) social aggressiveness. Research with adults has employed the Means-Ends Problem-Solving Procedure (MEPS) (cf. Spivack & Shure, 1974).

In an early study with residentially placed adolescents, Spivack and Levine (1963) found that youngsters diagnosed as "impulsive" and "emotionally disturbed" were significantly less successful than their "normal" peers in generating solutions to hypothetical problems. They also displayed less "foresight" in terms of considering the possible consequences of various actions. Several subsequent studies comparing the problem solving abilities of normal individuals and hospitalized psychiatric patients have replicated these findings. (Platt & Spivack, 1972a, b, 1973, 1974; Platt, Scura, & Hannon, 1973). In comparisons of "deviant" and normal children, two studies have suggested that children exhibiting maladaptive behaviors are often less capable of employing means-ends thinking (Shure & Spivack, 1972; Shure, Spivack, & Jaeger, 1971). Not only were there quantitative differences in the means they suggested for handling a problem, but disturbed youngsters frequently limited their solutions to impulsive and aggressive methods.

Other workers have also suggested that problem solving deficiences may play an important role in behavioral dysfunction. Levinson and Neuringer (1971), for example, speculate that suicidal behavior may reflect such a deficit. In a perceptual-motor laboratory task, they found suicidal adolescents less efficient in problem solving than a group of non-suicidal controls. Meichenbaum (in press) presents a valuable summary of some of the research suggesting that geriatric distress and thought disorders in the aged may be exacerbated by poor problem solving skills.

While the foregoing research is still preliminary, its findings are suggestive of a significant clinical consideration. Congruent with the statement made by D'Zurilla and Goldfried (1971), it appears that many distressed individuals display poor problem solving abilities. Whether these deficits are antecedents, consequences, or unrelated corollaries of maladjustment has yet to be extensively examined. Only a handful of studies have attempted to evaluate the effects of systematic training in problem solving on the adjustment and adaptation of "deviant" populations. In a series of three studies with normal and disruptive preschool children, Spivack and his colleagues evaluated the immediate and long-term effects of problem solving training (cf. Spivack & Shure, 1974). Using measures of means-end thinking (the PIPS) and a behavior rating scale, significant and relatively consistent improvements were observed:

> Thus data indicate that this training program has four major effects. First, it enhances alternative, consequential, and cause-and-effect thinking. Second, it decreases superfluous and irrelevant thinking. Third, it enhances problem-solving ability most among

> those who need it the most (those who are behaviorally aberrant). Fourth, it shifts the priority away from aggressive solutions and trains children to see nonforceful as well as forceful possibilities (p. 98).

Follow-up assessments at six months suggested that problem solving training had had an enduring impact. Not only were previously disruptive children substantially better adjusted at that time, but there was a lower frequency of maladjustment on the part of "normal" children who had received the training. That is, problem solving appeared to contribute to the *prevention* of maladjustment as well as to the improvement of previously disruptive subjects. Corroborative reports from parents and teachers further suggested that the children's newly acquired skills had generalized to playground and domestic settings. Some subjects were reported to be exhibiting consequential thinking in informing younger siblings of parental contingencies (e.g., "If you be good, Mommy might take us to the movies"). Frequent anecdotes related the parents' surprise at their children's use of reason, logic, and verbal resolutions to domestic conflicts. An amusing dialogue was shared by a mother whose preschooler had previously been bullied by a larger and older neighborhood boy:

STEVEN: Mama, Wayne hit me!
MOTHER: Go and tell his mother.
STEVEN: I did. She didn't give him no whoopin'.
MOTHER: Then go hit him back.
STEVEN: I can't, he's too big. (Steven then went out, was gone a long time, and returned.)
MOTHER: Where did you go so long?
STEVEN: I was out playin' with Wayne.
MOTHER: Was he fighting?
STEVEN: No, I told him if he don't hit me no more, he could have some candy.
MOTHER: Did you give him candy?
STEVEN: Yep, and he don't hit me no more (p. 115).

As indicated by the foregoing review, the area of problem solving is one of longstanding and multi-faceted inquiry. An extensive literature spans a range of topics from primate ponderings to industrial innovation. While it would be difficult to extrapolate clinical relevance directly from the evidence on animal problem solving and corporate creativity, we can at least concur that "instrumental thought" appears to have improved the efficiency of both hairy and well-shaven apes. Of more direct relevance are the literatures on human laboratory problem solving and systematized "inquiry training" in classrooms. Although research in the former has been disproportionately monopolized by relatively obtuse problem analogues, it has contributed impressively to our understanding of the processes and forms of efficient mediation. Educational applications have lent further corroboration to the clinical potential of systematic training in problem solving. On both academic and intellectual performance measures, individuals who have received such training often exhibit substantial improvement. Finally, the research on problem solving deficiencies in behavior disorders suggests that mediational dysfunctions are a frequent component in personal distress and maladaptive performance. This finding, of course, adds further support to several of the points made in Chapter 10 on the role of such processes in clinical dysfunction.

The direct application of problem solving training to behavioral disorders has only recently been pursued. In addition to the work of Spivack and his colleagues (cf. Spivack & Shure, 1974), a handful of studies have employed "thinking skills" training in their therapeutic procedures (e.g., Giebink, Stover, & Fahl, 1968; McGuire & Sifneos, 1970; Rosenthal & Meyer, 1971; Mahoney, 1973; Weiss, Hops, & Patterson, 1973). Component analyses and controlled empirical assessments, however, are sorely needed. Although some degree of tentative confidence is warranted by preliminary laboratory and classroom findings, the importance of accelerated explorations on this new frontier should be emphasized.

The *potential* relevance of problem solving to both clients and therapists needs little elaboration. In terms of adaptive versatility and the ability to cope with an ever-changing array of life problems, these cognitive skills may offer an invaluable personal paradigm for survival. Their potential contribution to therapeutic efficacy and independent self-improvement will hopefully become an issue of priority in future empirical scrutiny.

ATTRIBUTION

Another area of relevance to both the cognitive learning model and its associated therapies is that of *attribution*. If the quantity of literature generated in a field were any index of its heuristic worth, attribution theory would have to rank among the forerunners of current psychological perspectives. Despite its relative recency, the issue of causal attribution has already stimulated volumes of theory and a substantial body of associated research (cf. Heider, 1958; Kelley, 1967, 1973; de Charms, 1968; Jones, Kanouse, Kelley, Nisbett, Valins, & Weiner, 1971; Weiner, 1972). Although the vastness of this literature precludes any semblance of a detailed examination in the present writing, a brief overview of attribution theory and its clinical implications will be offered. In order to avoid encyclopedic boredom, reference will be made only to pivotal studies and reviews. The interested reader is directed to these sources for more comprehensive exposition.

The underlying premise in attribution theory is that *perceived causality may influence behavior.* As we saw in Chapter 10, the human organism frequently imposes order on experience by inferring relationships among experiential events. In Skinner's (1969) terms, contingency-shaped performances often evolve into "rule-governed behavior" via the individual's extrapolation of abstracts from particulars. According to attribution theory, one of the most common inferences made by the human being has to do with the causes of behavior—his own as well as others'. The fact that we assign causes to our actions is perhaps less than earthshaking; its clinical relevance lies in the nature of those causal attributions. For example, if we infer that our migraine headache and dizziness are due to an imminent psychotic break rather than the accidental inhalation of insecticides on the way home from work, our subsequent behavior may vary dramatically. Similarly, attributing a failing grade to the instructor's biases rather than our own incompetence may moderate the physiological and motoric performances which ensue. If our obesity, smoking, or depression are seen as caused by heredity, addiction, or a disease, we may be much less likely to instigate an active self-improvement enterprise.

The basic contention, then, is that causal attribution may exert a dramatic influence on behavior. In addition to this, the theory posits that the nature of our attributions will be affected by a variety of factors—prior experience, the amount and type of information currently available, and so on. There is even some evidence suggesting that the inferred causes of identical behaviors may vary depending on their owner (Jones & Nisbett, 1971). When observing someone else's performance (e.g., an academic success), we often attribute it to personality "traits" (intelligence, creativity, perseverance). Observing the same performance in ourselves, however, may lead to a "situational" attribution (luck, instructor bias, or an easy exam).

In its stimulation of a prolific literature, attribution theory has taken several different routes of inquiry. The three most relevant to cognitive behavior modification are *locus of control, misattribution therapy,* and *self-perception theory.*

Locus of Control

The role of perceived causality in both functional and dysfunctional behavior has been extensively examined by workers in personality theory, social psychology, and clinical research. Julian B.

Rotter, one of the pioneers and major contributors in this area, offers a succinct summary of the "locus of control" construct:

> The effect of a reinforcement . . . is not a simple stamping-in process but depends upon whether or not the person perceives a causal relationship between his own behavior and the reward. . . . When a reinforcement is perceived by the subject as . . . not being entirely contingent upon his action, then . . . it is typically perceived as the result of luck, chance, fate, as under the control of powerful others, or as unpredictable. . . . When the event is interpreted in this way by an individual, we have labeled this a belief in *external control.* If the person perceives that the event is contingent upon his own behavior . . . we have termed this a belief in *internal control* (1966, p. 1).

The basic theme of this construct deals with whether or not the individual perceives himself as an active causal agent rather than a passive recipient of environmental influences. A measure of internal-external self-perceptions is offered by the I-E Scale (Rotter, 1966) which asks respondents to choose between pairs of belief statements (e.g., "Many times I feel that I have little influence over the things that happen to me," versus "It is impossible for me to believe that chance or luck plays an important role in my life").

The experimental evidence on locus of control has suggested that it may, in fact, have substantial relevance for clinical applications (cf. Lefcourt, 1966, 1973; Throop & MacDonald, 1971; Rotter, Chance, & Phares, 1972; Phares, 1973). This generalization, however, must be moderated by the recognition that I-E measurements and experimental methodologies have often complicated evaluative conclusions (Averill, 1973). Two reviews by Lefcourt (1966) and Phares (1973) suggest that "internal" individuals—that is, those who see themselves as active agents in their own lives—differ from "externals" in a variety of ways. The internal person, for example, appears to take more initiative and responsibility in performance situations. He often seeks and utilizes information more efficiently, and seems to be more "in touch" with current environmental features. A number of studies with institutionalized psychiatric patients, prisoners, and various minority groups have suggested that these individuals are often more "external" than normal control populations. Classroom research has indicated that I-E scores may be a predictor of academic achievement—children who view their school performance as personally caused rather than chance-determined appear to be more active and successfull students.

Moreover, experiments on animals and humans have suggested that a belief in external causation may dramatically impair subsequent learning. Seligman, Maier, and Solomon (1969) have recently reviewed several years of research on "learned helplessness," an experimental analogue to despondency. Using shock avoidance paradigms, these researchers have found that early experiences of uncontrollable aversive stimulation may reduce the organism's likelihood of adaptive learning in subsequent avoidance experiments. Animals who are initially forced to endure unavoidable shocks are much less efficient in acquiring a coping avoidance response when one is later made available. On the other hand, subjects who have not experienced "helplessness" during early phases of these experiments are substantially more successful in subsequent avoidance learning. An extrapolation to human performance was recently reported by Thornton and Jacobs (1971). Subjects who were initially presented with unavoidable shock were less successful in acquiring a subsequent avoidance response.

Related to the active-passive orientation associated with internal-external beliefs is the recent experimental interest in the effects of perceived control over aversive stimulation. A number of studies have suggested that individuals often exhibit less autonomic distress when they perceive themselves as having some potential control over unpleasant experiences (cf. Lefcourt, 1973). Geer, Davison, and Gatchel (1970), for example, showed that subjects who falsely *believed* that they had control over shock duration in a reaction time experiment displayed fewer and smaller galvanic skin responses than individuals who believed that shock durations were predetermined. Similarly, Glass, Singer, & Friedman (1969) reported that the perception of control may be a more significant factor in coping with stress than the actual implementation of controlling options. Even though none of them actually exercised their option, subjects who believed they could control an unpredictable aversive noise showed less performance impairment than external perception subjects. As we shall see in Chapter 14, this "perceived freedom" may influence a variety of private and interpersonal experiences. A recent review by Averill (1973) points out some of the complexities in the theory and research on perceived control over aversive stimulation. In emphasizing that the relationship between personal control and subjective distress is far from a simple one, Averill concludes that:

> the stress-inducing or stress-reducing properties of personal control depend on such factors as the nature of the response and the context in which it is imbedded and not just upon its effectiveness in preventing or mitigating the impact of a potentially harmful stimulus (1973, p. 286).

The potential relevance of locus of control issues for clinical applications can hardly be ignored. Belief in internal or external control represents one of the mediational influences discussed in Chapter 10. Research within the formal paradigm of locus of control has suggested that a considerable amount of variance in task performance, academic achievement, and clinical outcome might be moderated by such beliefs. Although the relationship is far from simple, its practical implications should not be overlooked. As reviewed in preceding chapters, evidence from laboratory, field, and clinical realms strongly supports the contention that human behavior is often influenced by mediational factors. While I-E beliefs may be but one of those factors, their impact on therapeutic success and personal adaptation bear careful scrutiny.

Some of the broader implications of this area have already been addressed by Rotter, Chance, and Phares (1972). Brief mention will be made here of a few clinical and social issues posed by the locus of control evidence. First, what can we do when an individual *accurately* perceives himself as being at the mercy of external influences? The chronic mental patient, the prison inmate, the mental retardate, and the "socially underprivileged" often have very good reason to see themselves as impotent in their respective life situations. Politically and socially, they frequently have very little control over their own fate—which, of course, reinforces a passive despondence. The solution to this dilemma would seem to require extensive social and political reform, both inside and outside institutions.

A second issue relates to the modifiability of perceived control. Even when the individual's belief in externality is poorly supported, what is the likelihood of successful belief change? Preliminary evidence suggest that I-E beliefs are relatively malleable and can be affected by experiential feedback (cf. Phares, 1973; Rotter, Chance, & Phares, 1972). The programming of small but significant "success" experiences early in therapy, for example, may increase a client's internality. One of the intriguing considerations here relates to the inextricable interdependence of beliefs and (non-cognitive) behaviors (cf. Chapter 14). A child's poor school performance, for example, may be partly affected by his personally inferred incompetence. By systematically altering that perception, academic performance may improve. The future direction taken by the belief-behavior cycle may then be a function of myriad influences—whether the child incorporates his new experiential feedback into a modified pattern of self-statements, whether success experiences are appropriately scheduled to induce and maintain a resistant and enduring "internal" belief pattern, and so on.

A third consideration focuses on the importance of an active, coping orientation in therapy. If the individual perceives himself as a passive pawn rather than a responsible agent, he may be much less likely to seek or benefit from therapy. In the classic "you help me" fashion of all-too-many clients, he may view the therapist as a benevolent inoculator rather than a technical consultant in personal problem solving. As Phares (1973) indicates, there is suggestive evidence that the "external" client may not only be less aware of the situational influences in his life, but he may also exhibit retention deficits which could impair therapeutic change.

In conclusion it should be noted that the I-E dimension represents but one of many mediational processes which might moderate subjective distress and efficient performance. While it may be tempting to classify individuals as "internals" and "externals" as if perceived locus of control were an overriding and monolithic personality trait, we should keep in mind that I-E beliefs are often relatively situation-specific and modifiable. The pervasiveness of internal or external belief patterns may be a function of consistency in situational and experiential factors.

Misattribution Therapy

Another avenue of research on perceived causality has generated some specific therapeutic recommendations. In 1962, Schachter and Singer reported a classic study on the role of cognitive labeling in emotional arousal. They injected volunteer subjects with epinephrine, a drug which produces marked autonomic arousal (increased pulse, elevation of blood pressure, etc.). Some subjects were accurately informed about the effects of the drug, while others were given inaccurate information or remained uninformed. A group of control subjects were injected with inert saline solution. During a subsequent test phase, participants were exposed to an experimental confederate who modeled angry, euphoric, or neutral behavior. Behavioral ratings of subjects' actions during this phase revealed that the availability of a cognitive label for physiological arousal appeared to dramatically influence performance. Epinephrine-aroused individuals who attributed their autonomic activity to the drug showed significantly less angry or euphoric behavior than misinformed and uninformed subjects. The latter exhibited patterns generally congruent with the stimulus situation—i.e., in the presence of a euphoric model, they acted euphorically; an angry model occasioned more hostile performances. These and subsequent findings stimulated a theory on the role of cognition and labeling in subjective arousal (cf. Schachter, 1964). Briefly, that theory proposes that emotionality requires (a) experienced autonomic arousal and (b) a cognitive label which attributes the cause of that arousal to an emotionally relevant source:

> Given a state of physiological arousal for which an individual has no immediate explanation, he will "label" this state and describe his

> feelings in terms of the cognitions available to him (Schachter & Singer, 1962, p. 382).

The nature of the label assigned to autonomic arousal may, of course, dramatically influence both subjective distress and subsequent performance. If my distractability and heightened arousal are the result of sleep deprivation during finals week rather than an inferred mental disease, my actions may vary dramatically. This speculation has led to a series of attempted manipulations of attribution (labeling) in clinical analogues (Winett, 1970).

Ross, Rodin, and Zimbardo (1969), for example, gave subjects two insoluble puzzles to work on in an experiment purporting to deal with the effects of noise on performance. Subjects were told that solution of one of the puzzles would earn them money; solution of the other would allow them to avoid subsequent painful shock. An attribution manipulation was introduced regarding the side-effects of noise. Half of the subjects were told that the noise would probably produce hand tremors, heart palpitations, visceral upset, and an increased breathing rate (i.e., the autonomic correlates of fear). The other half were told that the noise would have fear-irrelevant side-effects (general numbness, a dull headache, etc.). The major dependent measure was the amount of time subjects spent working on the shock-avoiding versus money-earning puzzle. Figure 12-1 shows that subjects who attributed their arousal to the noise spent significantly less time on the shock-avoiding puzzle than did control subjects. Subjective measures also suggested that noise attribution subjects were less fearful than those for whom a fear-irrelevant label had not been provided.

The direct clinical relevance of programmed misattribution has been addressed by a number of workers in the last few years (cf. Valins & Nisbett, 1971; Kopel & Arkowitz, 1974). One of the seminal studies in this series involved the use of false heartrate feedback to modify subjects' cognitive labeling (Valins & Ray, 1967). Snake phobic volunteers were exposed to slides which either depicted the word "shock" or a scene from a fear-of-snakes hierarchy. Participants additionally heard falsified records of their own heartrates during slide presentations. On shock slides (which were paired with incremental shock over trials), their audible heart rate increased. During snake slide presentations, however, they heard their (falsified) heartrate decline. Subsequent measures of fear and snake avoidance suggested greater reductions by individuals who had inferred fear decrements from their bogus heartrate feedback.

Unfortunately, the Valins and Ray (1967) study suffered from several methodological inadequacies which limit the interpretation of its

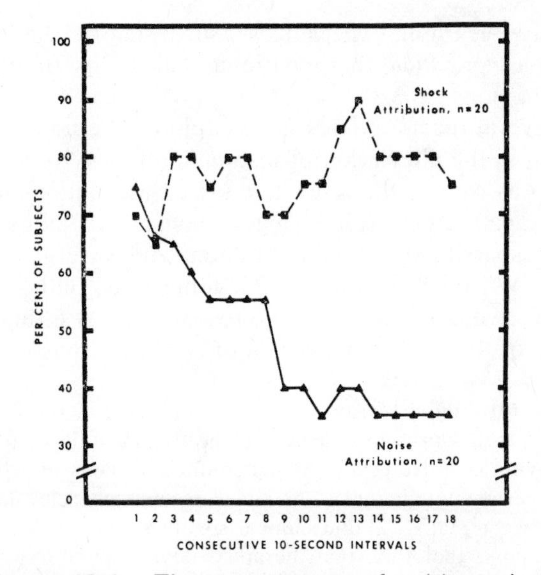

Figure 12-1. The percentage of subjects in each condition working to solve the shock-avoidance puzzle. (Reprinted with permission from Ross, Rodin, & Zimbardo, 1969.)

findings (cf. Bandura, 1969; Davison & Wilson, 1973). Moreover, repeated efforts to replicate these results under better controlled conditions have consistently failed (cf. Sushinsky & Bootzin, 1970; Rosen, Rosen, & Reid, 1972; Gaupp, Stern, & Galbraith, 1972; Stern, Botto, & Herrick, 1972; Kent, Wilson, & Nelson, 1972; Wilson, 1973b). Thus, the clinical promise of this specific procedure has yet to be confidently demonstrated. The contemporary status of misattribution therapies for fear reduction is aptly summarized by Bandura (1969):

> It should be remembered that cognitive claims have been mined many times with disappointing therapeutic yields. In the case of persons who display relatively weak inhibitions, erroneous explanations for physiological arousal to fear-provoking situations may lower their fear to the point where they can perform desired behavior. It is doubtful, however, that strong fears and inhibitions can be eliminated through either mislabeling internal reactions or attributing them to erroneous sources. . . . There is little reason to expect that auspicious cognitions induced through deceptive labeling can substitute for corrective learning experiences in the stable modification of human behavior (p. 448).

The "corrective learning experiences" suggested by Bandura (1969) do not, of course, preclude therapeutic modifications of other types of cognitive behavior.

Several recent studies have explored the potential benefits of misattribution in the alleviation of insomnia (cf. Davison, Tsujimoto, & Glaros, 1973) as well as the relevance of self-attributions in the maintenance of therapeutic behavior change (Davison & Valins, 1968, 1969). The extreme sparsity of data in this area and several non-supportive findings (e.g., Wilson & Thomas, 1973; Johnson & Gath, 1973) preclude even a speculative conclusion at the present time. A fitting commentary on the "state of the art," however, is offered by Davison et al. (1973):

> "Attribution therapy" has been enjoying increasing popularity in sociobehavioral approaches to the modification of maladaptive behavior. . . . However . . . when one evaluates the clinical utility of experimental findings, it becomes exceedingly relevant to distinguish between statistical and clinical significance. . . . We would not yet propose, therefore, that therapists devise actual treatment programs along the lines of our own methods; we would hope, however, that our findings will alert colleagues to the possibility that the manner in which clients and patients explain to themselves the reasons they have enjoyed therapeutic improvement may be one of an as yet undefined number of important factors in the maintenance of behavior change (p. 132).

The general conclusions to be drawn from the area of misattribution therapy are currently modest. First, in the paradigms and problem areas thus far explored, a relatively small percentage of outcome variance has been related to attributional influences. That is, its demonstrated therapeutic effects have been relatively meager. Second, the contribution of misattributional processes appears to be moderated by the function of an "autonomic nervous system override." In patterns involving weak inhibitions and mild autonomic arousal, deceptive labeling may influence subjective distress and subsequent performance. However, when stronger arousal-inducing stimuli are encountered, the therapeutic impact of misattribution is substantially reduced. Finally, there is some extremely preliminary evidence that therapeutic improvements may be more enduringly maintained when they are perceived as accruing from active self-involvement in therapy rather than from passive or extrinsic means. This last conclusion presents an important and research-worthy issue for future clinical investigations.

Before leaving the attribution area, several comments on the prevailing methodologies are worth noting. First, the relatively modest evidence thus far reported in support of attributional elements in therapy may derive from the fact that workers in this field have typically employed rather abrupt and ambitious paradigms in their efforts to alter subjects' beliefs. Telling a client that his subjectively labeled "fear of flying" is actually a mistaken reaction to the physiological effects of cabin pressurization will probably have little impact on the severe flight phobic. After years of sleep difficulties, giving the insomniac a drug and telling him that it will induce the symptoms of insomnia (restlessness, mind racing, etc.) may be a hard pill to swallow. Prior learning and the severity of autonomic arousal often lobby against a simple and swift relabeling of problematic behaviors. More promising possibilities are reflected in recent work by Bandura and his colleagues, who have developed procedures to encourage the *gradual* self-attribution of therapeutic improvement (Bandura, Jeffery, & Gajos, 1974; Bandura, Jeffery, & Wright, in press). An individual can be helped to overcome avoidance patterns through initially extensive external supports and then progressively weaned from such aids as he progresses. Similarly graduated procedures might dramatically improve the outcome in other utilizations of attribution principles. Moreover, since the induced belief in this refined strategy is veridical rather than deceptive, its enduring contribution to therapeutic maintenance may be enhanced.

Another area of potential relevance for attributional research deals with a frequently encountered clinical phenomenon: *arousal-induced arousal.* It is not uncommon for clients to report that they are depressed "because" they are depressed, or anxious "because" they are anxious. The act of perceiving oneself as "not handling it" is often an exacerbating element in subjective distress. To be depressed or anxious implies personal inadequacy and the inability to cope. The "fear of fear" maxim may deserve more credence than has yet been acknowledged. It is interesting to speculate that Frankl's (1959) technique of "paradoxical intention" may have bearing on this same vicious cycle. In paradoxical intention, the client is instructed to perform the very act which he finds distressing:

> A young physician consulted me because of his fear of perspiring. Whenever he anticipated an outbreak of perspiration, this anticipatory anxiety was enough to precipitate excessive sweating. In order to cut this circle formation I advised the patient, in the event that sweating should recur, to resolve deliberately to show people how much he could sweat. A week later he returned to report that . . . after suffering from his phobia for four years, he was able, after a single session, to free himself permanently of it within one week (p. 196).

The potential use of attributional relabeling in arousal-induced arousal has yet to be examined. Some individuals seem to maintain a cyclical self-arousal through chains of inferential labeling and critical self-statements. The premature ejaculator, for example, may exacerbate his own anxiety and performance inadequacies through such mediational processes. Beck (1972b) has described a similar spiral in depression. My own clinical records contain documented instances in which clients have reportedly panicked themselves through such a pattern. The cardiophobic detects a slight numbness in one hand and recognizes this as a possible symptom of cardiac dysfunction. This labeling induces heightened autonomic arousal which, in turn, provides more salient stimuli for self-arousal (palpitations, sweaty palms, etc.). Several cases of clients who thought they were "going crazy" offer further illustration. Vague and innocuous cues, when mislabeled as signs of imminent nervous breakdown, may effect dramatic and painful subjective distress. One client was convinced that his dizziness and feelings of "unreality" were indicative of impending mental illness. A brief interview revealed several alternative sources for these sensations (e.g., 68 hours of sleep deprivation).

Further research is needed to evaluate the speculation that attribution and relabeling procedures might assist in the interruption of arousal-induced arousal sequences. By temporarily terminating such spiraling patterns, therapeutic focus may be more efficiently received by other treatment concerns. Although anecdotal clinical evidence suggests some therapeutic relevance for these procedures, their evaluation must again await controlled empirical exploration.

Self-Perception Theory

One final area which we will briefly examine has to do with the theory of self-perception proposed by Daryl J. Bem (1967, 1970, 1972). Although originally presented as an alternative interpretation of popular "cognitive consistency" theories (cf. Abelson, Aronson, McGuire, Newcomb, Rosenberg, & Tannenbaum, 1968), Bem's self-perception theory has become one of the dominant paradigms in contemporary social psychology. Its relationship and contribution to "attribution theory" have been substantial.

Put most concisely, self-perception theory contends that:

> *Individuals come to "know" their own attitudes, emotions, and other internal states partially by inferring them from observations of their own overt behavior and/or the circumstances in which this behavior occurs. Thus, to the extent that internal cues are weak, ambiguous, or uninterpretable, the individual is functionally in the same position as an outside observer, an observer who must necessarily rely upon those same external cues to infer the individual's internal states* (Bem, 1972, p. 2).

An individual may thus infer an internal state of "hunger" from his self-observed eating behavior. Parallels between Bem's self-perception theory and Skinner's (1945, 1953) analysis of private events are both salient and intentional. Drawing upon a Skinnerian analysis of attitudes, Bem has argued that we infer our own private events in much the same way that we infer such events in others—namely, by observing behaviors and their associated environmental cues. Witnessing a lonely jogger on a pre-dawn San Diego beach may occasion our inference that the individual has positive attitudes about physical fitness. Very different attitudes might be attributed to this same jogger if he were accompanied by a platoon of fellow Marine recruits. In the same way, we may infer our own attitudes and emotions based on how we see ourselves behaving. The perenially badgered spouse may casually remark, "I must love him—otherwise, why would I put up with this?"

An area which has recently applied self-perception theory to research in behavior modification bears on the issue of extrinsic rewards and "intrinsic motivation." Pursuing some earlier work by Deci (1971, 1972), Lepper, Greene, & Nisbett (1973) have suggested that the receipt of extrinsic material reinforcement for a previously unrewarded performance may actually undermine an individual's intrinsic interest in the task. This hypothesis has obvious relevance for the recent trends toward increasing use of token economy programs in the classroom. If extrinsic contingencies are blanketly applied to an entire school or classroom, a number of formerly efficient students will now be receiving token reinforcement for performances which had not previously required supplementary incentives. According to Lepper et al., this "overjustification" of the rewarded activity may result in the individual's self-perception that his performance was extrinsically rather than intrinsically motivated. This inference, in turn, may jeopardize subsequent performance once external incentives have been removed. Lepper et al. describe a study addressed to this issue and cite the previous work of Deci as further corroboration of the undermining effects of extrinsic reward. Unfortunately, a number of methodological inadequacies seriously limit the empirical import of these inquiries. Moreover, a recent study exploring this hypothesis failed to encounter any undermining effects (Feingold & Mahoney, 1974). Despite a dramatic increase in performance during a token reinforcement phase, extended follow-up assessments did not reflect any deterioration of "intrinsic interest" subsequent to reward termination. The issue, of course, remains to be further examined. Hypotheses such as that regarding overjustification will hopefully continue to stimulate re-evaluations and refinements in applications of behavioral strategies.

A detailed examination of the vast literature devoted to self-perception theory would make the present chapter more of a tome than it already is. The reviews by Bem (1970, 1972) and Kopel and Arkowitz (1974) offer valuable summaries. Although its supporting evidence is not meager, Bem (1972) readily acknowledges a number of theoretical and methodological problems in the evaluation and assessment of self-perception research. With the qualification that replications, revisions, and refinements are unquestionably needed, however, the available data offer considerable support for the major premise of Bem's theory. Inferred attitudes, emotions, and beliefs appear to be dramatically influenced by the individual's perception of his own performance and its controlling variables.

The relevance of self-perception theory for clinical applications warrants brief comment. As with the other two avenues of attribution research, this one suggests some complex and potentially significant considerations for therapeutic practice. First, it should be noted that self-perception processes appear to be influenced by experiential feedback. Does this mean—as Skinner (1953, 1971) has contended—that all analyses of human behavior must ultimately return to an external (environmental) Prime Mover? If our attitudes, beliefs, and emotions are simply inferred results of behavioral observations, then why not restrict our analysis to the latter? The answer, of course, is that these inferences vary tremendously across individuals, situations, behaviors, and time. Moreover, variations in self-perception appear to be greatest when salient stimuli are lacking. Thus, as we have seen in the preceding chapters, two different individuals (or the same individual at two different times) may label and respond to the same event in quite discrepant manners. The moderating influence of mediational processes must again be underscored.

A second issue here brings us back to the "belief-behavior" relationship (cf. Chapter 14). If our beliefs (self-perceptions) are influenced by our observed behavior, and our behavior is itself influenced by our beliefs, then aren't we left with a complex reciprocity which staggers functional analysis? Exactly. The importance of that reciprocity will be reiterated and expanded in the next two chapters. For the time being, suffice it to say that a complex belief-behavior interdependence suggests that therapeutic strategies which focus on only one of these chain elements may seriously jeopardize the speed, extent, and duration of their positive impact.

The present chapter has examined three broad areas of relevance to both the cognitive learning model and its associated therapies. While the evidence on coping skills training is still extremely meager, preliminary findings have suggested the possibility of fertile yields from this unharvested area. Expanded research efforts are amply warranted.

The area of problem solving is one of longstanding and

multi-faceted inquiry. Research foci have included animal problem solving, industrial programs, human laboratory experiments, and inquiry training in the classroom. Recent investigations have suggested that a variety of behavioral disorders may be associated with problem solving deficits. Moreover, preliminary applications of systematic training in problem solving skills have yielded promising initial results. The converging evidence from laboratory, classroom, and clinical research suggests that this area may well represent one of the more exciting frontiers in the expansion of therapeutic procedures.

Theory and research on the phenomenon of causal attribution have stimulated an extensive and diversified literature. Three avenues of most direct relevance to cognitive behavior modification have been locus of control, misattribution therapy, and self-perception theory. Although the clinical yields of attributional perspectives have been relatively meager, their refinement and potential contribution to therapeutic improvements warrant continued empirical scrutiny.

Chapter Thirteen

Belief, Counter-Control, and Choice

The present chapter addresses several major foci which seem to loom large on the empirical horizon in cognitive behavior modification. While their current professional connotations range from "muddled" to "science fiction," their heuristic and clinical relevance continue to await close scientific examination.

BELIEF

The critical significance of cognitive contingencies and experiential assumptions has been amply documented in the last few chapters. The human organism responds to a "constructed" reality, and the nature of that "construction" seems to dramatically moderate performance variance. The pervasiveness of "assumptive worlds" (Frank, 1961) is perhaps camouflaged by the fact that they are shared and often culturally transmitted delusions. It is only when our beliefs (and associated actions) differ markedly from those which are socially approved that a label of "deviance" is applied.

The experimental analysis of belief could hardly be overemphasized in terms of its relevance for and potential impact upon future cognitive-clinical developments. While behaviorists from Pavlov to Skinner have repeatedly acknowledged the function of private symbolic processes in human performance, their controlled examination has remained safely outside of behavioral quarters. As token admissions to the complexity of human action, they have been solicited and energetically prostituted in *ad hoc* behavioral formulations but never allotted the legitimacy of formal empirical scrutiny. "Rules," "expectancies," and "symbolic events" are second-class citizens in the behavioral model—they do the hackwork of theory-saving when data force embarrassments on our scientific assumptions.

This Cognitive Inquisition, of course, may be related to both historical and methodological determinants (cf. Chapters 1–3). Hopefully, the historical conventions which have discouraged research on mediational processes have receded. We need no longer fear that our treasured self-perceptions as scientists will be challenged by dabbling a bit in the black box. Our colleagues in the physical sciences repeatedly exhibit how easily (and often profitably) the hard-nosed empiricist can be seduced by controlled inferences. But this raises the second determinant—namely, methodological problems. Common sense allegedly informs us that it is easier to arrive at a definition of "antimatter" than "belief." The former may therefore be talked about scientifically, while the latter must remain in the quagmire of metaphysics.

I shall not here belabor a point which has underscored virtually every chapter in the present writing—namely, that we have the technological skills to conceptually define and empirically examine mediational processes. Scientific definitions are rarely born of philosophy alone—they evolve from procedural considerations. Lamenting the absence of an unambiguous definition of "belief" is an expensive apologetic in behavior modification. It ostensibly absolves us of guilt for continuing to ignore these phenomena and effectively discourages the experimental operations which could germinate such a definition. Our negligence and stubborn defensiveness about scientific self-perceptions are long overdue for re-examination. If the "true" empiricist owes any fidelity at all, it is to the description of regularities in experience. Few would deny that beliefs are a pervasive factor and form in these regularities.

The foregoing comments hint that the experimental analysis of belief is anxiously awaiting the arrival of a behavior modifier in the laboratory. Does this mean that decades of research in social psychology have reaped no empirical benefits? Not exactly. Although I am less than enthusiastic about the practical contribution of belief and attitude research to date, some preliminary generalizations are beginning to bear the testimony of replication and refinement. While the ratio of literature to knowledge approaches infinity, we are at least more adequately aware of our ignorance.

What are beliefs? Definitions of this term in social psychology range widely and reflect the paradox of their own specification (i.e., the beliefs of their definers). Three of the most readable and provocative renditions on the structure of human thought are offered by Rokeach (1960), McGuire (1968), and Bem (1970). Bem's review is a valuable summary of the state of the art and bears considerable relevance to our current discussion. Although he does not offer a formal operationalization of the term, Bem (1970) draws together an impressive variety of assumptions and evidence. These inputs converge on the generalization that

> A man's beliefs and attitudes have their foundation in four human activities; thinking, feeling, behaving, and interacting with others (p. 2).

In terms of cognitive-symbolic structure, Bem distinguishes between *primitive beliefs* (the "givens" of a system) and *higher-order beliefs* (which are vertically and horizontally interdependent elements). Primitive beliefs are implicit "leaps of faith" which do not demand experiential confirmation or formal defense. Examples are the belief in the validity of our own sense data and such assumptions as causality. Higher-order beliefs, on the other hand, may require confirmation and/or defense. They are not "unconscious" or "intuitive" and often form complex superstructures with both parallel and hierarchical organization.

It is worth noting here that, aside from some structural embellishments, social psychology has added little terminological refinement to some long-standing conventions in epistemology. The philosopher Charles Peirce (1878), for example, defined "belief" as "a rule for action" having three components: cognitive, emotional, and behavioral. He contended that a belief entailed (a) sensations to be expected, and (b) behavior to be prepared. In his famous treatise on "The Will to Believe," William James (1896) defended the role of emotional satisfaction in justifying belief. A pervasive focus in virtually every epistemological definition of belief, however, has been behavioral—i.e., a "willingness to act" upon some predicative assumption. This "performance accountability" is illustrated in the fable about an irreligious vacationer who accidentally fell over the edge of the Grand Canyon and found himself dangling precariously from a small shrub. As he hung agonizingly close to imminent death, he mustered an awesome prayer of faith and conversion. Suddenly, his cries for supernatural intervention were answered by a thunderous question from the heavens, "Do you believe?" Startled and inspired, the dangling convert cried, "Yes . . . oh, yes, I *do* believe!" The voice thundered back, "Do you *really* believe?" "Yes, dear God . . . I really, really believe!" There was a brief silence before the heavenly voice wryly responded, "Then let go of the shrub. . ."

Belief entails a predicted performance—an accountability in action. The "strength" (degree, confidence) of a belief is reflected in the frequency and form of the actions it occasions. This behavioral component in belief has been sadly neglected by most social psychological inquiries. Our current knowledge about beliefs and attitudes is predominantly limited to verbal behavior. Subjects are seldom asked to "act" on their opinions and the physiological correlates of belief change are virtually unexamined. Notice that we may have again erred in focusing our empirical attention on only one of three possible nervous systems. The interaction of cognitive, affective, and motor elements in belief has been predominantly measured in cognitive-attitudinal terms. This harks back to the previous comment on the possible methodological benefits which might accrue were "behavioral" researchers to lend their inquiry skills to this area.

Two other features of the current "belief literature" warrant brief comment. First, the pervasive emphasis on a homeostatic drive toward "cognitive consistency" has been impressively prolific but pragmatically barren (cf. Abelson et al., 1968; Bem, 1970, 1972). In light of the plethora of studies addressed to this issue, its relatively meager support should offer a glaring guide to further formulations. Referring to the consistency theorists, Bem comments:

> Inconsistency, they seem to be trying to tell us, motivates belief and attitude change.
>
> But I don't believe it. At least not very much. In my view, a vision of inconsistency as a temporary turbulence in an otherwise fastidious pool of cognitive clarity is all too misleading. My own suspicion is that inconsistency is probably our most enduring cognitive commonplace. That is, I suspect that for most of the people most of the time and for all of the people some of the time inconsistency just sits there. . . . I believe, in short, that there is more inconsistency on earth (and probably in heaven) than is dreamt of in our psychological theories (1970, p. 34).

The upshot of this, of course, is that human beings are not inherently "rational." (Easy, Sigmund.) Consistency among beliefs or between beliefs and behavior is an acculturated value, not an inborn circuit. McGuire (1968), in qualifying his own earlier theorization (1960), has acknowledged the glaring inadequacies of assuming that human thought processes enjoy a tropism toward logic. While maintaining that cognitions are extensively interconnected, McGuire has conceded that their relationships are more often characterized by idiosyncratic "psycho-logic" than by formal logic.

A second comment deals with the dispositional reification of "cognitive styles." An extensive body of research has been addressed to the identification of "personality correlates" in attitude and belief change. The classic works on dogmatism/authoritarianism, for example, have sought to demonstrate that individuals can be reliably differentiated on the basis of their rigidity or openness to cognitive change (e.g., Adorno, Frenkel-Brunswik, Levinson, & Sanford, 1950; Rokeach, 1960; Ehrlich & Lee, 1969). A dated but exemplary summary by Rokeach (1960) illustrates this point:

> persons who are high in ethnic prejudice and/or authoritarianism, as compared with persons who are low, are more rigid in their problem-solving behavior, more concrete in their thinking, and more narrow in their grasp of a particular subject: they also have a greater tendency to premature closure in their perceptual processes and to distortions in memory, and a greater tendency to be intolerant of ambiguity (p. 16).

The cognitively "open" person is said to be more flexible and sensitive to accurate information processing, while the "closed" bigot is sanguinely stubborn in his reality distortions.

My comment here is cautionary—namely, while it may be tempting to impose pervasive "cognitive styles" on the hairless ape, doing so may itself be an act of perceptual dogmatism. The quest for dispositional consistency in human personality has not been a fruitful one (cf. Mischel, 1968, 1973), although the *belief* that it exists seems very resistant to extinction. Our inquiries into human mediation should remain open to the possibility that a diversity of "cognitive styles" may characterize the same person at different points in time and in varying environmental situations. On the other hand, the anti-trait behaviorist must entertain the possibility that ostensible performance consistencies across situations may be moderated by relatively homogeneous information processing systems. That is, the consistency perceived may be a consistency imposed, and this consistent imposition of consistency may be a human disposition. If there is any congruence between the processes involved in motoric and cognitive learning, then it becomes very plausible to speculate that economical mediational skills may develop. As limited capacity information processors, the selective filtration and distortion of experience may be inevitable.

There is nothing foreboding about the possibility that we may utilize relatively homogeneous filtration and distortion processes in constructing our realities. The source of that hypothetical homogeneity, however, poses a significant research issue. Some constraints (and consistency) are undoubtedly imposed by our physiological hardware and the symbol systems we employ. These, however, do not account for all the variance, and I would be willing to speculate that—if there are relatively pervasive "cognitive styles" which differentiate individuals—these "styles" are acquired mediational skills which are amenable to alteration.

Given that "belief" is such a promising area for future cognitive-behavioral research, where do we start? The preceding comments on the social psychological literature suggest that we enter the arena carefully, if at all. Its pay-off to previous entrants has been frustratingly meager. I would like, at this point, to provide a formal heuristic program of research to guide our imminent exploration of belief. I would also like to be six inches taller and have a mustache. Since neither of these desires is currently attainable, I shall compromise with some informal comments on where we might first attack our ignorance.

1. What Characterizes Belief?

I am not here reiterating our previous discussion of definitional problems, although their resolution might be facilitated by examination of some of the following issues. The primary question, I think, can be posed very succinctly: *What is the difference between saying something to yourself and believing it?* Pursuing for a moment the very fallible assumption that a "belief" is an implicit self-verbalization, what is it that distinguishes it from our various self-statements? Why do we believe some of the things we say to ourselves and not others?

One variable might be *rehearsal.* Do we assign greater confidence to self-statements which have been frequently repeated? Perhaps, but I doubt that it is all that simple. It seems unlikely that repeating the phrase "I like the President" would substantially alter the beliefs of a staunch political detractor. On trial one million and one, I doubt that our weary subject would have diametrically reversed his belief. Interestingly, when I posed this illustration to Professor Skinner, he suggested that trial one million and one might at least find the detractor more "understanding" of his political target. He then enumerated a self-change strategy which he employs in reducing interpersonal anger—namely, when upset by someone else's behavior, Skinner sits down and writes a list of the factors which might have generated the person's actions. By exploring these determinants, this cognitive practice may induce a more tolerant and understanding acceptance of the event.

This raises a second potential variable—*logical justification.* Much of the existing literature on belief has placed heavy emphasis on the internal consistency of "thought structures." Moreover, Ellis's rational psychotherapy (Chapter 11) is based on the explicit premise that logical self-examination can induce dramatic belief (and behavior) change. The belief researcher, then, should evaluate the role of logical relationships among cognitive elements. Four general suggestions from the previous work in this area are worth noting. First, there is evidence indicating at least some degree of "inter-relatedness" among cognitive processes (McGuire, 1960, 1968). That is, changes in some beliefs seem to effect changes in other related beliefs. In one illustrative study, McGuire (1960) showed that modifications of a syllogistic premise can effect reliable changes in associated conclusions—even though the inter-related cognitive events have not been presented in strict logical form. Interestingly, the impact of changing one belief on the status of other beliefs is not immediate. Time must be allowed for the effect to "filter down" through presumed organizational structure. This infiltration diminishes with time but may be bolstered by repeated exposure to the modified belief. I might comment here that the "delayed reaction" of a programmed belief change has some interesting clinical correlates.

A second consideration relates to the aforementioned evidence indicating that human thought processes are seldom as logical as some psychological theories have suggested. Although the data suggest that inter-relatedness and (to some degree) internal consistency may characterize many of our beliefs, their formal logical status is often very inadequate.

A related concern in evaluating the role of logical justification in belief has to do with the "Socratic effect" (McGuire, 1960; Rosen & Wyer, 1972). When individuals are allowed to examine and evaluate the rationality and coherence of their own beliefs, resulting cognitive changes are often more dramatic and enduring than when a didactic strategy is applied. This phenomenon can be induced by contiguously experiencing the discrepant beliefs or by Socratic interrogation. The clinical implications of this phenomenon—if it is veridical—bear thoughtful consideration. If cognitive behavior modification can be more efficiently and enduringly induced through a tactful encouragement of "self-examination," then methods like those suggested by Ellis may be in need of procedural refinement. It may be more therapeutic to be "gently directive" in self-discovery exercises than to beat a client over the head with the salience of his irrationality. Again, should the phenomenon hold up under continued empirical scrutiny, it may likewise present a double-edged clinical sword. There is preliminary evidence that individuals who are allowed to take the initiative in abstracting generalizations from particulars are more efficient problem solvers than subjects who are supplied with ready-made generalizations (Legrenzi, 1971). The former engage in more "testing" of their self-generated beliefs than do the latter. The superior strength and endurance of self-generated beliefs, however, poses a potential clinical problem. Namely, if these beliefs turn out to be nonveridical and maladaptive, they may be correspondingly less responsive to therapeutic revision. Recent work, for example, has shown that personal hypotheses in a problem solving situation may be extremely resistant to modification and virtually unaffected by disconfirming evidence (Wason, 1971). The cognitive clinician may therefore be facing a serious dilemma in his use of Socratic methods for belief change. While the procedure may induce powerful cognitive alterations, the therapist may need to be very surveillant regarding the form and adaptiveness of emerging beliefs. This speculation, of course, is one which goes well beyond our current data—and will remain so if the Cognitive Inquisition continues.

One final consideration in the analysis of logical coherence reflects on a finding which is gathering impressive documentation—namely, that the *homo sapiens* is a confirming rather than a disconfirming organism. Like many others, this contemporary "revelation" has been noted for some time:

> the human understanding, when any proposition has been once laid down . . . forces everything else to add fresh support and confirmation: and although most cogent and abundant instances may exist to the contrary, yet either does not observe, or despises them, or it gets rid of and rejects them by some distinction, with violent and injurious prejudice, rather than sacrifice the authority of its first conclusions (Francis Bacon, *Novum organum,* 1621, p. 46).

Despite the efforts of the falsificationists, the average human appears to be more responsive to experiential data which support rather than contradict his beliefs. A single instance of confirmation may have substantially more impact on belief maintenance than numerous disconfirmatory trials. Whether this is a cognitive recapitulation of the superiority of reinforcement over punishment or still another manifestation of the intermittent reinforcement effect has yet to be examined. Its processes, however, may have less immediate clinical relevance than its effects. Individuals not only selectively attend to belief-confirming experiences, but they appear to actively place themselves in environments which enhance the likelihood of such feedback. While Socrates may remind us that the "unexamined life is not worth living," the average person seems to equate examination with confirmation. Experiences which contradict our assumptive world are selectively ignored or distorted. The insulated inertia of this closed system is again well illustrated in the classical thought disorders (paranoia, delusions, etc.). Once a performance-guiding belief system has evolved, its refinement and adaptation to changing life circumstances may be effectively prevented by selective information processing. The believer becomes a "true believer" (Hoffer, 1951) with accelerating conviction and ever-accumulating confirmatory evidence. At a professional level, this phenomenon is documented by the technical isolation which frequently characterizes the "isms" (Krantz, 1971). The radical behaviorist and the cognitive psychologist often selectively expose themselves to predominantly confirmatory journals. Bolstered by this filtered "abundance" of empirical support, they may become progressively more skeptical of occasional "negative findings" and gradually more resistant to conceptual re-appraisal.

What are the clinical implications of the confirmation issue? One might begin by evaluating whether this "propensity" is a learned and modifiable one or one derived from our neurochemical circuitry. My hunch favors the former. In a society which places so much positive valuation on "being right," it isn't difficult to understand why individuals might be powerfully shaped in the focus of their selective attention. If and how that information processing bias can be therapeutically corrected poses a very different question. Should the cognitive therapist place more emphasis on the confirmation of incompatible and more adaptive beliefs rather than trying to destroy (disconfirm) previous cognitions? Should he stress the importance of critical self-examination as an adaptive process and strive to make the client less bigoted in his assimilation of experiential feedback? These and other significant issues await our concerted empirical attention.

The potential importance of logical justification in human belief formation has taken us on a circuitous tangent. We now return to the main theme—what is the difference between a self-statement and a belief? Two broadly defined foci have already been touched upon—rehearsal frequency and logical coherence.

A third influential variable might be the congruence between motoric behaviors and belief content. That is, our willingness to act on a predicative assumption may be influenced not only by its coherence with other assumptions (belief-belief consistency) but also by whether or not it coheres with our non-cognitive performances (belief-behavior consistency). This, of course, returns us to the arena of "cognitive consistency" with all of its myriad complications. As mentioned earlier, it does not appear likely that such congruence is either sufficient or necessary for belief formation and maintenance. However, there is some evidence to suggest that our own self-perceived performances do in fact leave their imprint on private assumptions. We often generate and revise our beliefs on the basis of what we see ourselves doing (Bem, 1970, 1972). The processes involved are certainly not clear and the form of cognitive change effected may vary tremendously. This latter point is well illustrated in the anecdote about a mental patient who believed that he was dead. Frustrated in his efforts to dissuade the patient of this belief, a psychiatrist chanced upon a miniature experiment to settle the issue. He asked the patient, "Do dead people bleed?" "No, of course not," came the reply, at which point the psychiatrist quickly produced a scalpel and pricked the patient's finger. He stood quietly as the amazed man watched a tiny drop of blood trickle from the incision. After an anguished silence and some obvious cognitive restructuring, the patient looked up and remarked, "I'll be damned! Dead people *do* bleed!"

We shall examine the relationship between (non-cognitive) behavior and belief more fully in the next section. For the time being, suffice it to say that it is neither clear, unidirectional, nor sufficient. That is, there seems to be a lot more going on than just belief-behavior alignment.

A fourth potential factor in the generation and maintenance of beliefs invokes the autonomic nervous system. Affective states, emotions, and similar "feeling" variables have unmistakable relevance for belief. One can trace the history of this observation well past the classical philosophers to the age-old differentiation of "feeling and knowing," "conation and cognition," and "head and heart." More recent analyses in the realm of attitude research have likewise documented the relationship. From Staats' classical conditioning of attitudes (cf. Chapter 4) to social psychology's emphasis on group influences, the significance of affective variables for belief has been amply demonstrated. While it would be an oversimplification to say that we believe things because it feels good to do so, there can be little doubt that our willingness to act on an assumption is often dramatically influenced by its associated and anticipated consequences. We are again nudging the ghost of William James and perhaps redescribing a camouflaged version of our former statement regarding our selective attention to confirmatory rather than contradictory experience. In either case, the variable remains a potent one. Its relevance is important not only to the functional analysis of belief, but also to a clinical phenomenon which is frequently observed but seldom cited. Namely, the client who complains of a "belief-feeling" discrepancy. "I *know* that rationally I should . . . but I just don't *feel* right about it." Analogous personal experience could probably be offered *ad infinitum*. Is there a viable distinction between belief and affect? Are autonomic changes a prerequisite to or consequence of cognitive changes (or neither)? When the head and the viscera are at variance, what are the variables which predict the winning influence in subsequent behavior?

The importance of social consensus in belief maintenance and change has been extensively examined in social psychological inquiries (cf. Bem, 1970). A *perceived* supportive culture appears to dramatically influence the rate and magnitude of belief modification. Interestingly, the available evidence suggests that relatively subtle, "non-coercive" social pressures may induce greater belief change than direct authoritarian efforts at manipulation. High pressure efforts to alter a person's attitudes or opinions may actually result in a "boomerang effect" wherein beliefs change in a direction opposite to that intended (Wicklund, 1974). The conspicuousness of efforts to induce belief change may moderate social pressure and social consensus factors. The relatively low rate of "conversions" in concentration camps, for example, may be partly attributed to the conspicuousness of brainwashing attempts. Despite severe physical deprivations and frequent isolation from a belief-supporting social environment, many prisoners endure prolonged manipulative efforts with remarkably little cognitive change. What are the variables which moderate this resistance? Are self-instructions and cognitive contingencies extensively involved?

The foregoing questions are only a few of those which face the belief researcher. Whether, in fact, self-statements can be differentiated from beliefs on the basis of rehearsal, logical coherence, behavioral congruence, or affective associates remains to be empirically examined. One final note of caution may be appropriate. The preceding discussion has singled out beliefs as *dependent* variables for the sake of speculative analysis. Unfortunately, nature isn't quite as cooperative. The preceding chapters have documented the pervasive role of beliefs as *independent* variables. We are again forced to acknowledge a complex reciprocal determinism. Not only may behavioral, affective, and symbolic organizational variables influence belief, but the belief most certainly retaliates. Anthropomorphisms aside, it is arbitrary to single out one element of a time-space sequence and call it the "cause" of a subsequent element. Our functional analysis of belief may be seriously impaired until we acknowledge the pervasive and inextricable interdependence of belief-behavior-environment combinations. Once we begin describing variables as if they were omnipotent Prime Movers which shape the destiny of certain events (be they beliefs, behaviors, or whatever), we have effectively removed ourselves from the empirical realm and entered the arena of metaphysical cosmology. Changes in belief appear to be related to changes in other phenomena (rehearsal, affective experience, etc.) and the prediction–description of belief change (if that is our current focus) may well require consideration of a complex interactive matrix. None of the above variables seem to be either sufficient or necessary associates in accounting for all of the variance. Our future inquiries might do well to abandon the search for a unified source and instead explore the relevance of integrated (and interdependent) phenomena.

2. What Are the Processes in Belief Change?

Another major avenue for continued and expanded analyses of belief relates to the processes and parameters of belief change. The foregoing discussion has already touched upon some of the potential phenomena which might be related to the formation and maintenance of belief. What are their implications for clinical practice? What are the most effective means for producing therapeutic belief change? How does one go about influencing the maladaptive assumptions of the depressed perfectionist or the paranoid schizophrenic?

The clinical and humane implications of these questions are as salient as they are research-deprived. We have distressingly little data on the practical effects of belief-change strategies in therapeutic realms. Our efforts toward changing cognitions have been prejudicially showered upon college sophomores, opinion polls, and the American consumer. We have devoted invaluable human skills and material resources in efforts to change beliefs about the relative merits of deodorants and political candidates. Meanwhile, our clinics, hospitals, and homes are inhabited by individuals whose existence and daily well-being are painfully jeopardized by dysfunctional beliefs. The clinical scientist has borne frequent testimony to the extreme personal suffering observed daily in our "mental" institutions. Had we devoted as much time and concerted research effort toward refining the techniques of therapeutic belief change as we have invested in marketing research, the pervasiveness of contemporary thought disorders might have been dramatically reduced. Needless to say, our priorities are in need of re-examination.

I shall not here belabor whether our "proper" focus in psychotherapy should be beliefs or behavior. That sterile controversy has already consumed more energy and professional talent than can be justified. Suffice it that a clinical program which disproportionately focuses upon one rather than both may be seriously limiting its own therapeutic impact. I do not agree with the popular behavioral dictum that, since attitude change seems to follow rather than precede behavior change, our major emphases should be directed toward improved performance. Conversely, I disagree with the notion that verbally-induced alterations in "self-image" and "insight" will result in the most humane and genuine therapeutic progress. The clinical scientist who views his client as a complex organism comprised of awesomely interrelated phenomena will aim at a broader improvement goal.

In the virtual absence of any clinical evidence on the relative effects of various belief-change strategies, we are left to speculate and extrapolate from other areas. From some of the social psychology literature and a few clinical analogue inquiries, it appears that a variety of procedures may contribute to mediational improvements. First, isolation of the belief in a formal symbol system may be important. Getting the client to represent his assumption tangibly may focus attention both on its content and its consequences. Second, relating the belief to related cognitive structures may be contributory. As Frank (1961) points out, most of our assumptive worlds are poorly mapped—we often remain relatively ignorant of our own performance blueprints. By clarifying both the belief and its associated structures, the client may be better able to effect revisions. Third, a "shared conceptual system" between therapist and client may be important. This point—again raised by Frank (1961)—may underlie the superiority of therapies that offer a relatively formal paradigm and rationale rather than isolated techniques. If the client buys into the paradigm, he may be much more likely to make (often) sweeping alterations in cognitive structure. Notice that this conceptual sharing may entail extensive "cognitive modeling" on the part of the therapist. In presenting his conceptual paradigm, he is also modeling some beliefs and encouraging an active self-examination on the part of the client. The potential contribution of this cognitive modeling component may be substantial. A fourth element may be rehearsal. While rote repetitions of a self-statement may not miraculously stamp in a belief, they appear to serve some facilitative function. Reinforcement constitutes a fifth possible factor; its potential importance need hardly be elaborated. By far the most significant factor, however, seems to be confirmatory experience. The client who engages in actual performances congruent with the desired belief frequently exhibits dramatic and often rapid cognitive restructuring. There is some evidence that these performances should be initially graduated but progressively more similar to naturalistic demands. Moreover, it appears that a supportive "perceived choice" assignment may induce greater impact on belief than an identical experience performed under the duress of authoritarian command. The parameters remain to be clarified—the generalization remains well established. Self-perceived behavior change can contribute powerfully to therapeutic belief change.

The potential relevance of information processing principles in belief change has yet to be examined systematically. Unfortunately, most human memory research has focused on discrete content items (e.g., consonant trigrams) rather than predicative relational inputs (e.g., "It is true that. . ."). Nevertheless, some relevancies and parallels are apparent. For example, encoding considerations may suggest enhanced belief change when assumptive statements are structurally coded (e.g., via mnemonics). Related to this are the issues of context and meaningfulness. A belief may need to be assimilated into some organizational schema, which again suggests the importance of a shared conceptual paradigm. Repetition frequency and recency may likewise influence belief formation and maintenance. Although these factors are frequently employed in religious proselytization, they have remained virtually unexamined by clinical researchers.

It is worth noting here that at least some of the processes in belief change may be "unconscious" in the sense that the individual is unaware of their operation. This speculation is, I think, firmly grounded in several diversified literatures. Evidence spanning the phenomena of incidental learning, biofeedback, and pre-attentive mechanisms testifies to the occurrence of at least some learning without awareness. While I agree with Bandura's (1969) summary that awareness is a facilitative (but not necessary) component in learning, we should remain apprised of the possibility that some learning can (and does) occur "unconsciously." Given that at least some nervous system alterations occur without awareness, our understanding of belief change processes may necessitate reliance on assessment methods other than introspection and verbal self-report. We must remain continually self-critical of even our most fundamental assumptions (e.g., that beliefs are predominantly in the domain of the central nervous system).

One intriguing issue in the processes of belief modification relates to whether it occurs in incremental or all-or-none fashion. Is the belief gradually shaped in the direction of therapeutic improvement, or is dichotomous "revelation" a more appropriate metaphor? When the depressed perfectionist alters his assumptive standards and self-evaluations, does it occur gradually or overnight? My noncommittal hunch is that both of these phenomena occur in most therapeutic modifications of belief. Conversations with colleagues and my own clinical experiences over the past few years have offered ample documentation of all-or-none belief change. As a matter of fact, a phenomenon which might be called the *cognitive click* seems to appear very frequently in a variety of therapy applications. Many practicing behavior therapists have related an observation that is seldom cited in our "technical" communications—namely, that there is often a discriminable point of "success" in desensitization, participant modeling and many other formalized procedures. A phobic client, for example, will often comment on a critical stage in hierarchy approach performance. Once this event has occurred (e.g., briefly touching the tail of a snake), subsequent tasks are reported as being "smooth sailing." More descriptive illustrations have been offered in over a dozen clinical cases involving programmed "thought-priming." Clients given "cue" cards to stimulate therapeutic self-statements have often displayed a remarkably similar pattern. They begin with protestations that the assignment is too "mechanical" or "artificial" and that it will certainly not work. However, within two weeks of initiating this exercise, they will often call the therapist with exclamations of "conversion." One young co-ed, for example, had sought therapy for her painful anxieties and self-criticisms regarding promiscuity—a pattern which she did not want to alter. With some therapist assistance, she generated several self-statements compatible with promiscuity and wrote them down on 3x5 cards (e.g., "The ability to be physically intimate is a sign of maturity and warmth"). Her assignment was to read each of the cards before each meal (the meals were conceptualized as useful and patterned cues, not clandestine reinforcers). She objected to the artificiality of the exercise but agreed to try it. After one week, there had been no change. Midway through the second week, however, she phoned the therapist at home and exclaimed, "I can't understand it—something has happened! I *believe* what I'm saying to myself!" Such clinical anecdotes, of course, are just that—clinical anecdotes. They offer weak but heuristic suggestions for further research endeavors.

I mentioned earlier that therapeutic belief change may be characterized as both an incremental and an all-or-none process. The cognitive click illustrates relatively dichotomous alterations. However, there are also some indications that the impact of cognitive restructuring may follow an incremental and relatively gradual generalization curve. That is, the client may change particular beliefs in all-or-none fashion and their alteration may in turn have a spreading impact on related or superordinate assumptions. When enough "particulars" have been modified, the "generalization" may itself be sieged. Somewhat analagous to Kuhn's (1962) "normal" and "revolutionary" science, the individual—as a personal scientist—may modify specific hypotheses until an entire paradigm shift is stimulated.

The tremendous variability of belief phenomena portend of a complexity which may stymie the behavioral researcher. The literature on superstition, for example, documents the frequency with which a single experience may induce a belief (Jahoda, 1969). Clinical and institutional records likewise illustrate the tenacity of dysfunctional beliefs even when disconfirmatory experience is abundant. As documented in Rosenhan's (1973) recent research on psychiatric labeling, this selective information processing is not restricted to the "deviant." Skilled professionals are often as expensively blind to disconfirming data as the astrologer and the paranoiac.

We remain a long way away from accounting for even a modest portion of the variance in human belief. However, our ignorance should be a stimulant rather than a deterrent to continued inquiry. The literatures of religion, psychopathology, and political ideology bear frequent witness to the painful dysfunctions and personal suffering which may accrue from adopting various beliefs. If we claim any semblance of humanistic philosophy in our professional pursuits, we cannot afford to continue ignoring this focus of human adjustment.

COUNTER-CONTROL

In the summer of 1970 I was invited to serve as a technical-consultant-teaching-parent in a family-style group home for "emotionally disturbed" children (Mahoney & Mahoney, 1973). The experience turned out to be one of the most exciting and humbling in my early career. I had my own "live-in laboratory" replete with six captive subjects and an enthusiastic staff. The amusing—and often endearing—anecdotes of our ambitious efforts to "control behavior" would constitute a novel in and of themselves. I relate a select few here because of their etiological impact on my own interests in cognitive behavior modification.

One of my most striking memories of our first ventures into the naturalistic application of learning principles focused on a naive frustration—children don't respond so neatly as rats (as least not the children in our program). Despite well formulated strategies and painstaking implementation efforts, we often got much more "misbehavior" than our operant consciences could tolerate.

An example is offered by six-year-old Aaron, a beautiful Chicano boy with a long history of family difficulties. Aaron was enuretic—an easily quantified "datum"—and we soon chose bedwetting as a preliminary focus in his treatment. One entire wall of the kitchen was covered with data charts, a column for each child. Bedwetting became Aaron's prime behavioral target, and we enthusiastically watched his progress as our contingencies took hold. Using an enuresis conditioning pad and contingent breakfast doughnuts, we had soon wrought our behavioral miracle—30 consecutive "dry nights." It was then time for the sage Behavior Modifier to shift reinforcement to an intermittent schedule. I sat down with Aaron and enthusiastically praised him for his improvement. "Now," I said, "you're going to graduate to an even better 'system'—one like grown-ups have. From now on, it will take *two* dry nights to earn a doughnut instead of just one." Aaron sat quietly for a minute, rubbed his six-year-old chin, and then responded, "Nope." I meekly echoed, "No?" "Nope," he said, "I think I'm gonna have a lot of wet nights."

He was right. In many successive attempts to regain his cooperation, we tried everything but a rubber band. Aaron would not stay dry and seemed to be thoroughly enjoying our futile antics to so coerce him. In desperation, we finally instituted a procedure which had been naively overlooked—extinction. After the failure of incentives ranging from roller skates to severe restrictions, we were amazed to find that all we had needed to do was ignore his transgressions.

Aaron taught us a very valuable lesson and one which was

replicated many times in the months that followed—behavior control is a bidirectional process. "Counter-control" became a frequent theme in our staff meetings, partly because it was not an uncommon observation in our research. A child who was "reinforced" for changing his school clothes would sometimes actually *decrease* the ostensibly rewarded behavior. Another who was "punished" for swearing would soon double his emission of obscenities. We introduced reversal phases in an attempt to identify the controlling variables; and sure enough, when we removed our contingencies the behaviors would often rapidly trend in desired directions. Were we dealing with reinforcement idiosyncrasies? Maybe we just hadn't found the "right" incentives? To test this, we gave counter-controlling subjects free access to the items and privileges which were later made contingent. On a non-contingent basis, they enthusiastically chose these "favorites." When the "favorites" were made contingent, however, they often seemed to suppress performances. The implication was obvious—some of our children were "purposely" acting opposite to our contingencies.

I soon became intrigued by "counter-control" as a research-worthy phenomenon and poured over the existing literature for suggestive evidence. Even though relatively cursory, my search was amply rewarded. We were certainly not alone in encountering performances exactly opposite to our desires. As a matter of fact, the literature seemed to abound with footnoted accounts of "oppositional" individuals who had gone awry in the face of learning principles. Cowan, Hoddinott, and Wright (1965), for example, reported a study with autistic children in which 10 out of 12 subjects responded opposite to experimenter instructions. Patterson and his colleagues have likewise documented the frequency of "negative set" in deviant children (cf. Patterson, Littman, & Brown, 1968; Patterson, 1969). In one laboratory assessment of a deviant preschooler, it was found that the child behaved in a manner which was diametrically opposite to his mother 100 percent of the time (Patterson, Hawkins, McNeal, & Phelps, 1967). In one token economy program, the counter-rebellion of "delinquent soldiers" was so extreme as to force immediate termination of the procedures (Boren & Coleman, 1970).

A recent study by Resnick and Schwartz (1973) offers a lucid illustration of counter-control. Subjects were asked to participate in a verbal learning experiment which required them to choose one of six pronouns and use it in a sentence. After 20 baseline trials, one group of subjects was informed that the experimenter would subsequently say "good," "mmm-hmmm," or "okay" whenever they chose the pronoun "I" or "we". It was explained to them that this verbal reinforcement procedure had been previously shown to increase the frequency of selected pronoun usage. Control subjects received identical experimenter reinforcement for their pronoun choices but remained uninformed of the explicit manipulative efforts. The resulting differences in performance are shown in Figure 13-1. Uninformed subjects increased their emission of reinforced pronouns, while subjects in the experimental group showed a slight but progressive suppression of "rewarded" behaviors.

Other illustrations of counter-control are not hard to provide—the human organism frequently "misbehaves" (cf. Meichenbaum, Bowers, & Ross, 1968; Browning, 1971; Nordquist, 1971; Betancourt & Zeiler, 1971; McCullough, 1972; Mahoney, Thoresen, & Danaher, 1972; Davison, 1973; Wicklund, 1974; Jeffrey, Hartmann, & Gelfand, in press). While these instances may be rare relative to the usual conformity reported in behavioral research, their mere existence is a seldom cited consideration in our discipline.

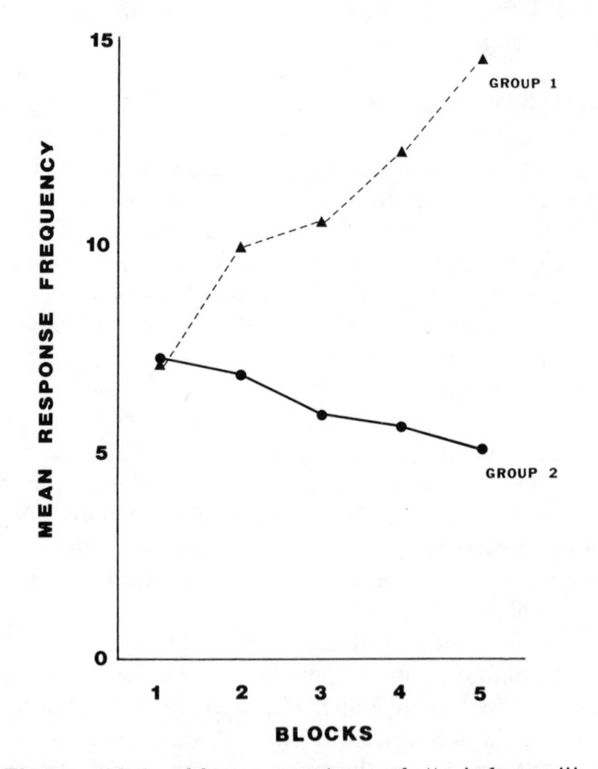

Figure 13-1. Mean number of "reinforced" pronouns emitted by subjects in the informed and uninformed groups. (Drawn from the data of Resnick & Schwartz, 1973.)

Deviation from prediction, however, should not be mistaken for a capriciousness in nature. Many of the studies reporting counter-control have found it to be a consistent and predictable pattern for that individual and /or situation. The subjects are being "deviant" only in the sense that they are responding in a manner which contradicts the experimenter's contingencies. This is a far cry from being indeterminate. They are still exhibiting performance regularities (albeit frustrating ones for their would-be controllers).

The phenomenon of counter-control is, I think, a sorely neglected area of research in contemporary behavior modification. Although our footnotes and informal discussions abound with anecdotes of the "screw you" phenomenon, we have been reluctant to grant this pattern a legitimate focus in our research. Despite the fact that oppositional patterns characterize many socially deviant minorities (e.g., delinquents, criminals, etc.), we have failed to bring counter-control into the laboratory for a closer functional analysis.

My experiences in the group home environment and a handful of pilot investigations over the past two years have suggested a number of possibly relevant variables in counter-control phenomena. First, it appears that the presence or absence of *choice* may moderate oppositional patterns. This possibility was first impressed upon me by six-year-old Aaron, our rebellious enuretic. Aaron was also a terror at bedtime—he refused to take his shower, threw temper tantrums, etc. We had painstakingly programmed reinforcement for more appropriate responses (e.g., with after-shower snacks) and consistently used the removal of privileges as negative consequences for transgressions (response cost and time-out). Nevertheless, Aaron's rebellious patterns persisted. One night, I serendipitously said, "Aaron, do you want to take your shower in the upstairs or the downstairs bathroom." He stopped, smiled broadly, and said, "Downstairs!" His compliance surprised me (partly because he usually showered downstairs). An equally amazed staff member asked me what I had done to win Aaron's cooperation. We set about a naturalistic experiment. Was it the choice? We arranged a series of ministudies which varied the presence or absence of choice and the type of choice involved (which bathroom, color of towel, etc.). Aaron's data were impressively consistent—when we gave him a choice, he complied enthusiastically. When we did not, he counter-controlled. Several subsequent experiences added to my hunch that choice may be an important variable in the moderation of oppositional patterns. It is interesting to note that some of the most effective treatment programs for delinquency have incorporated substantial choice options—the delinquents have some say-so in their own contingency management (e.g., Fixsen, Phillips, & Wolf, 1973).

A second possible parameter in counter-control may be the *conspicuousness* of manipulative or coercive efforts. An element in this conspicuousness, of course, is the presence or absence of an explicit prediction. In *Notes from the Underground,* a classic treatise on counter-control, Dostoyevsky (1864) commented that man would go to great extremes in order to avoid being predictable:

> And that is not all: even if man really were nothing but a piano-key, even if this were proved to him by natural science and mathematics, even then he would not become reasonable, but would purposely do something perverse out of simple ingratitude, simply to gain his point . . . . If you say that all this, too, can be calculated and tabulated . . . then man would purposely go mad in order to be rid of reason and gain his point! (p. 463)

Skinner aptly reminds us, however, that this statement by Dostoyevsky was itself a prediction—and one which closes the issue. Man's efforts toward being unpredictable are themselves predictable. The obnoxious car salesman and the overbearing clerk bear frequent witness to the effects of coercive pressure—we often counter-control.

A classroom demonstration of predictable unpredictability can be readily programmed. All the instructor need do is open his lecture with an overbearingly manipulative monologue on the "conditionability" of college students (who, after all, are simply overgrown rats). To demonstrate inflexible determinism in their behavior, he then predicts some relatively innocuous performance (e.g., that most of them will stand up at his simple command). When this performance is not forthcoming, the instructor can produce an hermetically sealed envelope containing his prediction of counter-control. (If most *do* stand up, he can marvel at the blind conformity induced by our culture.)

A third element in counter-control is that of *modeling*. If an individual is exposed to models who are either unresponsive or counter-responsive, he is much more likely to behave likewise (particularly if the models' oppositional performances have been rewarded or unpunished). The delinquent subculture and the gang leader offer ample illustrations of this phenomenon (Bandura, 1973).

Finally, there are several parameters which might interact in complex ways to influence the frequency and form of counter-controlling behaviors. The novelty of the task, the consequences of transgression, and the nature of the "request" are but a few. Since counter-control is probably a form of aggression, it may also be influenced by the many variables involved in such patterns (cf. Bandura, 1973). Likewise, since it often involves ascetic self-denial and ostensibly painful clashes with "the system," it probably entails some extensive cognitive contingencies and self-evaluative processes. The relative failure of coercive brainwashing techniques with prisoners of war attests to the power of these latter two elements in counter-control phenomena.

One methodological note closes our discussion of counter-control. It is a pattern which is defined arbitrarily by the non-correspondence between expected and observed behavior. To protect our inferential rigor, however, we may want to initially restrict our functional analyses and operational definitions to counter-responsiveness rather than non-responsiveness. The latter pattern may result from a variety of factors which have nothing to do with active counter-controlling processes. An inattentive or unmotivated individual may be non-responsive without necessarily being rebellious. Response patterns which are diametrically opposed to those requested or contingently programmed by an experimenter offer the strongest evidence for counter-control. The cardinal paradigm may involve a reversal design in which the same subject is shown to repeatedly reverse his performance in diametric opposition to the existing contingencies.

CHOICE

The relevance of choice for human behavior is not restricted to counter-control phenomena. There is now a rapidly increasing body of evidence suggesting that choice may be a significant factor in a number of complex response patterns. Recent animal research, for example, has indicated that the availability of multiple response options may have reinforcement properties. With consummatory variables held constant, both pigeons and rats have been shown to prefer conditions in which they can choose between two identical response options (cf. Catania, 1972b; Voss & Homzie, 1970). Whether these data reflect an incentive value in choice or the influence of such factors as stimulus complexity or survival-enhancing "control over the environment" remains to be determined (cf. Singh, 1970; Creed & Ferster, 1972). However, a substantial body of evidence has begun to suggest that at least some forms of choice have reinforcing properties for humans.

A series of classroom and laboratory studies have found, for example, that children exhibit higher performance rates when they are given choices and often show marked preferences for choice-enhancing activities (cf. Lovitt & Curtiss, 1969; Doke & Risley, 1972; Felixbrod & O'Leary, 1973; Brigham & Sherman, 1973; Brigham & Stoerzinger, 1974; Mahoney & Mahoney, 1974; Brigham & Bushell, in press). Interestingly, several of these studies have suggested that the observed performance increments may be directly attributable to the choice component itself rather than other experimental parameters. Superior performances were observed even when self-chosen activities or contingencies were *identical* to those previously or subsequently imposed by the experimenter. That is, it may not have been the consequences of the choosing which influenced responding as much as the act of choosing itself.

Corroborative evidence from two other areas lend additional impetus to the notion that some forms of choice may facilitate selected performance. MacDonough, Adams, and Tesser (1973), for example, found that desensitization subjects were significantly more successful when given choices in self-paced hierarchy presentation. Likewise, several recent studies have indicated that choice may enhance recall in paired-associate learning tasks (cf. Perlmuter, Monty, & Kimble, 1971; Monty & Perlmuter, 1972; Monty, Rosenberger, & Perlmuter, 1973). When compared with yoked control subjects, individuals who were allowed to choose their own response items showed substantially greater retention. Several intriguing results were reported in these inquiries. When subjects were given choices on some trials but not on others, their recall performances were consistently superior on the choice items. Likewise, continuous choice (100%) was more facilitative than intermittent (50%). Of particular note was the finding that subjects who were given choice options early in the experiment performed better than subjects who received later but quantitatively equal opportunities to choose.

Does all of this mean that "choice is a reinforcer"? Such a generalization might be a welcomely simple crystal in our search for human regularities. However, the phenomenon is again much more complex than can be characterized by simplistic maxims. The literatures on the stress-inducing effects of decision making strongly challenge a simple reinforcement equation. Animal studies have even shown that infrahumans will sometimes work to avoid difficult choices (e.g., Rachlin & Green, 1972). Political elections likewise demonstrate that the existence of options is not always an exhilarating experience.

All that can be gleaned from the existing evidence is the tentative generalization that some forms of choice seem to influence some types of performance in some subjects. A more definitive identification of the processes and paramenters involved must await careful empirical scrutiny. Two comments relevant to that scrutiny are offered.

First, our experimental analysis of choice must entail a thoughtful operationalization of the term. What do we mean by "choice"? A preliminary analysis suggests that the phenomenon could be conceptualized as 2x2 matrix which contrasts response and consequence options. The "choosing" organism may have access to two or more response options and these may be either identical or non-identical. (I shall here acknowledge but not belabor the phenomenological possibility that physically "identical" options may be subjectively perceived as non-identical.) Even when there is only one response available, however, the organism may have consequence options (again, identical or non-identical). This schema is illustrated below.

	Response	Consequence
Identical		
Non-Identical		

A molecular analysis suggests that in any given situation, the organism always has some minimal number of response options (e.g., pressing a lever, scratching its ear, etc.). What are the effects of increasing those options? For example, what happens if we install a second lever? How about a non-identical response option (e.g., a running wheel)? Each of the available response options, of course, has its associated consequences (ranging from food presentation to imperceptible proprioceptive events). What happens when a lever press produces either of two consequence options (e.g., a choice between two identical food pellets)? If a response gives the organism access to a choice between non-identical consequences (e.g., a food pellet or a sip of water), will it be preferred over a no-choice response? Notice that the response-consequence dichotomy breaks down when our molecular analysis examines consequence options. A choice between two consequences (pellet A or pellet B) is actually a choice between two responses. Viewing behavior as an ongoing chain of elements, we may need to reform our conceptualizations along the lines of stochastic processes. The question then becomes whether a perceived difference in subsequent choice options will influence differential probabilities of current alternatives. That is, is the current performance of response A or B affected by their respective effects on subsequent response options? For a specified subject-task combination, will the individual consistently perform responses which either expand or limit subsequent alternatives?

The above conceptual tangent should emphasize the complexities which face our experimental analysis of choice. It appears that all choice may be response choice and that it will be very difficult to separate the *act* of choosing from the *consequences* of choosing. Is it the existence of options or the ultimate consequences of those options which determine the influences of choice? Evolutionary analyses have suggested that diversification may have served a survival function in the species. Does this mean that some forms of choice may be inherently reinforcing? How does one isolate this from the pervasive cultural value attached to freedom and response options? Does the human organism value choice as an acquired reinforcer?

A related issue touches more explicity upon some of the possible cognitive components in choice. As we saw in Chapter 12, perceived choices may have significant clinical relevance in the moderation of stress reactions and in the initiation of active coping endeavors. In addition, there is substantial evidence that an individual's performance in a wide range of spheres may be affected by real and perceived freedom. In his reactance theory, Brehm (1966) has contended that an individual will actively strive to avoid or mitigate reductions in his personal freedom (response options). When that freedom is threatened or diminished, he will allegedly work to restore lost options—either directly, symbolically, or vicariously. Although the evidence is still preliminary, support for these hyphotheses is rapidly accumulating (cf. Wicklund, 1974). Of equal relevance is the literature on "perceived freedom" (cf. Steiner, 1970). Studies in this area have begun to identify some of the variables which seem to influence our perception of response options, as well as the effects of those perceptions on subsequent performance. Choice seems to be inferred, for example, when available response options are of near-equal valence. Interestingly, several studies have also suggested that subjects may attribute more freedom to experimenters who deliver intermittent rather than continuous consequences. Analyzing reinforcement as a communicative process, Steiner (1970) has suggested that parameters involved in reward presentation and scheduling may dramatically influence its meaning for the recipient.

An interesting clinical phenomenon related to the cognitive aspects of choice is observed in cases where the client complains about feeling "controlled." My research experiences with obesity in the past few years have offered ample illustrations of this "cognitive claustrophobia." The dieting individual will often report obsessive thoughts about virtually any restriction placed upon him. It is the age-old "forbidden fruit phenomenon"—tell a person they can't have something, and they want it all the more. How many parents have successfully induced spinach-eating by initially telling their child that he couldn't have any? The "greener pastures" psychology has even been documented in laboratory studies—children's reward preferences seem to be inversely related to the availability of the reward (Mischell & Masters, 1966).

The foregoing comments suggest a need for controlled examination of choice parameters and perceived freedom in clinical applications. What are the conditions which recommend or discourage choice as an emphasized therapeutic component? What are the parameters and determinants of ''cognitive claustrophobia''? These and other questions offer ample research options in our future empirical analyses.

Chapter Fourteen

Biological Relevancies

The main thesis of the present chapter is that biological factors may be relevant for the optimization of learning experiences in the human organism. It is ironic that the contemporary behaviorist often places himself on the horns of a self-contradictory dilemma. To his "mentalistic" colleagues, he energetically argues for the parsimony of a biological brain rather than an ephemeral mind; to his biological colleagues, however, he stubbornly minimizes the role of biological determinants in human behavior. Most of the anti-biology arguments, of course, are addressed to ethological and hereditary perspectives. The behaviorist contends that very little performance variance may be attributed to "inborn" mechanisms. However, in throwing out the biology of instinct, he has often thrown out the biology of learning.

To contend that most human behaviors are learned is not incompatible with the assumption that learning is biologically mediated. We presume that there are neurochemical changes underlying the process. Given a biological organism and a presumably neurochemical substratum for learning, it seems only reasonable to concede the possibility that the current physiological state of the individual may influence his ability to assimilate, retain, or utilize experiential information.

THE EVOLUTION OF THOUGHT

In an excellent theoretical review, Campbell and Spear (1972) have recently traced the "ontogeny of memory" and its physiological correlates. It is their contention that the inability of the adult human being to recall early infantile experiences may be due to retentional deficits rather than inadequacies of original learning experiences. They describe data on the development of information processing abilities and long-term memory in both animals and humans. In their analysis of the neurological correlates of memory development, Campbell and Spear suggest five possible variables:

(1) *myelinization of nerve fibers;* this biological process, which dramatically increases the speed of nerve conductance (and hence the rate and amount of potential information processing), may continue for several decades in the human being;
(2) *cell differentiation;* the number of synaptic connections among nerve cells increases rapidly with maturation and may influence retrieval capacities in memory mechanisms;
(3) *electrical activity;* increased electrical activity with maturational development implicates its possible role in learning and memory; since this activity is based on neurochemical processes, the importance of adequate chemical resources is noteworthy;
(4) *neural transmitters;* the development of memory correlates fairly well with increasing concentrations of serotonin, norepinephrine, dopamine, and acetylcholine; although their specific functions remain unclear, their role in central nervous system processes is amply documented;
(5) *DNA, RNA, and protein;* there is a growing consensus that some complex form of protein synthesis is involved in learning and memory, although specific mechanisms remain indeterminate.

While this overview is brief, it should emphasize the numerous possibilities for biological factors to interact with learning experiences. The protein-deficient organism, for example, may be unable to supply necessary enzymes, transmitters, or cellular elements for the appropriate processing of information.

Theories regarding the neural and biochemical basis of learning and memory, of course, are far from scarce. The analysis offered by Campbell and Spear (1972), however, raises some intriguing evolutionary speculations which warrant brief commentary.

It was mentioned earlier that mediation has presumably served a survival function in the continuation and differentiation of the species. Closer analysis reveals that the primary role of mediation may be "predictive" in nature. That is, the organism may learn to anticipate the consequences of various response options and correspondingly select the most adaptive alternative in a given situation. Contingencies are no more than systematic relationships (sequences) in experience. Their "awareness" (i.e., symbolic retention) may derive from past experience (direct or vicarious)[a] or from current symbol manipulation

[a] The technical distinction between direct and vicarious experience is difficult to defend, but its phenomenology is not.

(i.e., problem solving). This anticipatory function may economize effort by reducing trial-and-error learning. It may likewise avert fatal mistakes observed in the performance of peers. The ability to recall the location of edible food and the lairs of predators would have obvious survival value in atavistic environs. The development of symbol systems (e.g., language) in some of the higher primates probably enhanced capacities for symbolic learning experiences. As Terrace (1971) reminds us, man's acquisition of "covert speech" abilities may have derived from punitive contingencies which might ensue if our peers were apprised of our ruminations (plans, verbal aggressions, etc.). Many a spouse can attest to the survival value of covert speech.

The evolutionary development of cognitive processes is an alluring area of speculation. In Jaynes's (1974) analysis of the origins of consciousness, he discusses the role of developmental cognitive skills in man's current perception of his world. It has long been conjectured, for example, that the cave man's experience of dreams and nonveridical images may have occasioned many of our dualistic notions about existence (mind/brain, soul/body, current/afterlife, etc.). The development of symbolic activities must have indeed complicated at least some forms of human learning. Learning to discriminate between "real" and symbolic experiences is a phenomenon which is apparently repeated in every infant. It is also an ability which is sometimes lost by hallucinating individuals.

The development of language added further complexity to human performance. While dramatically enhancing opportunities for vicarious and symbolic learning experiences, it effectively introduced a biased filter between the organism and its environment. To accommodate the infinite diversity of experiential phenomena, regularities were artificially imposed by a symbol system. Language capacities allowed the organism to "tidy up" nature's frequent disarray, but in so doing they often constructed schema which were neither adaptive nor well correlated with "real world" sequences. Early scientific "thought" readily attests to the recurrence of erroneous generalizations derived from language-based sources (Kuhn, 1962). Moreover, Jaynes (1974) has contended that self-stimulatory "dialogues" in early man may have contributed to notions of supernatural voices and a bicameral mind.

Although speculations on the evolution of thought may be intellectually stimulating, their practical significance has been rarely demonstrated. The writings of Carl Jung, of course, attempt to relate evolutionary developments to current personal action. Piaget has likewise drawn on ontological phenomena in his theoretical analysis of cognitive development (cf. Piaget & Inhelder, 1969). While undeniably heuristic, these efforts have unfortunately received only sparse empirical examination in applied clinical realms.

The potential relevance of evolutionary considerations, however, should not be dismissed without careful examination of our implicit contemporary assumptions in the functional analysis of thought. While climbing inside the head of the caveman may have taught us little about clinical procedures, it has had apparent impact on our own ways of viewing symbolic processes. For example, the popular dichotomy between visual imagery and verbal encoding stems not only from phenomenological reports but also from evolutionary inferences. It is generally asserted that visual symbols (dreams, images, etc.) were earlier mediational forms than verbal (auditory). Data reflecting that "visual" memories require less rehearsal than auditory (Cohen, 1973) may lend some support to the implicit assumption that images are somehow more "primitive" than covert speech. Speculations about the role of imagery-mediated performance (Chapter 8) and possible differences in "verbal" versus "visual" cognitive therapies (Chapter 11) reinforce this dichotomy.

My point is that it may well be time to challenge the dichotomy. We have developed a technical language which describes cognitive events in terms of sense modalities and it is usually implied that a particular modality dominates in any given private experience. However, we may need to re-appraise our schema and remind ourselves that cognitive "modality" labels may derive more from our experimental operations than from any characteristics inherent in the symbolic event. The differences between "inner speech" and "inner speaking" have already been suggested (Leont'yev, 1969) and recent analyses of visual imagery have questioned whether one can simplistically separate sense modalities in cognitive events. Likewise, until we have demonstrated better correlation between sense modality brain activity and reported mediation forms (e.g., visual cortex activity and phenomenological imagery), we cannot assume an isomorphism between evolution of the senses and the evolution of quasi-sensory mediation.

Finally, it may behoove us as clinical scientists to maintain closer contacts with recent developments in the physiology of mediation. One line of inquiry, for example, has implicated deficiences in cerebral oxygenation as a possible moderator of intellectual impairment (Jacobs, Winter, Alvis, & Small, 1969). Recent work on hemispheric specialization has likewise suggested some intriguing complexities in the human brain (cf. Sperry, 1973; Nebes, 1974). Language skills and sequential information processing appear to be primarily executed by the left hemisphere in right-handed individuals. Spatial relationships and parallel processing, on the other hand, seem to be a specialization of the right hemisphere. While these functions are far from hemisphere-specific, evidence for their differential execution by the two cerebral divisions is considerable. There are even some data to suggest that the hemispheres often "compete" for control of motoric response systems. Although age-old speculations about "psychic conflicts" have already begun to enlist these findings as corroborative support, their clinical import is a long way from being determined. On the other hand, the potential significance of hemispheric specialization for a variety of clinical brain disorders need hardly be elaborated. More important, perhaps, is the emphasis this research places on physiological processes in cognitive functioning. The effective clinical scientist must remain an ambitiously diversified professional whose therapeutic skills and technical knowledge continue to grow with contemporary scientific progress. Interdisciplinary exposure and collaborative research endeavors offer valuable avenues for that growth.

SLEEP AND DREAMS

The potential relevance of sleep processes in therapeutic endeavors has remained virtually unexamined by contemporary behavioral researchers. Although insomnia has been an occasional clinical target, the contribution of sleep and dreams per se has been almost religiously avoided. In light of the lively animosities between behavioral and psychoanalytic quarters, this territoriality may not be surprising. However, recent evidence on sleep functions suggests that the applied clinical scientist (regardless of orientation) may be well advised to take a closer look at the therapeutic relevancy of this area.

The substantial evidence implicating sleep-dream functions in normal and abnormal human behavior has been reviewed by Dement (1972) and Hartmann (1973). The following represents a brief survey of a few major foci in sleep-dream research which seem to hold some promise for clinical extrapolation.

First, while far from unequivocal, the evidence on the effects of sleep deprivation suggest that it may be an important variable in a range of behavior disorders. The frequency of sleep disturbances prior to psychiatric hospitalization has been cited as one realm of data bearing on this relationship. Laboratory studies of sleep and dream deprivation have likewise offered some tentative support for the hypothesis that these phenomena can dramatically influence subjective distress. Self-reports of hallucinations, irritability, and psychotomimetic patterns in sleep-deprived "normal" individuals are not uncommon. Unfortunately, the validity of some of this research has been recently challenged on the grounds of methodological inadequacies and implicit demand characteristics. Its ultimate significance for clinical dysfunction must therefore await empirical refinements and controlled replication. Meanwhile, however, the therapist should remain apprised of the potential role of sleep disturbance in subjective distress and phenomenological experiences.

The possible influence of attributional labeling in sleep-related dysfunction is particularly noteworthy. The ramifications of labeling physiological signals as products of sleep deprivation rather than as signs of imminent psychosis have already been cited. A distressing arousal-induced arousal pattern might be averted if the initial physiological element is labeled appropriately. Analogous options for therapeutic (and veridical) attributions stem from recent work on circadian rhythms (cf. Segal & Luce, 1966; Dement, 1972). It is now widely accepted that a variety of physiological responses demonstrate a relatively consistent cyclic pattern every 24-28 hours. For example, blood pressure, body temperature, and blood glucose appear to follow wavelike biological rhythms with discernible peaks and reductions. The impact of these rhythms on phenomenological experience (e.g., "moods") has yet to be carefully examined. Their potential mislabeling and subsequent dysfunctional impact warrant controlled clinical inquiry.

A second broad area of clinical relevance bears on the recent research suggesting a relationship between dreaming and memory consolidation (Stokes, 1973). Although the evidence is again very preliminary, its contemporary convergence seems to implicate such a relationship. In correlational studies, amount of dream activity—as reflected in rapid eye movements (REMs)—appears to be positively related to measures of intellectual functioning. Laboratory investigations of human memory have likewise suggested that the interpolation of dreaming between learning and recall experiences may substantially facilitate performance. Conversely, the experimental deprivation of dream (REM) activity seems to impair memory retention. Interpretations of the relationships among dreaming, correlated increases in brain catecholamines, and protein synthesis theories of memory have likewise lent momentum to this avenue of inquiry. If, in fact, dream activity entails "store-and-organize" functions in human information processing, its relevance for clinical improvement may be substantial. The use of REM-inhibiting drugs in pharmacotherapy poses but one immediate target for reappraisal.

A third intriguing area deals with the phenomenon of dream recall and the potential relevance of dream processes in our understanding of human behavior change. Neisser (1967) and Cohen (1974) have suggested that the mechanisms of dreaming may be analogous to conventional information processing mechanisms. Thus, the analysis of dream contents might shed light on some of the parameters of associative memory, conceptual organization, and so on.

Although Skinner (1953) acknowledges the apparent validity of Freud's "wish fulfillment" hypothesis in dreaming, functional analyses of dream activity have remained a forbidden topic for the behavioral researcher. Clients are often discouraged from sharing their dreams with the behavior therapist, as if such an undertaking might contaminate his theoretical purity. Dreams, however, are data; their acknowledgment does not entail a defection to psychoanalysis or acceptance of a formal model of their function. While it is true that dream reports are verbal behaviors and may correspondingly be distorted by such variables as therapist attention and client expectancies, their potential relevance for therapeutic behavior change will remain empirically unexamined as long as the clinical scientist ignores or discourages their communication. Anecdotes from my own case records suggest that there may indeed be correlations between dream content and stages of therapeutic improvement. The phobic individual, for example, will frequently report more "coping" and realistic dreams about an avoided activity as therapy progresses. Similarly I have had several depressed clients recall dreams which reflected increasingly more competent and optimistic performances. These anecdotes, of course, could be interpreted in terms of therapeutic information processing and the "consolidation" of more adaptive mediational events.

Our tentative appraisal of the potential relevance of dreams for clinical behavior change need not entail the abstract embellishments and psychodynamic connotations of unconscious "dream work" and clandestine impulses. Recent evidence on dream recall suggests that stimulus salience and interference hypotheses may describe some of the component processes in dreaming more adequately than "repression" or "sublimation" (Cohen, 1974). Again, however, our appraisal must start with the data, and dream data have been too long neglected in clinical behavior modification.

NUTRITION

Having consumed several hundred pounds of wheat germ and soybeans in the past few years, I am undoubtedly biased in my suggestion of nutritional relevancies in cognitive behavior modification. That bias notwithstanding, however, I would contend that the preliminary data at least offer food for thought.

One of the problems in evaluating nutritional influences on behavior is the fact that the assumption of single factor causation is particularly pronounced in this area. Personal maladjustment is viewed as being solely the result of ingesting inappropriate nutrients. Popular food fads proselytize that "you are what you eat" and disorders ranging from acne to schizophrenia are said to be miraculously cured by organic foods and megavitamins. As Erhard (1973, 1974) points out, health food enthusiasts base their eccentric ingestion patterns on both religious and "scientific" sources. From the Zen macrobiotic diet (Oshawa, 1971) to the popular dietary rituals of Adelle Davis (1954), J. I. Rodale (1966), and Carlton Fredericks (1972), nutrition-conscious individuals often pursue their gastrointestinal gambits with fervid dedication and unbridled enthusiasm.

The health food enthusiast, however, is not alone in his monolithic prejudices about the causes and cures of personal distress and physical disease. The average clinician is correspondingly faithful to his assumption that the learning process which characterizes effective therapy transpires in a biological vacuum. Conditioning procedures are said to effect changes in response probabilities and—although a confession of presumed neurochemical substrata can be grudgingly extracted—the behavior therapist seldom acknowledges or evaluates possible biological influences. For example, the well established impact of calcium deficiency on an individual's muscular relaxation has yet to be examined in clinical procedures utilizing relaxation training.

The point here again emphasizes dichotomous thinking. It is probably not the case that the simple ingestion of specific nutrients will often effect clinical miracles. On the other hand, it is also unlikely that an individual's current biochemical resources have absolutely no effect on the speed, adequacy, and maintenance of therapeutic learning experiences. The "truth" probably lies somewhere in between—i.e., adaptive behavior change requires the interaction of biochemical prerequisites and appropriate environmental experience.

Unfortunately, the conventional guidelines for training in clinical psychology often ignore physiological relevancies. Like our medical colleagues, we often complete an exhaustive apprenticeship in only one relevant specialization without ever being exposed to some of the complex bio-social interactions which exist. Courses in "Nutrition and Behavior," for example, are seldom offered in graduate psychology programs. To exacerbate our ignorance, the availability of authoritative evidence often remains obscure. The clinician interested in nutritional relevancies is faced with a plethora of poorly documented "best sellers" which often sprinkle remote experimental data with generous personal biases. In the absence of a basic nutrition course, it is virtually impossible to separate the fact from the fiction in these popular treatises.

An integrated survey of the empirical evidence relating nutritional factors to behavior change processes would be an invaluable contribution to clinical science. Unfortunately, such a survey is not now available and the interested clinician is forced to integrate for himself. The comments which follow are intended to suggest some general relevancies and empirical justification for the expanded examination of nutritional factors in human adaptation. Formal textbooks in nutrition (e.g., Pike & Brown, 1967) offer background information and guidelines for the detection of serious nutrient deficits. Unfortunately the ratio of irrelevant-to-relevant clinical information in such texts is often staggeringly high. Comprehensive overviews of medical physiology and clinical nutrition, however, offer useful technical knowledge (e.g., Guyton, 1971; Williams, 1973). Finally, the publications *Nutrition Today* and the *American Journal of Clinical Nutrition* communicate empirical findings on a variety of clinical and nutritional topics.

The importance of *protein* deficiencies in human learning has been amply documented (e.g., Scrimshaw, 1967; Scrimshaw & Gordon, 1968; Kaplan, 1972). Although the severe conditions of *marasmus* (protein-calorie deficiency) and *kwashiorkor* (protein deficiency) are relatively rare, their effects on social, intellectual, and motoric function have received extensive investigation. As Kaplan (1972) points out, the adequacy of nutrition during prenatal development and during the first few years of growth appears to be critically important in the subsequent psychological functioning of the individual. Severe and prolonged deficiencies during that time result in serious and often irreversible nervous system damage. The critical role of protein in virtually all cell growth emphasizes its potential significance for the optimization of maturational processes. However, its equally critical functions in enzymatic processes and cellular energy suggest that its significance is not restricted to the neonate or infant. If memory mechanisms are in fact related to some form of protein synthesis, this nutrient may well be one of the more important in human clinical considerations.

Lappé (1971), however, points out that the average American adult probably ingests ten to twelve percent more protein than he needs. What is the likelihood, then, that clinical dysfunctions and behavior change processes might be influenced by this factor? Perhaps small. But the ingestion of protein must be distinguished from its absorption. Large quantities of protein can be eaten and the individual can still be deficient in "net protein utilization" (NPU). This is due to the fact that there are "limiting" amino acids which must be represented in appropriate proportions for the optimal absorption of other protein substances. Moreover, physiological and "emotional" stress have been shown to increase individual protein requirements by as much as thirty percent. Finally, there is some evidence that effective protein synthesis may be inhibited by a wide range of non-nutritive chemical agents (e.g., certain antibiotics, insecticides, etc.).

Fat and *carbohydrate* deficiencies are not common nutritional problems in contemporary Western culture. As a matter of fact, overabundance of these nutrients is probably responsible for our alarming rate of cardiovascular disease (Yudkin, 1972; Blumenfeld, 1964). However, several clinically relevant phenomena are noteworthy. First, it is not uncommon for the "starvation dieter" to self-induce the condition of *ketosis* through virtual elimination of carbohydrates from his diet (this strategy is actually recommended by one popular reducing method). In the absence of carbohydrates, body energy is derived predominantly from fats. This produces an accumulation of ketones in the blood and interstitial fluids. The end product of this process is the condition of *acidosis* (a high hydrogen ion concentration) whose major effect is the depression of central nervous system functioning. Interestingly, its counterpart (*alkalosis*) can also be induced through nutritional mismanagement (e.g., excessive intake of alkaline substances) and causes dramatic hypersensitivity of the nervous system.

Glucose absorption disorders offer another potential concern in clinical endeavors. The phenomena of diabetes and chronic alcoholism often bear witness to the importance of balanced glucose metabolism in normal functioning. The chronic alcoholic presents a more complicated picture due to the frequency of serious nutritional deficiencies which often result from near total reliance on alcohol as an energy source. One of the least understood and yet clinically relevant phenomena, however, is *hypoglycemia*—which is simply low blood sugar. The term is used to describe "normal" blood sugar deficiencies (e.g., in the fasting individual) as well as an undifferentiated syndrome thought to be characterized by chronic glucose absorption deficiencies. In terms of clinical patterns, the hypoglycemic individual often complains of fatigue, tremors, dizziness, headaches, and vague "mental confusion." Administration of a glucose tolerance test can often detect the "true" hypoglycemic, whose idiosyncratic absorption patterns can be easily corrected through dietary adjustments.

The possible relevance of temporary hypoglycemia in the average client bears thoughtful examination. Even though the brain accounts for less than three percent of total bodyweight, it consumes as much as 25 percent of available blood glucose. Its sensitive dependence on adequate glucose reserves has been well documented in brain neurochemistry. However, the average individual stores only enough glucose to last a few hours. Inadvertent mealskipping, unusual exertion, or stress-inflated calorie requirements might easily produce mild to moderate hypoglycemia and its associated phenomenological distress. Again, the clinical scientist may need to be perceptive of such possibilities and their remediation in optimal therapeutic treatment.

A number of *vitamin* deficiencies have been suggested as possible factors in psychiatric disorders (e.g., Milner, 1963; Shulman, 1967a, b; Pauling, 1968; Watson, 1972; Hawkins & Pauling, 1973; Sterner & Price, 1973). Most notable, perhaps, are the theories positing such a role for nicotinic acid (niacin), ascorbic asid (vitamin C), and the B vitamins (cf. Williams, 1971). The current evidence for these theories is extremely meager and methodologically inadequate. Pursuant to our previous discussion, many of the megavitamin therapies have unfortunately assumed that clinical dysfunction is *nothing but* hypovitaminosis and their treatment strategies have been restrictively ingestive.

It would be easy to marshal extrapolated evidence from body neurochemistry to substantiate the *possible* relevance of vitamin deficiencies in human maladjustment. Thiamine deficiency, for example, has been shown to reduce glucose absorption in the central nervous system by 50 to 60 percent (Guyton, 1971). It has likewise been implicated in the degeneration of myelin sheaths and a handful of studies have suggested that its experimental deprivation results in affective disturbance (depression, anxiety; cf. Pike & Brown, 1967). All of the B vitamins are known to function as co-enzymes, which again suggests their pervasive role in a range of diversified neurochemical processes. Similar extrapolations could be used in the defense of minerals as potentially significant factors in adaptive functioning. Magnesium concentrations, for example, are known to dramatically affect nervous system excitability and calcium has already been cited as a potential consideration in abnormal muscle tension. Unfortunately, extrapolated relevance is not sufficient to justify clinical revision. The existing data on actual therapeutic utility are hardly suggestive. While dietary inadequacies are often associated with some clinical dysfunctions (e.g., depression; cf. Beck, 1967), their contributory relevance remains noticeably devoid of examination.

This unfortunate dearth of evidence, however, may finally be under siege. There appears to be a growing empirical concern with the deleterious effects of malnutrition on personal functioning and intellectual growth. Warren (1973) cites well over a dozen recent reviews on this topic. Many of these have focused on the phenomena of prenatal and early childhood malnutrition, although the beginnings of an adult-clinical focus are apparent. Unfortunately, as Warren also notes, methodological inadequacies seriously limit the empirical contribution of most existing studies. The data are not only meager; they are weak.

Why, then, the present excursion into nutrition? What empirical justification can be offered for the recommendation that behavior modifiers begin to consider biochemical relevancies in their clinical endeavors? My defense rests squarely in that data vacuum. That is, the data will probably remain nonexistent as long as our conventional research prejudices discourage our participation in their collection. It may, in fact, turn out that very little therapeutic outcome variance will be attributable to biochemical factors. Until adequate data are available, however, our judgment must remain suspended. The burden of responsibility cannot be assigned to nonexistent data. The pragmatic fertility of an area is determined by its empirical harvest and a harvest can hardly be expected without the sowing of seeds.

Two final comments: first, there is a popular assumption that the average member of contemporary Western culture is a well-fed (and often over-fed) organism. Malnutrition is viewed as a concern for underprivileged nations and the socio-economic minorities. While it is certainly true that the most severe forms of malnutrition are encountered in these populations, it is equally true that a "well-fed" organism is not necessarily a "well-nourished" one (Jacobson, 1972, 1973). In a recent national survey, for example, it was found that a surprisingly large number of Canadians suffer from a range of mild to moderate nutritional deficiencies (Sabry, Campbell, Campbell, & Forbes, 1974).

Second, our examination of nutritive relevancies in clinical research should not maintain the dichotomy which has already impaired investigations in this area. A nutritive deficiency need not induce consistent hallucinatory patterns in order to have potential therapeutic significance. There may be a significant difference between national recommendations (Minimum Daily Allowances) and optimal nutrition. Our research inquiries should be addressed to evaluating the practical utility of conceptualizing therapy as a complex bio-social process in which *optimal* biochemical substrata are brought into contiguity with appropriate learning experiences.

The present and previous chapter have been admittedly speculative and well byond the data. Their intention, however, has not been to draw a premature knot of finality or to suggest a unified model for absolving our ignorance. The explicit task has been to acknowledge that ignorance and to hopefully offer some heuristic suggestions for needed areas of investigation. We must be careful here not to equate "speculative" with "unscientific" and thereby ignore the crucial importance of theory in our empirical pursuits. I concur with the comments of a colleague who recently defended his own theoretical excursions in a similar manner:

> Much of the argument goes beyond the established facts . . . . Every scientific field has a boundary beyond which discussion, though necessary, cannot be as precise as one might wish. . . . Speculation is necessary, in fact, to devise methods which will bring a subject matter under better control (Skinner, 1974, p. 19).

The major intention of our biological excursion has been to suggest that we divest ourselves of the "learning supremacy" convention and begin to view the human being as a complex bio-social organism. The potential value of a collaborative interdisciplinary approach is an oft lauded but seldom realized ideal. By expanding our own conceptual horizons to encompass more diverse parameters of human functioning, we may enhance both our knowledge and our humanistic potential as clinical scientists.

Chapter Fifteen

An Emerging Paradigm: The Personal Scientist

Simplification is often a sacrifice. Abstracting generalizations from particulars frequently requires a prejudicial de-emphasis of inconsistencies. However, in our own finite and fallible theories of reality, distillation and inference appear to be unavoidable. We construct our broad hunches about regularities in experience, often at the expense of non-conforming details. While our "abridged reality" sometimes bears only remote resemblance to the way things "really" are, continued evaluations and revisions of our conceptual bifocals will hopefully minimize distortion.

In drawing tentative conclusions from the foregoing chapters, the simplification sacrifice should be borne in mind. Extrapolating generalizations from an area as recent and rudimentary as cognitive behavior modification is undoubtedly presumptuous. Only further empirical research, however, can decide whether it was preposterous.

Were I asked to summarize the first twelve chapters of this book in 100 words or less, its crystallization would be:

(1) There are ample data to suggest that mediational processes are pervasive and powerful elements in complex human behavior—the inadequacies of a non-mediational model are salient;
(2) As a mediational perspective, the covert conditioning model has offered few and modest conceptual improvements; moreover, with few exceptions, the treatment strategies germinated by that model have generally demonstrated variable and meager therapeutic promise; and
(3) even in fetal form, the cognitive learning model has offered a comprehensive and potentially more adequate theory of complex human action; while derived clinical applications have lagged far

behind conceptual heuristics, preliminary inquiries offer ample justification for continued and expanded research.

Tentative generalizations, of course, should acknowledge the fallibility of our evaluative criteria. Many investigations on covert conditioning and cognitive restructuring, for example, have utilized poor empirical methodologies. We must be careful not to invoke a double standard in our interpretation of findings from such studies. It is tempting to "reject" reported successes which derive from a poorly executed experiment, but to "accept" negative results despite this same inadequacy. This is particularly true when the disconfirming data apply to a "competing" paradigm while the supportive evidence relates to our personally preferred strategy. Such double standards merit continued re-appraisal. A poor experiment yields poor data regardless of their directionality.

We must likewise acknowledge the possible fallibility of conventional "null hypothesis" testing. The arbitrary criteria in statistical analyses bear frequent consideration. As Meehl (1967) points out, the research consequences of conventional behavioral methodologies are often paradoxically detrimental to the field. The limitations and license of relying so heavily on simple directionality in hypotheses and the reinforcement of *ad hoc* explanations and "cuteness" in behavioral science may have an expensive price:

> Meanwhile our eager-beaver researcher, undismayed by logic-of-science considerations and relying blissfully on the 'exactitude' of modern statistical hypothesis-testing, has produced a long publication list and been promoted to a full professorship. In terms of his contribution to the enduring body of psychological knowledge, he has done hardly anything. His true position is that of a potent-but-sterile intellectual rake, who leaves in his merry path a long train of ravished maidens but no viable scientific offspring (p. 114).

Relevant to this point is the continuing denigration of data which fail to "refute" the null hypothesis. Steeped in a long and seemingly inflexible tradition of "justificationism" we continue to propagate the delusion that "negative results" are somehow less informative or valuable than "positive results." Although I have already belabored this point, it warrants reiteration. Our journal publication policies and selective professional attention force us into a filtered feedback paradigm in which only "successful" experiments are communicated. The pervasiveness of this element in contemporary behavioral research should not be underestimated. Several of the unpublished studies reporting "negative results" were given to me with profuse apologies for their empirical "failure." The effects of this prejudicial theory-saving policy warrant thoughtful re-evaluation. Numerous conversations with colleagues convince me that the communication of data *qua* data (regardless of "directionality") could substantially reduce the waste and redundancy of research endeavors which now plague our discipline. Moreover, as our own literature readily attests, the selective reinforcement of a behavior can often dramatically increase its occurrence. To the extent that "positive" results are professionally rewarded, they will be obtained—even at the expense of perceptual distortions, selective reporting, and outright deception. Colleagues may thus be stimulated by the published effectiveness of a strategy and remain expensively ignorant of the fact that the reported success may have been drawn from a sample of procedurally identical failures.

Data are valenced only if we place a presumptuous value on our hypotheses. In a science as rudimentary as ours, we cannot afford the luxury of such policies. Data are data regardless of their implications for pet hypotheses. Moreover, one might argue that disconfirmatory evidence warrants particular attention since the likelihood of its detection is probably reduced by our selective data processing. As behavioral scientists, we are delinquent in our own reinforcement practices. Future contingencies will hopefully place greater emphasis on expository information gathering rather than on selective and value-laden hypothesis testing.

Finally, we must acknowledge the differences among weak, sparse, and nonsupportive data. Our relative confidence in the validity of a relationship is based on the (a) extent, (b) quality, and (c) content of its associated evidence. When the data are sparse, our confidence can only be tentative. When they are abundant but derived from inadequate experimentation, we are again obliged to defer all but the most modest of evaluative leaps. Stronger degrees of confidence are warranted only by ample and methodologically adequate data which bear meaningfully on the relationship in question (supportively *or* nonsupportively).

From a practical standpoint, the foregoing synopsis poses a difficult clinical dilemma. Although the evidence seems to warrant a mediational approach to human performance, the form and efficacy of such an approach have only recently received empirical scrutiny. The data suggest very modest promise from covert conditioning endeavors. On the other hand, research on cognitive therapies has yet to offer sufficient and methodologically adequate support for "gearing up" our therapeutic procedures along these lines. As clinicians we are ethically obliged to offer our clients the most powerful and effective strategies available. On the other hand, our data preclude any semblance of confident complacency in the current state of our art. While Matson

(1971) may be partially correct in stating that we Grand Conditioners "have no clothes," he must at least acknowledge that we are aware of our nudity.

The foregoing pessimism is, I think, only partially warranted and should be qualified by several relevant clinical research considerations. First, we do not have the option of waiting for the data to "arrive." In a self-appraising scientific discipline, the data are never completely "in"—they are always "coming." Second, our knowledge of effective therapeutic procedures will grow only if we take an active role in its harvest. The age-old dichotomy of "clinician" versus "researcher" should be buried with the many other bifurcations which currently polarize our search for knowledge. The most effective therapist is one who is in close touch with the "data" and who sensitively adjusts therapeutic strategies to the ebb and flow of relevant feedback. While component analyses and controlled evidence may be slow in arriving, the utility of clinical case report findings should not be underemphasized. Weak data are better than no data, particularly when the supportive evidence on our previous therapeutic strategies is less than overwhelming. Again, we must distinguish among weak, nonsupportive, and nonexistent evidence. Controlled single subject inquiries by the practicing clinician offer invaluable sources of potential knowledge in this area. Data from an empirical case study need not be inherently "weaker" than that offered in group research. The data will remain sparse or nonexistent, however, so long as we continue to view therapy as a marketed product rather than an exploratory endeavor.

Finally, we may derive some clinical optimism from the realization that our empirical confidence falls along a relativity continuum. While we may not be as comfortable as we would like regarding the current state of the art, we should not allow our perfectionistic standards to subvert continued examinations. Our confidence in the processes and procedures of humane therapeutic improvement must remain tentative and exploratory. We must learn to supplant our frustrated certainty-striving with a more exciting and adaptive commitment to open re-evaluation and continual refinement.

CONVERGING TRENDS

My tentative optimism regarding cognitive behavior modification does not rest solely on a specific technique or a commitment to further evaluation. It claims additional support from what I think are converging trends from some very divergent areas. Few contemporary behaviorists would deny that "something is afoot" in the traditional learning model. Whether that "something" is a sinister force or a timely reformation depends on one's biases; my own need hardly be elaborated. It is apparent that something is finally starting to filter down from the massive literature generated by first and second generation behavior modifiers. Steadfast truisms are falling faster than Noyes pellets, and our former conceptual complacency is rapidly turning into an excited inquisitiveness. In short, the conventional "learning model" is under critical review by its own constituents. As briefly reviewed in Chapter 8, a rapidly accumulating literature is beginning to question and refine many long-standing principles. I shall not here reiterate or expand upon the myriad studies which have challenged "traditional" learning theory. A brief glance at virtually any behavioral journal in the last few years offers adequate corroboration of that trend. The growing self-criticism in behavioral quarters is, I think, an optimistic sign of a maturing discipline and portends of exciting advances in the decade to come.

One convergence in recent behavioral research is the focus on mediation. As documented in the preceding chapters, cognitive-symbolic activities have become a popular research topic in contemporary behavior modification. Similar trends may be found in areas ranging from motivation theory to perception. As Dember (1974) puts it, "Psychology has gone cognitive (p. 161)."

Related to the above focus is the emergence of a new medium for describing and conceptualizing experiential effects—namely, "information." Central processes have edged into the limelight of peripheral associations, and data supporting their candidacy have not been meager. A large percentage of the variance observed in human performance appears to be influenced by central, information transfer processes. Literatures spanning the areas of vicarious learning, awareness, expectancy, and problem solving readily attest to this focus. Although the groans of transition are clearly audible, behavior modifiers are slowly beginning to reform their hypotheses to include information transfer and symbolic activity as well as peripheral associationism.

A third convergence may be detected in the preceding chapters on mediational therapies. Although varying widely in their means, these therapies have focused (sometimes exclusively) on the systematic alteration of thoughts and images. The assumption that these covert events play a crucial role in behavior dysfunction has become almost implicit. Unfortunately, this has often resulted in failures to assess the contribution of mediational factors in specific cases. It is interesting to note, however, that several of the most impressive therapeutic paradigms in contemporary behavior modification (covert modeling and self-instruction) have employed structured training in the modification of these cognitive behaviors. A third (participant modeling) relies heavily on a range of mediational processes.

Finally, research on coping skills training illustrates a trend which has accelerated dramatically in the last few years. The clinical and empirical focus of behavior modification has begun to shift away from discrete responses toward more general strategies of adjustment. Generalization and maintenance have become primary interests and broad-spectrum treatment packages have begun to emerge. Literatures ranging from self-control to problem solving have contributed generously to this convergence.

Where does all of this leave us? Aside from our glaring need for continued empirical input, what has cognitive behavior modification to offer the contemporary clinician-researcher? The data are preliminary, the trends are suggestive, and the future looks hopeful. But what about tomorrow's client? Can any clinically useful crystals be distilled from our currently meager knowledge?

My admittedly apprehensive answer is "yes." It is apprehensive because clinical recommendations—even when explicitly qualified as tentative and preliminary—are often adopted and adhered to with uncritical enthusiasm and infrequent re-evaluation. My own commitment to empiricism is too strong to allow a complacent "how to do it" summary. On the other hand, my own experiences as a clinician-researcher keep me frequently apprised of the value of consultation and collaboration in therapy. There comes a time when, in the absence of adequate data, inadequate data must temporarily suffice. Regrettably, such is the case in much of contemporary clinical science and particularly in cognitive behavior modification.

The following clinical suggestions should be "processed" with due caution. I do not propose a monolithic "cognitive therapy" nor do I hesitate to admit that my tentative suggestions blend controlled empirical support with my own clinical experience. What follows is a commentary, not a conclusion. It represents a summary of the features and elements I believe to be potentially significant in therapeutic behavior change. Their formal supporting data range from relatively strong to virtually nonexistent and my confidence in their power is proportionately guarded. I present them in the hope that so doing will facilitate expanded efforts toward their empirical evaluation.

There are two basic considerations in virtually every clinical case: (1) the therapeutic goals, and (2) the procedural means for achieving those goals. While the experienced clinician may enter each case with some broad perspective biases and a few prepotent treatment strategies, he should remain sufficiently open to idiosyncracies and exploratory innovations. The effective clinical scientist is sensitive to his data and adjusts his therapeutic procedures in due accordance—regardless of conventional procedures, popular technology, or his own prejudicial hypotheses. This "seat-of-the-pants empiricism" is an invaluable clinical skill. It should not be confused, however, with a glorification of eclecticism. Whether they are explicit or implicit, the clinician always enters his arena with predilections toward types of assessment and treatment. As a mediating organism, these biases are probably unavoidable. On the other hand, they should be constantly self-examined and sufficiently balanced so that flexible, data-directed innovations are possible. In other words, the primary commitment in clinical science is to the "data." Theoretical and procedural biases—even when they are based on ample empirical data—must remain secondary (albeit unavoidable) elements.

The foregoing should emphasize the need to approach each case as a clinical experiment which may require unique goals and innovative means. The therapist must adapt his diversified skills to accommodate each kaleidoscopic client. This is not to deny that some broad and flexible guidelines may not be helpful in directing therapeutic efforts. The clinician is unavoidably influenced by his own value-laden beliefs on the outcome of "successful" therapy. He is likewise affected by technological biases reflecting his training and experience. The following comments on general therapeutic goals and efficacious clinical means reflect my own values and experience. As such, they are intended to be communicative and heuristic, not persuasive.

PARADIGM FOR SURVIVAL: THE PERSONAL SCIENTIST

My own bias in clinical goal-setting suggests that the most humane therapeutic pursuits strive to provide clients with broad and effective coping skills. While discrete strategies have routinely been applied to specific problems in conventional behavior therapy, their effects have often been painfully limited. Unidimensional presenting problems appear to be a myth propagated by behavioral research conventions. The average client is not simply snake phobic—he often expresses desires to improve personal adjustment along a wide range of foci. While broader therapeutic goals may require more ambitious and skillful functional analyses, these are neither impossible nor inherently less empirical than the problem-specific diagnoses currently popular in behavioral quarters. The client presenting multiple complaints *could* be treated with assembly-line technologies in piecemeal fashion. However, in my opinion, this approach is not only wasteful of valuable therapist time, but it also involves a disservice to the client in terms of his ability to independently cope with future adjustment problems. Broad-based survival skills may incur a bit more therapist effort and ingenuity, but they probably return substantially greater humanistic impact in the realms of generalization, maintenance, and independent functioning.

A related bias suggests that we are obliged to share our scientific commitments with clients. Although their parameters and autonomic associates may vary, there are few qualitative differences between an empirical research problem and a distressing personal problem. However, we often dichotomize their alleged solutions. "Professional" problems are approached via scientific method—systematic observation, hypothesis generation, evaluative tests, and so on. "Personal" problems, on the other hand, are treated as if they were a different kind of animal. In my opinion, this double standard is both unwarranted and potentially detrimental to optimal clinical impact. We should strive to provide our clients with the same technical skills we employ as researchers in approaching and resolving problematical situations. That is, we should share our commitment to empiricism and view therapy as an apprenticeship designed to train *personal* scientists—individuals who are skillful in the functional analysis and systematic improvement of their own behavior. We should model and teach an "intimate empiricism" replete with skills training in problem analysis, hypothesis generation, evaluative experimentation, and so on.[a] If the clinician considers the scientific approach a useful paradigm for his own problem solving endeavors, he can hardly discourage a personal science paradigm for his client.

Given that broad coping skills and a personal (scientific) paradigm for survival are defensible therapeutic goals, their constituent elements must be specified. Although I shall omit detailed excursions, the following general suggestions offer an approximate component analysis.

Orientation.

The client is provided with a general overview of therapy as an apprenticeship in problem solving. Some brief conceptual didactics may be required to challenge notions about "inherent" personality deficits and insoluble dilemmas. Personal distress and performance deficiencies are described as deterministic results of individual and environmental influences. The client is placed in the role of an active and responsible agent in his own adjustment. Therapy will entail the acquisition of more adaptive skills via instruction, modeling, and graduated performance assignments. Accurate record keeping is a critical element in personal science, since solution refinements are sensi-

[a] This type of paradigm is similar to that suggested by Kelly (1955) and draws upon the literatures of self-control and social learning theory as well as cognitive behavior modification.

tively adjusted to these data. The client is asked to view himself as an active participant in a self-corrective enterprise. The therapist presents himself as a technical consultant, sharing both a conceptual commitment and an accumulation of relevant knowledge and skills.

The role of programmed "expectancy" in this orientation would require a much finer analysis than we are currently permitted. Suffice it to say that I do not consider "expectancy" to be an illegitimate or "nonspecific" artifact in clinical science. As outlined in Chapter 10, expectancy may be viewed as a complex of mediational processes which influence selective attention, response utilization, and anticipated consequences. Viewed in this manner, it is a justified and significant element in therapeutic behavior change. A client who does not anticipate improvement from a procedure will be less likely to attend to, retain, or implement its features. The expectancy suggested in the personal science paradigm, however, is not one of unbridled enthusiasm. It is rather a tentative optimism based upon a philosophy of empiricism and a commitment to enduring self-corrective refinement. Just as the applied scientist is dedicated to a methodology rather than a subject matter, the personal scientist is encouraged to value the process over the outcome of his intimate experiments. There are no therapeutic "failures," only inefficient solutions and the paradigm is designed to feed "negative findings" back into a self-corrective loop of continued problem solving.

Problem Definitions.

For heuristic purposes, the client is trained to clearly specify representative problems in his personal adjustment. The development of this skill often entails substantial therapist assistance and may be a critical prerequisite to problem analysis. General categories of dysfunction may be facilitative—e.g., performance deficit or excess, unsatisfactory response form, incentive deficiencies, stimulus-related disorders, etc. Whenever possible, specific improvement goals are delineated.

Problem Analysis.

This phase involves active self-examination through systematic observation and self-records. Its purpose is to discover and describe regularities in problematical patterns. Temporal, social, cognitive, and situational associates are scrutinized. The client may be given self-monitoring assignments to structure accurate observations of antecedent–behavior–consequence patterns. Guided training and practice may be employed to evaluate and improve the accuracy of personal data collection. Categories of observation may be altered in accordance with their suggestive relevance. Joint therapist–client data analyses model the detection of regularities and the generation of solution hypotheses. Since mediational processes frequently exacerbate personal dysfunction, particular attention is given to such factors as perceptual errors and cognitive elements in distress (e.g., self-statements, performance standards, maladaptive self-evaluations, inferential errors, cognitive contingencies, and so on).

An important component in problem analysis may be the utilization of Socratic dialogue. Rather than bestowing a formal problem summary on the client, the therapist encourages self-exploration of personal data and tentative hypotheses. Through a series of questions and summaries, focus is placed on self-discovery of problematical patterns and potential solutions. This procedure not only facilitates the development of independent problem analysis skills, but it may effect more pervasive and enduring changes in relevant cognitive elements of the pattern (cf. Chapter 13).

Solution Generation.

Once the problem has been defined and analyzed, potential solutions are delineated and discussed. Whenever possible, emphasis is placed on generating multiple solutions from which to choose. When solutions involve skills already present in the client's repertoire, immediate focus is placed on a considered evaluation of the probable consequences of various options. Therapist input is centered around technical information on probable outcomes and assistance in the examination of all relevant options.

When generated solutions require skills or skill integrations which are currently deficient in the client, therapist input focuses on technical procedures which might effect improvement. Although this could entail use of problem-specific therapeutic strategies (e.g., desensitization), it is more often geared to the provision of general coping skills. Frequent foci are relaxation training, general self-regulatory skills, and "remedial mediation" (coping self-instructions, covert modeling, etc.). When inferential errors, cognitive contingencies, and similar relational dysfunctions are involved, training in remedial mediation may entail Socratic self-examination of premises, written homework assignments, and informal instruction in the forms of reasoning.

Personal Experimentation.

The fifth phase entails preliminary testing of one or more solutions. The selected course of action is often divided into unit assignments and care is taken to increase the likelihood that initial implementations will meet with success. Continuing personal data collection is emphasized as an invaluable source of feedback on the appropriateness and progress of the selected option. Care is taken to insure an adequate test of the solution and to discourage premature termination due to client impatience. A *minimum* of two weeks' experimentation is usually devoted to preliminary analysis.

Evaluation.

After adequate preliminary testing, personal data records are reviewed and the client is asked to offer an evaluation of progress to date. Unless that evaluation reflects unreasonable expectations, the therapist abides by it in subsequent consultation (i.e., it is the client's criteria—not the therapist's—which primarily determine the adequacy of change). If the evaluation is positive, attention is focused on the refinement, expansion, and/or maintenance of improvement. If it is negative, the personal experiment is reviewed as a valuable learning experience which has provided important information on the viability of a specific option. This information is integrated and examined in the subsequent selection, modification, or generation of an alternative solution. The personal experimentation phase is then resumed.

Graduation.

Even though emphasis throughout the paradigm has been placed on independent functioning, it is often difficult to avoid the development of at least some dependency on the technical skills and social/professional feedback of the therapist. To facilitate a weaning from this situation, the client is oriented toward a positive valuation of independent adjustment. Progressively more extensive demonstrations of personal initiative are encouraged throughout consultation and a graduated fading of therapist input is employed. Rather than abrupt case termination, a programmed series of graduated re-evaluations is pursued. Care is taken here to avoid reinforcement of minor relapses via re-initiation of therapy. Faded contacts are continued for at least one year and often entail gradual transition from prior role stimuli (i.e., therapeutic assistance) to cues more congruent with the client's continued independent functioning (e.g., social meetings).

Several comments are warranted regarding the viability and clinical breadth of the foregoing personal science paradigm. First, it is obviously geared toward primary application with non-institutional adult clients. One would hardly embark on an analogous paradigm with a nonverbal enuretic child. On the other hand, evidence reviewed in the preceding chapters suggests that appropriate alterations might easily allow its use with children, adolescents, and institutionalized individuals. The research on problem solving, for example, indicates that the acquisition of these skills may not be strongly correlated with measures of intelligence. The importance of an individualized paradigm over a routine package, however, bears constant acknowledgment.

A second point relates to the focus on effecting both cognitive and non-cognitive change during clinical apprenticeship. The cumulative evidence on both covert conditioning and cognitive therapies suggests that strategies which emphasize only one of these elements yield correspondingly limited results. "Verbal" therapies induce greatest changes in verbal behavior. Although the intricate interdependence of cognitive and non-cognitive performances may result in some degree of transfer, this generalization is probably substantially improved when both receive systematic clinical focus. Depressive clients who are trained to modify mediational elements as well as overt actions, for example, may show dramatically better improvement than clients who alter only one of these classes (cf. Taylor, 1974). This point will be reiterated in subsequent discussions. For the time being, suffice it to say that a treatment paradigm which limits its focus to a single performance modality can expect to harvest clinical effects which are correspondingly limited. Changes in motoric, affective, and mediational behaviors require multifaceted therapeutic strategies.

A third consideration is the apparent valuation of structured logical problem solving in the resolution of personal distress. Like Ellis's RET (Chapter 11), the personal scientist paradigm appears to presume that the client wants to be rational and methodical in his remedial adjustment. This connotation may stem from the elaborated metaphor of a "personal scientist," an image which may appeal to the intelligent adult out-patient. However, it is my speculation that the metaphor could be adjusted to meet the needs of specified clients. The goal of the paradigm is to be effective, not to play scientist. Its cardinal feature is the utility of an active, coping self-theory. Thus, for clients who might not like to view themselves as apprentices in personal science, the metaphor can be altered. A mystery novel buff, for example, might be asked to view therapy as a "personal detective" paradigm. Everyday illustrations of problem solving may likewise offer valuable metaphors. An auto mechanic often turns out to be a pretty shrewd "scientist." He translates vague complaints about an engine noise into a specific kind of noise (e.g., a metallic click). He then isolates the situations in which it occurs (e.g., usually in second gear). Possible causes are then hypothesized and evaluated as to relative likelihood. Data collection processes are utilized throughout (e.g., driving the car, engine disassembly, etc.) and the chosen solution (e.g., replacement of a transmission gear) is subsequently tested. Thus, naturalistic illustrations and non-scientist metaphors might be useful in adapting the coping paradigm to individual client characteristics.

One final comment. The personal scientist paradigm is a general recommendation, not a monolithic package. The client who requests brief and specific assistance for a circumscribed area of adjustment should not be forced into a coping mold. Again, our efforts as clinicians should be scientific, self-examining, and adapted to the individualized needs of the client in question. We owe fidelity to the person, not the paradigm.

IMPLEMENTING THE PARADIGM: SOME CLINICAL MEANS

The foregoing comments, of course, raise the issue of *means*. Given that a personal science paradigm is chosen as a general therapeutic goal, one is faced with the question of how best to implement it. Abundant research on the relative efficacy of various clinical procedures offers invaluable suggestions in this consideration. I shall again be selective, brief, and admittedly biased in surveying what I consider to be our best contemporary options for effecting paradigm implementation.

Modeling.

One of the most impressive therapeutic strategies thus far evaluated emphasizes the role of vicarious learning in clinical improvement. The demonstrated "power" of modeling therapies has been almost awesome when compared with many alternative clinical means (cf. Bandura, 1969, 1971 a, b, c, d, 1972, 1973; Rachman, 1972). A prime and promising candidate, then, for effecting a chosen therapeutic goal seems to be one which draws heavily on vicarious learning processes.

This, of course, may impose substantial responsibilities on the therapist in terms of his demonstrating and modeling adaptive personal skills. In the privacy of their own evaluative reveries, most clinicians have probably experienced professional and ethical anxieties stimulated by their own personal problems. The "Physician, heal thyself!" platitude incurs an implicit dictum that if you can't handle your own problems, you can hardly be of assistance to clients. The frequency with which professional therapists exhibit mild to moderate personal maladjustment is not an uncommon topic. (An early interest of mine questioned whether therapist maladjustment was a cause or an effect of vocation choice. My current speculation is that psychology is one of two professions which allow exemption from social constraints on eccentricity and deviance—comedians and psychotherapists are often reinforced for zany patterns).

The therapist's burden of responsibility as a personal model for his clients, however, may be less taxing than one might think.

Recent evidence on the coping-versus-mastery distinction suggests that the clinician who portrays himself as the paragon of adjustment may actually reduce his therapeutic impact. A coping commitment to personal adjustment and remedial problem solving may be a powerful and humane therapist contribution. While this may not require intimate self-disclosure by the clinician, it suggests the potential importance of sharing personal illustrations of the survival paradigm (both retrospective and contemporary).

Optimal clinical improvement may require not only a "coping model" therapist but also multi-modal modeling. That is, effectiveness may be moderated by the form and frequency of motoric, affective, and cognitive modeling. Through strategies of role playing, participant modeling, and guided practice, the therapist can demonstrate both cognitive and non-cognitive skills which will enhance clinical impact. Cognitive modeling may be particularly beneficial since it is rarely available in non-therapeutic settings. By "thinking out loud" and sharing his own mediational skills, the therapist may provide valuable assistance in the development, integration, and adaptive revision of client cognitions.

Reinforcement.

A second major means for facilitating the implementation of a personal scientist paradigm deals with the use of systematic reinforcement for progress. I need hardly elaborate on the demonstrated role of motivation and therapist approval in effective therapy. Three brief comments, however, are woth noting.

First, although the behavior therapist is often well aware of the literature documenting social reinforcement influences in client performance, few counselors actually monitor their own dispensations in the clinic. Video-tape replays of my own and others' therapeutic efforts have convinced me that the practicing behavior modifier might frequently benefit from the examination of his own verbal and nonverbal therapy behaviors. Communication skills are a critical and virtually neglected component in behavior therapy. We are delinquent in their analysis and refinement. Besides becoming attuned to molecular session contents, the clinical scientist must remain apprised of molar trends in his reinforcement practices. Initially dense social praise may be gradually faded toward an intermittent schedule which facilitates subsequent client independence.

Related to this thinning of therapist praise is the issue of differential focus. What is reinforced in early sessions may be a less appropriate target at a later stage. In my own supervision of therapy, I have labeled this transition the *critical shift*. It is well illustrated in the phenomenon of depression. Few behavior therapists initiate counseling for depression by rigidly ignoring depressive statements; such a strategy would probably keep their waiting rooms empty. Therapy is usually begun with some preliminary reassurances, empathic responses, and an assimilation of the depressive complaints. Following this development of "rapport" (which, I think, can be operationalized), selective reinforcement practices are gradually implemented. It is this "critical shift" of attention which merits careful scrutiny. Therapy is too often portrayed as a scene for complaining rather than coping. By systematically directing session content away from "what's wrong" to "what's right," the therapist may facilitate inculcation of an active coping orientation in his client.

Finally, I draw a distinction between sincere and manipulative reinforcement. The latter, in my opinion, is a potentially dangerous practice. Praising a client for nonveridical progress may seriously undermine the extent and duration of therapeutic improvement. An academically "sub-normal" student, for example, or a physically "unattractive" client should not be given inaccurate therapist evaluations simply to alleviate subjective distress. Unfounded flattery may induce unrealistic expectations and painful discoveries in future performance. The therapist who cannot find ample opportunities for sincere reinforcement might do well to evaluate his own criteria. The gist of this admittedly biased suggestion is that accurate feedback is a more important therapist contribution than indiscriminate "supportiveness." While encouragement should certainly be emphasized its focus should be realistic.

It is interesting to note that our clinical paradigms continue to portray the behavior therapist as an emotionless (albeit skilled) technician. Just as his communication skills (both verbal and nonverbal) have remained virtually unexamined due to their prohibition from the popular fare of "acceptable" research, so has his autonomic nervous system escaped our scrutiny. We often measure our clients' emotional responses during therapy, and assume that the therapist's physiology has nothing important to offer. Might "empathy" be partially reflected in the clinician's autonomic responsiveness? Are some forms of therapist arousal facilitative during treatment? How frequently do behavioral clinicians actually exhibit the intellectual stoicism portrayed in their procedural descriptions? These speculations will remain "only" speculations as long as our empirical bifocals limit our potential areas of data collection. Therapy is not a consummatory response—there are two organisms in the chamber and we need to take a much closer look at *both* sides of their interaction.

Graduated Performance Tasks.

With remarkably few exceptions, the most effective strategies in contemporary psychotherapy have incorporated direct performance experience as a therapeutic element. This consideration reiterates our previous discussion regarding the importance of both cognitive and non-cognitive foci in paradigm implementation. Clinical dysfunctions are seldom restricted to a single nervous system. Central, somatic, and autonomic components often interact with substantial complexity. The indiscriminate emphasis of a single form of input may seriously jeopardize optimal therapeutic improvement. Traditional "verbal" therapies (which can be easily distinguished from those previously described) offer ample documentation to the limitations of a procedure which overemphasizes central nervous system input. Autonomic and peripheral feedback appear to be important therapy elements. This does not deny, of course, that the nervous systems are reciprocally interdependent. However, conjoint improvements in motoric, affective, and mediational performances appear to be facilitated by a therapeutic approach which balances inputs to the respective systems.

The importance of *graduated* performance tasks remains to be fully delineated. Initially modest and progressively more demanding assignments may provide early success experiences and enhance a positive coping orientation. They may likewise facilitate continued pursuit of therapeutic goals. On the other hand, there is some evidence to suggest that task gradation may not be a necessary feature in many client-task combinations. A minimization of clinical risk might recommend use of graduated tasks until more definitive data are available.

The contribution of participant modeling, guided practice, and response-induction aids in initial task assignments bears thoughtful consideration. By maximizing the likelihood of preliminary progress, these procedures may dramatically facilitate continued improvement. Their gradual withdrawal may then enhance independent maintenance and generalization.

Self-Evaluation.

A fourth component in the successful implementation of the personal scientist paradigm focuses on the acquisition of adaptive self-evaluative skills. The literature reviewed in previous chapters lends ample support to the contention that most human behaviors do not receive immediate external consequences. However, many are accompanied by evaluative self-reactions. The critical significance of these private consequences can hardly be overemphasized. The lifetime consequences of most individuals are predominantly self-presented. Not only do we have more access to our own behavior, but we live in a culture which often demands self-evaluation.

Unfortunately, that culture also encourages predominantly dysfunctional self-evaluations. The literatures on depression and self-regulation attest to the disproportionate frequency of self-criticism over self-praise. From cradle to coffin we are taught to be self-disparaging. Apologies, religious confessions, and self-critical statements are rewarded with reassurance and the avoidance of external attack. By admitting our own deficiencies or misdeeds, we mitigate the criticisms of others. Self-praise, on the other hand, is religiously discouraged. Humility and asceticism are lauded "virtues" and self-confidence is tolerated only if it is quiet and justified.

My biases regarding the current cultural shaping of self-evaluation should be apparent. Clinical records abound with distressing illustrations of the extreme personal suffering induced by culturally condoned masochism. I have elaborated elsewhere my conviction that the human being is often least "humane" in his private self-treatment (Mahoney, 1974b). We are acculturated self-critics who plod through a chaotic life of often capricious and meager reinforcements, passively relegating our happiness to an external rather than internal environment. The nature and accessibility of most of our deeds, however, suggests that it is often the case that if we don't reinforce ourselves, we won't be reinforced at all.

On a more empirical plane, the dysfunctional tenacity of maladaptive self-evaluations has been amply documented. Unreasonable standards and idiosyncratic self-reactions may seriously jeopardize therapeutic input. The clinical scientist is well advised to carefully examine and systematically improve his clients' self-evaluative patterns. The potential use of modeling in this endeavor need hardly be defended.

A COMMENT ON ETHICS

One issue which is frequently faced in clinical behavior modification involves the therapist's role in value decisions. That issue is probably even more critical in *cognitive* behavior modification because of its frequent involvement with belief systems. What does the therapist do when a client's distress is exacerbated by a value premise which he does not share? What are the professional and ethical obligations, for example, when a devoutly religious client is anxious and guilt-ridden due to belief-behavior discrepancies? Can a therapist who supports equality of the sexes conduct marital counseling without being biased by his own values? When we systematically assess and modify thought patterns, are we pursuing a "benevolent brainwashing" which is unwittingly subversive and pervasively immoral?

The currently popular stance taken by behavior therapists is both ironic and inadequate. It is ironic because it invokes "client choice" as a factor which absolves the clinician of both guilt and responsibility. As Bandura (1969) says:

> To the extent that the client serves as the primary decision-maker in the value domain, the ethical questions that are frequently raised concerning behavioral control become pseudo issues (p. 101).

Thus, the client allegedly chooses his own therapeutic goals and the therapist assumes the role of a technical consultant who suggests the means for goal attainment. The irony, of course, stems from the fact that the behaviorist views choice from a deterministic framework. The client's choices are not manifestations of "free will"; they are products of current influences and prior learning history.

And here the inadequacy of the "client choice" maneuver becomes apparent. If choice is, in fact, a determined behavior resulting from past and current influences, the therapist cannot magically exempt himself as an influence. The evidence documenting therapist impact on client verbal behavior strongly challenges the behavior modifier's complacent self-perception as an unresponsive catalyst in value decisions. The "choice" proposal may satisfy some legal, political and public relations dilemmas; but it does not remove us either from involvement or ethical responsibility in the value domain.

There is an interesting (and culturally approved) "psycho-logic" employed in this area; namely, it is assumed that an individual's previous learning history has "squatter's rights" on his beliefs and values. The client's culturally determined choice preferences are considered sacrosanct. Pre-therapy influences on belief (e.g., parents, religious training, etc.) are deemed "better" and more legitimate than influences during the therapeutic enterprise. The clinician is explicitly told to keep his hands off clients' beliefs and values. By leaving ethical decisions to the client, we place "responsibility" in the safe distance of his experiential past. In essence, we have conceded that we want to avoid becoming a new element in the learning history which has produced current value biases.

I am here suggesting that we acknowledge the inadequacy of the "client choice" argument in absolving ourselves of ethical responsibilities in therapy. I am not, however, suggesting that we abandon our respect for clients' values and plunge headlong into attitude reconditioning. The alluring paternalism of a psychological prophet is something which must be continually guarded against—it is easy for the therapist to assume that *his* values are inherently "better" than those of his client.

My main point here is that we should stop deluding ourselves into thinking that we can wash our hands of ethical involvement by simply leaving value choices to the client. Even if it *were* possible to exempt ourselves as an influence in therapeutic decisions, this would itself constitute a value commitment. Just as "not deciding is a decision," relegating ethical issues to the client's prior learning history is itself a value decision—it implies that prior influences *should* dominate over present ones. This consideration, however, may be a pseudo-issue because it is unlikely that the therapist can actually avoid influencing at least some client choices.

Given this last concession, what are the implications for the clinical scientist? That question is one which deserves thoughtful consideration and frequent re-appraisal. The value domain is not easily amenable to logical analysis or empirical evaluation. The therapist must therefore realize that his own conclusions on this issue inevitably result from his own individual learning history.

The following suggestions are value-derived and represent but one possible set of guidelines for therapist behavior. My own learning history suggests that the clinical scientist's obligations are:

(1) to recognize his own value biases in the therapeutic enterprise;
(2) to *honestly* acknowledge those biases to the client in all instances wherein major value issues arise; therapist inputs should be labeled as "empirically-based" technical knowledge or "value-derived" opinions so that the client can process them accordingly;
(3) to assist the client in discriminating those instances of personal distress and/or performance dysfunction which appear to be related to a particular value or value system (e.g., a religion); and
(4) to provide assistance in anticipating the consequences of value system modifications when these are considered as a possible therapeutic option.

Thus, a client who is experiencing anxiety and religion-based guilt over his sexual behavior might be aided in discriminating the incongruity between his values and his behavior. Four fundamental options may be perceived: (a) a change in behavior, (b) a change in values, (c) changes in both, and (d) no change. The therapist's obligation is to assist in problem definition, solution generation, and anticipation of consequences. He may not, however, be able to avoid influencing the direction of client choice. Therefore, his biases and probable influence should be openly and honestly acknowledged as an element to be considered in the decision in question. When therapist and client values are at extreme variance, this should be acknowledged and—with mutual respect—efforts should be made to avail the client of assistance from a more compatible clinical scientist.

In my opinion, the therapist who *unwittingly* shapes the values of his clients is more deserving of our professional concern than one who acknowledges his probable impact on client choice and introduces that element as an important consideration in the clinical enterprise. This opinion, of course, and the foregoing statements are themselves reflections of my value bias—i.e., that honest and explicit acknowledgment of such biases should be made. I am aware that this stance is an ethical rather than an empirical one, and that it may well contradict the current value premises of many readers. However, I feel as professionally obliged to express my own biases here as I do to acknowledge and respect contrary opinions on the part of my colleagues.

The foregoing summary of a broad-based therapeutic paradigm has been admittedly brief, terminologically informal, and pervasively value-laden. I shall not again belabor its tentative nature nor implore caution and critical examination in its implementation. It represents a loose configuration of my own current assumptions and procedures in clinical research. My commitment to self-appraising scrutiny and therapeutic refinement predict both my surprise and disappointment should that paradigm remain unaltered.

Chapter Sixteen

The Thinking Behaviorist: A Postscript

We have covered a considerable distance in a few short chapters. Whether the direction of that journey has been wanton or worthwhile depends to a large extent on the reader's biases. It was mentioned in the first chapter that the goal of this undertaking was to offer more questions than answers. That goal derives from an assumption which I consider to be invaluable in our scientific journeying—namely, that it is better to travel hopefully than to arrive.

We began with an evaluation of the historical and methodological factors which have stubbornly discouraged controlled behavioral research on mediational events. Some of the popular conceptual arguments against inference were evaluated and found to be both logically and pragmatically inadequate. Moreover, the pervasive role of inference in all human behavior—and therefore all scientific research—transformed the issue from *whether* we should infer to *when* and *what* should be inferred.

An analysis of the non-mediational model showed it to be strikingly inadequate to deal with behaviors ranging from simple to complex and spanning both human and infra-human populations. Although this fundamental perspective has contributed invaluably to our first generation understanding of basic behavior principles, its practical utility has been unduly limited by its conceptual boundaries. It has restricted its focus to a relatively small fraction of human behavior—i.e., that which is publicly observable.

The covert conditioning model and its derivative therapies were then examined. Unfortunately, neither the model nor its clinical applications has been impressive. The existing data were summarily considered extremely sparse, qualitatively poor, and generally equivocal in their implications.[a]

Our journey then proceeded to two alternative mediational models—information processing and cognitive learning. The former was presented as a perspective which might have considerable relevance for clinical applications. The cognitive learning model attempted a tentative integration of several converging perspectives and briefly outlined some of their clinical parallels. Therapies relevant to this cognitive approach were then examined. Again, the evidence reviewed was found to be relatively meager and often methodologically inadequate. While several sub-areas have mustered exciting preliminary support, a conservative empirical standard recommends cautious optimism and continued inquiry.

At this point, our travels left the formal avenues of conceptual–empirical analysis and turned more explicitly to speculation. Imminent research foci and a few unexamined horizons were briefly noted. The areas of belief, counter-control, choice, and bio-social interactions were suggested as being among the areas needing further scrutiny. In the applied clinical realm, some tentative (and apprehensive) generalizations were then drawn and a personal scientist paradigm was presented. This perspective was distilled from the foregoing research and from some value-based personal derivations.

Several explicit biases were recurrent themes in our tour. A dedication to "data" rather than theory, for example, was repeatedly defended. If research in cognitive behavior modification continues at its current pace, the need for that fidelity can hardly be overemphasized. Human beings are theoretical animals and the allure of speculative generalization is ever present. As reflected in Chapter 10, the area of cognitive-clinical functioning has already generated an initial model and—if the history of psychology is any predictor—we may soon be drowning in theories while still barely moistened by data. While I readily acknowledge the utility (and inevitability) of theories, I must agree with Francis Bacon (1621) regarding their desirable rate of development:

> The understanding must not be allowed to jump and fly from particulars to remote axioms and of almost the highest generality;

[a] Although it has probably been readily apparent in the tenor of the present writing, I should perhaps explicitly acknowledge that my own views on the nature of "private events" have undergone a "paradigm shift" in the last few years. Covert conditioning constituted my former perspective. Having re-examined that model and found it less adequate than a cognitive learning perspective, I am now filtering the data through the latter. Hopefully, a re-appraisal several years hence will suggest further revisions or an even more adequate paradigm.

> . . . it must not be supplied with wings, but rather hung with weights to keep it from leaping and flying (p. 104).

A second bias in the present writing has dealt with many of the unquestioned assumptions which seem to permeate contemporary behavioristic perspectives. The belief in unilinear causation, for example, rests on an indefensible premise. Reciprocal determinism was suggested as a more viable alternative viewpoint. Similarly, we noted the frequency of dichotomous thinking and "mono-topical" biases in current viewpoints. Conventional models assign major causal responsibility to a particular class of variables (cognitive versus non-cognitive, experiential versus biological, etc.). Their intervention strategies are often relatively restricted and correspondingly limited in their impact. My intention has been to challenge these monolithic models and invite consideration of a more ambitious (but hopefully more adequate) perspective emphasizing experiential, mediational, and biological interactions.

In addition to questioning some of our frequent conceptual bifurcations, I have encouraged a scientific relativism which is at variance with contemporary publication practices and conventional scientific fidelities in behavior modification. More specifically, I have taken a few swings at the "falsifying," hypothesis-testing model and have criticized the denigration of "negative results" in our empirical endeavors. These philosophy of science biases derive from a more general prejudice about the processes involved in the growth of knowledge. That prejudice will be more clearly reflected in the next section. First, however, a comment on the relevance of our journey for our work as clinical scientists.

As mentioned in Chapter 10, there is one datum which has more than adequate empirical support—the human being "thinks" a lot. Evidence reviewed in the preceding chapters suggests that mediational processes are pervasive and critically influential factors in human performance. We selectively filter environmental input and actively construct experiential regularities. We anticipate future events and often distort our perception of them to enhance conformity with our expectations. All of this suggests that the human being is a frequently deluded organism whose beliefs and behaviors are stubbornly molded by perceptual bigotry. The implications of this view of man, however, strike a little closer to home when we are reminded that most scientists are human and that scientific research is comprised of belief-behavior patterns.

In my opinion, one of the most important conclusions to be drawn from the literature reviewed in this book is that we need to examine some of the mediational components in our own scientific behaviors. Once again, the realization that we actively construct and distort our scientific "facts" is far from recent:

> For man's sense is falsely asserted to be the standard of things: on the contrary, all the perceptions, both of the senses and the mind, bear reference to man and not to the universe; and the human mind resembles those uneven mirrors which impart their own properties to different objects . . . and distort and disfigure them (Francis Bacon, 1621, p. 41).

Not only are we selective in the way we see the data, but we are very selective in the data we look for. In an entertaining philosophical critique, Karl Popper (1972) addresses this issue in contrasting the "bucket" and the "searchlight" theories of scientific knowledge. In the bucket theory, the content and direction of empirical research is determined by experimental findings and observational data. This perspective, which is analogous to Skinner's (1950) "atheoretical" argument, de-emphasizes hypothesis-testing as a model. However, as Popper and others have pointed out, all research inquiries involve assumptions, expectancies, and hypothetical biases. Although our empirical hunches may occasionally be "tacit" (Polanyi, 1958, 1966), their role in selecting the data we will entertain can hardly be exaggerated.

The scientist is a human being and, as such, is not exempt from the mediational influences which dramatically affect human action. While awareness of those influences may reduce their distortional impact, it is unlikely that it can be totally eliminated. Moreover, the average scientist seldom applies his technical knowledge to himself. Ostensibly, his is the only immaculate perception.

The realization of personal fallibility as a scientist suggests two major conclusions. First, our pursuit of knowledge is far from "objective" in any technical sense of that term. The data are *always* filtered. Second, the growth of knowledge is not self-directed. Our successive approximations toward "truth" might be more accurately described as successive embellishments of assumptive worlds. That is, the growth of knowledge is dramatically influenced by our expectancies and selective questioning of nature.

These two conclusions bear corresponding implications for some of our future pursuits in clinical science.

PHILOSOPHY OF SCIENCE: A RE-APPRAISAL

The first implication, and one which has permeated many earlier discussions, deals with the conventional methodology of science in behavior modification research. With rare exceptions, the behavioral scientist complacently pursues his empirical inquiries feeling comfortably justified that there are logical foundations for his efforts. Although exposure to philosophy of science is sometimes offered in graduate training programs, it is seldom presented in a manner which emphasizes its relevance to everyday research endeavors. Moreover, the prevailing philosophy promulgated in behavioral quarters (i.e., logical positivism)[b] is sorely outdated and unquestionably inadequate as a "meta-theory." Unaware that his philosophical foundations have disintegrated, however, the behavioral researcher continues to energetically implement his inquiries and faithfully model revered standards of falsifiability, operationism, null hypothesis testing, and so on.

The logical and conceptual inadequacies of "justificationist" philosophies of science are commendably presented by Weimer (in press). Although he constructs a few straw men in process, Weimer's incisive critique of conventional scientific assumptions in psychological research warrants thoughtful consideration by the experimental clinician. For example, the notion that scientific growth involves the gradual accumulation of "facts" does not fit with the observation that "victorious" psychological theories often deny the "facts" of their predecessors. The "facts" are apparently not immutable; they are theory-specific relativisms. Moreover, the assumption that empirical knowledge grows only through falsification (refutation) or confirmation of hypotheses has been decisively challenged (cf. Kuhn, 1962; Popper, 1963, 1972; Lakatos, 1970; Lakatos & Musgrave, 1970). Finally, there is evidence to suggest that our knowledge progresses through plural selection processes[c] and paradigm revolutions rather than through molecular hypothesis reformation and sequential theoretical revisions. We do not test theories one at a time. They are evaluated pluralistically—an observation which has stimulated some workers to actually recommend an accelerated proliferation of theories (Feyerabend, 1970). Moreover, the growth of our knowledge seems to be more often characterized by sweeping conceptual revolutions than by gradual theoretical refinements (Kuhn, 1962).

Having challenged the long-revered justificationist philosophies, Weimer (in press) reviews the contemporary non-justificationist perspectives characterized by Bartley (1962, 1968), Kuhn (1962, 1970a,b), Popper (1959, 1963, 1972), and himself. An illustration is

[b] Contemporary psychological methodologies often blend threee separate "isms" (logical positivism, operationism, and falsificationism—cf. Turner, 1967; Weimer, in press).

[c] That is, we evaluate a number of paradigms simultaneously and select those which currently seem more adequate.

"comprehensively critical rationalism" (Bartley), which recommends a pervasive and continuous scrutinization of all theories, including itself. The scientist is urged to maintain a kind of patient paranoia about everything—his data, his theory, and even his technical paranoia. Consistent with this view and more relevant to some of our foregoing comments is the perspective of "psychological fallibilism" (Kuhn, Weimer) which contends that the growth of scientific knowledge can only be understood from a psychological viewpoint. Drawing on the point made earlier, our understanding of the processes involved in empirical growth may require a greater appreciation for the scientist as a fallible information processor.

Where does all of this leave us? Are we still appropriately described by William James's (1890) comment that, "This is no science, it is only the hope of a science"? I don't think so. We have at least come to realize that our search for knowledge is a fallible and relative enterprise. There are no universal standards for reality—our "facts," our purest data, are inevitable distortions of a presumed real world. The roughness of their approximation can never be evaluated. We are inextricably caught up in a collective solipsism of science and can never completely transcend the Platonic "shadows" imposed by our inherent information processing mechanisms. Our only methodological option in reducing the distortion of those mechanisms may be to re-appraise our naive justificationist perspectives and commit ourselves to a scientific paradigm which deals more effectively with our knowledge gathering fallibilities.[d]

TOWARD AN EMPIRICAL HUMANISM

Thus, our pursuit of knowledge is far from being "objective." It is also not self-directed. One of the myths of the justificationist tradition is that a sufficient accumulation of data will force a distillation of principles. Collect enough facts and nature's regularities will become self-apparent. This assumption is amply illustrated in the frenzied and often directionless data collection witnessed in some psychological quarters. The implicit ideal is quantity, not quality, and its effects are sadly reflected in both our *vita* and our journals.

Unfortunately, the direction of scientific "searchlights" is seldom evolutionary or self-corrective. The *content* of our inquiries is

[d] The proposition that our pursuit of knowledge must take into account the perceptual—psychological limitations of the knowledge-seeker (scientist) is itself a limited solution. Our understanding of human data processing fallibilities must itself undergo *fallible* empirical scrutiny, leaving us at best with a relativistic "converging confidence" epistemology.

dramatically influenced by our own acculturated beliefs and preconceptions. We may come closer and closer to scientific consensus of a specific problem, but we seldom acknowledge the values and assumptions which make that problem more worthy of empirical attention than some other. There are unwritten conventions about what can and should be researched and these tacit rules determine which efforts will be professionally reinforced as relevant and contributory.

I have argued elsewhere (Mahoney, 1974b) that the myth of an amoral technology in an applied science must be energetically challenged. It might be premature to say at this point that we are approaching the Los Alamos stage of behavior control; however, the rapidly expanding precision of our technology can scarcely be ignored. Recent political demonstrations and legal controversies regarding behavior modification bear witness to its ominous growth and public portent. Minority groups have argued that our ostensibly amoral technologies have been used to strengthen the *status quo*. We have armed the teacher, the parent, and the prison warden with skills which are frequently employed in ethic-laden enterprises. Even though we can retreat to the logical argument that scientific principles are amoral descriptions of nature, such a maneuver will certainly do little to influence the continuing abuse of our technology by its consumers.

In my opinion, the clinical scientist can and should address himself to the ethical implications of his research and its assimilation. The means for pursuing that involvement are varied. One of the more salient issues deals with the direction of our empirical searchlights. Given that we are rapidly refining our knowledge of behavior change processes, where will our findings leave us? What guidelines are we to follow in humane clinical research? It is, of course, difficult to give directions when you don't know where you are going; and this, I think, is part of our problem. We have energetically maintained our pursuit of knowledge without first examining or evaluating some of the value issues inherent in that pursuit.

The scientist invariably relies upon at least two "commitments" in his professional endeavors. He is committed to a *means* of acquiring knowledge which dictates "how" he asks questions of nature. More tacit, perhaps, is his commitment to unspecified *ends* which constitute a value system directing "what" he will research. The complete scientist, in my opinion, will be sensitively apprised of both of these commitments in his own pursuits and will pursue an unending re-appraisal of their merits.

My own methodological (means) commitments have permeated virtually every chapter of this book. Less explicit until the last few chapters have been my value objectives (end commitments). Some of my ethical biases regarding humanistic guidelines for future clinical research have been presented elsewhere (Mahoney, 1974b). Briefly, I have suggested four general foci for preliminary attention:

1. *personal freedom,* with its associated emphases on responsible choice and independent coping skills;
2. *social sensitivity,* a balanced consideration of both personal and social consequences without disproportionate preoccupation with either;
3. *management of temporal gradients,* again balancing immediate and delayed consequences in a manner which allows both spontaneity and reasoned anticipation; and
4. *cognitive ecology,* cleaning up our private environs and modeling a self-acceptance based on the process rather than outcome of our endeavors.

Needless to say, I think each of the above can be specified in terms which will enable their empirical scrutiny.

Like most value systems, my own probably derives more from the autonomic than from the central nervous system. I shall not pretend to offer a logical defense in its behalf. However, I shall confess to taking consolation from the belief that humanistic philosophy can contribute substantially to the survival and betterment of our species.

We are now, I think, on the verge of an era which holds exciting promise in both conceptual and clinical realms. The "science" of the next decade looks to be provocatively more personal in both method and focus. While it may still be a vast "darkness in which we grope" (William James, 1890), it is at least now illuminated by a humility born of ignorance. Our analysis of the scientist as a fallible information processor offers promising potential in the understanding of human epistemology. More striking, however, is the apparent emergence of a personalized science dedicated to the implementation of a humanistic philosophy. We may well be nearing an interface of values and science which will offer unprecedented contributions.

Previous efforts to integrate science and humanism have, of course, left a bloody arena in their wake. The battles have been lively and lengthy; their results uniformly unproductive (Mahoney, Kazdin, & Lesswing, 1974). It should be obvious from the foregoing that I consider an integration of these two perspectives to be not only feasible but excitingly fertile. Hopefully, the behaviorist and the humanist have outgrown their adolescent rivalries. If either claims to adopt as his personal and professional goal the elimination of human suffering and individualized growth of the person, a collaborative and personalized science must be pursued. The current world crises and the prevalence of human distress bear sad and frequent witness to our need for an intimate and empirical humanism. It is to be hoped that the decade to come will find us united in our aspirations toward becoming sensitive scientists who are dedicated to the empirical refinement of man's humanity to himself and to his fellow man.

References

Abelson, R. P., Aronson, E., McGuire, W. J., Newcomb, T. M., Rosenberg, M. J., & Tannenbaum, P. H. (Eds.), *Theories of cognitive consistency: A sourcebook.* Chicago: Rand McNally, 1968.

Ackerman, P. D. Extinction of covert impulse responses through elimination of consummatory events. *Psychological Record,* 1972, *22,* 477–486.

———. Formulations regarding an experimental analysis of covert impulse and depression responses as mediators of consummatory S–R sequences. *Psychological Record,* 1973, *23,* 477–486.

Adams, J. A. *Human memory.* New York: McGraw-Hill, 1967.

Adorno, T. W., Frenkel-Brunswik, E., Levinson, D. J., & Sanford, R. N. *The authoritarian personality.* New York: Harper, 1950.

Agras, W. S. Transfer during systematic desensitization therapy. *Behaviour Research and Therapy,* 1967, *5,* 193–199.

———. Covert conditioning. *Seminars in Psychiatry,* 1972, *4,* 157–163.

Allen, G. J. The behavioral treatment of test anxiety. *Behavior Therapy,* 1972, *3,* 253–262.

Alston, W. P. Can psychology do without private data? *Behaviorism,* 1972, *1,* 71–102.

Alumbaugh, R. V. Use of behavior modification techniques toward reduction of hallucinatory behavior: A case study. *Psychological Record,* 1971, *21,* 415–417.

Anant, S. S. A note on the treatment of alcoholics by a verbal aversion technique. *Canadian Psychologist,* 1967, *8,* 19–22.

Anderson, J. R., & Bower, G. H. *Human associative memory.* Washington, D.C.: Winston & Sons, 1973.

Annon, J. S. The therapeutic use of masturbation in the treatment of sexual disorders. In R. D. Rubin, J. P. Brady, & J. D. Henderson (Eds.), *Advances in behavior therapy.* Vol. 4. New York: Academic Press, 1973. Pp. 199–215.

Apter, M. J. *The computer simulation of behavior.* New York: Harper, 1970.

Argabrite, A., & Nidorf, L. 15 questions for rating reason. *Rational Living,* 1968, *3,* 9–11.

Ascher, L. M. An experimental analog study of covert positive reinforcement. In R. D. Rubin, J. P. Brady, & J. D. Henderson (Eds.), *Advances in behavior therapy*. Vol. 4. New York: Academic Press, 1973. Pp. 127–138.

Ascher, L. M., & Cautela, J. R. Covert negative reinforcement: An experimental test. *Journal of Behavior Therapy and Experimental Psychiatry,* 1972, *3,* 1–5.

Ashem, B., & Donner, L. Covert sensitization with alcoholics: A controlled replication. *Behaviour Research and Therapy,* 1968, *6,* 7–12.

Atkinson, R. C., & Shiffrin, R. M. The control of short-term memory. *Scientific American,* 1971, *225,* 82–90.

Atkinson, R. C., & Wickens, T. D. Human memory and the concept of reinforcement. In R. Glaser (Ed.), *The nature of reinforcement.* New York: Academic Press, 1971. Pp. 66–120.

Averill, J. R. Personal control over aversive stimuli and its relationship to stress. *Psychological Bulletin,* 1973, *80,* 286–303.

Ayllon, T., & Azrin, N. H. Reinforcement and instructions with mental patients. *Journal of the Experimental Analysis of Behavior,* 1964, *7,* 327–331.

Babladelis, G. Personality and conditioning: A series of attempts to modify self-concept. *Psychological Record,* 1973, *23,* 553–559.

Bachrach, A. J. *Psychological research: An introduction.* (2nd ed.) New York: Random House, 1965.

Bacon, F. *Novum organum.* (original 1621) Oxford: Oxford University Press, 1889.

Baer, D. M., & Sherman, J. A. Reinforcement control of generalized imitation in young children. *Journal of Experimental Child Psychology,* 1964, *1,* 37–49.

Bain, J. A. *Thought control in everyday life.* New York: Funk & Wagnalls, 1928.

Baker, J. N. Reason versus reinforcement in behavior modification. Unpublished doctoral dissertation, University of Illinois, 1966.

Bandura, A. Vicarious processes: A case of no-trial learning. In L. Berkowitz (Ed.), *Advances in experimental social psychology*. Vol. II. New York: Academic Press, 1965. Pp. 1–55.

———. A social learning interpretation of psychological dysfunctions. In P. London & D. Rosenhan (Eds.), *Foundations of abnormal psychology.* New York: Holt, Rinehart & Winston, 1968. Pp. 293–344.

———. *Principles of behavior modification.* New York: Holt, Rinehart & Winston, 1969.

———. (Ed.), *Psychological modeling: Conflicting theories.* Chicago: Aldine-Atherton, 1971. (a)

———. Psychotherapy based upon modeling principles. In A. E. Bergin & S. L. Garfield (Eds.), *Handbook of psychotherapy and behavior change.* New York: Wiley, 1971. Pp. 653–708. (b)

———. *Social learning theory.* Morristown, N.J.: General Learning Press, 1971. (c)

———. Vicarious and self-reinforcement processes. In R. Glaser (Ed.), *The nature of reinforcement.* New York: Academic Press, 1971. Pp. 228–278. (d)

———. The process and practice of participant modeling treatment. Paper presented to the Conference on the Behavioral Basis of Mental Health, Galway, Ireland, 1972.

———. *Aggression: A social learning analysis.* Englewood Cliffs: Prentice-Hall, 1973.

Bandura, A., & Barab, P. G. Conditions governing nonreinforced imitation. *Developmental Psychology,* 1971, *5,* 244–255.

Bandura, A., Blanchard, E. B., & Ritter, B. Relative efficacy of desensitization and modeling approaches for inducing behavioral, affective, and attitudinal changes. *Journal of Personality and Social Psychology,* 1969 *13,* 173–199.

Bandura, A., Grusec, J. E., & Menlove, F. L. Observational learning as a function of symbolization and incentive set. *Child Development,* 1966, *37,* 499–506.

Bandura, A., & Jeffery, R. W. Role of symbolic coding and rehearsal processes in observational learning. *Journal of Personality and Social Psychology,* 1973, *26,* 122–130.

Bandura, A., Jeffery, R. W., & Bachicha, D. L. Analysis of memory codes and cumulative rehearsal in observational learning. Unpublished manuscript, Stanford University, 1974.

Bandura, A., Jeffery, R. W., & Gajos, E. Generalizing change by participant modeling with self-directed mastery. Unpublished manuscript, Stanford University, 1974.

Bandura, A., Jeffery, R. W., & Wright, C. L. Efficacy of participant modeling as a function of response induction aids. *Journal of Abnormal Psychology,* in press.

Bandura, A., & Menlove, F. L. Factors determining vicarious extinction of avoidance behavior through symbolic modeling. *Journal of Personality and Social Psychology,* 1968, *8,* 99–108.

Bandura, A., & Rosenthal, T. L. Vicarious classical conditioning as a function of arousal level. *Journal of Personality and Social Psychology,* 1966, *3,* 54–62.

Bandura, A., & Walters, R. H. *Adolescent aggression.* New York: Ronald Press, 1959.

Bannister, D. Psychology as an exercise in paradox. *Bulletin of the British Psychological Society*, 1966, *19*, 21–26.

Barber, T. X., & Hahn, K. W. Experimental studies in "hypnotic" behavior: Physiological and subjective effects of imagined pain. *Journal of Nervous and Mental Disease*, 1964, *139*, 416–425.

Barlow D. H. Increasing heterosexual responsiveness in the treatment of sexual deviation: A review of the clinical and experimental literature. *Behavior Therapy*, 1973, *4*, 655–671.

Barlow, D. H., Agras, W. S., Leitenberg, H., Callahan, E. J., & Moore, R. C. The contribution of therapeutic instruction to covert sensitization. *Behaviour Research and Therapy*, 1972, *10*, 411–415.

Barlow, D. H., Leitenberg, H., & Agras, W. S. Experimental control of sexual deviation through manipulation of the noxious scene in covert sensitization. *Journal of Abnormal Psychology*, 1969, *74*, 596–601.

Barlow, D. H., Leitenberg, H., Agras, W. S., & Wincze, J. The transfer gap in systematic desensitization: An analogue study. *Behaviour Research and Therapy*, 1969, *7*, 191–196.

Bartlett, F. C. *Remembering*. Cambridge: Cambridge University Press, 1932.

Bartley, W. W. *The retreat to commitment*. New York: Alfred A. Knopf, 1962.

———. Theories of demarcation between science and metaphysics. In I. Lakatos & A. Musgrave (Eds.), *Problems in the philosophy of science*. Amsterdam: North Holland Publishing Company, 1968. Pp. 40–64.

Bass, B. A. An unusual behavioral technique for treating obsessive ruminations. *Psychotherapy: Theory, Research and Practice*, 1973, *10*, 191–192.

Bayroff, A. G., & Lard, K. E. Experimental social behavior of animals: III. Imitational learning of white rats. *Journal of Comparative Psychology*, 1944, *37*, 165–171.

Beck, A. T. *Depression: Clinical, experimental, and theoretical aspects*. New York: Hoeber, 1967.

———. Cognitive therapy: Nature and relation to behavior therapy. *Behavior Therapy*, 1970, *1*, 184–200. (a)

———. Role of fantasies in psychotherapy and psychopathology. *Journal of Nervous and Mental Disease*, 1970, *150*, 3–17. (b)

———. Cognition, affect, and psychopathology. *Archives of General Psychiatry*, 1971, *24*, 495–500.

———. Cognition, anxiety, and psychophysiological disorders. In C. D. Spielberger (Ed.), *Anxiety: Current trends in theory and research*. New York: Academic Press, 1972. Pp. 343–354. (a)

———. The phenomenon of depression: A synthesis. In D. Offer & D. X. Freedman (Eds.), *Modern psychiatry and clinical research*. New York: Basic Books, 1972. (b)

———. Cognitive modification in depressed, suicidal patients. Paper presented to the Society for Psychotherapy Research, Denver, 1974.

Beck, A. T., & Greenberg, R. L. Cognitive therapy with depressed women. In V. Franks & V. Burtle (Eds.), *Women in therapy*. New York: Brunner/Mazel, in press.

Beck, A. T., Laude, R., & Bohnert, M. Ideational components of anxiety neurosis. Unpublished manuscript, University of Pennsylvania, 1974.

Belmont, J. M., & Butterfield, E. C. Learning strategies as determinants of memory deficiencies. *Cognitive Psychology*, 1971, *2*, 411–420.

Bem, D. J. Self-perception: An alternative interpretation of cognitive dissonance phenomena. *Psychological Review*, 1967, *74*, 183–200.

———. *Beliefs, attitudes, and human affairs*. Monterey: Brooks/Cole, 1970.

———. Self-perception theory. In L. Berkowitz (Ed.), *Advances in experimen-*

tal social psychology. Vol. 6. New York: Academic Press, 1972. Pp. 1–62.

Bem, S. L. Verbal self-control: The establishment of effective self-instruction. *Journal of Experimental Psychology*, 1967, *74*, 485–491.

Benjamin, A. C. *Operationism*. Springfield, Ill.: Charles C. Thomas, 1955.

Berecz, J. Modification of smoking behavior through self-administered punishment of imagined behavior: A new approach to aversion therapy. *Journal of Consulting and Clinical Psychology,* 1972, *38*, 244–250.

Berger, S. M. Conditioning through vicarious instigation. *Psychological Review*, 1962, *69*, 450–466.

Berger, S. M., & Johansson, S. L. Effect of a model's expressed emotions on an observer's resistance to extinction. *Journal of Personality and Social Psychology*, 1968, *10*, 53–58.

Bergin, A. E. A self-regulation technique for impulse control disorders. *Psychotherapy: Theory, Research and Practice*, 1969, *6*, 113–118.

———. Cognitive therapy and behavior therapy: Foci for a multidimensional approach to treatment. *Behavior Therapy*, 1970, *1*, 205–212.

Bernard, C. *An introduction to the study of experimental medicine*. (original 1865) New York: Dover, 1957.

Bernstein, D. A. Modification of smoking behavior: An evaluative review. *Psychological Bulletin*, 1969, *71*, 418–440.

———. Situational factors in behavioral fear assessment: A progress report. *Behavior Therapy*, 1973, *4*, 41–48.

Betancourt, F. W., & Zeiler, M. D. The choices and preferences of nursery school children. *Journal of Applied Behavior Analysis*, 1971, *4*, 299–304.

Blackwood, R. O. The operant conditioning of verbally mediated self-control in the classroom. *Journal of School Psychology*, 1970, *8*, 251–258.

Blanchard, E., & Draper, D. O. Treatment of a rodent phobia by covert reinforcement: A single subject experiment. *Behavior Therapy*, 1973, *4*, 559–564.

Blanshard, B., & Skinner, B. F. Is the concept of consciousness necessary?: A debate. *Philosophy and Phenomenological Research*, March, 1967.

Blumenfeld, A. *Heart attack: Are you a candidate*? New York: Pyramid, 1964.

Bolles, R. C. Reinforcement, expectancy, and learning. *Psychological Review*, 1972, *79*, 394–409.

Boren, J. J. Some variables affecting the superstitious chaining of responses. In P. B. Dews (Ed.), *Festschrift for B. F. Skinner*. New York: Appleton-Century-Crofts, 1970. Pp. 119–129.

Boren, J. J., & Coleman, A. D. Some experiments on reinforcement principles within a psychiatric ward for delinquent soldiers. *Journal of Applied Behavior Analysis*, 1970, *3*, 29–37.

Bourne, L. E., & Dominowski, R. L. Thinking. *Annual Review of Psychology*, 1972, *23*, 105–130.

Bower, G. H. Imagery as a relational organizer in associative learning. *Journal of Verbal Learning and Verbal Behavior*, 1970, *9*, 529–533.

———. Mental imagery and associative learning. In L. Gregg (Ed.), *Cognition and learning in memory*. New York: Wiley, 1972.

Breger, L. (Ed.), *Clinical-cognitive psychology*. Englewood Cliffs: Prentice-Hall, 1969.

Brehm, J. W. *A theory of psychological reactance*. New York: Academic Press, 1966.

Breland, K., & Breland, M. The misbehavior of organisms. *American Psychologist*, 1961, *16*, 681–684.

Breznitz, S. A study of worry. *British Journal of Social and Clinical Psychology*, 1971, *10*, 271–279.

Bridger, W. H., & Mandel, I. J. A comparison of GSR fear responses produced by threat and electric shock. *Journal of Psychiatric Research*, 1964, *2*, 31–40.

———, & ———. Abolition of the PRE by instructions in GSR conditioning. *Journal of Experimental Psychology*, 1965, *69*, 476–482.

Bridgman, P. W. *The logic of modern physics*. New York: Macmillan, 1927.

———. Remarks on the present state of operationism. *Scientific Monthly*, 1954, *79*, 224–226.

Brigham, T. A., & Bushell, D. Notes on autonomous environments: Effects of student-selected and teacher-selected rewards on academic performance. *Educational Technology*, in press.

Brigham, T. A., & Sherman, J. A. Effects of choice and immediacy of reinforcement on single response and switching behavior of children. *Journal of the Experimental Analysis of Behavior*, 1973, *19*, 425–435.

Brigham, T. A., & Stoerzinger, A. Choice as a consequence: A concurrent analysis. Unpublished manuscript, Washington State University, 1974.

Brown, P. L., & Jenkins, H. M. Auto-shaping of the pigeon's key-peck. *Journal of the Experimental Analysis of Behavior*, 1968, *11*, 1–8.

Brown, R., & McNeill, D. The "tip of the tongue" phenomenon. *Journal of Verbal Learning and Verbal Behavior*, 1966, *5*, 325–337.

Browning, R. M. Treatment effects of a total behavior modification program with five autistic children. *Behaviour Research and Therapy*, 1971, *9*, 319–327.

Bruch, H. *Eating disorders*. New York: Basic Books, 1973.

Bruner, J. S., Goodnow, J. J., & Austin, G. A. *A study of thinking*. New York: Wiley, 1956.

Bucher, B., & Fabricatore, J. Use of patient-administered shock to suppress hallucinations. *Behavior Therapy*, 1970, *1*, 382–385.

Buchwald, A. M. Extinction after acquisition under different verbal reinforcement combinations. *Journal of Experimental Psychology*, 1959, *57*, 43–48. (a)

———. Experimental alterations in the effectiveness of verbal reinforcement combinations. *Journal of Experimental Psychology*, 1959, *57*, 351–361. (b)

———. Supplementary report: Alteration in the reinforcement value of a positive reinforcer. *Journal of Experimental Psychology*, 1960, *60*, 416–418.

Burkhead, D. E. The reduction of negative affect in human subjects: A laboratory investigation of rational-emotive psychotherapy. Unpublished doctoral dissertation, Western Michigan University, 1966.

Burmester, M. A., Garth, R. E., Koos, E. M., & Stothart, J. R. *Explorations in biology*. Kansas City, Mo.: Mid-continent Regional Educational Laboratory, 1970.

Burstein, S., & Meichenbaum, D. The work of worrying in children undergoing surgery. Unpublished manuscript, University of Waterloo, 1974.

Butterfield, E. C., Wambold, C., & Belmont, J. M. On the theory and practice of improving short-term memory. *American Journal of Mental Deficiency*, 1973, *77*, 654–669.

Butts, D. P. The relationship of problem solving ability and science knowledge. *Science Education*, 1965, *49*, 138–146.

Butts, D. P., & Jones, H. L. Inquiry training and problem solving in elementary school children. *Journal of Research in Science Teaching*, 1966, *4*, 21–27.

Callahan, E. J., & Leitenberg, H. Aversion therapy for sexual deviation: Contingent shock and covert sensitization. *Journal of Abnormal Psychology*, 1973, *81*, 60–73.

Campbell, B. A., & Spear, N. E. Ontogeny of memory. *Psychological Review*, 1972, *79*, 215–236.

Campbell, D. T., & Stanley, J. C. *Experimental and quasi-experimental designs for research*. Chicago: Rand McNally, 1963.

Campbell, L. M. A variation of thought-stopping in a twelve-year-old boy: A case report. *Journal of Behavior Therapy and Experimental Psychiatry*, 1973, *4*, 69–70.

Cannon, W. B. "Voodoo" death. *American Anthropologist*, 1942, *44*, 169–181.

———. "Voodoo" death. *Psychosomatic Medicine*, 1957, *19*, 182–190.

Carnegie, D. *How to stop worrying and start living*. New York: Simon & Schuster, 1948.

Castaneda, C. *A separate reality: Further conversations with Don Juan*. New York: Pocket Books, 1972.

Catania, A. C. Chomsky's formal analysis of natural languages: A behavioral translation. *Behaviorism*, 1972, *1*, 1–15. (a)

———. The pigeon's preference for free choice over forced choice. Paper presented to the Psychonomic Society, St. Louis, November, 1972. (b)

Catania, A. C., & Cutts, D. Experimental control of superstitious responding in humans. *Journal of the Experimental Analysis of Behavior*, 1963, *6*, 203–208.

Cautela, J. R. Treatment of compulsive behavior by covert sensitization. *Psychological Record*, 1966, *16*, 33–41.

———. Covert sensitization. *Psychological Reports*, 1967, *20*, 459–468.

———. The use of imagery in behavior modification, Paper presented to the Association for the Advancement of Behavior Therapy, Washington, D.C., 1969. (a)

———. Behavior therapy and self-control: Techniques and implications.

In C. M. Franks (Ed.), *Behavior therapy: Appraisal and status*. New York: McGraw-Hill, 1969. Pp. 323–340. (b)

———. Covert negative reinforcement. *Journal of Behavior Therapy and Experimental Psychiatry*, 1970, *1*, 273–278. (a)

———. Covert reinforcement. *Behavior Therapy*, 1970, *1*, 33–50. (b)

———. The treatment of alcoholism by covert sensitization. *Psychotherapy*, 1970, *7*, 86–90. (c)

———. Treatment of smoking by covert sensitization. *Psychological Reports*, 1970, *26*, 415–420. (d)

———. Covert conditioning. In A. Jacobs & L. B. Sachs (Eds.), *The psychology of private events: Perspectives on covert response systems*. New York: Academic Press, 1971. Pp. 109–130. (a)

———. Covert extinction. *Behavior Therapy*, 1971, *2*, 192–200. (b)

———. Covert modeling. Paper presented to the Association for the Advancement of Behavior Therapy, Washington, D.C., 1971. (c)

———. Rationale and procedures for covert conditioning. In R. D. Rubin, H. Fensterheim, J. D. Henderson, & L. P. Ullmann (Eds.), *Advances in behavior therapy*. New York: Academic Press, 1972. Pp. 85–96.

———. Covert processes and behavior modification. *Journal of Nervous and Mental Disease*, 1973, *157*, 27–36.

Cautela, J. R., & Baron, M. G. Multifaceted behavior therapy of self-injurious behavior. *Journal of Behavior Therapy and Experimental Psychiatry*, 1973, *4*, 125–131.

Cautela, J. R., Flannery R. B., & Hanley, E. Covert modeling: An experimental test. *Behavior Therapy*, in press.

Cautela, J. R., Steffan, J., & Wish, P. Covert reinforcement: An experimental test. *Journal of Consulting and Clinical Psychology*, in press.

Cautela, J. R., Walsh, K., & Wish, P. The use of covert reinforcement in the modification of attitudes toward the mentally retarded. *Journal of Psychology*, 1971, *77*, 257–260.

Cautela, J. R., & Wisocki, P. A. The use of imagery in the modification of attitudes toward the elderly: A preliminary report. *Journal of Psychology*, 1969, *73*, 193–199.

Cautela, J. R., & Wisocki, P. A. Covert sensitization for the treatment of sexual deviations. *Psychological Record*, 1971, *21*, 37–48.

Chapman, J. Visual imagery and motor phenomena in acute schizophrenia. *British Journal of Psychiatry*, 1967, *113*, 771–778.

Chapman, R. F., Smith, J. W., & Layden, T. A. Elimination of cigarette smoking by punishment and self-management training. *Behaviour Research and Therapy*, 1971, *9*, 255–264.

Chapman, R. M. Evoked potentials of the brain related to thinking. In F. J. McGuigan & R. A. Schoonover (Eds.), *The psychophysiology of thinking*. New York: Academic Press, 1973. Pp. 69–108.

Chappell, M. N., & Stevenson, T. I. Group psychological training in some organic conditions. *Mental Hygiene*, 1936, *20*, 588–597.

Cherry, E. C. Some experiments on the recognition of speech, with one and with two ears. *Journal of the Acoustical Society of America*, 1953, *25*, 975–979.

Chesen, E. S. *Religion may be hazardous to your health*. New York: Collier, 1972.

Church, R. M. Transmission of learned behavior between rats. *Journal of Abnormal and Social Psychology*, 1957, *54*, 163–165.

Cohen, D. B. Toward a theory of dream recall. *Psychological Bulletin*, 1974, *81*, 138–154.

Cohen, G. How are pictures registered in memory? *Quarterly Journal of Experimental Psychology*, 1973, *25*, 557–564.

Cooke, G. Evaluation of the efficacy of the components of reciprocal inhibition psychotherapy. *Journal of Abnormal Psychology*, 1968, *73*, 464–467.

Corson, J. A. Observational learning of a lever pressing response. *Psychonomic Science*, 1967, *7*, 197–198.

Coué, E. *The practice of autosuggestion*. New York: Doubleday, 1922.

Covington, M. V., Crutchfield, R. S., & Davies, L. B. *The productive thinking program. Series one: General problem solving*. Berkeley: Brazelton, 1966.

Cowan, P. A., Hoddinott, B. A., & Wright, B. A. Compliance and resistance in the conditioning of autistic children: An exploratory study. *Child Development*, 1965, *36*, 913–923.

Craig, K. Physiological arousal as a function of imagined, vicarious, and direct stress experiences. *Journal of Abnormal Psychology*, 1968, *73*, 513–520.

Craighead, W. E. The role of muscular relaxation in systematic desensitization. In R. D. Rubin, J. P. Brady, & J. D. Henderson (Eds.), *Advances in behavior therapy*. Vol. 4. New York: Academic Press, 1973. Pp. 177–197.

Crawford, M. P., & Spence, K. W. Observational learning of discrimination problems by chimpanzees. *Journal of Comparative Psychology*, 1939, *27*, 133–147.

Creed, T. L., & Ferster, C. B. Space as a reinforcer in a continuous free-operant environment. *Psychological Record*, 1972, *22*, 161–167.

Crosby, R. M., & Cahoon, D. D. Superstitious responding as an artifact in investigations of shock elicited aggression. *Psychological Record*, 1973, *23*, 191–196.

Crowder, J. E., & Thornton, D. W. Effects of systematic desensitization, programmed fantasy, and bibliotherapy on a specific fear. *Behaviour Research and Therapy*, 1970, *8*, 35–41.

Curtis, R. H., & Presly, A. S. The extinction of homosexual behavior by covert sensitization: A case study. *Behaviour Research and Therapy*, 1972, *10*, 81–83.

Danaher, B. G. An experimental analysis of coverant control: Cuing and consequation. Paper presented to the Western Psychological Association, San Francisco, April, 1974.

———. The theoretical foundations and clinical applications of the Premack Principle: A review and critique. *Behavior Therapy*, in press.

Danaher, B. G., & Thoresen, C. E. Imagery assessment by self-report and behavioral measures. *Behaviour Research and Therapy*, 1972, *10*, 131–138.

Darby, C. L., & Riopelle, A. J. Observational learning in the rhesus monkey. *Journal of Comparative and Physiological Psychology*, 1959, *52*, 94–98.

Darrow, C. W. Differences in the physiological reactions to sensory and ideational stimuli. *Psychological Bulletin*, 1929, *26*, 185–201.

Davis, A. *Let's eat right to keep fit*. New York: Harcourt, Brace and Jovanovich, 1954.

Davis, D., McLemore, C. W., & London, P. The role of visual imagery in desensitization. *Behaviour Research and Therapy*, 1970, *8*, 11–13.

Davis, G. A. Current status of research and theory in human problem solving. *Psychological Bulletin*, 1966, *66*, 36–54.

———. *Psychology of human problem solving: Theory and practice*. New York: Basic Books, 1973.

Davis, G. A., & Scott, J. A. (Eds.), *Training creative thinking*. New York: Holt, 1971.

Davison, G. C. Differential relaxation and cognitive restructuring in therapy with a "paranoid schizophrenic" or "paranoid state." *Proceedings of the 74th Annual Convention of the Amercian Psychological Association*, 1966, 177–178.

———. Elimination of a sadistic fantasy by a client-controlled counterconditioning technique: A case study. *Journal of Abnormal Psychology*, 1968, *73*, 84–89. (a)

———. Systematic desensitization as a counterconditioning process. *Journal of Abnormal Psychology*, 1968, *73*, 91–99. (b)

———. Self-control through "imaginal aversive contingency" and "one-downmanship": Enabling the powerless to accommodate unreasonableness. In J. D. Krumboltz & C. E. Thoresen (Eds.), *Behavioral counseling: Cases and techniques*. New York: Holt, Rinehart & Winston, 1969. Pp. 319–327.

———. Counter-control in behavior modification. In L. A. Hamerlynck, L. C. Handy, & E. J. Mash (Eds.), *Behavior change: Methodology, concepts, and practice*. Champaign, Ill.: Research Press, 1973. Pp. 153–167.

Davison, G. C., Tsujimoto, R. N., & Glaros, A. G. Attribution and the maintenance of behavior change in falling asleep. *Journal of Abnormal Psychology*, 1973, *82*, 124–133.

Davison, G. C., & Valins, S. On self-produced and drug-produced relaxation. *Behaviour Research and Therapy*, 1968, *6*, 401–402.

Davison, G. C., & Valins, S. Maintenance of self-attributed and drug-attributed behavior change. *Journal of Personality and Social Psychology*, 1969, *11*, 25–33.

Davison, G. C., & Wilson, G. T. Processes of fear-reduction in systematic desensitization: Cognitive and social reinforcement factors in humans. *Behavior Therapy*, 1973, *4*, 1–21.

Day, W. F. Radical behaviorism in reconciliation with phenomenology. *Journal of the Experimental Analysis of Behavior*, 1969, *12*, 315–328. (a)

———. On certain similarities between the philosophical investigations of

Ludwig Wittgenstein and the operationism of B. F. Skinner. *Journal of the Experimental Analysis of Behavior*, 1969, *12*, 489–506. (b)

———. Methodological problems in the analysis of behavior controlled by private events: Some unusual recommendations. Paper presented to the Americn Psychological Association, Washington, D.C., 1971.

deBono, E. *Lateral thinking*. New York: Harper, 1970.

deCharms, R. *Personal causation: The internal affective determinants of behavior*. New York: Academic Press, 1968.

Deci, E. L. Effects of externally mediated rewards on intrinsic motivation. *Journal of Personality and Social Psychology*, 1971, *18*, 105–115.

———. Intrinsic motivation, extrinsic reinforcement, and inequity. *Journal of Personality and Social Psychology*, 1972, *22*, 113–130.

Dember, W. N. Motivation and the cognitive revolution. *American Psychologist*, 1974, *29*, 161–168.

Dement, W. C. *Some must watch while some must sleep*. Stanford: Stanford Alumni Association, 1972.

DeNike, L. D. The temporal relationship between awareness and performance in verbal conditioning. *Journal of Experimental Psychology*, 1964, *68*, 521–529.

Denny, D. Modeling effects upon conceptual style and cognitive tempo. *Child Development*, 1972, *43*, 105–119.

Dewey, J. *How we think*. Boston: Heath, 1933.

———. *Logic: The theory of inquiry*. New York: Holt, 1938.

DiLoreto, A. O. *Comparative psychotherapy: An experimental analysis*. Chicago: Aldine-Atherton, 1971.

Doke, L. A., & Risley, T. R. The organization of daycare environments: Required vs. optional activities. *Journal of Applied Behavior Analysis*, 1972, *5*, 405–420.

Dostoyevsky, F. M. *Notes from the Underground*. (original 1864) In B. G. Guerney (Ed.), *A treasury of Russian literature*. New York: Vanguard Press, 1943. Pp. 442–537.

Dulany, D. E. The place of hypotheses and intentions: An analysis of verbal control in verbal conditioning. In C. W. Eriksen (Ed.), *Behavior and awareness*. Durham, N.C.: Duke University Press, 1962. Pp. 102–129.

———. Awareness, rules, and propositional control: A confrontation with S-R behavior theory. In T. R. Dixon & D. L. Horton (Eds.), *Verbal behavior and general behavior theory*. Englewood Cliffs: Prentice-Hall, 1968. Pp. 340–387.

D'Zurilla, T. Recall efficiency and mediating cognitive events in "experimental repression." *Journal of Personality and Social Psychology*, 1965, *1*, 253–257.

D'Zurilla, T. J., & Goldfried, M. R. Problem solving and behavior modification. *Journal of Abnormal Psychology*, 1971, *78*, 107–126.

D'Zurilla, T. J., Wilson, G. T., & Nelson, R. A preliminary study of the effectiveness of graduated prolonged exposure in the treatment of irrational fear. *Behavior Therapy*, 1973, *4*, 672–685.

Edwards, M. W. A survey of problem-solving courses. *Journal of Creative Behavior*, 1968, *2*, 33–51.

Efron, R. The conditioned inhibition of uncinate fits. *Brain*, 1957, *80*, 251–262.

Ehrlich, H. J., & Lee, D. Dogmatism, learning, and resistance to change: A review and a new paradigm. *Psychological Bulletin*, 1969, *71*, 249–260.

Ellis, A. Outcome of employing three techniques of psychotherapy. *Journal of Clinical Psychology*, 1957, *13*, 344–350.

———. *Reason and emotion in psychotherapy*. New York: Stuart, 1962.

———. A cognitive approach to behavior therapy. *International Journal of Psychotherapy*, 1969, *8*, 896–900.

———. *The essence of rational psychotherapy: A comprehensive approach to treatment*. New York: Institute for Rational Living, 1970.

———. *Growth through reason*. Palo Alto: Science & Behavior Books, 1971.

———. *How to master your fear of flying*. New York: Curtis, 1972.

———. Are cognitive behavior therapy and rational therapy synonymous? *Rational Living*, 1973, *8*, 8–11. (a)

———. *Humanistic psychotherapy: The rational-emotive approach*. New York: Julian Press, 1973. (b)

Ellis, A., & Harper, R. A. *A guide to rational living*. Hollywood: Wilshire, 1961.

Epstein, L. H., & Peterson, G. L. Differential conditioning using covert stimuli. *Behavior Therapy*, 1973, *4*, 96–99.

Erhard, D. The new vegetarians. *Nutrition Today*, 1973, *8*, 4–12.

———. The new vegetarians: Part II. *Nutrition Today*, 1974, *9*, 20–27.

Eriksen, C. W., & Kuethe, J. L. Avoidance conditioning of verbal behavior without awareness: A paradigm of repression. *Journal of Abnormal and Social Psychology*, 1956, *53*, 203–209.

Estes, W. K. Reward in human learning: Theoretical issues and strategic choice points. In R. Glaser (Ed.), *The nature of reinforcement*. New York: Academic Press, 1971, Pp. 16–36.

Estes, W. K., Koch, S., MacCorquodale, K., Meehl, P. E., Mueller, C. G., Schoenfeld, W. N., & Verplanck, W. S. *Modern learning theory*. New York: Appleton-Century-Crofts, 1954.

Farber, I. E. The things people say to themselves. *American Psychologist*, 1963, *18*, 185–197.

Farr, J., & Tucker, D. Extension of the covert sensitization paradigm with sexual deviance. Unpublished manuscript, Pennsylvania State University, 1974.

Feigenbaum, E. A., & Feldman, J. C. *Computers and thought*. New York: McGraw-Hill, 1963.

Feingold, B. D., & Mahoney, M. J. Reinforcement effects on intrinsic interest: Undermining the overjustification hypothesis. *Behavior Therapy*, 1974 (in press).

Feldhusen, J. F., Treffinger, D. J., & Bahlke, S. J. Developing creative thinking: The Purdue creativity program. *Journal of Creative Behavior*, 1970, *4*, 85–90.

Felixbrod, J. J., & O'Leary, K. D. Effects of reinforcement on children's academic behavior as a function of self-determined and externally imposed contingencies. *Journal of Applied Behavior Analysis*, 1973, *6*, 241–250.

Feyerabend, P. Consolations for the specialist. In I. Lakatos & A. Musgrave (Eds.), *Criticism and the growth of knowledge*. Cambridge: Cambridge University Press, 1970. Pp. 197–230.

Fixsen, D. L., Phillips, E. L., & Wolf, M. M. Achievement Place: Experiments in self-government with pre-delinquents. *Journal of Applied Behavior Analysis*, 1973, *6*, 31–47.

Flannery, R. B. A laboratory analogue of two covert reinforcement procedures. *Journal of Behavior Therapy and Experimental Psychiatry*, 1972, *3*, 171–177. (a)

———. Use of covert conditioning in the treatment of a drug-dependent college dropout. *Journal of Counseling Psychology,* 1972, *19,* 547–550. (b)

Foreyt, J. P., & Hagen, R. L. Covert sensitization: Conditioning or suggestion? *Journal of Abnormal Psychology*, 1973, *82*, 17–23.

Fox, E. E., & Davies, R. L. Test your rationality, *Rational Living*, 1971, *5*, 23–25.

Foxman, J. Effect of cognitive rehearsal on rat phobic behavior. *Journal of Abnormal Psychology*, 1972, *79*, 39–46.

Frank, J. D. *Persuasion and healing*. Baltimore: Johns Hopkins Press, 1961.

Frankl, V. E. *Man's search for meaning: An introduction to logotherapy*. New York: Washington Square Press, 1959.

Fredericks, C. *Eating right for you*. New York: Grosset & Dunlap, 1972.

Gagne, R. M. Problem solving. In A. W. Melton (Ed.), *Categories of human learning*. New York: Academic Press, 1964. Pp. 293–317.

Galton, F. Statistical inquiries into the efficacy of prayer. *Fortnightly Review,* 1872, *12*, 125–135.

———. *Inquiries into human faculty and its development*. New York: Macmillan, 1883.

Garcia, E., Guess, D., & Byrnes, J. Development of syntax in a retarded girl using procedures of imitation, reinforcement, and modelling. *Journal of Applied Behavior Analysis*, 1973, *6*, 299–310.

Gardiner, R. M. A test of coverant control therapy to reduce cigarette smoking. Unpublished doctoral dissertation, University of Louisville, 1971.

Garfield, Z. H., McBrearty, J. F., & Dichter, M. A case of impotence treated with desensitization combined with *in vivo* operant training and thought substitution. In R. D. Rubin & C. M. Franks (Eds.), *Advances in behavior therapy*. New York: Academic Press, 1969.

Gaul, D. J., Craighead, W. E., & Mahoney, M. J. The relationship between eating rates and obesity. *Journal of Consulting and Clinical Psychology*, in press.

Gaupp, L. A., Stern, R. M., & Galbraith, G. G. False heart-rate feedback and reciprocal inhibition by aversion relief in the treatment of snake avoidance behavior. *Behavior Therapy*, 1972, *3*, 7–20.

Geer, J. H., Davison, G. C., & Gatchel, R. J. Reduction of stress in humans through non-veridical perceived control of aversive stimulation. *Journal of Personality and Social Psychology*, 1970, *16*, 731–738.

Gentry, W. In vivo desensitization of an obsessive cancer fear. *Journal of Behavior Therapy and Experimental Psychiatry*, 1970, *1*, 315–318.

Gerst, M. D. Symbolic coding processes in observational learning. *Journal of Personality and Social Psychology*, 1971, *19*, 7–17.

Gershman, L. Case conference: A transvestite fantasy treated by thought-stopping, covert sensitization and aversive shock. *Journal of Behavior Therapy and Experimental Psychiatry*, 1970, *1*, 153–161.

Gewirtz, J. L. The roles of overt responding and extrinsic reinforcement in "self-" and "vicarious-reinforcement" and in "observational learning" and imitation. In R. Glaser (Ed.), *The nature of reinforcement*. New York: Academic Press, 1971. Pp. 279–309.

Giebink, J. W., Stover, D. S., & Fahl, M. A. Teaching adaptive responses to frustration to emotionally disturbed boys, *Journal of Consulting and Clinical Psychology*, 1968, *32*, 366–368.

Glass, D. C., Singer, J. E., & Friedman, L. N. Psychic cost of adaptation to an environmental stressor. *Journal of Personality and Social Psychology*, 1969, *12*, 200–210.

Glucksberg, S., & King, L. J. Motivated forgetting mediated by implicit verbal chaining: A laboratory analog of repression. *Science*, 1967, *158*, 517–519.

Gold, S., & Neufeld, I. L. A learning approach to the treatment of homosexuality. *Behaviour Research and Therapy*, 1965, *2*, 201–204.

Goldfried, M. R. Systematic desensitization as training in self-control. *Journal of Consulting and Clinical Psychology*, 1971, *37*, 228–234.

———. Reduction of generalized anxiety through a variant of systematic desensitization. In M. R. Goldfried & M. Merbaum (Eds.), *Behavior change through self-control*. New York: Holt, Rinehart & Winston, 1973. Pp. 297–304. (a)

———. Self-control training in anxiety reduction. Paper presented to the American Psychological Association, Montreal, August, 1973. (b)

Goldfried, M. R., Decenteceo, E. T., & Weinberg, L. Systematic rational restructuring as a self-control technique. *Behavior Therapy*, 1974, *5*, 247–254.

Goldfried, M. R., & Trier, C. S. Effectiveness of relaxation as an active coping skill. *Journal of Abnormal Psychology*, in press.

Goldiamond, I. Self-control procedures in personal behavior problems. *Psychological Reports*, 1965, *17*, 851–868.

———. Perception, language and conceptualization rules. In B. Kleinmuntz (Ed.), *Problem solving: Research, method, and theory*. New York: Wiley, 1966. Pp. 183–224.

Goldstein, A. P. *Therapist-patient expectanicies in psychotherapy*. New York: Pergamon, 1962.

Gonzalez-Wippler, M. *Santeria: African magic in Latin America*. New York: Julian Press, 1973.

Goodman, D. S., & Maultsby, M. C. *Emotional well-being through rational behavior training*. Springfield, Ill.: Charles C. Thomas, 1974.

Gordon, S. B. Self-control with a covert aversive stimulus: Modification of smoking. Paper presented to the Association for the Advancement of Behavior Therapy, Washington, D.C., 1971.

Gordon, W. J. J. *Synetics*. New York: Harper & Row, 1961.

Gotestam, K. G., & Melin, L. Covert extinction of amphetamine addiction. *Behavior Therapy*, 1974, *5*, 90–92.

Grings, W. W. The role of consciousness and cognition in autonomic behavior change. In F. J. McGuigan & R. A. Schoonover (Eds.), *The psychophysiology of thinking*. New York: Academic Press, 1973. Pp. 233–256.

Grossberg, J. M., & Wilson, H. Physiological changes accompanying the visualization of fearful and neutral situations. *Journal of Personality and Social Psychology*, 1968, *10*, 124–133.

Guess, D., & Baer, D. M. An analysis of individual differences in generalization between receptive and productive language in retarded children. *Journal of Applied Behavior Analysis*, 1973, *6*, 311–329.

Gustav, A. "Success is —"; Locating composite sanity. *Rational Living*, 1968, *3*, 1–6.

Guthrie, E. R. *The psychology of learning*. New York: Harper, 1935.

Guyton, A. C. *Textbook of medical physiology*. Philadelphia: W. B. Saunders, 1971.

Haggerty, M. E. Imitation in monkeys. *Journal of Comparative Neurology*, 1909, *19*, 337–455.

Hall, J. F. *Verbal learning and attention*. Philadelphia: J. B. Lippincott, 1971.

Hall, K. R. L. Observational learning in monkeys and apes. *British Journal of Psychology*, 1963, *54*, 201–226.

Hallam, R. S. Extinction of ruminations: A case study. *Behavior Therapy*, in press.

Hamerlynck, L. A., Handy, L. C., & Mash, E. J. (Eds.), *Behavior change: Methodology, concepts, and practice*. Champaign, Ill.: Research Press, 1973.

Hark, R. D. An examination of the effectiveness of coverant conditioning in the reduction of cigarette smoking. Unpublished doctoral dissertation, Michigan State University, 1970.

Harsch, O. H., & Zimmer, H. An experimental approximation of thought reform. *Journal of Consulting Psychology*, 1965, *29*, 475–479.

Hart, J. T. Memory and the feeling-of-knowing experience. *Journal of Educational Psychology*, 1965, *56*, 208–216.

Hartig, M., & Kanfer, F. H. The role of verbal self-instructions in children's resistance to temptation. *Journal of Personality and Social Psychology*, 1973, *25*, 259–267.

Hartman, B. J. 60 revealing questions for 20 minutes. *Rational Living*, 1968, *3*, 7–8.

Hartmann, E. L. *The functions of sleep*. New Haven: Yale University Press, 1973.

Haslan, M. The treatment of an obsessional patient by reciprocal inhibition. *Behaviour Research and Therapy*, 1965, *2*, 213–216.

Hawkins, D., & Pauling, L. (Eds.), *Orthomolecular psychiatry*. San Francisco: W. H. Freeman, 1973.

Hayes, K. J., & Hayes, C. Imitation in a home-raised chimpanzee. *Journal of Comparative and Physiological Psychology*, 1952, *45*, 450–459.

Haynes, S. N., & Geddy, P. Suppression of psychotic hallucinations through time-out. *Behavior Therapy*, 1973, *4*, 123–127.

Hefferline, R. F., Bruno, L. J. J., & Camp, J. A. Hallucinations: An experimental approach. In F. J. McGuigan & R. A. Schoonover (Eds.), *The psychophysiology of thinking*. New York: Academic Press, 1973. Pp. 299-342.

Heider, F. *The psychology of interpersonal relations*. New York: Wiley, 1958.

Hekmat, H., & Vanian, D. Behavior modification through covert semantic desensitization. *Journal of Consulting and Clinical Psychology*, 1971, *36*, 248–251.

Herbert, J. J., & Harsh, C. M. Observational learning by cats. *Journal of Comparative Psychology*, 1944, *37*, 81–95.

Hilgard, E. R., & Bower, G. H. *Theories of learning*. (3rd ed.) New York: Appleton-Century-Crofts, 1966.

Hodgson, R., & Rachman, S. The effects of contamination and washing in obsessional patients. *Behaviour Research and Therapy*, 1972, *10*, 111–117.

Hodgson, R., Rachman, S., & Marks, I. The treatment of chronic obsessive compulsive neurosis: Follow-up and further findings. *Behaviour Research and Therapy*, 1972, *10*, 181–189.

Hoffer, E. *The true believer*. New York: Harper, 1951.

Hogan, R. A. Implosive therapy in the short-term treatment of psychotics. *Psychotherapy: Theory, Research and Practice*, 1966, *3*, 25–32.

Holmes, D. S., & Schallow, J. R. Reduced recall after ego threat: Repression or response competition? *Journal of Personality and Social Psychology*, 1969, *13*, 145–152.

Homme, L. E. Perspectives in psychology: XXIV. Control of coverants, the operants of the mind. *Psychological Record*, 1965, *15*, 501–511.

Hook, S. (Ed.), *Determinism and freedom in the age of modern science*. New York: Collier, 1958.

Horan, J. J. "In vivo" emotive imagery: A technique for reducing childbirth anxiety and discomfort. *Psychological Reports*, 1973, *32*, 1328.

Horan, J. J., Baker, S. B., Hoffman, A. M., & Shute, R. E. Weight loss through variations in the coverant control paradigm. Paper presented to the American Educational Research Association, Chicago, April, 1974.

Horan, J. J., & Dellinger, J. K. "In vivo" emotive imagery: An experimental test. *Psychological Reports*, in press.

Horan, J. J., & Johnson, R. G. Coverant conditioning through a self-management application of the Premack principle: Its effect on weight reduction. *Journal of Behavior Therapy and Experimental Psychiatry*, 1971, *2*, 243–249.

Horowitz, M. J., & Becker, S. S. Cognitive response to stress and experimental demand. *Journal of Abnormal Psychology*, 1971, *78*, 86–92. (a)

———., & ———. Cognitive response to stressful stimuli. *Archives of General Psychiatry*, 1971, *25*, 419–428. (b)

———., & ———. The compulsion to repeat trauma: Experimental study of intrusive thinking after stress. *Journal of Nervous and Mental Disease*, 1971, *153*, 32–40. (c)

Horowitz, M. J., Becker, S. S., & Moskowitz, M. L. Intrusive and repetitive thought after stress: A replication study. *Psychological Reports*, 1971, *29*, 763–767.

Hudgins, C. V. Conditioning and voluntary control of the pupillary light reflex. *Journal of General Psychology*, 1933, *8*, 3–51.

Hull, C. L. *Principles of behavior*. New York: Appleton-Century-Crofts, 1943.

Huxley, F. *The invisibles*. New York: McGraw-Hill, 1969.

Ince, L. P. The self-concept variable in behavior therapy. *Psychotherapy: Theory, Research and Practice*, 1972, *9*, 223–225.

Jackson, B. Treatment of depression by self-reinforcement. *Behavior Therapy*, 1972, *3*, 298–307.

Jacobs, A., & Sachs, L. B. (Eds.), *The psychology of private events: Perspectives on covert response systems*. New York: Academic Press, 1971.

Jacobs, A., & Wolpin, M. A second look at systematic desensitization. In A. Jacobs & L. B. Sachs (Eds.), *The psychology of private events: Perspectives on covert response systems*. New York: Academic Press, 1971. Pp. 77–108.

Jacobs, E. A., Winter, P. M., Alvis, H. J., & Small, S. M. Hyperoxygenation effects on cognitive functioning in the aged. *New England Journal of Medicine*, 1969, *281*, 753–757.

Jacobson, E. The electrophysiology of mental activities. *American Journal of Psychology*, 1932, *44*, 677–694.

———. *Progressive relaxation*. Chicago: University of Chicago Press, 1938.

———. Electrophysiology of mental activities and introduction to the psychological process of thinking. In F. J. McGuigan & R. A. Schoonover (Eds.), *The psychophysiology of thinking*. New York: Academic Press, 1973. Pp. 3–31.

Jacobson, M. F. *Eater's digest*. Garden City, New York: Anchor, 1972.

Jacobson, M. *Nutrition scoreboard*. Washington, D.C.: Center for Science in the Public Interest, 1973.

Jahoda, G. *The psychology of superstition*. Baltimore: Penguin, 1969.

James, W. *The principles of psychology*. New York: Holt, 1890.

———. *The will to believe*. (original 1896) New York: Longmans, Green, 1912.

Janda, L. H., & Rimm, D. C. Covert sensitization in the treatment of obesity. *Journal of Abnormal Psychology*, 1972, *80*, 37–42.

Janis, I. *Psychological stress*. New York: Wiley, 1958.

Jaynes, J. *The origin of consciousness in the breakdown of the bicameral mind*. Unpublished manuscript, Princeton University, 1974.

Jeffrey, D. B., Hartmann, D. P., & Gelfand, D. M. A comparison of the effects of contingent reinforcement, nurturance and non-reinforcement on imitative-identificatory learning. *Child Development*, in press.

Johnson, D., & Gath, D. Arousal levels and attribution effects in diazepam-assisted flooding. *British Journal of Psychiatry*, 1973, *123*, 463–466.

Johnson, S. S. The effects of self control techniques upon differing types of smoking behavior. Unpublished doctoral dissertation, University of Colorado, 1968.

Johnson, W. G. Some applications of Homme's coverant control therapy: Two case reports. *Behavior Therapy*, 1971, *2*, 240–248.

Jones, E. E., Kanouse, D. E., Kelley, H. H., Nisbett, R. E., Valins, S., & Weiner, B. (Eds.), *Attribution: Perceiving the causes of behavior*. Morristown, N. J.: General Learning Press, 1971.

Jones, E. E., & Nisbett, R. E. *The actor and the observer: Divergent perceptions of the causes of behavior*. Morristown, N. J.: General Learning Press, 1971.

Jones, R. G. A factored measure of Ellis's irrational belief system, with personality and maladjustment correlates Unpublished doctoral dissertation, Texas Technological College, 1969.

Kanfer, F. H. The maintenance of behavior by self-generated stimuli and reinforcement. In A. Jacobs & L. B. Sachs (Eds.), *The psychology of private events: Perspectives on covert response systems*. New York: Academic Press, 1971, Pp. 39-59.

Kanfer, F. H., Cox, L. E., Greiner, J. M., & Karoly, P. Contracts, demand characteristics and self-control. *Journal of Personality and Social Psychology*, in press.

Kanfer, F. H., & Goldfoot, D. A. Self-control and tolerance of noxious stimulation. *Psychological Reports*, 1966, *18*, 79–85.

Kanfer, F. H., & Karoly, P. Self-control: A behavioristic excursion into the lion's den. *Behavior Therapy*, 1972, *3*, 398–416.

Kanfer, F. H., & Phillips, J. S. *Learning foundations of behavior therapy*. New York: Wiley, 1970.

Kanfer, F. H., & Seidner, M. L. Self-control: Factors enhancing tolerance of noxious stimulation. *Journal of Personality and Social Psychology*, 1973, *25*, 381–389.

Kaplan, A. *The conduct of inquiry*. Scranton: Chandler, 1964.

Kaplan, B. J. Malnutrition and mental deficiency. *Psychological Bulletin*, 1972, *78*, 321–334.

Kaufman, A., Baron, A., & Kopp, R. E. Some effects of instructions on human operant behavior. *Psychological Monograph Supplements*, 1966, *1*, 243–250.

Karst, T. O., & Trexler, L. D. Initial study using fixed-role and rational-emotive therapy in treating public-speaking anxiety. *Journal of Consulting and Clinical Psychology*, 1970, *34*, 360–366.

Kazdin, A. E. Methodological and assessment considerations in evaluating reinforcement programs in applied settings. *Journal of Applied Behavior Analysis*, 1973, *6*, 517–531. (a)

———. Covert modeling and the reduction of avoidance behavior. *Journal of Abnormal Psychology*, 1973, *81*, 87–95. (b)

———. The effect of suggestion and pretesting on avoidance reduction in fearful subjects. *Journal of Behavior Therapy and Experimental Psychiatry*, 1973, *4*, 213–221. (c)

———. Effects of covert modeling and reinforcement on assertive behavior. *Proceedings of the 81st Annual Convention of the American Psychological Association*, 1973, *8*, 537–538. (d)

———. Self-monitoring and behavior change. In M. J. Mahoney & C. E. Thoresen (Eds.), *Self-control: Power to the person*. Monterey: Brooks/Cole, 1974. Pp. 218–246.

———. Covert modeling, model similarity, and reduction of avoidance behavior. *Behavior Therapy*, in press. (a)

———. The effect of model identity and fear-relevant similarity on covert modeling. *Behavior Therapy*, in press. (b)

Keat, R. A critical examination of B. F. Skinner's objections to mentalism. *Behaviorism*, 1972, *1*, 53–70.

Keller, F. S., & Schoenfeld, W. N. *Principles of psychology*. New York: Appleton-Century-Crofts, 1950.

Kelley, H. H. Attribution theory in social psychology. In D. Levine (Ed.), *Nebraska symposium on motivation*. Vol. 15. Lincoln: University of Nebraska Press, 1967. Pp. 192–238.

———. The processes of causal attribution. *American Psychologist*, 1973, *28*, 107–128.

Kelly, G. A. *The psychology of personal constructs*. New York: Norton, 1955.

Kendler, H. H., & Kendler, T. S. Vertical and horizontal processes in problem solving. *Psychological Review*, 1962, *61*, 442–448.

Kendrick, S. R., & McCullough, J. P. Sequential phases of covert reinforcement and covert sensitization in the treatment of homosexuality. *Journal of Behavior Therapy and Experimental Psychiatry*, 1972, *3*, 229–231.

Kenny, F. T., Solyom, L., & Solyom, C. Faradic disruption of obsessive ideation in the treatment of obsessive neurosis. *Behavior Therapy*, 1973, *4*, 448–457.

Kent, R. N., Wilson, G. T., & Nelson, R. Effects of false heart-rate feedback on avoidance behavior: An investigation of "cognitive desensitization." *Behavior Therapy*, 1972, *3*, 1–6.

Keutzer, C. S. Behavior modification of smoking: The experimental investigation of diverse techniques. *Behaviour Research and Therapy*, 1968, *6*, 137–157.

Kingsley, R. G. An evaluation of contingency content in covert conditioning. Unpublished master's thesis, Rutgers University, 1973.

Kintsch, W. *Learning, memory, and conceptual processes*. New York: Wiley, 1970.

Kirkham, J. F., Levy, S., & Crotty, W. J. *Assassination and political violence*. Washington, D.C.: United States Government Printing Office, 1969.

Kleinmuntz. B. (Ed.), *Problem solving: Research, method, and theory*. New York: Wiley, 1966.

Klinger, E. *Structure and functions of fantasy*. New York: Wiley, 1971.

Koch, S. Psychology and emerging conceptions of knowledge as unitary. In T. W. Wann (Ed.), *Behaviorism and phenomenology*. Chicago: University of Chicago Press, 1964. Pp. 1–41.

Köhler, W. *The mentality of apes*. New York: Harcourt, Brace, 1925.

Kolvin, L. Aversive imagery treatment in adolescents. *Behaviour Research and Therapy*, 1967, *5*, 245–249.

Kopel, S. A., & Arkowitz, H. The role of attribution and self-perception in behavior change: Implications for behavior therapy. Unpublished manuscript, University of Oregon, 1974.

Krantz, D. L. The separate worlds of operant and non-operant psychology. *Journal of Applied Behavior Analysis*, 1971 *4*, 61–70.

Krop, H., Calhoon, B., & Verrier, R. Modification of the "self-concept" of emotionally disturbed children by covert self-reinforcement. *Behavior Therapy*, 1971, *2*, 201–204.

Krop, H., Perez, F., & Beaudoin, C. Modification of "self-concept" of psychiatric patients by covert reinforcement. In R. D. Rubin, J. P. Brady, & J. D. Henderson (Eds.), *Advances in behavior therapy*. Vol. 4. New York: Academic Press, 1973. Pp. 139–144.

Kuhn, T. S. *The structure of scientific revolutions*. Chicago: University of Chicago Press, 1962.

———. Logic of discovery or psychology of research? In I. Lakatos & A. Musgrave (Eds.), *Criticism and the growth of knowledge*. Cambridge: Cambridge University Press, 1970. Pp. 1–23. (a)

———. Reflections on my critics. In I. Lakatos & A. Musgrave (Eds.), *Criticism and the growth of knowledge*. Cambridge: Cambridge University Press, 1970. Pp. 231–278. (b)

Kumar, K., & Wilkinson, J. C. M. Thought stopping: A useful treatment for phobias of "internal stimuli." *British Journal of Psychiatry*, 1971, *119*, 305–307.

Kushner, A. W. Two cases of auto-castration due to religious delusions. *British Journal of Medical Psychology*, 1967, *40*, 293–298.

Lakatos, I. Falsification and the methodology of scientific research programmes. In I. Lakatos & A. Musgrave (Eds.), *Criticism and the growth of knowledge*. Cambridge: Cambridge University Press, 1970. Pp. 91–196.

Lakatos, I., & Musgrave, A. (Eds.), *Criticism and the growth of knowledge*. Cambridge: Cambridge University Press, 1970.

Langfeld, H. S. (Ed.), Symposium on operationism. *Psychological Review*, 1945, *52*, 241–294.

Lappé, F. M. *Diet for a small planet*. New York: Ballantine, 1971.

Lawson, D. M., & May, R. B. Three procedures for the extinction of smoking behavior. *Psychological Record*, 1970, *20*, 151–157.

Lazarus, A. A. New methods in psychotherapy: A case study. *South African Medical Journal*, 1958, *32*, 660–663.

———. *Behavior therapy and beyond.* New York: McGraw-Hill, 1971.

Lazarus, A. A., & Abramovitz, A. The use of "emotive imagery" in the treatment of children's phobias. *Journal of Mental Science,* 1962, *108,* 191–195.

Lazarus, A. A., Davison, G. C., & Polefka, D. A. Classical and operant factors in the treatment of a school phobia. *Journal of Abnormal Psychology,* 1965, *70,* 225–229.

Leacock, S., & Leacock, R. *Spirits of the deep: A study of an Afro-Brazilian cult.* New York: Doubleday, 1972.

Lefcourt, H. M. Internal versus external control of reinforcement: A review. *Psychological Bulletin,* 1966, *65,* 206–220.

———. The function of the illusions of control and freedom. *American Psychologist,* 1973, *28,* 417–425.

Legrenzi, P. Discovery as a means to understanding. *Quarterly Journal of Experimental Psychology,* 1971, *23,* 417–422.

Lehman, A. *Superstition and magic.* Stuttgart: Enke, 1898.

Leont'yev, A. A. Inner speech and the processes of grammatical generation of utterances. *Soviet Psychology,* 1969, *7,* 11–16.

Lepper, M. R., Greene, D., & Nisbett, R. E. Undermining children's intrinsic interest with extrinsic reward: A test of the "overjustification" hypothesis. *Journal of Personality and Social Psychology,* 1973, *28,* 129–137.

Levinson, M., & Neuringer, C. Problem-solving behavior in suicidal adolescents. *Journal of Consulting and Clinical Psychology,* 1971, *37,* 433–436.

Lick, J., & Bootzin, R. Covert sensitization for the treatment of obesity. Paper presented to the Midwestern Psychological Association, Detroit, 1971.

Lindsley, O. R. Should we decelerate urges or actions? Thou shalt not covet. Paper presented to the American Psychological Association, Washington, D.C., 1969.

Litvak, S. B. A comparison of two brief group behavior therapy techniques on the reduction of avoidance behavior. *Psychological Record,* 1969, *19,* 329–334.

Lobitz, W. C., & LoPiccolo, J. New methods in the behavioral treatment of sexual dysfunction. *Journal of Behavior Therapy and Experimental Psychiatry,* 1972, *3,* 265–271.

Locke, E. A., Cartledge, N., & Koeppel, J. Motivational effects of knowledge of results: A goal-setting phenomenon? *Psychological Bulletin,* 1968, *70,* 474–485.

Loeb, A., Beck, A. T., Diggory, J. C., & Tuthill, R. Expectancy, level of aspiration, performance, and self-evaluation in depression. *Proceedings of the 75th Annual Convention of the American Psychological Association,* 1967, *2,* 193–194.

Lomont, J. F., & Edwards, J. E. The role of relaxation in systematic desensitization. *Behaviour Research and Therapy,* 1967, *5,* 11–25.

London, P. The end of ideology in behavior modification. *American Psychologist.* 1972, *27,* 913–920.

Lovitt, T. C., & Curtiss, K. Academic response rate as a function of teacher- and self-imposed contingencies. *Journal of Applied Behavior Analysis,* 1969, *2,* 49–53.

Lowe, G. R. The phenomenology of hallucinations as an aid to differential diagnosis. *British Journal of Psychiatry,* 1973, *123,* 621–633.

Luria, A. *The role of speech in the regulation of normal and abnormal behavior.* New York: Liveright, 1961.

———. Psychological studies of mental deficiency in the Soviet Union. In N. R. Ellis (Ed.), *Handbook of mental deficiency.* New York: McGraw-Hill, 1963, Pp. 353–387.

MacCorquodale, K., & Meehl, P. E. On a distinction between hypothetical constructs and intervening variables. *Psychological Review,* 1948, *55,* 95–107.

MacDonald, A. P., & Games, R. G. Ellis' irrational values: A validation study. *Rational Living,* 1972, *7,* 25–28.

MacDonough, T. S., Adams, H. E., & Tesser, A. The effects of choice in systematic desensitization. *Psychological Record,* 1973, *23,* 397–404.

Maes, W. R., & Heimann, R. A. The comparison of three approaches to the reduction of test anxiety in high school students. Unpublished manuscript, Arizona State University, 1970.

Mahoney, K., & Mahoney, M. J. Children's preferences for choice: An experimental analysis. Unpublished manuscript, Pennsylvania State University, 1974.

Mahoney, M. J. Toward an experimental analysis of coverant control. *Behavior Therapy,* 1970, *1,* 510–521.

———. The self-management of covert behavior: A case study. *Behavior Therapy,* 1971, *2,* 575–578.

———. Research issues in self-management. *Behavior Therapy,* 1972, *3,* 45–63.

———. Clinical issues in self-control training. Paper presented to the American Psychological Association, Montreal, 1973.

———. Behavior therapy: Some critical comments. Paper presented to the American Psychopathological Association, Boston, 1974. (a)

———. The sensitive scientist in empirical humanism. Paper presented to the American Educational Research Association, Chicago, April, 1974. (b)

Mahoney, M. J., Kazdin, A. E., & Lesswing, N. J. Behavior modification: Delusion or deliverance? In C. M. Franks & G. T. Wilson (Eds.), *Annual review of behavior therapy theory and practice.* Vol. 2. New York: Brunner/Mazel, 1974.

Mahoney, M. J., & Mahoney, F. E. A residential program in behavior modification. In R. D. Rubin, J. P. Brady, & J. D. Henderson (Eds.), *Advances in behavior therapy.* Vol. 4. New York: Academic Press, 1973. Pp. 93–102.

Mahoney, M. J., Moore B. S., Wade, T. C., & Moura, N. G. M. The effects of continuous and intermittent self-monitoring on academic behavior. *Journal of Consulting and Clinical Psychology*, 1973, *41*, 65–69.

Mahoney, M. J., Moura, N. G. M., & Wade, T. C. The relative efficacy of self-reward, self-punishment, and self-monitoring techniques for weight loss. *Journal of Consulting and Clinical Psychology*, 1973, *40*, 404–407.

Mahoney, M. J., Thoresen, C. E., & Danaher, B. G. Covert behavior modification: An experimental analogue. *Journal of Behavior Therapy and Experimental Psychiatry*, 1972, *3*, 7–14.

Maletzky, B. M. "Assisted" covert sensitization: A preliminary report. *Behavior Therapy*, 1973, *4*, 117–119.

———. "Assisted" covert sensitization in the treatment of exhibitionism. *Journal of Consulting and Clinical Psychology*, 1974, *42*, 34–40.

———. Assisted covert sensitization for drug and alcohol abuse. *International Journal of the Addictions*, in press.

Maletzky, B. M. & George, F. S. The treatment of homosexuality by "assisted" covert sensitization. *Behaviour Research and Therapy*, 1973, *11*, 655–657.

Maltz, M. *Psycho-cybernetics*. Englewood Cliffs: Prentice-Hall, 1960.

Maltzman, I. Theoretical conceptions of semantic conditioning and generalization. In T. R. Dixon & D. L. Horton (Eds.), *Verbal behavior and general behavior theory*. Englewood Cliffs: Prentice-Hall, 1968. Pp. 291–339.

Mandel, I. J., & Bridger, W. H. Interaction between instructions and ISI in conditioning and extinction of the GSR. *Journal of Experimental Psychology*, 1967, *74*, 36–43.

Manno, B., & Marston, A. R. Weight reduction as a function of negative covert reinforcement (sensitization) versus positive covert reinforcement. *Behaviour Research and Therapy*, 1972, *10*, 201–207.

Marks, I. M. New approaches to the treatment of obsessive-compulsive disorders. *Journal of Nervous and Mental Disease*, 1973, *156*, 420–426.

Marks, I. M., Crowe, M., Drewe, E., Young, J., & Dewhurst, W. Obsessive-compulsive neurosis in identical twins. *British Journal of Psychiatry*, 1969, *115*, 991–998.

Marks, I. M., & Gelder, M. G. Transvestism and fetishism: Clinical and psychological changes during faradic aversion. *British Journal of Psychiatry*, 1967, *113*, 711–729.

Marks, I. M., Rachman, S., & Gelder, M. G. Methods for assessment of aversion treatment in fetishism with masochism. *Behaviour Research and Therapy*, 1965, *3*, 253–258.

Marmor, J. The psychodynamics of realistic worry. *Psychoanalysis and Social Science*, 1958, *5*, 155–163.

Marquis, J. N. Orgasmic reconditioning: Changing sexual object choice through controlling masturbation fantasies. *Journal of Behavior Therapy and Experimental Psychiatry*, 1970, *1*, 263–271.

Marshall, W. L. Cognitive functioning in schizophrenia. *British Journal of Psychiatry*, 1973, *123*, 413–433.

———. The modification of masturbation. Unpublished manuscript, Kingston Psychiatric Hospital, 1974.

———. A combined treatment approach to the reduction of multiple fetish-related behaviors. *Journal of Consulting and Clinical Psychology,* in press. (a)

———. The modification of phobic behavior by covert reinforcement. *Behavior Therapy,* in press. (b)

Marshall, W. L., Polgrin, D., & Boutilier, J. Reinforcement contingencies in covert reinforcement. Unpublished manuscript, Kingston Psychiatric Hospital, 1974.

Marshall, W. L., Strawbridge, H., & Keltner, A. The role of mental relaxation in experimental desensitization. *Behaviour Research and Therapy,* 1972, *10,* 355–366.

Marx, H., & Hillix, W. A. *Systems and theories in psychology.* New York: McGraw-Hill, 1963.

Masters, W. H., & Johnson, V. E. *Human sexual response.* Boston: Little, Brown, 1966.

———., &———. *Human sexual inadequacy.* Boston: Little, Brown, 1970.

Mather, M. The treatment of an obsessive-compulsive patient by discrimination learning and reinforcement of decision making. *Behaviour Research and Therapy,* 1970, *8,* 315–318. (a)

———. Obsessions and compulsions. In C. Costello (Ed.), *Symptoms of psychopathology.* New York: Wiley, 1970. Pp. 302–319. (b)

Matson, F. W. Matson replies to Skinner. *Humanist,* 1971, *31,* 2.

Matson, W. I. *The existence of god.* Ithaca: Cornell University Press, 1965.

Maultsby, M. Rational emotive imagery. *Rational Living,* 1971, *6,* 24–26. (a)

———. Systematic written homework in psychotherapy. *Rational Living,* 1971, *6,* 17–23. (b)

Max, L. W. An experimental study of the motor theory of consciousness: II. Action-current responses in deaf mutes during sleep, sensory stimulation and dreams. *Journal of Comparative Psychology,* 1935, *19,* 469–486.

———. Experimental study of the motor theory of consciousness: IV. Action-current responses in the deaf during awakening, kinaesthetic imagery, and abstract thinking. *Journal of Comparative Psychology,* 1937, *24,* 301–344.

May, J. R., & Johnson, H. J. Physiological activity to internally elicited arousal and inhibitory thoughts. *Journal of Abnormal Psychology,* 1973, *82,* 239–245.

McClellan, T. A., & Stieper, D. R. A structured approach to group marriage counseling. *Rational Living,* 1973, *8,* 12–18.

McCullough, J. P. An investigation of the effects of model group size upon response facilitation in the high school classroom. *Journal of Behavior Therapy and Experimental Psychiatry,* 1972, *3,* 561–566.

McCullough, J. P., & Powell, P. O. A technique for measuring clarity of imagery in therapy clients. *Behavior Therapy,* 1972, *3,* 447–448.

McGuigan, F. J. Covert oral behavior during the silent performance of language tasks. *Psychological Bulletin,* 1970, *74,* 309–326.

———. Electrical measurement of covert processes as an explication of "higher mental events." In F. J. McGuigan & R. A. Schoonover (Eds.), *The psychophysiology of thinking.* New York: Academic Press, 1973. Pp. 343–385.

McGuigan, F. J., & Schoonover, R. A. (Eds.), *The psychophysiology of thinking.* New York: Academic Press, 1973.

McGuire, M. T., & Sifneos, P. E. Problem solving in psychotherapy. *Psychiatric Quarterly,* 1970, *44,* 667–673.

McGuire, R., & Vallance, M. Aversion therapy by electric shock: A simple technique. *British Medical Journal,* 1964, *1,* 151–153.

McGuire, R. J., Carlisle, J. M., & Young, B. G. Sexual deviation as conditioned behaviour: A hypothesis. *Behaviour Research and Therapy,* 1965, *2,* 185–190.

McGuire, W. J. A syllogistic analysis of cognitive relationships. In C. I. Hovland & M. J. Rosenberg (Eds.), *Attitude organization and change.* New Haven: Yale University Press, 1960. Pp. 65–111.

———. Theory of the structure of human thought. In R. P. Abelson, E. Aronson, W. J. McGuire, T. M. Newcomb, M. J. Rosenberg, & P. H. Tannenbaum (Eds.), *Theories of cognitive consistency: A sourcebook.* Chicago: Rand McNally, 1968. Pp. 140–162.

McGeogh, J. A. The formal criteria of a systematic psychology. *Psychological Review,* 1933, *40,* 1–12.

McKeachie, W. J. The decline and fall of the laws of learning. *Educational Researcher,* 1974, *3,* 7–11.

McLemore, C. W. Imagery in desensitization. *Behaviour Research and Therapy,* 1972, *10,* 51–57.

Meehl, P. E. Theory-testing in psychology and physics: A methodological paradox. *Philosophy of Science,* 1967, June, 103–115.

Mees, H. L. Sadistic fantasies modified by aversive conditioning and substitution. *Behaviour Research and Therapy,* 1966, *4,* 317–320.

Meichenbaum, D. The effects of instructions and reinforcement on thinking and language behaviors of schizophrenics. *Behaviour Research and Therapy,* 1969, *7,* 101–114.

———. Examination of model characteristics in reducing avoidance behavior. *Journal of Personality and Social Psychology,* 1971, *17,* 298–307. (a)

———. The nature and modification of impulsive children. Paper presented to the Society for Research in Child Development, Minneapolis, 1971. (b)

———. Ways of modifying what clients say to themselves: A marriage of behavior therapies and rational-emotive therapy. *Rational Living,* 1972, *7,* 23–27. (a)

———. Cognitive modification of test anxious college students. *Journal of Consulting and Clinical Psychology,* 1972, *39,* 370–380. (b)

———. Cognitive factors in behavior modification: Modifying what clients say to themselves. In C. M. Franks & G. T. Wilson (Eds.), *Annual review of behavior therapy theory and practice.* Vol. 1. New York: Brunner/Mazel, 1973. Pp. 416–431. (a)

———. Enhancing creativity by modifying what *S*'s say to themselves. Unpublished manuscript, University of Waterloo, 1973. (b)

———. *Cognitive behavior modification.* Morristown, N.J.: General Learning Press, 1974. (a)

———. Self-instructional methods. In F. H. Kanfer & A. P. Goldstein (Eds.), *Helping people change.* New York: Pergamon, 1974. (b)

———. Therapist manual for cognitive behavior modification. Unpublished manuscript, University of Waterloo, 1974. (c)

———. Self-instructional training: A cognitive prosthesis for the aged. *Human Development,* in press.

Meichenbaum, D., Bowers, K., & Ross, R. R. Modification of classroom behavior of institutionalized female adolescent offenders. *Behaviour Research and Therapy,* 1968, *6,* 343–353.

Meichenbaum, D., & Cameron, R. Training schizophrenics to talk to themselves: A means of developing attentional controls. *Behavior Therapy,* 1973, *4,* 515–534. (a)

———., & ———. An examination of cognitive and contingency variables in anxiety relief procedures. Unpublished manuscript, University of Waterloo, 1973. (b)

———., & ———. Stress inoculation: A skills training approach to anxiety management. Unpublished manuscript, University of Waterloo, 1973. (c)

———., & ———. The clinical potential of modifying what clients say to themselves. In M. J. Mahoney & C. E. Thoresen (Eds.), *Self-control: Power to the person.* Monterey: Brooks/Cole, 1974. Pp. 263–290.

Meichenbaum, D., Gilmore, J., & Fedoravicius, A. Group insight vs. group desensitization in treating speech anxiety. *Journal of Consulting and Clinical Psychology,* 1971, *36,* 410–421.

Meichenbaum, D., & Goodman, J. The developmental control of operant motor responding by verbal operants. *Journal of Experimental Child Psychology,* 1969, *7,* 553–565. (a)

———., & ———. Reflection-impulsivity and verbal control of motor behavior. *Child Development,* 1969, *40,* 785–797. (b)

———., & ———. Training impulsive children to talk to themselves: A means of developing self-control. *Journal of Abnormal Psychology,* 1971, *77,* 115–126.

Meichenbaum, D., & Turk, L. The implications of research on disadvantaged children and cognitive training for educational television: Ways of improving Sesame Street. *Journal of Special Education,* 1972, *6,* 27–42.

Melton, A. W. Implications of short-term memory for a general theory of memory. *Journal of Verbal Learning and Verbal Behavior,* 1963, *2,* 1–21.

Melton, A. W., & Martin, E. (Eds.), *Coding processes in human memory.* New York: Wiley, 1972.

Menzies, R. Conditioned vasomotor responses in human subjects. *Journal of Psychology,* 1937, *4,* 75–120.

Metraux, A. *Voodoo in Haiti.* (H. Charteris, translator) New York: Schocken, 1972.

Meynen, G. E. A comparative study of three treatment approaches with the obese: Relaxation, covert sensitization, and modified systematic desensitization. Unpublished doctoral dissertation, Illinois Institute of Technology, 1970.

Miller, G. A. The magical number seven, plus or minus two: Some limits on our capacity for processing information. *Psychological Review,* 1956, *63,* 81–97.

Miller, G. A., Galanter, E., & Pribram, K. *Plans and the structure of behavior.* New York: Holt, Rinehart & Winston, 1960.

Miller, M. M. Treatment of chronic alcoholism by hypnotic aversion. *Journal of the American Medical Association,* 1959, *171,* 1492–1495.

———. Hypnotic-aversion treatment of homosexuality. *Journal of the National Medical Association,* 1963, *55,* 411–415.

Miller, N. E. The influence of past experience upon the transfer of subsequent training. Unpublished doctoral dissertation, Yale University, 1935.

———. Learning of visceral and glandular responses. *Science,* 1969, *163,* 434–445.

Miller, N. E., & Dollard, J. *Social learning and imitation.* New Haven: Yale University Press, 1941.

Milner, G. Ascorbic acid in chronic psychiatric patients—A controlled trial. *British Journal of Psychiatry,* 1963, *109,* 294–299.

Mischel, W. *Personality and assessment.* New York: Wiley, 1968.

———. *An introduction to personality.* New York: Holt, Rinehart & Winston, 1971.

———. Toward a cognitive social learning reconceptualization of personality. *Psychological Review,* 1973, *80,* 252–283.

———. Processes in delay of gratification. In L. Berkowitz (Ed.), *Advances in experimental social psychology.* Vol. 7. New York: Academic Press, in press.

Mischel, W., & Ebbesen, E. B. Attention in delay of gratification. *Journal of Personality and Social Psychology,* 1970, *16,* 329–337.

Mischel, W., Ebbesen, E. B., & Zeiss, A. R. Cognitive and attentional mechanisms in delay of gratification. *Journal of Personality and Social Psychology,* 1972, *21,* 204–218.

Mischel, W., & Masters, J. C. Effects of probability of reward attainment on responses to frustration. *Journal of Personality and Social Psychology,* 1966, *3,* 390–396.

Monahan, J., & O'Leary, K. D. Effects of self-instruction on rule-breaking behavior. *Psychological Reports,* 1971, *29,* 1059–1066.

Montgomery, A. G. Comparison of the effectiveness of systematic desensitization, rational-emotive therapy, implosive therapy, and no therapy, in reducing test anxiety in college students. Unpublished doctoral dissertation, Washington University, 1971.

Monty, R. A., & Perlmuter, L. C. The role of choice in learning as a function of meaning and between- and within-subjects designs. *Journal of Experimental Psychology,* 1972, *94,* 235–238.

Monty, R. A., Rosenberger, M. A., & Perlmuter, L. C. Amount and locus of choice as sources of motivation in paired-associate learning. *Journal of Experimental Psychology,* 1973, *97,* 16–21.

Morgan, C. L. *Habit and instinct.* London: Edward Arnold, 1896.

———. *Introduction to comparative psychology.* 2nd ed. London, W. Scott, 1899.

Morganstern, K. P. Implosive therapy and flooding procedures: A critical review. *Psychological Bulletin,* 1973, *79,* 318–334.

Morse, W. H., & Skinner, B. F. A second type of superstition in the pigeon. *American Journal of Psychology,* 1957, *70,* 308–311.

Mowrer, O. H. *Learning theory and the symbolic processes.* New York: Wiley, 1960.

Mullen, F. G. The effect of covert sensitization on smoking behavior. Unpublished manuscript, Queens College, 1968.

Nagel, E. *The structure of science.* New York: Harcourt, 1961.

Nawas, M. M. Wherefore cognitive therapy? A critical scrutiny of three papers by Beck, Bergin, and Ullmann. *Behavior Therapy,* 1970, *1,* 359–370.

Nawas, M. M., Welsch, W., & Fishman, S. The comparative effectiveness of pairing aversive imagery with relaxation, neutral tasks and muscular tension in reducing snake phobia. *Behaviour Research and Therapy,* 1970, *8,* 63–68.

Nebes, R. D. Hemispheric specialization in commissurotomized man. *Psychological Bulletin,* 1974, *81,* 1–14.

Neisser, U. *Cognitive psychology.* New York: Appleton-Century-Crofts, 1967.

Neuringer, A. J. Animals respond for food in the presence of free food. *Science,* 1969, *166,* 399–401.

———. Many responses per food reward with free food present. *Science,* 1970, *169,* 503–504. (a)

———. Superstitious key pecking after three peck-produced reinforcements. *Journal of the Experimental Analysis of Behavior,* 1970, *13,* 127–134. (b)

Neuringer, C. Self- and other-appraisals by suicidal, psychosomatic, and normal hospitalized patients. *Journal of Consulting and Clinical Psychology,* 1974, *42,* 306.

Newbury, E. Current interpretation and significance of Lloyd Morgan's canon. *Psychological Bulletin,* 1954, *51,* 70–74.

Newell, A., & Simon, H. A. *Human problem solving.* Englewood Cliffs: Prentice-Hall, 1972.

Nordquist, V. M. The modification of a child's enuresis: Some response-response relationships. *Journal of Applied Behavior Analysis,* 1971, *4,* 241–247.

Norman, D. A. *Memory and attention.* New York: Wiley, 1969.

Norman, W. The efficacy of cognitive restructuring versus skills training in generating behavior change. Unpublished doctoral dissertation, Pennsylvania State University, 1974.

Notterman, J. M., Schoenfeld, W. N., & Bersh, P. J. A comparison of three extinction procedures following heart rate conditioning. *Journal of Abnormal and Social Psychology,* 1952, *47,* 674–677.

Nydegger, R. V. The elimination of hallucinatory and delusional behavior by verbal conditioning and assertive training: A case study. *Journal of Behavior Therapy and Experimental Psychiatry,* 1972, *3,* 225–227.

O'Connor, R. D. Modification of social withdrawal through symbolic modeling. *Journal of Applied Behavior Analysis,* 1969, *2,* 15–22.

O'Donnell, J. M., & Brown, M. J. K. The classical conditioning of attitudes: A comparative study of ages 8 to 18. *Journal of Personality and Social Psychology,* 1973, *26,* 379–385.

O'Leary, K. D. The effects of self-instruction on immoral behavior. *Journal of Experimental Child Psychology,* 1968, *6,* 297–301.

Olton, R. M., & Crutchfield, R. S. Developing the skills of productive thinking. In P. Mussen, J. Langer, & M. V. Covington (Eds.), *Trends and issues in developmental psychology.* New York: Holt, Rinehart & Winston, 1969. Pp. 68–91.

O'Neill, D. G., & Howell, R. J. Three modes of hierarchy presentation in systematic desensitization. *Behaviour Research and Therapy,* 1969, *7,* 289–294.

Orne, M. T. Demand characteristics and the concept of quasi-controls. In R. Rosenthal & R. L. Rosnow (Eds.), *Artifact in behavioral research.* New York: Academic Press, 1969. Pp. 147–179.

Osborn, A. F. *Applied imagination.* 3rd ed. New York: Scribner's, 1963.

Osgood, C. E. *Method and theory in experimental psychology.* New York: Oxford University Press, 1953.

Oshawa, G. *Macrobiotics: An invitation to health and happiness.* San Francisco: George Oshawa Memorial Foundation, 1971.

Paivio, A. *Imagery and verbal processes.* New York: Holt, Rinehart & Winston, 1971.

———. Psychophysiological correlates of imagery. In F. J. McGuigan & R. A. Schoonover (Eds.), *The psychophysiology of thinking.* New York: Acadmic Press, 1973. Pp. 263–295.

Palkes, H., Stewart, M., & Freedman, J. Improvement in maze performance of hyperactive boys as a function of verbal training procedures. *Journal of Special Education,* 1972, *5,* 337–342.

Palkes, H., Stewart, M., & Kahana, B. Porteus maze performance of hyperactive boys after training in self-directed verbal commands. *Child Development,* 1968, *39,* 817–826.

Papanek, V. J. Tree of life: Bionics. *Journal of Creative Behavior,* 1969, *3,* 5–15.

Patterson, G. R. Behavioral techniques based upon social learning. In C. M. Franks (Ed.), *Behavior therapy: Appraisal and status.* New York: McGraw-Hill, 1969. Pp. 323–374.

Patterson, G. R., Hawkins, N., McNeal, S., & Phelps, R. Reprograming the social environment. *Journal of Child Psychology and Psychiatry,* 1967, *8,* 181–195.

Patterson, G. R., Littman, I., & Brown, T. R. Negative set and social learning. *Journal of Personality and Social Psychology,* 1968, *8,* 109–116.

Paul, G. L. Outcome of systematic desensitization. I: Background, procedures, and uncontrolled reports of individual treatment. In C. M. Franks

(Ed.), *Behavior therapy: Appraisal and status.* New York: McGraw-Hill, 1969. Pp. 63–104. (a)

———. Outcome of systematic desensitization. II: Controlled investigations of individual treatment, technique variations, and current status. In C. M. Franks (Ed.), *Behavior therapy: Appraisal and status.* New York: McGraw-Hill, 1969. Pp. 105–159. (b)

———. Behavior modification research: Design and tactics. In C. M. Franks (Ed.), *Behavior therapy: Appraisal and status.* New York: McGraw-Hill, 1969. Pp. 29–62. (c)

Pauling, L. Orthomolecular psychiatry. *Science,* 1968, *160,* 265–271.

Pavlov, I. P. *Selected works.* Moscow: Foreign Languages Publishing House, 1955.

Peale, N. V. *The power of positive thinking.* Englewood Cliffs: Prentice-Hall, 1960.

Peirce, C. S. How to make our ideas clear. (original 1878) In J. Buchler (Ed.), *The philosophy of Peirce.* London: Routledge, 1940.

Pelman Institute of America, *Pelmanism: Lesson V—Will and Effort.* New York: Pelman Institute, 1919.

Penfield, W. The interpretive cortex. *Science,* 1959, *129,* 1719–1725.

Perlmuter, L. C., Monty, R. A., & Kimble, G. A. The effect of choice on paired-associate learning. *Journal of Experimental Psychology,* 1971, *91,* 47–53.

Phares, E. J. *Locus of control: A personality determinant of behavior.* Morristown, N.J.: General Learning Press, 1973.

Piaget, J. *The language and thought of the child.* New York: Meridian, 1955.

Piaget, J., & Inhelder, B. *The psychology of the child.* New York: Basic Books, 1969.

Pike, R. L., & Brown, M. L. *Nutrition: An integrated analysis.* New York: Wiley, 1967.

Platonov, K. I. *The word as a physiological and therapeutic factor.* Moscow: Foreign Languages Publishing House, 1959.

Platt, J., Scura, W. C., & Hannon, J. R. Problem-solving thinking of youthful incarcerated heroin addicts. *Journal of Community Psychology,* 1973, *1,* 278–281.

Platt, J., & Spivack, G. Problem-solving thinking of psychiatric patients. *Journal of Consulting and Clinical Psychology,* 1972, *39,* 148–151. (a)

———., & ———. Social competence and effective problem-solving thinking in psychiatric patients. *Journal of Clinical Psychology,* 1972, *28,* 3–5. (b)

———., & ———. Studies in problem-solving thinking of psychiatric patients: I. Patient-control differences; II. Factorial structure of problem-solving thinking. *Proceedings of the 81st Annual Convention of the American Psychological Association,* 1973, *8,* 463–464.

———., & ———. Means of solving real-life problems: I. Psychiatric patients versus controls, and cross-cultural comparisons of normal females. *Journal of Community Psychology,* 1974, *2,* 45–48.

Plummer, L. S., & Das, S. S. A study of dichotomous thought processes in accident-prone drivers. *British Journal of Psychiatry*, 1973, *122*, 289–294.

Plutchik, R. Operationism as methodology. *Behavioral Science*, 1963, *8*, 234–241.

Polanyi, M. *Personal knowledge*. Chicago: University of Chicago Press, 1958.

———. *Personal knowledge*. New York: Harper, 1964.

———. *The tacit dimension*. Garden City, N.Y.: Doubleday, 1966.

Polya, G. *How to solve it*. 2nd ed. Princeton: Princeton University Press, 1957.

Popper, K. R. *The logic of scientific discovery*. New York: Harper, 1959.

———. *Conjectures and refutations*. New York: Harper, 1963.

———. *Objective knowledge: An evolutionary approach*. London: Oxford University Press, 1972.

Premack, D. Reinforcement theory. In D. Levine (Ed.), *Nebraska symposium on motivation: 1965*. Lincoln: University of Nebraska Press, 1965. Pp. 123–180.

———. Catching up with common sense or two sides of a generalization: Reinforcement and punishment. In R. Glaser (Ed.), *The nature of reinforcement*. New York: Academic Press, 1971. Pp. 121–150.

Proctor, S., & Malloy, T. E. Cognitive control of conditioned emotional responses: An extension of behavior therapy to include the experimental psychology of cognition. *Behavior Therapy*, 1971, *2*, 294–306.

Rachlin, H., & Green, L. Commitment, choice and self-control. *Journal of the Experimental Analysis of Behavior*, 1972, *17*, 15–22.

Rachman, S. The role of muscular relaxation in desensitization therapy. *Behaviour Research and Therapy*, 1968, *6*, 159–166.

———. Obsessional ruminations. *Behaviour Research and Therapy*, 1971, *9*, 229–235.

———. Clinical applications of observational learning, imitation, and modeling. *Behavior Therapy*, 1972, *3*, 379–397.

Rachman, S., Hodgson, R., & Marks, I. The treatment of chronic obsessive-compulsive neurosis. *Behaviour Research and Therapy*, 1971, *9*, 237–247.

Rachman, S., Marks, I. M., & Hodgson, R. The treatment of obsessive-compulsive neurotics by modelling and flooding *in vivo*. *Behaviour Research and Therapy*, 1973, *11*, 463–471.

Razran, G. A quantitative study of meaning by conditioned salivary technique (semantic conditioning). *Science*, 1939, *90*, 89–91.

———. The observable unconscious and the inferable conscious in current Soviet psychophysiology. *Psychological Review*, 1961, *68*, 81–147.

———. Russian physiologists' psychology and American experimental psychology. *Psychological Bulletin*, 1965, *63*, 42–64.

Reese, H. W. The study of covert verbal and nonverbal mediation. In A. Jacobs & L. B. Sachs (Eds.), *The psychology of private events: Perspectives on covert response systems*. New York: Academic Press, 1971. Pp. 17–38.

Rehm, L. P. Relationships among measures of visual imagery. *Behaviour Research and Therapy,* 1973, *11,* 253–264.

Resnick, J. H., & Schwartz, T. Ethical standards as an independent variable in psychological research. *American Psychologist,* 1973, *28,* 134–139.

Richardson, A. *Mental imagery.* New York: Springer, 1969.

Richardson, F. C., & Suinn, R. M. A comparison of traditional systematic desensitization, accelerated massed desensitization, and anxiety management training in the treatment of mathematics anxiety. *Behavior Therapy,* 1973, *4,* 212–218.

Ridberg, E., Parke, R., & Hetherington, M. Modification of impulsive and reflective cognitive styles through observation of film mediating models. *Developmental Psychology,* 1971, *5,* 369–377.

Rimm, D. C. Thought stopping and covert assertion in the treatment of phobias. *Journal of Consulting and Clinical Psychology,* 1973, *41,* 466–467.

Rimm, D. C., & Bottrell, J. Four measures of visual imagination. *Behaviour Research and Therapy,* 1969, *7,* 63–69.

Rimm, D. C., & Litvak, S. B. Self-verbalization and emotional arousal. *Journal of Abnormal Psychology,* 1969, *74,* 181–187.

Rimm, D. C., & Masters, J. C. *Behavior therapy: Techniques and empirical findings.* New York: Academic Press, 1974.

Rimm, D. C., Saunders, W. D., & Westel, W. Thought stopping and covert assertion in the treatment of snake phobics. Unpublished manuscript, Southern Illinois University, 1974.

Riopelle, A. J. (Ed.) *Animal problem solving.* Baltimore: Penguin, 1967.

Rodale, J. I. *Rodale's system for mental power and natural health.* New York: Pyramid, 1966.

Rohan, W. A. A comparison of two aversive conditioning procedures for problem drinking. Paper presented at the Brockton V. A. Hospital, Brockton, Mass., 1970.

Rokeach, M. *The open and closed mind.* New York: Basic Books, 1960.

Rosen, G. M., Rosen, E., & Reid, J. B. Cognitive desensitization and avoidance behavior: A reevaluation. *Journal of Abnormal Psychology,* 1972, *80,* 176–182.

Rosen, N. A., & Wyer, R. S. Some further evidence for the "Socratic effect" using a subjective probability model of cognitive organization. *Journal of Social Psychology,* 1972, *24,* 420–424.

Rosen, R. C., & Schnapp, B. J. The use of a specific behavioral technique (thought-stopping) in the context of conjoint couples therapy: A case report. *Behavior Therapy,* 1974, *5,* 261–264.

Rosenhan, D. L. On being sane in insane places. *Science,* 1973, *179,* 250–258.

Rosenthal, R. *Experimenter effects in behavioral research.* New York: Appleton-Century-Crofts, 1966.

Rosenthal, R., & Rosnow, R. L. (Eds.) *Artifact in behavioral research.* New York: Academic Press, 1969.

Rosenthal, T. L., & Meyer, V. Case report: Behavioral treatment of clinical abulia. *Conditional Reflex,* 1971, *6,* 22–29.

Ross, L., Rodin, J., & Zimbardo, P. G. Toward an attribution therapy: The reduction of fear through induced cognitive-emotional misattribu-

tion. *Journal of Personality and Social Psychology,* 1969, *12,* 279–288.

Rotter, J. B. Generalized expectancies for internal versus external control of reinforcement. *Psychological Monographs,* 1966, *80:* Whole No. 609.

Rotter, J. B., Chance, J. E., & Phares, E. J. (Eds.), *Applications of a social learning theory of personality.* New York: Holt, Rinehart & Winston, 1972.

Royce, J. E. Does person or self imply dualism? *American Psychologist,* 1973, *28,* 883–886.

Russell, P. L., & Brandsma, J. M. A theoretical and empirical integration of the rational-emotive and classical conditioning theories. *Journal of Consulting and Clinical Psychology,* 1974, *42,* 389–397.

Rutner, I. T. The modification of smoking behavior through techniques of self-control. Unpublished master's thesis, Wichita State University, 1967.

Rutner, I. T., & Bugle, C. An experimental procedure for the modification of psychotic behavior. *Journal of Consulting and Clinical Psychology,* 1969, *33,* 651–653.

Ryle, G. *The concept of mind.* New York: Barnes & Noble, 1949.

Sabry, Z. I., Campbell, J. A., Campbell, M. E., & Forbes, A. L. Nutrition Canada. *Nutrition Today,* 1974, *9,* 5–13.

Sachs, L. B., Bean, H., & Morrow, J. E. Comparison of smoking treatments. *Behavior Therapy,* 1970, *1,* 465–472.

Sachs, L. B., & Ingram, G. L. Covert sensitization as a treatment for weight control. *Psychological Reports,* 1972, *30,* 971–974.

Sarason, I. G. Test anxiety and cognitive modeling. *Journal of Personality and Social Psychology,* 1973, *28,* 58–61.

Sargant, W. *Battle for the mind.* New York: Harper & Row, 1957.

Schachter, S. The interaction of cognitive and physiological determinants of emotional state. In L. Berkowitz (Ed.), *Advances in experimental social psychology.* Vol. 1. New York: Academic Press, 1964. Pp. 49–80.

Schachter, S., & Singer, J. E. Cognitive, social, and physiological determinants of emotional state. *Psychological Review,* 1962, *69,* 379–399.

Schmickley, V. G., Johnson, R. G., Elson, S. E., Rate, L. T., Ripstra, C. C., & Yager, G. G. Covert operant reinforcement of remedial reading learning tasks. Paper presented to the American Educational Research Association, Chicago, April, 1974.

Scrimshaw, N. S. Malnutrition, learning and behavior. *American Journal of Clinical Nutrition,* 1967, *20,* 493–502.

Scrimshaw, N. S., & Gordon, J. E. (Eds.), *Malnutrition, learning, and behavior.* Cambridge, Mass.: MIT Press, 1968.

Segal, J., & Luce, G. G. *Sleep.* New York: Arena, 1966.

Segal, S. J. (Ed.), *Imagery: Current cognitive approaches.* New York: Academic Press, 1971.

Seligman, M. E. P., Maier, S. F., & Solomon, R. L. Unpredictable and uncontrollable aversive events. In F. R. Brush (Ed.), *Aversive conditioning and learning.* New York: Academic Press, 1969.

Shaffer, L. F. The problem of psychotherapy. *American Psychologist,* 1947, *2,* 459–467.

Shapiro, A. K. Placebo effects in medicine, psychotherapy, and psychoanalysis. In A. E. Bergin & S. L. Garfield (Eds.), *Handbook of psychotherapy and behavior change.* New York: Wiley, 1971. Pp. 439–473.

Shaw, W. A. The relation of muscular action potentials to imaginal weight lifting. *Archives of Psychology,* 1940, No. 247, p. 50.

Sheehan, P. W. (Ed.) *The function and nature of imagery.* New York: Academic Press, 1972.

Sheerer, M. Problem solving. *Scientific American,* 1963, *208,* 118–128.

Shulman, L. S. Seeking styles and individual differences in patterns of inquiry. *School Review,* 1965, *73,* 258–266.

Shulman, R. Vitamin B-12 deficiency and psychiatric illness. *British Journal of Psychiatry,* 1967, *113,* 252–256. (a)

———. A survey of vitamin B-12 deficiency in an elderly psychiatric population. *British Journal of Psychiatry,* 1967, *113,* 241–251. (b)

Shure, M., & Spivack, G. Means-ends thinking, adjustment and social class among elementary school-aged children. *Journal of Consulting and Clinical Psychology,* 1972, *38,* 348–353.

Shure, M., Spivack, G., & Jaeger, M. Problem-solving thinking and adjustment among disadvantaged preschool children. *Child Development,* 1971, *42,* 1791–1803.

Sidman, M. *Tactics of scientific research.* New York: Basic Books, 1960.

Singer, J. L. Imagery and daydream techniques employed in psychotherapy: Some practical and theoretical implications. In C. D. Spielberger (Ed.), *Current topics in clinical and community psychology.* New York: Academic Press, 1972.

Singh, D. Preference for bar pressing to obtain reward over freeloading in rats and children. *Journal of Comparative and Physiological Psychology,* 1970, *73,* 320–327.

Sirota, A. D. A take-off on reinforcement: Or, how to get high on raisins. Unpublished manuscript, Pennsylvania State University, 1974.

Skinner, B. F. The operational analysis of psychological terms. *Psychological Review,* 1945, *52,* 270–277.

———. "Superstition" in the pigeon. *Journal of Experimental Psychology,* 1948, *38,* 168–172.

———. Are theories of learning necessary? *Psychological Review,* 1950, *57,* 193–216.

———. *Science and human behavior.* New York: Macmillan, 1953.

———. What is psychotic behavior? In B. F. Skinner, *Cumulative Record.* New York: Appleton-Century-Crofts, 1959. Pp. 202–219.

———. Behaviorism at fifty. *Science,* 1963, *140,* 951–958.

———. An operant analysis of problem solving. In B. Kleinmuntz (Ed.), *Problem solving: Research, method, and theory.* New York: Wiley, 1966. Pp. 225–257.

———. *Contingencies of reinforcement: A theoretical analysis.* New York: Appleton-Century-Crofts, 1969.

———. *Beyond freedom and dignity.* New York: Alfred A. Knopf, 1971.

———. *About behaviorism.* New York: Alfred A. Knopf, 1974.

Slovic, P., & Lichtenstein, S. Comparison of Bayesian and regression approaches to the study of information processing in judgment. *Organizational Behavior and Human Performance,* 1971, *6,* 694–744.

Solyom, L., & Kingstone, E. An obsessive neurosis following morning glory seed ingestion treated by aversion relief. *Journal of Behavior Therapy and Experimental Psychiatry,* 1973, *4,* 293–295.

Sperling, G. A. The information available in brief visual presentation. *Psychological Monographs,* 1960, *74,* Whole No. 498.

Sperry, R. W. Lateral specialization of cerebral function in the surgically separated hemispheres. In F. J. McGuigan & R. A. Schoonover (Eds.), *The psychophysiology of thinking.* New York: Academic Press, 1973. Pp. 209–229.

Spielberger, C. D., Bernstein, I. H., & Ratliff, R. G. Information and incentive value of the reinforcing stimulus in verbal conditioning. *Journal of Experimental Psychology,* 1966, *71,* 26–31.

Spielberger, C. D., & DeNike, L. D. Descriptive behaviorism versus cognitive theory in verbal operant conditioning. *Psychological Review,* 1966, *73,* 306–326.

Spivack, G., & Levine, M. *Self-regulation in acting-out and normal adolescents.* Report M-4351. Washington D.C.: National Institute of Health, 1963.

Spivack, G., & Shure, M. B. *Social adjustment of young children: A cognitive approach to solving real-life problems.* San Francisco: Jossey-Bass, 1974.

Staats, A. W. An integrated-functional learning approach to complex human behavior. In B. Kleinmuntz (Ed.), *Problem solving: Research, method, and theory.* New York: Wiley, 1966. Pp. 259–339.

———. *Learning, language, and cognition.* New York: Holt, Rinehart, & Winston, 1968. (a)

———. Social behaviorism and human motivation: Principles of the attitude-reinforcer-discriminative system. In A. G. Greenwald, T. C. Brock, & T. M. Ostrom (Eds.), *Psychological foundations of attitudes.* New York: Academic Press, 1968. Pp. 33–66. (b)

———. Language behavior therapy: A derivative of social behaviorism. *Behavior Therapy,* 1972, *3,* 165–192.

Staats, A. W., Gross, M. C., Guay, P. F, & Carlson, C. C. Personality and social systems and attitude-reinforcer-discriminative theory: Interest (attitude) formation, function, and measurement. *Journal of Personality and Social Psychology,* 1973, *26,* 251–261.

Staats, A. W., & Hammond, O. W. Natural words as physiological conditioned stimuli: Food-word-elicited salivation and deprivation effects. *Journal of Experimental Psychology,* 1972, *96,* 206–208.

Staats, A. W., Minke, K. A., Martin, C. H., & Higa, W. R. Deprivation-satiation and strength of attitude conditioning: A test of attitude-reinforcer-discriminative theory. *Journal of Personality and Social Psychology,* 1972, *24,* 178–185.

Staddon, J. E. R., & Simmelhag, V. L. The "superstition" experiment: A reexamination of its implications for the principles of adaptive behavior. *Psychological Review,* 1971, *78,* 3–43.

Stampfl, T. G., & Levis, D. J. Essentials of implosive therapy: A learning-theory-based psychodynamic behavioral therapy. *Journal of Abnormal Psychology,* 1967, *72,* 496–503.

Steffan, J. J. The effects of covert reinforcement upon hospitalized schizophrenics. Paper presented at the Eastern Psychological Association, New York, 1971.

———. Effect of covert reinforcement upon male and female college students. Unpublished master's thesis, Rutgers University, 1972.

Steffy, R. A., Meichenbaum, D., & Best, J. A. Aversive and cognitive factors in the modification of smoking behavior. *Behaviour Research and Therapy,* 1970, *8,* 115–125.

Steiner, I. D. Perceived freedom. In L. Berkowitz (Ed.), *Advances in experimental social psychology.* Vol. 5. New York: Academic Press, 1970. Pp. 187–248.

Steinfeld, G. The use of covert sensitization with institutionalized narcotic addicts. *International Journal of Addiction,* 1970, *5,* 225–232.

Stern, R. M., Botto, R. W., & Herrick, C. D. Behavioral and physiological effects of false heart rate feedback: A replication and extension. *Psychophysiology,* 1972, *9,* 21–29.

Stern, R. M., & Kaplan, B. E. Galvanic skin response: Voluntary control and externalization. *Journal of Psychosomatic Research,* 1967, *10,* 349–353.

Stern, R. M., & Lewis, N. L. Ability of actors to control their GSRs and express emotions. *Psychophysiology,* 1968, *4,* 294–299.

Stern, R. S. Treatment of a case of obsessional neurosis using thought-stopping technique. *British Journal of Psychiatry,* 1970, *117,* 441–442.

Sterner, R. T., & Price, W. R. Restricted riboflavin: Within-subject behavioral effects in humans. *American Journal of Clinical Nutrition,* 1973, *26,* 150–160.

Stokes, J. P. The effects of rapid eye movement sleep on retention. *Psychological Record,* 1973, *23,* 521–531.

Stoyva, J. Biofeedback techniques and the conditions for hallucinatory activity. In F. J. McGuigan & R. A. Schoonover (Eds.), *The psychophysiology of thinking.* New York: Academic Press, 1973. Pp. 387–414.

Strel'chuk, I. V. New contemporary methods of treating patients with alcoholism. *Soviet Medicine,* 1957, *21,* 26–33.

Stuart, R. B. *Trick or treatment: How and when psychotherapy fails.* Champaign, Ill.: Research Press, 1970.

———. Situational versus self-control. In R. D. Rubin, H. Fensterheim, J. D. Henderson, & L. P. Ullmann (Eds.), *Advances in behavior therapy.* New York: Academic Press, 1972. Pp. 129–146.

Stunkard, A. F., & Mahoney, M. J. Behavioral treatment of the eating disorders. In H. Leitenberg (Ed.), *Handbook of behavior modification.* New York: Appleton-Century-Crofts, in press.

Suchman, J. R. Inquiry training in the elementary school. *Science Teacher,* 1960, *27,* 42–47.

———. J. R. *Evaluating inquiry in physical science.* Chicago: Science Research Associates, 1969.

Suinn, R. M. Behavior rehearsal training for ski racers. *Behavior Therapy,* 1972, *3,* 519–520. (a)

———. Removing emotional obstacles to learning and performance by visuomotor behavioral rehearsal. *Behavior Therapy,* 1972, *3,* 308–310. (b)

Suinn, R. M., & Richardson, F. Anxiety management training: A nonspecific behavior therapy program for anxiety control. *Behavior Therapy,* 1971, *2,* 498–510.

Sushinsky, L. W., & Bootzin, R. R. Cognitive desensitization as a model of systematic desensitization. *Behaviour Research and Therapy,* 1970, *8,* 29–33.

Taylor, F. G. The modification of depression. Unpublished doctoral dissertation, Queen's University, 1974.

Taylor, J. G. Personal communication (1955) in J. Wolpe, *Psychotherapy by reciprocal inhibition.* Stanford: Stanford University Press, 1958.

———. A behavioural interpretation of obsessive-compulsive neuroses. *Behaviour Research and Therapy,* 1963, *1,* 237–244.

Terrace, H. S. Awareness as viewed by conventional and by radical behaviorism. Paper presented at the American Psychological Association, Washington, D.C., 1971.

Thomson, M. J. C. The disinhibition of a memory during systematic desensitization. *Journal of Behavior Therapy and Experimental Psychiatry,* 1971, *2,* 301–302.

Thoresen, C. E., & Mahoney, M. J. *Behavioral self-control.* New York: Holt, Rinehart & Winston, 1974.

Thorndike, E. L. Animal intelligence: An experimental study of the associative processes in animals. *Psychological Review Monograph Supplement,* 1898, *2* (4, Whole No. 8).

———. *Animal intelligence.* New York: Macmillan, 1911.

Thornton, J. W., & Jacobs, P. D. Learned helplessness in human subjects. *Journal of Experimental Psychology,* 1971, *87,* 367–372.

Throop, W. F., & MacDonald, A. P. Internal-external locus of control: A bibliography. *Psychological Reports,* Monograph Supplement 1-V28, 1971, 175–190.

Todd, F. J. Coverant control of self-evaluative responses in the treatment of depression: A new use for an old principle. *Behavior Therapy,* 1972, *3,* 91–94.

Tolman, E. C. *Purposive behavior in animals and men.* New York: Appleton-Century-Crofts, 1932.

Tooley, J. T., & Pratt, S. An experimental procedure for the extinction of smoking behavior. *Psychological Record,* 1967, *17,* 209–218.

Tori, C., & Worell, L. Reduction of human avoidant behavior: A comparison of counter-conditioning, expectancy, and cognitive information approaches. *Journal of Consulting and Clinical Psychology,* 1973, *41,* 269–278.

Torrance, E. P., & Myers, R. E. *Creative learning and teaching.* New York: Dodd, 1970.

Treisman, A. M. Verbal cues, language and meaning in selective attention. *American Journal of Psychology,* 1964, *77,* 206–219.

Trexler, L. D., & Karst, T. O. Rational-emotive therapy, placebo, and no-treatment effects on public-speaking anxiety. *Journal of Abnormal Psychology,* 1972, *79,* 60–67.

———., & ———. Further validation for a new measure of irrational cognitions. *Journal of Personality Assessment,* 1973, *37,* 105–155.

Turner, M. B. *Philosophy and the science of behavior.* New York: Appleton-Century-Crofts, 1967.

Tyler, V. O., & Straughan, J. H. Coverant control and breath holding as techniques for the treatment of obesity. *Psychological Record,* 1970, *20,* 473–478.

Ullmann, L. P. On cognitions and behavior therapy. *Behavior Therapy,* 1970, *1,* 201–204.

Ullmann, L. P., & Krasner, L. *A psychological approach to abnormal behavior.* Englewood Cliffs: Prentice-Hall, 1969.

Valins, S., & Nisbett, R. E. *Attribution processes in the development and treatment of emotional disorders.* Morristown, N.J.: General Learning Press, 1971.

Valins, S., & Ray, A. A. Effects of cognitive desensitization on avoidance behavior. *Journal of Personality and Social Psychology,* 1967, *7,* 345–350.

Verplanck, W. S. Unaware of where's awareness: Some verbal operants—notates, monents, and notants. In C. W. Eriksen (Ed.), *Behavior and awareness.* Durham, N.C.: Duke University Press, 1962. Pp. 130–158.

Viernstein, L. Evaluation of therapeutic techniques of covert sensitization. Unpublished manuscript, Queens College, 1968.

von Bertalanffy, L. *Robots, men and minds.* New York: George Braziller, 1967.

Voss, S. C., & Homzie, M. J. Choice as a value. *Psychological Reports,* 1970, *26,* 912–914.

Vygotsky, L. S. *Thought and language.* Cambridge: M.I.T. Press, 1962.

Wagner, M. Smokers of the world unite. *Association for the Advancement of Behavioral Therapies Newsletter,* 1969, *4,* 12.

Wagner, M. K. & Bragg, R. A. Comparing behavior modification approaches to habit decrement—smoking. *Journal of Consulting and Clinical Psychology,* 1970, *34,* 258–263.

Walters, O. S. Religion and psychopathology. *Comprehensive Psychiatry,* 1964, *101,* 24–35.

Walton, D., & Mather, M. The application of learning principles to the treatment of obsessive-compulsive states in the acute and chronic phases of illness. *Behaviour Research and Therapy,* 1963, *1,* 163–174.

Warden, C. J., Fjeld, H. A., & Koch, A. M. Imitative behavior in Cebus and Rhesus monkeys. *Pedagogical Seminary and Journal of Genetic Psychology,* 1940, *56,* 311–322.

Warren, N. Malnutrition and mental development. *Psychological Bulletin,* 1973, *80,* 324–328.

Wason, P. C. Problem solving and reasoning. *British Medical Bulletin,* 1971, *27,* 206–210.

Waters, W. F., & McDonald, D. G. Autonomic response to auditory, visual and imagined stimuli in a systematic desensitization context. *Behaviour Research and Therapy,* 1973, *11,* 577–585.

Watson, G. *Nutrition and your mind: The psychochemical response.* New York: Bantam, 1972.

Watson, J. B. Imitation in monkeys. *Psychological Bulletin,* 1908, *5,* 169–178.

———. Psychology as the behaviorist views it. *Psychological Review,* 1913, *20,* 158–177.

———. *Behaviorism.* Chicago: University of Chicago Press, 1924.

Watts, F. N., Powell, G. E., & Austin, S. V. The modification of abnormal beliefs. *British Journal of Medical Psychology,* 1973, *46,* 359–363.

Weimer, W. B. *Psychology and the conceptual foundations of science.* Englewood Cliffs, N. J.: Prentice-Hall, in press.

Weiner, B. *Theories of motivation: From mechanism to cognition.* Chicago: Rand McNally, 1972.

Weiner, H. Real and imagined cost effects upon human fixed-interval responding. *Psychological Reports,* 1965, *17,* 659–662.

Weiner, I. Behavior therapy in obsessive-compulsive neurosis: Treatment of an adolescent boy. *Psychotherapy: Theory, Research and Practice,* 1967, *4,* 27–29.

Weiss, R. L., Hops, H., & Patterson, G. R. A framework for conceptualizing marital conflict: A technology for altering it, some data for evaluating it. In L. A. Hamerlynck, L. C. Handy, & E. J. Mash (Eds.), *Behavior change: Methodology, concepts, and practice.* Champaign, Ill.: Research Press, 1973. Pp. 309–342.

Weisz, A. E., & Taylor, R. L. American Presidential assassinations. In D. N. Daniels, M. F. Gilula, & F. Ochberg (Eds.), *Violence and the struggle for existence.* Boston: Little, Brown, 1970. Pp. 291–307.

Wickelgren, W. A. The long and the short of memory. *Psychological Bulletin,* 1973, *80,* 425–438.

Wicklund, R. A. *Freedom and reactance.* New York: Wiley, 1974.

Wilkins, W. Desensitization: Social and cognitive factors underlying the effectiveness of Wolpe's procedure. *Psychological Bulletin,* 1971, *76,* 311–317.

———. Expectancy of therapeutic gain: An empirical and conceptual critique. *Journal of Consulting and Clinical Psychology,* 1973, *40,* 69–77.

Williams, D. R., & Williams, H. Auto-maintenance in the pigeon: Sustained pecking despite contingent non-reinforcement. In P. B. Dews (Ed.), *Festschrift for B. F. Skinner.* New York: Appleton-Century-Crofts, 1970, Pp. 279–288.

Williams, J. G., Barlow, D. H., & Agras, W. S. Behavioral measurement of severe depression. *Archives of General Psychiatry,* 1972, *27,* 330–333.

Williams, R. J. *Nutrition against disease: Environmental prevention.* New York: Pitman, 1971.

Williams, S. R. *Nutrition and diet therapy.* Saint Louis: C. V. Mosby Company, 1973.

Wilson, G. T. Innovations in the modification of phobic behaviors in two clinical cases. *Behavior Therapy,* 1973, *4,* 426–430. (a)

———. Effects of false feedback on avoidance behavior: "Cognitive" desensitization revisited. *Journal of Personality and Social Psychology,* 1973, *28,* 115–122. (b)

———. Aversive control of maladaptive behavior. Paper presented at Pennsylvania State University, January, 1974. (a)

———. Behavior therapy in adults. Paper presented at the American Psychopathological Association, Boston, March, 1974. (b)

Wilson, G. T., & Davison, G. C. Processes of fear-reduction in systematic desensitization: Animal studies. *Psychological Bulletin,* 1971, *76,* 1–14.

———., & ———. Behavior therapy and homosexuality: A critical perspective. *Behavior Therapy,* 1974, *5,* 16–28.

Wilson, G. T., & Thomas, M. Self- versus drug-produced relaxation and the effects of instructional set in standardized systematic desensitization. *Behaviour Research and Therapy,* 1973, *11,* 279–288.

Wine, J. Investigations of an attentional interpretation of test anxiety. Unpublished doctoral dissertation, University of Waterloo, 1970.

———. Test anxiety and direction of attention. *Psychological Bulletin,* 1971, *76,* 92–104.

Winett, R. A. Attribution of attitude and behavior change and its relevance to behavior therapy. *Psychological Record,* 1970, *20,* 17–32.

Wisocki, P. A. Treatment of obsessive-compulsive behavior by covert sensitization and covert reinforcement: A case report. *Journal of Behavior Therapy and Experimental Psychiatry,* 1970, *1,* 233–239.

———. The empirical evidence of covert sensitization in the treatment of alcoholism: An evaluation. In R. D. Rubin, H. Fensterheim, J. D. Henderson, & L. P. Ullmann (Eds.), *Advances in behavior therapy,* Vol. 3. New York: Academic Press, 1972, Pp. 105–113.

———. A covert reinforcement program for the treatment of test anxiety. *Behavior Therapy,* 1973, *4,* 264–266. (a)

———. The successful treatment of a heroin addict by covert conditioning techniques. *Journal of Behavior Therapy and Experimental Psychiatry,* 1973, *4,* 55–61. (b)

Wisocki, P. A., & Rooney, E. J. A comparison of thought stopping and covert sensitization techniques in the treatment of smoking: A brief report. *Psychological Record,* 1974, *24,* 191–192.

Wolpe, J. *Psychotherapy by reciprocal inhibition.* Stanford: Stanford University Press, 1958.

———. *The practice of behavior therapy.* New York: Pergamon, 1969.

———. Dealing with resistance to thought-stopping: A transcript. *Journal of Behavior Therapy and Experimental Psychiatry,* 1971, *2,* 121–125.

Wolpe, J., & Lazarus, A. A. *Behavior therapy techniques.* New York: Pergamon, 1966.

Wolpin, M., & Raines, J. Visual imagery, expected roles and extinction as possible factors in reducing fear and avoidance behavior. *Behaviour Research and Therapy,* 1966, *4,* 25–38.

Wooley, S. C. Physiologic versus cognitive factors in short term food regulation in the obese and nonobese. *Psychosomatic Medicine,* 1972, *34,* 62–68.

Yamagami, T. The treatment of an obsession by thought-stopping. *Journal of Behavior Therapy and Experimental Psychiatry,* 1972, *2,* 133–135.

Yudkin, J. *Sweet and dangerous.* New York: Bantam, 1972.

Zangwill, O. L. *Remembering* revisited. *Quarterly Journal of Experimental Psychology,* 1972, *24,* 123–138.

Zeller, A. An experimental analogue of repression. II. The effect of individual failure and success on memory measured by relearning. *Journal of Experimental Psychology,* 1950, *40,* 411–422.

Zimmerman, B. J., & Rosenthal, T. L. Observational learning of rule-governed behavior by children. *Psychological Bulletin,* 1974, *81,* 29–42.

Zingle, H. W. A rational therapy approach to counseling underachievers. Unpublished doctoral dissertation, University of Alberta, 1965.

About the Author

The author received his B.A. degree from Arizona State University and his Ph.D. from Stanford University. He is currently Assistant Professor of Psychology at Pennsylvania State University. A frequent contributor to professional journals, he is also the co-author of *Behavioral Self-Control* and *Self-Control: Power to the Person.* His avocational interests range from philosophy and humanism to dirt riding and country music. Reflecting some of the conceptual breadth evinced in the text, he is a member of the *Behavior Therapy* editorial board as well as the American Humanist Association.

Name Index

Subject Index